T0342396

Codes of Finance

VINCENT ANTONIN LÉPINAY

Codes of Finance

Engineering Derivatives
in a Global Bank

Princeton University Press
Princeton and Oxford

Published by Princeton University Press, 41 William Street,
Princeton, New Jersey 08540

In the United Kingdom: Princeton University Press, 6 Oxford Street,
Woodstock, Oxfordshire OX20 1TW

press.princeton.edu

Library of Congress Cataloging-in-Publication Data

Lépinay, Vincent Antonin.
    Codes of finance : engineering derivatives in a global bank / Vincent Antonin Lepinay.
        p.   cm.
    Includes bibliographical references and index.
    ISBN 978-0-691-15150-2 (cloth : alk. paper)   1. Financial engineering—Case studies.
2. Derivative securities—Case studies.   3. Bank management—Case studies.   4. Selling—
Banks and banking—Case studies.   I. Title.
    HG176.7L47 2011
    332.64'57—dc23   2011020249

British Library Cataloging-in-Publication Data is available

This book has been composed in Minion Pro with Myriad Pro display
Printed on acid-free paper ∞
Printed in the United States of America
10 9 8 7 6 5 4 3 2 1

CONTENTS

ACKNOWLEDGMENTS

Michel Callon and Bruno Latour generously read versions of this book. Its felicitous moments owe them much: in different styles, they have always been present, extending their supervision to a protective attention that nurtured a unique environment and great relationships. At the Centre de Sociologie de l'Innovation, other scholars also were helpful readers; Fabian Muniesa stands out as a great intellectual companion. A group of us initiated the Associations d'Etudes Sociales de la Finance ("Social Studies of Finance Association") in Paris in 2000. Made up of young social scientists, we have met consistently since then, creating an environment that fosters lively conversations informed by a common interest in financial, monetary, and banking issues. With its members coming from different intellectual schools and endowed with very limited financial means—not to say surviving on a shoestring—the association has forced participants to engage the technicality of finance and dare to theorize from the technique itself.

Soon after, other clusters of scholars from the social sciences working on finance—sociologists in Germany around Karin Knorr Cetina and Alex Preda, in Scotland around Donald MacKenzie and Yuval Millo, and in the United States around David Stark and Daniel Beunza, geographers in England around Nigel Thrift, and anthropologists in the United States around Bill Maurer and Annelise Riles—came together in an informal social studies of finance community. The community took shape through a series of conferences in New York, Konstanz, London, and Paris. *Codes of Finance* was born from this protracted discussion. Its many contributors—too many to name each—are here warmly thanked for fueling a growing interest for financial matters. Ellen Hertz occupies a special role as she became a co-writer while I was finishing my dissertation. She opened my eyes to what has become my next project, the complex relation between finance and law.

A few individuals have helped shape the book and deserve special mention. In New York City, from 2002 to 2006, Peter Bearman, David Stark, and Harrison White helped me open up to American sociology after a solid indoctrination in continental sociology. I owe special thanks to David Stark, who saved me from the prospect of a slow death in French academia when he invited me to Columbia University. Later Bruce Kogut and Josh Whitford generously read and commented on the manuscript. During the academic year 2004–2005, Tim Mitchell ran an exciting seminar at the International Center for Advanced Studies at New York University. It offered amazing conditions and fruitful intellectual conversations. The fellows who shared their views of the market are all thanked for some solid intellectual engagements. Koray Caliskan is owed a special mention for his help throughout the New York University years. The year after, Faye Ginzburg and Angela Zito offered me a year of fellowship at their Center for Religion and Media. Although religion is not featured prominently in this book, they provided time and space for the maturing of some ideas tried here. Bill Maurer, Doug Holmes, Hiro Miazaki, and Annelise Riles all provided comments at various stages of this project.

My colleagues at the Massachusetts Institute of Technology (MIT) have helped me in many ways, formal and informal, and I owe to them my smooth transition from New York City to the academic bubble of Cambridge, Massachusetts. Michael Fisher, David Jones, David Mindell, Natasha Schull, and Roz Williams eased this transition. David Kaiser kindly accepted to help me through the process of revisions of drafts of the manuscript, and he has been a superb interlocutor, bringing rigor where it was needed and experience in all matters. I have also been fortunate to teach a new class (formalism) with him, which helped me clarify what I was doing. The students from this class have been generous readers: Alma Steingardt, Michael Rossi, Tom Schilling, and Canay Ozden deserve special mention for their generous help. Susan Silbey has taught me much at MIT, and I look forward to maintaining a strong intellectual conversation with her.

An MIT/Harvard reading group formed late in the process of my writing, and it was decisive in pushing the manuscript through its last stretch. All its members are warmly thanked, and Stefan Helmreich deserves special acknowledgment; he offered much intellectual encouragement. Eric Schwarz and Beth Clevenger have been efficient, patient and helpful editors at Princeton University Press. At a different press, this book had a previous life under the auspices of Trevor Pinch and Margy Avery. Their numerous pieces of advice, as well as their reviewers, have been much appreciated.

This book has been long in the making. The fieldwork and the interviews themselves spanned only two years—December 1999 through December 2001—but once the academic exercise of the dissertation was over in 2004, life resumed, and its grip has been felt in many ways and has slowed the transformation of the dissertation into a book that is enjoyable to readers outside its circle of committee members. As the book waited patiently in the Drawer of Dissertations, my wife Verena gave birth to our daughter and son, happily slowing down the process of rewriting. More than anybody else, they made the experience more enjoyable.

PREFACE

Financial Innovation from within the Bank

This book sets out to make sense of financial innovation by documenting how a new product—the capital guarantee product (CGP)—that was used by a bank, General Bank[1], caused disruption to the bank's orderly organization. It is an attempt to understand what happened to financial actors (engineers, traders, salespeople, regulators) after they began to invent services that changed their way of making deals, eventually unsettling their businesses.[2] Disruptive financial engineering not only left regulators puzzled and often unable to make sense of the risks generated by the innovative financial products, but also unsettled the bank that was expecting to adopt and exploit the innovations.[3] What happens to an institution that sells products that undermine its organizational structure? Peeking into General Bank's radical financial engineering offers us a rare glimpse of the relations among otherwise distinct modalities of innovations. In this text, products, processes, and organizations are studied together. This book uncovers a self-defeating form of innovation whereby a bank's organization undermines its financial practices, and unstable securities designed by the bank destroy its infrastructure.

Over the past thirty years, financial innovations have dramatically changed the way in which companies and individuals can manage their assets. Now, as many companies and even more households observe the dire consequences of innovative financial products, it is fair to wonder whether any of these products are well understood by the financial actors themselves.[4] Once set loose in General Bank, these innovative products produce a number of unexpected consequences, straining the ability of dozens of operators who are baffled by these tortured formulas—physicists, mathematicians, legal scholars, and, last but not least, folk psychologists in search of the ultimate law of the market. But who really understands the language of this new breed of finance? *Codes of Finance* is not a narrow book about the financial crisis that has struck the world economy since 2007. Many studies (MacKenzie, 2010; Tett, 2009) provide interested readers with illuminating accounts of the factors that led to that crisis, but they adopt a focus that both takes them close to the unfolding of events and can make them lose sight of the bigger picture. They characterize the crisis against the backdrop of a nonfailing financial system, which allows them to avoid questioning the proper object of finance. Critical accounts of finance, predating the current situation, have long pictured finance as a genetic expression of the capitalist economy's crisis-in-the-making (Minsky, 1982, 1986). *Codes of Finance* scrutinizes the consequences of financial engineering on a specific bank by looking at the disruption triggered by products that pushed finance—in the form of derivations—to its ultimate consequence. As such, the book documents closely and engages the ever more sophisticated financial innovations upon which finance critics have long glossed, yet without grounding them in the manufactures of finance themselves. CGPs are instances of *derivative finance*. Despite being designed and traded in the civilized business district of La Defense situated in the wealthy and orderly western suburbs of Paris, they are part of a world of finance that plays cat and mouse with regulation. Financial economists, chief among them Nobel Prize laureate Merton Miller (1986), have famously characterized financial engineering innovation as a market reaction to regulations.[5] This binary opposition—regulation versus innovation—has the drawback of caricaturing the process of engineering. It portrays innovation as a one-sided escape, whereas in actuality it is a complex dance where innovators simultaneously dodge *and* exploit existing rules and infrastructures. If innovations operate in a preexisting ecology of financial rules and products, then the key question becomes that of their insertion therein; and if the task of social scientists should be more than the production of propaganda for financial engineering, then it could very well be to document the consequences of such innovations. Over the past decades, some sectors of the financial industry have pushed these operations to their limits and have shown that innovation can have disastrous effects on the economy. This destruction was no real surprise. Economist Joseph Schumpeter (1942) had long pointed to the inner paradox of capitalist economies that thrive through destructive creations. With his sober assessment of these economies, Schumpeter could anticipate that they would run out of steam should innovators be stifled. But what if the unleashing of financial innovation were to destroy capitalist economies? What if creative destruction were to lack any creation?

Codes of Finance sides with neither Schumpeter nor Miller's account of innovation in relation to regulation. Rather, it dissects an episode of highly innovative financial engineering and lays bare the specificity of derivative finance. If derivation denotes a mode of operation that survives by a high level of innovation and by a lack of accountability, then it entertains more complex relations with the ecology of economic goods than the "creative destruction" motto captures. Derivation entails quick remobilization of the organization of the bank. As such, it has consequences for the way the bankers work. Before articulating more fully the specific mechanism of derivation, it is necessary to zoom in on the agent of this mode of operation, the financial product itself. To document this, *Codes of Finance* adopts an ethnographic method and gives the same attention to the technical and organizational conditions of the exercise of finance as it does to the human operators (traders, engineers, and salespeople). The ethnographic genre applied to financial institutions is now well established and boasts a variety of approaches ranging from full immersion (Hertz, 1998; Ho, 2009; Miyazaki, 2006) to more varied methods combining oral histories and on-site observations (Beunza and Stark, 2004; Knorr Cetina, 2002; Knorr Cetina and Brueggers 2002; Zaloom, 2006). These monographs provide excellent documentation of the organization of trading rooms, but they disconnect these morphologies from the matter of exchange itself. *Codes of Finance* adds to the organizational and cultural dimensions a distinctive understanding of financial engineering. It does not provide a technical account of contemporary finance for the sake of technicality; rather, it assesses the weight of financial formalisms on the bank's organization and the reciprocal transformation of financial engineering exposed to the temporality of a trading room and its back offices. With that objective in sight, *Codes of Finance* tracks with great detail the CGP's trajectory within the bank and the transformations that the derivative mode of value creation entails for its organization. Borrowing humbly from the famous preface to the first German edition of Karl Marx's *Capital*:

> In bourgeois society, the commodity-form of the product of labour—or the value-form of the commodity—is the economic cell-form. To the superficial observer, the analysis of these forms seems to turn upon minutiae. It does in fact deal with minutiae, but they are of the same order as those dealt with in microscopic anatomy.[6]

Codes of Finance applies this call for microscopic anatomy of unleashed financial engineering to a bank whose dedication to innovation foreshadowed other economic experiments that failed, thus leading to our current financial crisis.

One legitimate question the reader may ask this far into the book concerns the focus on the financial product itself. Why should we follow its chaotic trajectory in the first place? Will it not distract us from more structural considerations? Pragmatic considerations guided this choice.[7] Designing new products and selling them to clients is the business of the bank; this is where changes occur in the bank. A bank that does not innovate using new products or financial services is not likely to survive for very long. There is obviously room for a large variety of financial service firms in the market, and some firms are more aggressive than others, but the odds that a non-innovative firm might thrive are low. This is where changes are imposed from outside the bank. Regulations that set the playing field for financial institutions respond to the existing ecology of financial products and to the risks of financial engineering. There, too, it is not possible to reduce the variety of regulations framing financial transactions to a simple or one-way reaction. Rules are analyzed, and financial engineers spend much of their time detecting regulatory loopholes to be exploited through the design of new products. The ingenuity of these designers is fed by these rules. Products are not invented from scratch but through the animation of financial transactions by engineers rather than by regulators.

Structuring and Packaging Finance

CGPs started to be sold to clients in the mid-1990s, along with other new financial services belonging to the class of *structured finance* (*structured* is the name given by the industry to that type of finance). CGPs were not innovative from that perspective, as the structuring of finance had already been practiced for a few decades. The bank thought of CGP structuration as part of a global service offered to clients (whether corporate clients or individual investors) with a special need. Packaging is the modus operandi of the structuring of finance: it builds new services from existing ones, aggregates securities that are disconnected, and transforms the scattered and spotty ecology of financial instruments by adding new instruments. Most of the time, structuring involved combining existing assets and liabilities and finding ways to qualify them in an advantageous way for the client. The kind of "advantages" derived from structuring assets could range from exploiting legal and regulatory loopholes with an appropriate new qualification to excluding some assets from supervision by investors and regulatory authorities. Structuring ranged from playing with the rules to circumventing them, but even when these products followed the rules, offshore legal vehicles were used to enable packages that would not be possible under more stringent regulations.[8] But, first and foremost, structuring entailed a unique commercial relationship that brought the bank and its clients closely together. The CGP created much space for clients to maneuver around the floor of the design's negotiation of the specific structured products.

CGPs offer and combine a spectrum of generic solutions to specific needs. The bank must marry well-known tools to each client: the packaging that it strives to achieve demands customization and tailored design. The clients are given exotic names—high net worth individuals (HNWI) and, for the very rich, ultrahigh net worth individuals (UHNWI)—when they are not companies in search of solutions to treasury problems. The minimum amount of money that a client or a company had to possess to have access to these services made CGPs elite financial instruments.[9] So, although it shares many features with more traditional mass financial services, structured finance repeats a form that finance took at its birth, when services were not standardized but personal and fully customized.[10]

In financial parlance, the term "negotiable financial instruments" has a special meaning. It points to instruments that have a secondary market and can be transferred. Once a negotiable instrument is bought by owner B from owner A, B can sell it to C and so on through an infinite cycle of ownership. Through these negotiations, the object of negotiations—the financial instrument—remains stable. It is a legal convention creating rights and duties over time so that successive owners can negotiate exclusively the transaction price. The situation changes when the object of transaction is itself included in the negotiation. Then, the qualities of this object become part of the discussion, and the price is only one feature among others. Not only the price of the instrument but also all its qualities are negotiable. The real estate market offers such a case, where successive owners can modify the good to be sold in response to prospective buyers' preferences. In that case, negotiability applies along both axes of qualities and prices. The art market offers a counter example to the negotiability of a good's properties. Much like standard securities, each transaction leaves the art piece as it was created, but unlike financial products, the series of owners—individuals or institutions—who once held the piece are factors in its value during a transaction.[11]

CGPs are negotiable along these two directions but, unlike securities and units on the real estate market, negotiability involves only two instead of an infinite chain of owners, former owners, and prospective owners. The rounds of negotiations over the composition of the product involve exclusively General Bank and its client. No third party joins the negotiation because the nature of the customized service rules out a transfer and a cycle of successive ownership. Although the negotiability of CGPs involved only the bank and its client in a much simpler pattern of products' circulation than the generalized exchange, the close interaction between clients and General Bank actually made that relation more complex by blurring the lines of separation between the product designer and the product purchaser.

The waltz between the client and the bank that *Codes of Finance* documents is both an old story in the long history of banking and a new one created because of the porosity of lending and borrowing institutions—lenders want to make sure they will retrieve the money invested in uncertain business ventures. Businesses seeking capital from banks or venture capitalists have to allow these lenders access to their companies—if not always literally, as there is normally not much of the physical premises themselves to assess, at least the business plans are usually reviewed thoroughly and the conduct of the business itself is often under close scrutiny. The distinction between this long-standing characteristic of relational banking and what *Codes of Finance* is purporting is that in our case clients invite themselves to the bank, as opposed to bankers reining in company managers. This intrusion seizes the occasion of products' design but far from simply reversing the relation of trespassing, and proving that relational banking is about wielding power by holding the purse strings, the new presence of clients among financial salespeople, engineers, traders, and back-office managers transforms the long-established relations between these centers of operation. The orderly division

-100% Capital Guarantee at Maturity
-120% Participation in the Quarterly Average Rise of the Portfolio
-120% Participation in the Best Performing Index in Case of Portfolio Underperformance

Maturity date	February 25, 2008
Underlying	Equally weighted basket composed of the following indices:
	-DJ EUROSTOXX 50 (STX)
	-S&P 500 (SP)
	-NIKKEI 225 (NIX)
Capital Guarantee	100% of Nominal Amount at Maturity
Redemption at Maturity	Maturity, the holder will receive the greater of the following:
	-Nominal x 100%
	-Nominal x (100% + 120% [Max($BKT_m - 1$;0)])

with

$$BKT_m = \frac{1}{32}\sum_{t=1}^{32} BKT_t$$

$$BKT_t = \left[\frac{1}{3}\times\frac{SPt}{SPi}\right] + \left[\frac{1}{3}\times\frac{STXt}{STXi}\right] + \left[\frac{1}{3}\times\frac{NIXt}{NIXi}\right]$$

Double Chance   If $BKT_m < BKT_i$, the Note pays

$$\text{Nominal}\times\left(100\% + 120\%\times MAx\left[\frac{SPm}{SPi} - 1; \frac{STXm}{STXi} - 1; \frac{NIXm}{NIXi} - 1;0\right]\right)$$

with

$$SPm = \frac{1}{32}\sum_{t=1}^{32} SPt \;\; ; STXm = \frac{1}{32}\sum_{t=1}^{32} STXt \;\; ; NIXm = \frac{1}{32}\sum_{t=1}^{32} NIXt$$

Figure 1. A Prospectus of a Capital Guarantee Product[12]

of labor between the front, middle, and the back office is disrupted by clients who invent themselves as designers for the occasion.

Documenting a team that designs and manages new products, rather than tracking a lonely trader who deals with standard securities, changes quite dramatically the account of finance. When financial engineering becomes part of the picture, the "securities" designed by growing numbers of engineers are no longer true to their etymology. The term *securities* was originally used to designate financial products that were standardized in such a way that they would not demand much attention beyond a close look at their prices. Securities were literally "free of care." This freedom enjoyed by traders referred to the derivation of value created by property rights over equities (buildings, equipment, and all the assets, whether material or immaterial, coming with business ventures). This derivation did not demand care of the equities themselves, so that owning securities freed capitalists from managing businesses. With financial engineering, these previously carefree vehicles are combined into a new business venture, and care is once again an imperative. Traders now must understand not only the market as a whole but also the very specific characteristics of the new product that is to sit in their portfolios for long stretches of time. The products designed are long-lived. They remain with the bank issuing them and with the client who acquires them. Throughout their lives, they continue to require management by the partners of these deals; that is, whether the products are assets or liabilities.

The principle of the CGP was simple: clients (institutional or individual clients) would pay the bank to manage their capital for a period varying from three to fifteen years. This initial fee would amount to a variable percentage of the total capital invested by the client.[13] This capital would then be in the possession of the bank, which would manage it the way it believed most appropriate. This management would take place in the trading rooms of the bank, outside the purview of the clients, according to principles that the bank jealously protected. At the end of three to fifteen years, the bank would return this initial amount (*capital guarantee*: 100 percent of nominal amount at maturity) plus a return based on a formula, the bank's crown jewel and the distinctive mark of this financial service,[14]

At maturity, the holder will receive the greater of the following:

Nominal $\times$ 100% or Nominal $\times$ {100% + 120% $\times$ [Max(BKT$_m$ – 1;0)]}.

It is good to restate the distinction between the formula of the CGP (guarantee and mechanical performance of the basket) and the promise of hedge funds (performance of a secret investment recipe).[15] For the latter, the only source for high returns is the talent of the manager and his or her traders. The client who trusts such a manager and team of traders does not have access to the final return through an explicit formula, and the style of managing the client's capital is fully black-boxed. If things go bad and if strategies turn out to be flawed, clients can lose most of their money. When managers engage in fraudulent activities, clients can lose all their capital. Against this background, the CGP offered a unique combination of insurance (through the guarantee) and investment (through the performance of the formula). CGPs were not the black boxes theorized by Bruno Latour to characterize the irreversibility engineered by scientists in their attempt to build strong facts.[16] Rather, they were *white boxes*, transparent formulas exposing the mechanism of value without restraints.[17] Unlike other investment in mutual funds or hedge funds, the uncertainty of the payoff was only driven by the fluctuating values of the underlying financial products lodged in the basket (BKT) and bent by the formula (100% + 120% . . .). The bank itself has no control over this uncertainty, and no artistic or scientific means enter into setting the return more or less high. The only work of the trader is to guarantee that the bank can make the payoff to the client when the contract comes to term. With the prospectus in hand, the client knows as much as he or she can hope of the future gain; knowing more would entail some superior knowledge or some form of market manipulation.

Unlike the client who can only observe the return of his or her wager—and negotiate with the bank the boundaries of a product—the bank actively manages the capital lent by the client. The formulas and recipes of this management will be central themes of *Codes of Finance*. These recipes have a technical name in finance: hedging. Unlike the literal and explicit payoff formula served to the client, hedging methods and strategies are kept away from everybody outside the trading room. Even more restricted, these techniques do not circulate beyond the trading desk and its few operatives. These hedging techniques are the crown jewels of the bank and are the outcomes of sophisticated engineering prowess.

It is the thesis of this book that the engineers of these products had largely overlooked the puzzle of understanding and hedging the risks thereby created. Thinking quasi-exclusively with numbers-engendered prices and smooth scenarios, such as the one just supplied, had allowed bankers to get carried away and made them lose touch with the actual costs of financial innovation. Innumerable events during the life of a CGP could disrupt its sleek imagined trajectory and make it fall in a chaos of competing interpretations. Responsibility for these failures was the hubris of derivation that had seized the engineers of General Bank.

The Business of Derivation

It is the ambition of this book to document closely the impact of an innovation in financial engineering on a bank and use these insights to address the major question of the origin of value in political economy. What do financial engineering innovations do to economic value? Which economic mechanisms do these products help us understand? In particular, what is economic derivation? The one benefit of the most recent financial crisis is undoubtedly the creation of a space of public critique around financial engineering. Yet, despite the timely embracing of a major political economy question, critics of recent innovations involving financial derivatives have often turned to either flawed and hasty characterizations or apologetic technical accounts, both of which miss the gist of the derivative gesture. If people with even cursory knowledge of economic mechanisms know of some "derivatives," like futures and options whose prices are contingent upon underlying commodities or securities, these products are often understood as *secondary* or *metaeconomic* entities and defined in purely contractual terms by the contingency of the claim that characterizes them. Despite the considerable amount of money that they mobilize and their centrality to many industrial enterprises, derivatives are considered peripheral to "real economies."[18] They are also described as parasitic to the sound working of real production factors. In these accounts, the very notion of "real economies" is problematic to the extent that it points to an *economic substratum*, a substance that economic enterprises either respect or derail. If the need to investigate whether derivation brings chaos or felicity, is well taken, the investigation cannot borrow the path of a regression toward a theory of labor value when the pressing issue is rather to grasp the composition of economic entities.[19]

Codes of Finance is a case study of economic derivation, but rather than look at derivatives as a class of economic goods, this ethnography studies derivation as a process. In so doing, it fills the gap between propagandists of financial engineering and its blunt critics by offering some elements of an analysis of economic derivation.[20] Against the common views that alternate between overlooking derivation's role and demonizing it, I posit that derivation is the central operation behind economic value creation.

Derivatives have recently received much scholarly and journalistic coverage. If financial economists have mostly praised the diffusion of innovations springing from the 1970s-era solution to the pricing of simple derivative products through the Black–Scholes formula, then historians and sociologists have shown a greater interest in understanding the process through which pricing recipes have reinforced market mechanisms. The rich and rapidly growing body of scholarship started by Michel Callon's economic reformulation of the performativity thesis (Callon, 1998) has mostly been centered around the framing of transactions through the design of institutions and their market devices. Donald MacKenzie has taken up such a program and developed it in the direction of finance, focusing on the 1970s innovations and the transformations of Stock Exchanges they induced.[21] Against the idea that there are two regimes of transactions, natural prices and man-made rules, the performativity scholars point to the coexistence of these modes but in a chronological order: behind each price, a design. Change the design and the price will follow suit. The consequences of this inscription of the price within the design show a renewed role granted to the organization of markets and to the political decisions thus far kept out of the picture by economists brandishing the threat of inefficiency.

Codes of Finance is also a story of designs, but unlike the performativity of scholars who look at the invention of a frame coordinating actors around economic transactions, it dissects another regime of value. Derivations are shifts and flights from existing frames. The shifts are designed to benefit from the stability engineered by the frame without incurring the costs of instituting this stability. If the frame creates a public good and a site of coordination for the actors willing to play by its rules, then derivation only draws on existing goods. It does not institute; rather, it latches onto and derives value from this operation. Derivation is a regime that quickly takes and offers nothing in return, at least not in the form of a contract setting the rights and duties of parties. Once these economic gestures have become the primary characters of this mode of value creation, the emphasis on framing found in performativity studies loses its relevance.

In one way, the mechanism of derivation operates along terms exactly opposite to those of the performativity thesis. Whereas scholars who have embraced or rejected Callon's program focused on the active design of economies through scripts written by economists and social engineers, *Codes of Finance* investigates how finance has become an exercise of turning economies into infinite texts by derivation.[22] The drive of derivation is opposite to that of social engineers' shaping of the economy through scripts: building and stabilizing the morphology of economies is not the goal but the resource to be exploited without reciprocity. Existing institutions, and the wealth of untapped information and resources they exude, are the building blocks of derivative enterprises. The moment of formation is skipped altogether and a restless and unstable business venture replaces an organization.

Locating themselves at the end of a chain of derivations, General Bank's formulas manipulate securities and indices *as if* they are nothing but inscriptions detached from their foundations (respectively, the publicly traded capital of companies and the securities of these companies). From the engineers' perspective, the building blocks of these shrewd formulas can be thought of as words that combine in unlimited numbers to form imaginary new formulas to be sold to clients. Engineers dream of turning General Bank into a storyteller ("give us $1 million, we will make it grow to $1.2 million effortlessly") without dealing with lower levels of the economy (physical plants, national economies) and without worrying about the stability of these stories—finance as a pure promise, disembodied and detached from the rest of the economy. Of course, derivation never eschews completely the building of even so transitory a frame. Although this gesture lacks accountability, it is constantly caught up in regulations that hinder its guiding principles. But, more important than the chase between regulators and innovators, derivation as an extreme and purified form of value creation has consequences on the organization that carries it. When it is practiced by a large investment bank, like General Bank, derivation becomes a self-annihilating mechanism through which innovation and organization undermine each other. Derivations are premised on an ability to quickly move assets, work forces and in general investments in order to rapidly exploit the business opportunities foreseen by the bank's engineers. Deriving and organizing are not easily married, as one pulls in the direction of exploration when the other pushes toward exploitation along the lines of stable rules. The study of General Bank's organization will clarify the problems created through the use of derivation and shed light on a series of dilemmas that the bank faced once it adopted this technique:

- Mobility versus stability of its organization
- Mobility versus stability of its products
- Secrecy versus openness
- Concentration of the trading room versus dispersion of the maintenance sites of its products
- Multiplication of the modes of calculation versus presentation of a unique bottom line to the shareholders

Overview of Chapters

The introduction presents the bank to the reader by focusing on the practical conditions of the fieldwork and on the various populations studied in the book's three parts. The main questions of the book are presented as mechanisms for charting the threads from concrete descriptions to the more theoretical ending of the book.

Part I of our voyage into financial engineering—From Models to Books scrutinizes the product and its models. This close focus has one objective: to understand how the economic imagination of engineers materializes into financial services, subsequently maintained by traders on actual markets.

Chapter 1 focuses on financial operators' use of codes and languages in the trading room to articulate new financial products. It lays out the coding and modeling conflicts that arise between the various disciplines (physicists, mathematicians, computer scientists). Codes can either be formal or ad hoc, but the (ironic) bottom line is that no one knows for sure how best to describe these products. The problem is not a paucity of descriptions, but rather an embarrassment of riches. CGPs have too many competing depictions that were derived from the multiplicity of languages adopted by different groups operating within the financial industry. The lack of synthesis of these languages is both a resource for and a threat to the financial industry. Banks have a particular incentive to encourage proliferation, at least to the extent that it does not jeopardize their own integrity: each new code casts light on a dimension of the product and helps to anticipate potential reactions. Yet the accumulation of codes may turn the bank into a Tower of Babel. The dispersion of the product's characteristics into so many languages exposes the bank to the risk of losing sight of its actual holdings.

Traders of CGPs sit at the intersection of several Exchanges.[23] This delicate position owes much to the design of the products they manage: CGPs involve sophisticated combinations of underlying securities that traders are not expert in but must still buy and sell. Chapter 2 provides a detailed description of the management of the traders' huge portfolios. It introduces a crucial actor in the trading room: the pricer (a computational machine that provides traders with the market values of their contracts). In a market in which products are designed to create asymmetry between the bank and its clients or other competing banks, pricers that provide traders with values and risks produce the only knowledge available. Portfolios aggregate so many products that traders cannot easily develop tacit knowledge of the reactions of their assets to market shifts. Unable to speculate about products with values derived from several Exchanges, traders simulate various strategies before hedging. But such simulations make them lose touch with their running price and disrupt the hedging scenario designed by engineers.

Part II of this book—Topography of a Secret Experiment—analyzes the territories of the bank. Codes generate new milieus in and around the bank. They allow engineers and traders to map the risks and promises of new financial species, and they create new populations of operators as well as a gradient of skills that are required to translate this information from the language of the bank to the language of the customers.

The profusion of languages that the bank uses to define its products takes place in an environment that is highly competitive. Chapter 3 describes how the trading room is itself a market with a fierce competition around the allotment of its most profitable sectors among the traders. Not only financial instruments but also skills are being traded in the room. Each operator prefers to be outfitted with the most lucrative line of products, but faced with a strong hierarchy the operators themselves end up circulating from bank to bank in much the same way as products circulate from the bank to the client. Thus, these two parallel circulations in the space of the trading room and beyond create unprecedented competition. But this competition must eventually give way to collaboration because uncertainty about the definitions of the products and their possible reactions may well jeopardize all the actors.

The dream of ubiquity encapsulated in the formulas of these products runs counter to the storage imperative imposed upon the bank for products held for several years. The new demands that these products create in terms of location vis-à-vis the market have significant effects on the organization of the bank. Chapter 4 reviews the difficulties encountered by the variety of operators trying to keep track of the changes a typical product goes through. The customized nature of the services offered by General Bank and the right of the clients to revise their products along the way creates a puzzle for an organization needing to be collectively reactive to these changes. The question facing the bank is now: Where should the products be located so that traders can hedge them on a daily basis and clients can change them?

Part III of this book—Porous Banking: Clients and Investors in Search of Accounts—looks at the economy of customized financial products. It moves outward from the hermetic environment of the bank to bring new populations into the picture: clients, investors, and regulators now become the main characters of the CGP. Part III first looks at the process of selling financial products that are essentially mathematical formulas. Clients tend to be both knowledgeable and inconstant in their preferences, a combination that poses a difficult task for the bank operators: the operators must accept the intrusion of an expert client in the design of the product while stabilizing their preferences. Chapter 5 examines the notion of client preference by showing how clients are affected by interactions related to the properties of products as these are staged by salespeople. The interaction between salesperson and client is set up to control the uncertainty around the product and the client. To anticipate and control the preferences of clients, the salespeople have to *become* clients. On the other end, General Bank has to tailor its commercial pitch to differentiate its services from liquidity while luring the client into freezing his or her capital for 5 to 10 years. How does one coin a marketing strategy that conveys the idea of a two-headed instrument, both investment and insurance?

Clients were not the only group excluded from the privacy of the bank's design of exotic finance.[24] Investors owning General Bank shares had no direct way of monitoring the secret and opaque strategies conducted by the bank. Indeed, the bank itself did not always assess properly its risks and costs. Only after having launched these innovative products did it try to devise ways of counting them and measuring their costs. Chapter 6 introduces the other side of the bank where the costs of the CGPs are revealed. These high-maintenance products create new costs (organizational and human) and challenge existing accounting techniques. Against this opacity, investors have demanded that specific accounting rules be adopted. They have pressed for more transparent disclosure requirements and a new bank organizational strategy.

These intimate relations between the bank and its clients and investors strain the bank's boundaries. This intrusion from investors reversed the privileges of the trading room: from being an aggressively calculating center, it became itself subjected to calculations by investors; from being an engineer of finance, it became engineered by finance. Chapter 7 describes how this enforced porosity spurred a reaction among financial operators to engage in "reverse finance" to slow down the process of commoditization that threatened them.

The conclusion addresses the underlying economic question raised by derivation. CGPs can be described as combinations of existing securities; as such, their value is derived from existing values. I use them as a purified case of economic derivation. The quest for foundations and origins that has driven economic theorists, as well as their critics, for the past three centuries prevents us from fully understanding this regime of derivation. The conclusion of the book provides a timely question in view of the most recent financial crisis: If we have lost the hope of assigning a site to value creation (labor, land, etc.) and must now live with long cascades of derivation, how do we set the criteria for good and bad cascades?

Codes of Finance

A Day in a Trader's Life

Codes of Finance examines a bank to reveal how financial operators and financial products coexist. This coexistence is tense because the bank deals with innovative products that yield unexpected reactions on unevenly charted markets. Because the designs of the financial products introduced here is coextensive to the lives of traders, engineers, and salespeople, these innovations are major protagonists and need to be fleshed out. How can we describe a world that is a patchwork of individuals, machines, and products? A series of sharp definitions up front is tempting, but would miss the crucial uncertainty surrounding many of the latest innovations of finance. Understanding, defining, and controlling new products are indeed central concerns of the operators we are about to study. To introduce the reader to the concrete daily practices of these characters, I offer a snapshot of the typical day of the trader.

At 8:00 A.M., Alan arrives in the General Bank equities and derivative products trading room. Alan is in charge of maintaining a portfolio of financial products, much like an art collector would maintain a collection of paintings. He sells some products, buys others, and tries to figure out what will facilitate success in the market and where the market is headed. Upon arriving, he indulges for a few minutes in the usual small talk with colleagues. He catches sight of the quantitative engineer (the "quant"), who specializes in creating price models for the financial products that Alan trades. For a good twenty minutes, Alan quizzes the quant on the puzzles that the market has created the day before. Much like a Formula One driver would report to mechanics the reactions experienced while driving on a test circuit, Alan briefs the quant on the ups and downs of his portfolio's value and seeks an account that will help him anticipate future market configurations that are similar. He cannot afford to watch his portfolio lose value, and he presses the quant for some simple accounts of his products on the market. He sees himself as part of an engineering collective working to innovate and understand its innovations. Alan has been a trader at General Bank for five years. He graduated from a Parisian engineering school and, after specializing for a year in applied mathematics, he went straight to the bank to work at a desk famous for its financial engineering prowess.

The trader—as his title suggests—buys and sells "things." But unlike other traders who roam other floors of the same building, Alan does not trade goods and commodities like silk, oil, or cotton. He specializes in financial products, *securities* in finance parlance, whose values depend on the economic activities of companies, groups of companies, and sometimes countries. That difference matters for Alan: he deals exclusively with flows of currency located in bank accounts spread across the world so that, unlike most commodity traders, he never has to worry about the physical delivery of perishable goods. Finance is a *derived* modality of economy that does not preoccupy itself with dealing in things, like bushels of wheat or barrels of crude oil; rather, it elaborates and derives new economic vehicles (equities, bonds, futures, options) from existing economic activities. Unlike silk or cotton, financial products are nothing but contractual documents that define the volume and direction of money between the partners in a deal. Yet these contracts, because they are innovative, can be more difficult to understand and control than physical commodities. Alan sits at one end of such a deal.

Alan works at a desk alongside other traders and engineers sitting side-by-side and facing rows of monitors. He turns on his computer and connects to a suite of software—hidden in his computer but easily accessible by the click of his mouse. It is the beginning of a long day that may last until 6:00 or 7:00 P.M. if things go well. During the day he will access the market through his computer to check the value of his financial products. Figuring out the value of the entire set of financial products he owns is Alan's quasi-exclusive activity. These products are organized in a portfolio—in practical terms, a window on his computer with the list of all owned products and their relevant characteristics. Before computers came to occupy center stage in the trading room, portfolios were comprised of sheets of paper held together by binders that contained all the information in a contract. Alan stands at the end of a long evolutionary line that marks the transformation of paper agreements to digital bits, but he regularly has to go back to paper for information. First among the pieces of information he consults are the prices and their variations, also called volatility. Remember that Alan is not going to have much use for these products: if anything, he expects to get a return from holding a debt that provides interest or from owning a piece of property that offers a dividend. Alternatively, he anticipates being able to sell back the products to another trader, at a price higher than the one he paid for the initial acquisition.[1] He needs to get money out of his products because the paper or digital bits modes of transaction offer little else.[2]

After much consideration and consultation with other traders in the room, Alan turns to his other principal activity—figuring out a way of buying and selling financial products according to a scheme derived from his analysis of the market. How does he make up his mind? He looks at the variations in prices of his products and sees what their correlation looks like. *Correlation* is the most crucial indicator for Alan: it tells him whether the price changes of securities translate into a loss for his portfolio. With many products in his portfolio, Alan can easily lose track of the composition of price changes. Some products go up, others go down, and when hundreds of them move continuously in unpredictable directions and react to even the smallest piece of news, predicting the value of the portfolio is no easy task. His attention is sharpened by the omnipresence of the "pricer," a piece of software crucial to his strategies and plans. This piece—designed by the quant and turned into a computational tool by the computer engineers of the research and development (R&D) unit of the bank—computes many calculations at a speed that greatly surpasses Alan's. It contains pieces of information pertaining to all the products owned by Alan and processes that mass of data on a continuous basis. As his portfolio grows, the task of figuring out the risk entailed by collections of financial products is largely given to the pricer. By simulating transactions, this tool performs a crucial function that explains some of the most central features of financial markets. Thanks to the pricer, Alan can assess the value of his portfolio without having to engage in transactions: the products that Alan has in his portfolio do not move from this place. The pricer simulates real-world markets enough so that Alan can be confident that its estimate approaches what another trader would offer.

Although Alan delegates much analytical authority to the pricer when making decisions, he retains a much praised quality among traders. He has developed a *sense* of the market. He knows not to buy too much at a time so as to not raise suspicion among other traders in the market monitoring the price changes. He also knows that markets have temporal moods: not all hours offer the same response from other traders because of the limited window of intervention. Alan buys and sells financial products on Exchanges located in Asia, Europe, and North America, each of which operates on local time. This dispersion adds to the problems already plaguing Alan's day: He sits in a Parisian trading room, and as he turns on his pricer, he has to deal with markets that are on the verge of closing or are already closed. A Japanese financial product is assessed in parallel with a Canadian financial product, but one recapitulates into its prices all the trading-day vicissitudes, whereas the other stumbles on the first bits of information. As a partial remedy to this geographic dilemma of his trading activities, Alan works with collaborators in these other financial centers. When he sleeps, they look after his portfolio and debrief him (for the Asia-based collaborators) before he takes over. When Alan leaves the desk after the French Exchange has closed, he passes his portfolio to his North America–based collaborator. But unlike an air controller who handles airplanes when they move into his or her assigned zone and passes them to another controller when they exit the zone, Alan has the final call on the portfolio and handles over 8 or 9 hours of a plane flying 24 hours.[3] For more than 14 hours, the plane is on its own.

Alan is thus one among thousands of traders who dedicate their lives to monitoring prices and selling in anticipation of a downturn while buying when they expect a price rise. But Alan does not simply trade financial products. He does much more than that inasmuch as he *adds* to the existing pool of economic goods and services. He has made his reputation—and much money—as part of a group that designs new and sometimes unique financial products for banks.

As a consequence of this foray into engineering, the dialogue that traders of simpler and more standard products would entertain with their pricers alone is replaced by communication with a much larger population in the bank; salespeople, engineers, and quants become interlocutors and part of a complex chorus. This slight modification to the life of the trader has far-ranging consequences: The design of a new security begs the question of its nature. Although financial products are not exactly products—unlike commodities such as cotton or oil—their characteristics can easily be captured on paper. For Alan, innovative and unique securities can also be defined, but as they are "produced" and negotiated between the engineers and salespeople on the bank's side with the client, it is not rare that the text of the contract changes several times before the transaction itself and even after. With a portfolio full of these customized products, each with changing characteristics, Alan is often interrupted by a back-office manager in the middle of his portfolio assessment asking him to check on the actual terms of a contract.

Around 4:00 P.M., in the middle of balancing his portfolio risk exposure—selling risky securities, purchasing other more promising ones—Alan gets such a call. One of the contracts sold by General Bank to a wealthy client requires the payment of interest twice a year. The back-office manager phones to make sure that the front office (the site of product design, marketing, and management; Alan's world) and the back office (the site of product maintenance and of the posttransaction client relationship) are referencing the *same* product. This call comes on the heels of a series of mismatches between the two offices. Financial products registered as X in the front office were simultaneously registered as Y in the back office, and during discussions about individual contracts, each office believed it was talking about the same, unique contract. In some cases, the client had still another version of the contract, turning a financial deal into a genuine cacophony.

The reason for such inadvertent mistakes in an otherwise cautious industry is the two-headed nature of the bank in its relationships with its clients. Also, there is a crucial clause in the contracts allowing clients to demand modifications of the products once they are already issued. Alan initiates the deal with the help of salespeople, who bring wealthy clients to the bank; the back-office operators maintain the contract and close the deal. In particular, the back office settles the circulation of money between the bank and its clients. With thousands of outstanding contracts, warnings have been automated and attached to each contract when it reaches the time of payment. But in between the design of a contract tailored to a client's needs and its term (3, 5, or 10 years down the road), the product can undergo significant changes. A series of events, duly listed in the contract, can authorize the client—and the bank—to renegotiate the terms of the deal, but this appealing characteristic to the client can quickly become a nightmare for the bank. Seemingly simple questions crop up: What is the latest deal? What service do we owe the client and when do we need to pay him?

Alan leaves the trading room. He has done what he is employed to do, relentlessly, on a daily basis: hedging. He has adjusted the composition of his portfolio to protect its value against anticipated changes. But as he embarks on the subway journey that takes him to the center of Paris, he cannot help but worry about the ongoing value variation that the portfolio is undergoing. Even though the French Exchange is now closed, his products do not enjoy much rest. Behind his back, so to speak, other Exchanges are in full swing, and their moves cannot be hedged by Alan as they unfold.

Questioning Finance

Access

This book tells the story of a financial innovation from the inside. But one might legitimately ask: Do we really want another insider's account? Are we not already paying a high price for having left insiders to organize financial markets at their convenience for too long? If financial operators acknowledge that they erred, then the accounts that they give of their inability to control a situation that went out of control are short of illuminating. Threatened as scapegoats of a major financial crisis, those who have attempted to articulate the failure of the financial system usually spend more time shifting the blame over to another group of experts than shedding light on the system's inherent complexity. When experts are in a bubble, it is safe to burst it open, but not just any tool will reveal its inner complexity. Indeed, who will gain an intellectual grasp of these financial innovations and their ripple effects without a firm grip on the technical mechanisms that triggered the current collapse?

In this book, I neither sing the praise of the wunderkind of the booming financial engineering world nor do I encourage the trial of a "den of thieves." Rather, I invite the reader to travel with me and observe one of the actors of a play gone sour, without initial prejudices about finance, markets, and big money. Instead of hasty and premature judgments, it is more fruitful to paint an accurate portrait of the manufacture of complex finance. The identity of financial operators, the name of the bank, counterparts (clients), and the name of the software I document and analyze have been disguised. The point of *Codes of Finance* is not to uncover "juicy stories," but rather to shed light on the intellectual and organizational consequences of financial engineering.

I entered General Bank in January 2000 and left it in July 2001. I did fieldwork there in my capacity as a PhD student in "economics of innovation." The people who recruited me cared little about my actual training or the questions that would occupy me as an apprentice scholar. They let me in because I was attending one of the prestigious master's programs in mathematical finance at the Universite Paris 6 Jussieu.[1] Students of this program were required to spend six months as interns in a bank. This opportunity became my fieldwork. Another reason they accepted me—a more obscure one, although one that explains some crucial features of the General Bank population—was my "education."[2] I came to the bank as a student of one of the *Grandes Ecoles*, and although I did not brag about it, it inevitably came up in the interviews with my employers. It immediately eased my introduction to the bank. General Bank may not have been a den of thieves, but it was unquestionably a den of alumni of elite schools, selectively cultivating peers rather than searching the general work force for vacancies. I transferred three times in the bank, occupying successively the position of research assistant (early 2000), trader assistant (spring 2000), and middle-office manager (2001). The first position entailed designing an overhaul of market research in the fixed-income trading room. The second position brought me to the equities and derivatives trading room, the main site of this investigation. There, I was asked to design an application to rationalize the circulation of information between traders, engineers, and salespeople. My third and last position was in the middle office of the fixed-income room. I was in charge of remodeling their exotic derivative products and managing their transfer from one database to another. Fortunately for me and for the research agenda I had set for myself, these positions allowed me to meet all the other actors of the investment banking unit of General Bank: I ended up spending a year and a half documenting the product that the bank was hailing as a revolution in market finance.

The perspective of this book is that of an outside observer who lived in and around a bank and made himself a quasi-expert.[3] But it was not just any bank: General Bank was one of the central actors in the financial revolutions of the 1990s. This French bank was the darling of the financial derivatives markets: It repeatedly won the award of "best derivatives house" of the year given by *Risk* magazine, one of the bibles of the discipline.[4] It was the epitome of financial engineering, pioneering a new economic landscape for firms and individuals willing to bring high-tech finance to their lives. More recently, in January 2008, General Bank also made the headlines, albeit for less savory reasons: Kevin Voldevieille, a trader, fraudulently convinced his management to allow him to invest far above his limits.[5] This now infamous trader spent a few years working in the exact same sites that this book documents. He started his career in the little-known and unglamorous back offices of General Bank, and he made his way to the site of all envy: the trading room, also roamed by our more anonymous Alan. I crossed paths with Voldevieille but never got the chance to study him personally. As I started investigating the fancy world of the front office, I realized that most of the action—and the most interesting actions—were taking place in the back office. Both Voldevieille and I were at General Bank to understand the consequences of highly structured financial products—laden with mathematics and equipped with the latest computing technologies—on the maintenance of the bank.

When Voldevieille's scheme was exposed, English-speaking commentators reveled in depicting the typical French arrogance and the lack of adequate risk supervision. They immediately adopted a mix of psychological and sociological approaches to understanding what had led such a young, hardworking, and successful member of the French middle class to spin such a tangled web of document fabrication and database manipulation. These accounts contained a number of the stock prejudices that journalists often invoke to pepper their pieces with cultural veracity: Parisian versus provincial opposition; class society; monopoly of power in the hands of polytechnicians; hubris of the French way of engineering finance. Voldevieille was a modern version of Rastignac, the famous character created by French writer Honore de Balzac: aspiring and striving, ready to bend the rules laid down by the established elite to make a name in Parisian circles. Few pieces went further than this storyline or questioned whether their repetition of the word "French" was adding much light in uncovering the fraudulent strategies used by Voldevieille and to his ability to go unnoticed for so long.

Although these writings comforted a few readers' worldviews, they often focused on cultural platitudes and did not help much in understanding the underlying causes of such behaviors. *Codes of Finance* documents financial innovation *as it took place* in a French bank. Its scene is the new financial district of La Defense on the western edge of Paris. Yet, it is not primarily a book about France or French characters. The "old boy network" culture experienced during my recruitment is not particularly French. Every elite education institution operates along these lines; anthropologist Karen Ho, for example, has recently shown how graduates from Harvard, Princeton, Stanford, and MIT select incoming interns among the ranks of their alma maters (Ho, 2009). Similarly, the kinds of experiments that General Bank entertained were carried forth simultaneously in other countries. Swiss bank *Union des Banques Suisses* had initiated the move toward similar products and French engineers had learned from its failure. U.S. banks were also in full swing trying to devise similar formulas.

An exclusively cultural account, focused on national specificities and overlooking the technicality of financial innovation, would inflate factors that were not central to the vicissitudes of the General Bank enterprises.[6] This lesson was learned from the methods of Actor Network Theory scholars and from one of its most fruitful applications, offered by Bruno Latour (1993) in his study of the failure of a *personal public transportation* system, *Aramis*. In discarding a blunt cultural approach, I do not assume a sphere of finance, detached from its context; rather, I expect the relevant issues to surface in the course of the investigation. The preeminence of engineers in French higher administration and boards of directors of major companies is of major import. The freedom that financial engineers enjoyed in the trading room, the support that they received from other engineers at higher levels, and the relative lack of supervision that they experienced in their interactions with the risks department all came from their perceived importance. Yet, this prestige alone would not have allowed them to steer the bank into one of the riskiest finance operations. In the venture that this book documents, the companion pieces of these powerful engineers—CGPs, products of the engineers' financial imagination—have to be seen as the primary characters if we are to understand the story about to unfold.

The Population in and around the Bank

Inside General Bank, communities with different and distinct expertises collaborate around whatever product is pushed. It is worth highlighting these groups to give visibility to the chaotic nature of the conversations circling around the products; an added payoff is to get a sense of their relative location in the bank. Because the purpose of this study is to track the ripple effects of innovative products on the bank as an institution, it is useful to lay out the *functions* that this methodology will discover through its meandering. Front, middle, and back offices will feature in the coming account, but not as the cleanly distinct entities that the functional approach offers. If the dream of the CGP designers was to dissipate geographic differences by designing a product that straddled Paris, Tokyo, New York, and any other Exchange around the globe, this book will tell a story of highly localized practices and competing idioms struggling to live up to the blueprint of a global financial product.[7]

Front Office

The front office of a bank is the best-known operation center that this book will document. Yet, I argue that its perceived status has hidden some of its most interesting features. It is a profitable site to study because, through its tortured topography, the stability of the firm comes into play. It is, first, a site of exceedingly secretive calculations among engineers, salespeople, and traders collectively designing new products. Secrecy rules here, as these products cannot be protected by patents: derivation of value achieved by the bank never lasts long in the face of intense competition. Simultaneously, it is also a site of great porosity. In the front office, clients get involved in the very design process, inviting themselves into the already crowded chorus of traders, engineers, and legal advisors. Traders also hedge their products here by tempering them with the daily changes of underlying markets. Front offices are worth a close look, as the tension between secrecy and transparency in the trading room is fully observable.

The trading room's financial and quantitative engineers (quants) are closest to the formal expression of products. Quants[8] were brought to the trading rooms when derivative products started to lend themselves to precise calcu-

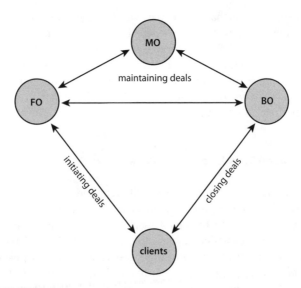

Figure 2. Sequences of Intervention in the Making of the Deal
This diagram presents one topography of the font/middle/back offices. As the story unfolds, other topographies will emerge.[10]

lative methods imported from mathematics and physics. For quants, prices can be studied either as equations to be solved or as Brownian motions[9] to be simulated. Financial engineers, in contrast, bring a less quantitative perspective to financial products. They are responsible for the final version of the contracts between the bank and its clients. They do not create these formulas from scratch. Instead, they devise them based on the complex interactions between the bank's salespeople and the traders' experience of the market. For all their differences, these two groups do not labor in isolation. Long conversations have to take place between financial engineers and quants to bridge different approaches to what a price is and how mathematical formulations of a financial product should be understood.

Also in the front office, the traders are in charge of the daily hedging of their portfolios of products. They buy and sell to make sure that the bank will be able to honor each product's payoff without incurring a loss, and they also seek to benefit from market opportunities. This activity allows them to develop an expertise akin to that of the financial engineers in the trading room: each needs to figure out how much a contract will be worth in a week, a month, or a couple of years. Yet, their paths to understanding the fluctuations in the values of these products are not always compatible.[11] Traders are immersed in the market, surrounded by "noises" that they factor into their analyses—data that would be ignored by financial engineers working with mathematical price functions instead of actual market prices.

The salespeople in the trading room work very closely with the traders and the financial engineers when new products are issued. They believe they understand whether a new product will sell and generate a large profit or whether it will go unnoticed, hidden by the growing list of products offered by competitors. The descriptions generated by this prominent group reflect their interactions with the bank's clients. Inserting themselves, via the proximity of salespeople, into the cozy conversation of the trading room, clients open this conversation up to an outside world populated by competitors and other agencies. Clients, too, want to control their risks and to tailor financial products to their specific needs.[12]

Salespeople want the bank to issue as many contracts as possible: this represents their bonus, a quasi-direct function of the number of transactions from the desk. Whether a contract turns out to be a good deal for the bank when it comes to term, and whether all the payments have been made, is of no direct relevance for salespeople. That last consideration is crucial to the traders and, to a lesser extent, engineers. Their remuneration is a function of the performance of their portfolios of products. If they are managing products that cause the bank to lose money, they and the financial engineers and quants are first to be chastised. The salespeople are only selling: they are neither designers nor managers of the products, hence they escape the regular inquiries of cause and effect.

Middle Office .

The middle-office operators have much looser task definitions. To put it briefly, they stand between the front office and the back office. Whereas the front office sits closest to the clients and closest to the sites of transaction (Exchanges on which traders buy and sell, invest the clients' money, and hedge their portfolios), the middle office bridges two centers within the bank. Middle-office operators check information flowing between the hectic world of the trading room and the steadier, slower world of the back office. A position in the middle office is not prestigious compared with that of traders or of front-office engineers. In some instances, middle offices have been made irrelevant when transactions are so straightforward that back-office staff and traders can communicate smoothly without the need of an interpreter.[13] At General Bank, their task was still much needed, and some of them were located close to the front office—in the same room.[14] Much to their frustration, they were located in the trading room but did not engage in front-office activities.

Back Office

If the middle-office operations are not easy to describe without entering further into the activities and the types of products, back-office functions are much easier to grasp. "Records" is the word that captures the predominant task. Back-office operators deal with past and current transactions with a focus on data accuracy that traders do not always understand. Front-office populations are focused on prices and investment opportunities: they monitor market changes on a daily basis and with an attention to very high frequencies. Seconds are their relevant units of intervention. Back-office operators look at deals across a different timescale. Their emphasis is on accurate records and on meticulously respected due dates—notions often derided by traders. Back-office managers scrupulously check on deals and make sure payments are processed on a timely basis. Closing prices, start dates, and end dates are their universe. Every day, they track indices and stock prices and fill out electronic forms that end up feeding databases preciously guarded. Yet, the designs of these products and the reversibility clause dearest to the clients add complication to the function described thus far. In the course of retrieving market information, checking product characteristics, and general maintenance, the back office crosses paths with the front office, the middle office, and the clients. When contracts must be amended on the fly, the temporal division of labor between traders and back-office managers undergoes a shift that rubs against the privilege of front-office employees.

This tension created by the unstable product–client combination comes from the two-headed nature of the bank. During the negotiations, the front office speaks for the bank through the salesperson and the trader; once the contract has been signed, the back office takes over and conducts the client relationship. This bifurcation would work fine if the contract were not occasionally to morph midway through its term, forcing back and front offices to become partners for a day in a new round of negotiations with the client. Whereas the goal of these products was to contract the dispersion of financial markets into one place—the bank—and invent a global financial vehicle, these very products had the unexpected consequence of exacerbating fragmentation in the bank. Overlapping prerogatives, conflicting speaking rights for the bank, and porosity threatened the balance of power and the orderliness of General Bank.

Beyond Front, Middle, and Back Offices

Close to the back office—but technically different and organizationally very different from the back office—two other centers interact with the front office–middle office–back office chain of circulation. The accounting department and the risk department act as satellites of the chain: they have elliptical orbits and come and go more or less frequently. Whereas the two external determinants of trading-room activities were thus far the client and the markets for hedging, the risk and accounting departments introduce other important figures to this story. Investors in publicly traded companies have been increasingly vocal over the past thirty years. Central to their concerns as investors is their ability to see through the opaque corporate structures that banks such as General Bank generate. The CGP belongs to a family of prod-ucts that has triggered much worry among investors due to the customiza-tion that these products force on the bank. Contracts carried for up to fifteen years would be fine if only they could be assessed before their term. If these contracts evade the accounting capture that the bank offers its current and prospective owners, they are seen as black boxes. Their value cannot be as-sessed and investors' strategies cannot be adjusted accordingly. In a nutshell, and most problematically, these products do not have a price. In response to the challenges raised by the customization of these products and as part of a movement in tune with the growing power of investors over managers, the boundaries of managerial control in the bank have been increasingly tested.

Who is peripheral and who is central in the composition of financial prod-ucts are stakes that are fiercely fought over by the communities who partake in the definition of the CGP. Studying this class of products shows how the design of a seemingly innocuous new financial vehicle can shake the com-mon language of a bank, and beyond the bank itself, the financial industry that struggles to make sense of the potential consequences of its ripple effects on markets. The disruptive power of such innovative products shakes off the clean distinction of these groups into front, middle, and back, as well as insid-ers and outsiders in a way that is not trivial. With the main actors (operators and products) now visible, it is possible to present the main topics of *Codes of Finance*—derivation materializes, and its consequences on the world of operators and on the bank itself become tangible.

Topics

A difficulty of this book comes from the very definition of its object (CGPs). Surprising as it may sound, even among those who design, trade, and manage CGPs, it is not possible to define them unequivocally. Engineers will summa-rize them as "a zero-coupon and a call option"; back-office managers will see them as "a contract and 32 quarterly fixing dates"; traders will define them as "the indices' futures hedging scheme"; clients will define them as "aggressive insurance." The dispersion of their definition along the network of operators is a challenge for the social scientist setting out to describe what is at stake in these products. Any definition that I offer at the start of my analysis runs the risk of simply adding another competing definition to the chorus of existing definitions, put forth in other venues.[15] Definitions thus become the central characters in this research.[16]

Financial Conversations: Codes, Models, and Secrets

The frequent issuance of new products by the trading room prompts a pro-liferation of codes and models that offer new perspectives on their properties.[17] In the context of the bank, differentiation multiplies cognitive handles on the product: all the definitions of a CGP mentioned above are right and they are all useful to their users but this multiplication also jeopardizes the unity of the bank. Each local language draws boundaries around an isolated "clan" and hinders the communication demanded by the sensitivity of these products.

The simultaneous push to issue more and more customized products—designed for the idiosyncratic needs of customers in the context of an assembly-line mentality—adds to the puzzle of designing special codes. It is easy to reckon the magnitude of problems created by the conflict between customization and mass production: If Alan had the luxury of real customization and was to deal with only a few products, he would keep them closely under his sight. There, they would stand at his fingertips. Yet, in real life Alan's products exist in different formats—scattered between his computer's hard drive, a server shared with the rest of the trading room, still other digital versions on his assistant's workstation, and a few other paper versions at a couple of sites a few floors above. And that multiplication of the product into many versions is true for each and every one of them. So, faced with such a proliferation of versions, coding them is not a luxury: it is the only survival strategy of traders overwhelmed with documents, whose characteristics must be at their *quasi-fingertips* on demand. Codes and models invented to describe and manipulate products are technologies of *adjustable distance* and simplification. These technologies accept the loss of the *whole* of each product—no longer under the gaze of the trading-room operators—in return for the relevant features of *all* the products.[18]

The dilemma here is, again, simple. Should operators use an arbitrary language and arbitrary characterizations to describe their products, they might quickly lose track of their value to the bank. They will also endanger the bank by postponing communication around the characteristics of the product. Deciding how to speak about and define these products is a nontrivial operation as a result, as the struggle between the demand for precision and the *sociality* of these products gets in the way.[19] An example of this tension will clarify things.

A language widely shared in General Bank—as in most banks across the world— was that of profit and loss (P&L); that is, how much money the bank was making on the product under scrutiny at the time of the calculation. One of the reasons for such a widespread use of this language stemmed from its apparent market stamp. These quasi-experimental conditions, amidst a world fraught with a large variety of idioms, proved a blessing for this study. It seemed to submit other idioms to the market test. P&L seemed to be the raison d'être of such products, so much so, in fact, that it would shut out other languages. However, even this test, as specific as it was, could not help from remaining open-ended and underdetermined. Although P&L appeared to limit the variety of idioms to the one-dimensional, scientific, and final account of the return yielded by the financial products, the actual reality was far from the case. The notion of profit was constantly reshaped by conflicting languages and by the perimeter of its circulation in the bank. Whether one looked at the CGP dealt by the trader alone or the CGP maintained by the long list of operators working in the wake of its issuance, its relevant characteristics changed substantially. These products' value was site-sensitive, so that a notion so alluring as profit captured only portions of their career. Indeed, profit can span different lengths of time (over a year, a week, etc.), and it needs an accounting apparatus to reduce multiple financial engagements into a single economic metric.[20] Profit is sometimes pure liquidity—the holding of cash in the present, without any claims over the future—but it rarely comes down to this perfect form, as the calculation of P&L usually takes place while the assets are still on the market, that is, no longer or not yet liquid. They cannot be withdrawn temporarily, measured, and then silently returned to the markets. They are experimented upon in vivo.[21]

If P&L is a public code—used by most banks and present in all traders' minds at bonus time, but already open to challenges as to the perimeter of calculation, it is not surprising that such profit-driven institutions as banks are also sites of many other less public forms of product categorization and modeling. These more private codes are designed with a view to better capture and control the risky properties unleashed by these innovative products. The tensions created by innovations are well known. Old notions do not do justice to new realities; radically new notions disrupt conversations around existing objects and tend to leave the current audience behind. This tension is exacerbated in the financial industry by the need to maintain secrecy while allowing for *multiple* bodies of experts to congregate around the *same* product, among thousands of like products. In a booming labor market that facilitates the movement of operators from bank to bank, secrecy protects the precious, short-lived, and exclusive know-how of the bank. The bank struggles to figure out how to invest time and money developing new specialized local languages while retaining a work force that could easily transfer these languages to more rewarding competitors. Legal protections through confidentiality pledges do little to maintain secrecy: most of the knowledge gained is neither formal nor codified and it is easy for a trader to carry ways of categorizing products or portfolios to competing banks.

Codes are everywhere in the bank: one finds them in the primitive forms of conversation between traders and salespeople, as well as in a more articulate form when quants design models to capture the relevant price features of a product or portfolio. On-the-go classifications simplify in ways similar to the transformations achieved by a scientific model. In both cases, traders and quants need to invent appropriate ways of sorting out these products and their versions so that they can respond to their calls. That is the meat of the code puzzle: to take good care of the product, the classifications and the codifications achieved need to respect their seams.

Codes are refrains. They turn chaos—"organized" chaos, in a bank in search of ever-more profit and turned into a market with fierce competition among different traders—into order through simplification. Gilles Deleuze offers penetrating, if difficult, insights in a theory of the code as refrain in *A Thousand Plateaus* (1987 [1980]). He defines refrains as always simultaneously cognitive and topographical: they bring order into the world by acting as frames that pacify the chaos of the surrounding activities that threaten to shatter each and every form of stability. Simultaneously, refrains also define topographies. Often, they are used with a special intent to set the boundaries of understanding: enabling some, disabling others.[22] They can only be uttered in special situations, within a circle of authorized operators and distant enough from others not privy to their formulas and their powers to decode. Traders and engineers do not share the computer codes of their pricers with the salespeople: they strive fiercely to retain their monopoly as price makers over that crucial instrument in the room so that they can exclude every other employee from that zone. Salespeople do not share with the back-office manager the detailed history of the deals they have negotiated with their biggest clients or the written notes they have on these clients. During the tense period of product issuance, they engage in complex dances with clients across the perimeter of the bank. When mastered, the codes put the operator in control of his or her perimeter and help define his or her milieu. These codes offer an entry into the competitive topography of the bank: all operators want to make money by selling as many contracts as possible, but they also have to borrow circuitous routes to achieve that goal. Some need to use computer programs churning out prices, while others need to accumulate information about clients to better anticipate their preferences.

The Problematic Nature of the Firm Selling Complex and "Sticky" Finance

If the first unit of analysis in this book is the CGP, the site of analysis is the firm. I conducted fieldwork there; most interviews also took place there and if I radiated outward to further understand the extended business of CGP and its calibration by clients, I always followed channels of information that tied back to the firm.[23] But focusing on the bank was not just a decision made for the sake of simplicity and feasibility. Dwelling on this manufacture of profit and documenting the mechanisms used in achieving its goals offered a unique access into the contradictory nature of a financial firm, torn apart by the two imperatives of being a closed, self-sustaining legal unit while serving customized financial services to clients who did not hesitate to trespass its boundaries. This self-annihilating feature of finance is best understood by documenting the series of operators dancing around the products: the product designers sit (literally) next to the traders who maintain and hedge these products; this small population inhabits the same building as back-office operators, who wrap up the contract and make sure that, at least for a while, the commercial relation is closed for good. Yet, the very design of the product introduces much disruption in that division of labor and challenges the stability of the firm.

Scholars of finance have documented sites other than firms, bringing much clarity to their mechanisms. Among these sites, Exchanges have attracted attention for their centrality to the emergence of a mass market and to the long-sought desire to show what modes of organization are most conducive to transactions.[24] This study does not indulge in documenting another Exchange, because it focuses on a stage of financial innovation that precedes the orderly working of Exchanges. When products are first released, their space of circulation is not yet settled; they strive for a market, initially just a niche in the distant future. Their prospect as Exchange listings usually lies far ahead. In some cases, when their business model is based on constant transformations—as was the case of CGPs—they can only survive outside of Exchanges that impose standardization. Exchanges are fascinating sites of dense interactions but the relative orderliness of their functioning can easily hide the even more fascinating moment of product design.

Exchanges have long been sites of financial innovation, with new contracts created to attract business and generate revenue fees. Yet, *Codes of Finance* deals with a different kind of financial innovation, based on the derivation of excess information produced by existing Exchanges. Unlike Exchanges, General Bank does not involve all the parties in its deal. Its operating principle is that of an asymmetric transfer, and its success as a derivation hinges precisely on that absence of reciprocity. The Exchange could itself issue such contracts, but it would need to have the same infrastructure as General Bank to be in a position to hedge such risky positions and it would also need to be a global actor operating on many other Exchanges. These characteristics are quite the opposite of those of the Exchange, which is grounded and central. The main interest in studying General Bank comes from the tension created by its need to capture the excess information produced by Exchanges while maintaining a speed and mobility that protects it from being caught up and made to face the duty of reciprocity, built in the institutional principles of Exchanges.

The design of these financial products and the subsequent imperative to maintain them make for a unique look into the manufacture of profit, but one of the features that engineers have built into the CGP adds a further interest to the study of an innovative firm. By design, these are long and sticky commercial relations: the bank and the client are on board, and they have to coexist, regardless of the moving economic conditions and the likely change of prospect for the success of the deal. In other words, when a predefined set of events occurs, the client is given the opportunity to redesign the letter of the contract in order to benefit from it. A company goes bankrupt and is no longer publicly traded; two companies merge and carry new risks; an index's composition changes. These are the conditions that can authorize a CGP client to become an engineer and redesign the contract.[25] This forced coexistence is different from the regular customer-service clauses embedded in most commercial contracts. Customer services limit the ability of the client to alter the parameters of their deals after the transaction. The definition of the good and its customary use ("cats not to be dried in the microwave oven" and other common-sense tips) stabilizes the relation. The definition choreographs a series of roles that have to be played by the manufacturer, the customer, and the commodity, and it is in place to protect the customer from faulty manufacturing as much as to protect the manufacturer from relentlessly litigious customers. What CGPs propose works against this stabilization and exacerbates the contention around the liability created by the service. Although the bank and its clients agree on many things through the contract, much can still be negotiated once the contract has been written up and signed. Clients who are otherwise kept at a distance from the design of products find here the occasion to weigh in on some key contractual terms and subvert the division of labor between service providers and service users.

At the same time, the firm is also a problematic site of conversation inasmuch as the operations conducted there require the mobilization of all the bodies of experts reviewed in the previous section. As with most international banks, General Bank had offices in all major economic centers. Some of the biggest of these foreign offices featured trading rooms dedicated to dealing financial securities traded on the local Exchanges. General Bank was in London, New York, and Tokyo, among other economic centers, to increase its exposure to local businesses and to be situated closer to major Exchanges. "Distributed firms" are common in the financial industry, but the trading-room engineers in Paris not only relied on their local branches to carry out some of the operations that they designed, they also tried to make two philosophies of the firm coexist: a centralized site where French traders maintained the products, and a globalized service needing constant attention at all its nervous articulations, (i.e., at all the local foreign offices concerned with its hedging necessities). The firm finds itself strangely *crowded from a distance*: many bodies of experts and embarrassingly present clients, who take advantage of a contractual clause that keeps a door open into an institution that values secrecy. As this book will document in great detail, this globalized product hedged from Paris ended up tearing the firm apart.

The lack of a unique and stable site for these transactions of services—that have no clear material configuration if it was not for their contractual apparatus—makes the bank a conflicted entity. Several decades ago, Ronald Coase (1937), in his article "The Nature of the Firm," launched what was to become a research program and one of the most written about questions in economics. Coase was trying to understand why firms exist in market economies and why organizations with their *rules-based coordination*, as opposed to *price-based transactions*, are sometimes more efficient forms. According to Coase, the moment of transition from a market efficiency to a firm efficiency is decided by the costs incurred by market transactions.[26] The Coasian insights force us to question the boundaries of firms and to understand how the specific characteristics of a firm's business act as incentives for more or less tight organizational forms. This research program has given birth to a schism between sociologists and economists around the question of the nature of the firm. This study does not take sides but rather leverages the rare access to a bank—in the process of designing products and animating their markets—to resuscitate the Coasian question. Yet, the tension that occurs from having to organize and innovate new products demanding to be simultaneously in and out of the bank creates an added twist. Capturing and exploiting information entails some form of organization, whereas the imperative of mobility pulls General Bank toward a lighter structure.

A firm such as General Bank is itself a Coasian case study. It is a complex organization with several units carrying different businesses, but the reward system of the market activities (Alan and his colleagues designing and taking care of products) is premised on measures of performance and achievement that usher in a market-flavored competition between employees. At the same time, the enforced secrecy around these activities caused by the very volatile recipe for success with financial innovation, sets all sorts of barriers around the bank against competing banks. Yet, this tension between the reward system and the nature of the financial knowledge is further exacerbated by the design of products, which require constant back and forth between the organization and the outside markets (i.e., the clients and the Exchanges on which traders hedge their products). These vectors of communication thin the organization and undermine the roles buttressing it amidst a chaotic and intensely competitive environment.

In this study, I add to the usual Coasian concern for the firm a special attention to the nature of the products that are its raison d'être. A close study of the circulation of the products and operators within the allegedly bounded firm displays a much more complex topography than the market/organization dichotomy hints at. In truth, the two polar notions that frame the Coasian approach bracket the varieties of disruptions that innovative products and services can usher into an organization operating on markets. *Codes of Finance* goes beyond that dichotomy and documents the limits of this form of financial innovation. What happens to a firm endeavoring to sell a financial product that is never quite sold (a blow to the market) and that needs to be hedged on a daily basis (a blow to the organization)?

Bodies of Finance

The etymology of the word firm reminds us that there is a spatial element to the term. It is solid and resistant, enduring and steadfast. Yet, is it groundedness that financial firms need most? Firms also denote that which can be trusted—with the notable Italian contraction of the holding (*la firma*) and of the guarantee provided by the signature (*la firma*) of the business owner. But how does trust travel thousands of miles, when operators such as Alan are stuck in their seats and when firms do not move?[27] A tension tears apart the firm. Ubiquity is General Bank's aim, but it is grounded firmly on the western edge of Paris. General Bank's engineers design financial products that derive their value from economic activities unfolding in remote places *and* they need to keep in contact with these places and their Exchanges. They are the sites where traders manage the risk entailed by the issuance of these global beasts, and they are there either in person or under some sociotechnical extension that immediately exposes them to possible disruptions. Ideally, the firm would need to literally span these Exchanges, *enabling* a collective of traders to live up to the dream of the globalized CGP, but that would create other conversations and negotiations among traders and engineers dispersed across the globe and remove General Bank even further away from the project of a purified economic vehicle, contracting the world economy into a formula. *Codes of Finance* documents the clash between the dream of ubiquitous and instantaneous finance and the necessary bodies that strain to achieve this version of a purified economy. Financial engineers would do away with the bodies of the bank altogether in their wildest vision: the physical bank provides resistance to the purification of the economy into prices, and nothing but prices. They slow down what could be body-less transactions and, going back to Coase's dichotomy, they are part of the costly organization.

"Bodies" needs to be understood broadly here.[28] They are the predictable *flesh-and-bones* bodies of traders striving to seamlessly convey the message of the products they have in charge. But they are also the instruments heavily populating the trading room roamed by Alan and his colleagues, mathematical models simplifying the products' prices, and binders containing folders with all the versions of the products. What unites these multiple instantiations of bodies is their inability to differ quickly *on their own*. In an environment in which the ability to change and redirect one's course upon the slightest modifications of prices is key, bodies stand out as slow.[29] They can certainly transform themselves when they connect with other entities—other bodies with more or less momentum—but left by themselves, they will stick to their trajectories. And the survival of the trading room hinges on quick reorganizations. From that perspective, bodies are central to the story of CGPs because they are the instantiation of the organization and its dreaded Coasian transaction costs.

Financial engineers designing CGPs think beyond the bodies of finance: they envision products freed from the weight of the organization and able to live up to the dream of prices reacting to other prices. This dream of ethereal financial engineering—happily overlooking the cost of communication—painfully meets those bodies that deliver the message that derivations of value do not come without costs. The CGP, through its bold projection as a global product deriving its value from dispersed financial places, fuels the dream of a space- and time-free world where economic activities are all part of a global village. This dream is easy to propagate and to entertain *on paper*, and that is what General Bank's clients were receiving. That is *where* they were investing their money. Traders and the other operators in charge of maintaining the contracts experienced, as wine connoisseurs will appreciate, much more *full-bodied* operations. They were the ones affected by these innovations because the speed built into the hedging blueprint of CGPs and the imperative that their risks be balanced by continuous hedging on Exchanges across the world exceeded greatly their ability *qua* isolated traders. CGPs were no angels despite their engineers' confidence that they were the closest things to a godly invention.[30]

The curse of bodies experienced by traders unable to live up to the engineers' ethereal financial blueprints became a blessing and a resource when the business of derivation developed by General Bank's exotics desk started to become an asset itself and the prospect of it being turned into a commodity materialized. When investors started to take a close peek at these operations—not as clients of CGPs but as shareholders and potential owners of a lucrative unit, detachable from the rest of the bank and sellable to competitors willing to catch up quickly—what used to be itself a sophisticated subject of calculation became an object of financial calculations. General Bank's financial operators who were so far working to exacerbate the project of finance by pushing the economic gesture of derivation to its extreme, suddenly became its most committed critics. Instead of creating purified economic bodies as prices, they organized their activities around a tentacular information software that pervaded the various activities involved in pricing by maintaining the precious products and integrating them strongly into the rest of the bank. Becoming a body again, in the midst of a corporate governance culture that preached the modularity of firms and their reduction to prices, was an achievement.

Deleuze's concept of assemblage is useful to describe the tension between the efforts to articulate the engineered opacity of these new products and the resistance to commoditization through technical tentacular integration.

> a multiplicity which is made up of heterogeneous terms and which establishes liaisons, relations between them, across ages, sexes and reigns—different natures. Thus the assemblage's only unity is that of a co-functioning: it is a symbiosis, a "sympathy". It is never filiations which are important, but alliances, alloys; these are not successions, lines of descent, but contagions, epidemics, the wind. (Deleuze and Parnet, 2002, 69)

None of these efforts—articulation and integration—entail homogeneity. Rather, they gather different bodies and discover solutions to the problems at hand. In one case, the imperative is to make a new product talk and express its unique risks and promises by penetrating its formula. In the other case, ruling out the commercial isolation of a unit in the bank is important. In one case, the assemblage produces a price and an assessment of risk; in the other, it engineers a magma-like organization and blurs the seams of the unit by anchoring its core to the rest of General Bank's business in such a way that no price can be attached to the exotics desk.

Financial engineering pushes the limit of the bank as a firm. It creates services that both need organization for various teams of operators and at the same time strive for constant mobility. This tension seizes all of the holdings of the trading room, whether operators or instruments, rules or space organization. This imperative draws a fault line that cuts through previous divisions (operators vs. products; space vs. discipline) and makes fruitful another gradient based on the *animation* of the network that the room tries to stimulate. The success of CGP depended on the happy integration of these bodies through a rhythm that would carry the information intact from one end of the network to the other.

PART I

From Models to Books

We start our journey into financial engineering by scrutinizing the product. This close focus has one objective: understanding how the theoretical imaginings of financial engineers become financial services, which are then maintained by traders on actual Exchanges. The development of new products is one of the secret steps of market operations. The genesis of products is protected because that is where the know-how of the engineers shows itself the most clearly. For the bank to survive and attract new clients, new financial services must embody new possibilities for investors and their money. Banks are in a race against other financial service firms, but they are also in a race against themselves: they have to survive the tyranny of the formula they have sold and make sure that when the time comes, they can return the client's capital and its formula-based performance.

CGPs are synthetic products drawing on existing securities. As compilations of outstanding financial products twisted by the formula, they need to be outfitted with their own models. The appeal of the product— as a combination of insurance and investment—also creates the central puzzle that the trading room wrestles with: finding the model that suits the product. Given that this articulation is the source of major difficulties in the trading room, it is worth clarifying the terms of the product/model dance using an older derivative.

A "call" on a listed stock, traded on an Exchange, is a product designed to meet what are supposed to be needs of a class of clients. The description of a "call" can assume many forms, but when a client wants to buy one, he or she is usually handed a series of documents that contain the following information:

A definition:

A call option is a *contract* that gives the *holder* the *right* ("the option" not the obligation) to buy a certain *quantity* of an *underlying* security from the *writer* of the *option*, at a specified *price* (*strike price*) up to a specified *date* (*expiration date*).[1]

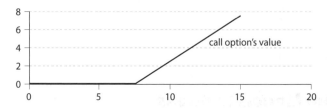

Figure 3. A Call Option's Value with a Strike Price of 7.7
This graph does not factor in the cost of the option. Should it do so, it would shift the curve downward of the cost of the option itself. The horizontal line across the bottom (the *x*-axis) represents the underlying instrument's price. The vertical axis shows the profit/loss as the underlying instruments move up or down. The heavy line is our payoff.

A formula of its payoff:

Call option payoff = Max (0, [Underlying price – Strike price]).

With the definition and the formula, a visual representation of the call's value is also usually offered [see figure 3].

The simplicity of its payoff is disarming: one underlying and a linear deduction of the call's value. This instrument derives its value from a mechanical relation between a price, defined by the contracting parties, and a fluctuating price, beyond the parties' control. Nothing else interferes in the value of the call: the whole economy could go wild, but as long as the underlying exhibits a price, the call has a value. When the term of the product has come due, the owner of such a contract can say how much money it is worth and replace the value with the price by replacing "(Underlying price – Strike price)" by its amount. Now, clients who purchase such contracts may have good reasons to sell them before they mature. As a treasurer, you may discover that the company on which you held a call option is no longer among your priorities. You had simplistically imagined that it was a direct competitor of yours and that any market share it would acquire would be a negative against you. Holding call options automatically allowed you to benefit from its stock performance so that you would balance the loss of market shares by a financial gain. You realize other factors weigh on the competition, and the mechanical relation between your business performance and competitors' stock performance does not hold true. It is time to get rid of a useless insurance. But how much should it be worth? The current difference (Underlying price – Strike price) may be positive on one day, but who guarantees it will still be so in the next few days? The one certainty offered by the product comes from its term. Then, and only then, assessing the value of the contract requires nothing but good reading skills so as to compare the current price and the strike price.[2] Before that final moment, however, the value of the contract is much trickier to discover, and that is when models are taken out of the drawer and applied to the contract to figure out its value; that is, how much money another person who needs such a service should pay for it.

Derivatives offer contrasting qualities: they are literal but engineered—some would say tortured. The range of their prices is fully covered by their literal formula, so that once I have the statistical qualities of its underlyings (price and volatility, or higher order variations of prices to some of its parameters) one cannot know additional factors of future price changes. Yet, they are also engineered into sometimes long and tortured formulas in such a way as to make their value difficult to anticipate for a client. Obviously, a possibly infinite number of factors will influence the ups and downs of the underlying but once captured, the value of the derivative is given by the formula's mechanical relation to the underlying.

The engineered component, coupled with their novelty, explain why it is difficult for clients to deal with the uncertainty of these products' value by resorting to "inner experience." The engineering of derivatives challenges even chief financial officers (CFOs), who swim daily in the sea of big figures—thousands and millions of Euros. Even products as plain as calls contain numbers with clauses and conditions that make difficult the calculation of their value. The innovative engineering offered by the bank makes all forms of personal expertise by the client irrelevant, as finance becomes nothing but numbers folded in so many ways as to render calculation a distant dream.

One could suspect that more competition will help solve the dilemma of traders and clients from the indeterminacy of engineered derivatives' value before their term comes. In what sounds like good economic reasoning, let the market do what it does best and produce information; let thousands of other interested traders do the work of valuation. Yet, even if a client was ready to use an existing market to let competition point to the efficient price, he or she could not find the perfect determination of value because the constant innovations outpace the production of a market where competition could take place.

Those studying the series of problems that derivatives created have been quick to equate these features—literal but engineered into opaque products—with fraud. The contention points to the asymmetry of information: designers engineer products in such a way as to protect their expertise against clients' clear and informed assessment; they sell fancy formulas, but they are mostly smoke and mirrors and marketing ploys, at best. At worst, derivatives are fraudulent. In this book, I do not aim to settle this long-held question. Rather, I document how financial engineering and its tortured formulas burden the operators and disrupt the conduct of operations in the bank. One of the consequences of these products' indeterminacy is the need to have a sense of the value of the financial product through models. Sometimes, these models are publicly available and anyone interested in the price of these transactions can use them.

▌ A Model

Models are central to assessing financial derivatives' value because these products are fully synthetic: their value can be captured through an equation that feeds on a few variables from the underlyings that can easily be extracted from the market.[3] One famous model for such simple products as the call, bought in order to hedge businesses with foreign partners is the Black–Scholes pricing formula. Its equation is as follows:

$$c = s\Phi(d_1) - xe^{-rt}\Phi(d_2),$$

where

$$d_1 = \frac{\log(s/x) + (r + \sigma^2/2)t}{\sigma\sqrt{t}}$$

$$d_2 = d_1 - \sigma\sqrt{t}$$

Log denotes the natural logarithm, and

c = the value of the call option
s = the price of the *underlying* stock
x = the *strike* price
r = the *continuously compounded* and *risk-free interest rate*
t = the time in years until the *expiration* of the option
σ = the *implied volatility* for the underlying stock
Φ = the *standard normal* cumulative distribution function.[4]

Even readers with a taste for mathematics or physics formalisms will pause temporarily to decipher the terms of the equation and its components. At first sight, one does not recognize the simple terms of the call behind the equation. What occurred between the literal expression of a product and its particular expression in formal terms is the science and art of modeling. When the product disappears behind its model, what is left of its relevant features? The Black–Scholes model works by leaving the literal terms of the product's payoff (Max [0, . . .]) only to capture its possible value over a wide range of underlying price variations. During this apparent digression and roundabout route, sight of the product is lost, and risks are taken as quantitative engineers test the market to assess the quality of their model. If the model simplifies the product, despite the more intimidating equation, the operators working in the trading room also expect the new model expressions of their risky contracts to be sharper. If the product comes under the guise of a model and is filtered by a model, and if it is novel enough to challenge existing models—which would make its price common knowledge and its issuance tied to very low commercial margins—and if in addition it needs to renew itself on a regular basis to dodge competition, then the question becomes: How do engineers know when a model is good, when a product is risky, and when they are maintaining it properly?

The constant mandate to innovate or perish creates a quasi-experimental environment within the bank, with experts bringing to the room a variety of approaches and different timings of interventions. The quasi-experiment is polarized by two modes of knowledge production: the *secluded*[5] exploration of models by the bank researchers and the *practical* exploration of products by traders when they attend to their portfolios. The practical exploration engaged by traders addresses these financial products fully dressed—decked out with all of their technological apparatus. They do have their say in the choice of these launches, but their intimate, daily experience of the markets does not take precedence over the engineers' more theoretical elaborations. Traders' complex experience, rarely put into words or made explicit, positions them differently from the bank's more confined researchers. During the course of their market explorations, traders regularly discover new properties of the products they manage. These products return information about the markets in which they are launched as well as about their design.[6] Variations in prices of products offer some indications concerning a segment of their market, and the multiple cross-checks carried out by traders on their products may coax the market to reveal relationships that were not necessarily anticipated.[7]

This exercise in the extraction of the properties of financial products under real-world circumstances becomes even more central when the trading room innovates aggressively and its operators are faced with unknown products. They learn about them as they test them under a variety of conditions. Some tests are simulations and attempt to re-create the market environment in a computer; some others are carried out in the market itself. But this exploration of commercial products is not that of mathematics or physics. Here, properties are more akin to weather system anticipation, with goals set to the short to medium terms. Engineers and traders know that understanding and controlling the future payoffs of CGPs is more than brandishing the law of supply and demand, since translating new designs into such notions remains unkown. And when knowledge is forthcoming, it never holds true for long. These dynamics make fruitful the conversation between confined researchers and those active on the markets: traders, and, to a lesser extent, salespeople, communicate things to the engineers, which the latter cannot anticipate or imagine. Traders preceded engineers in the financial markets. They developed skills through contact with transactions and they formulated ad-hoc theories of how markets worked. Confined researchers appeared only later, bringing with them the legitimacy earned in fields connected to finance (physics, mathematics, and accounting). This crossover was not an obvious one, and the rules of these other disciplines did not always satisfy the needs of the type of experimentation required by finance.

CHAPTER 1

Thinking Financially and Exploring the Code

The trading room is a place where new financial products are created, sold, and maintained. This process might seem simple, at least in its fundamentals. It involves the purchase and sale of new and traditional products with the aim of guaranteeing the greatest income for the bank while minimizing the risk of losses. It turns out, however, that having even an approximate idea of the value of some of these products is not at all intuitive. Such is the payoff *and* risk of financial innovations. Typically, clients and competitors do not know how to assess these products and find themselves having to rely on the initial inventor. These are simply the dynamics of product innovation: new products create temporary rents for the innovator. Yet, this very inventor is also frequently working in the dark, searching for the value of his or her creations. As a consequence of this uncertainty, the trading room is also a place where models are developed to figure out the value of these inventions. In this chapter,[1] I document and analyze the imperatives and the uncertainty that innovative structured financial products create for the grammar and lexicon of the "penser financierement" (thinking financially), the motto among engineers and traders. By its composition, the trading room is heterogeneous, with several bodies of experts claiming to "think financially." The languages that are adopted for thinking through and communicating new products reflects this discontinuity. This chapter documents a series of such languages. The chronology of their presentation does not itself reflect either ontological preeminence or the order of emergence. Nevertheless, it is not an arbitrary order. After a clarification of the trading room motto and the two primary approaches to financial engineering that were at play at General Bank, the chapter starts from the least stabilized forms of codifications, with operators figuring out the reactions to products by hand. Escalating from hands-on to program-based, codes gain resistance and become full-fledged characters of the financial conversation in the room.

| *Penser Financierement*

"Thinking financially" was a recurring theme in the trading room.[2] Operators would rank each other along the line of this gradient: whatever one's training, one was assessed on one's ability to think more or less financially. Yet, no one could articulate clearly what this mode of thinking entailed; it lent itself to at least two interpretations. The most mundane of these sees finance as a domain to which "thinking" must apply. Finance is seen as a set of products, rules, and institutions different from competing sets of other rules and goods, such as those that govern cultural goods, for example. In other words, people in finance must reckon with financial objects and treat them on their own terms. This first reading of the trading-room motto isolates the thinking from its domain of application. A second, more challenging interpretation of the motto, sees thinking as being subverted by the objects it embraces: thinking is not a faculty independent of and anterior to the financial domain under consideration. On the contrary, it is a mode of thinking writ large, a total cognitive style necessary to capture financial activities and products. Thinking this way requires not a cold head and a quiet room but rather is contaminated by the objects of investigation themselves. Grasping these innovations entails letting their form of existence seep into the operator, whether an engineer or a trader. This second understanding of the penser financierement motto established a much higher bar for operators, as they had to first discover and then learn a style. And the discovery component was to be collective. Complicating the attempt to penetrate new products and weigh their specific risk, operators from different disciplinary backgrounds were at work simultaneously: mathematicians and physicists, computer scientists and salespeople, traders and lawyers. Each discipline had a claim on the proper way of speaking about financial products and on the way that would minimize the risks taken by issuing them en masse. The variety of expertise brought together from the first moment of innovations to the end of the deal and the settlement of the payoff forced operators to master idioms that were often foreign to their educational backgrounds.

At stake in the imperative of *thinking financially* is the nontrivial problem of the locutor who does not speak the language of finance and lets the risk of a deal hover uncharted. The possibility of chaos threatening a community that receives money and commits to return at least as much (the guarantee) in the distant future looms high in this tense environment. Whoever issues products without a firm grasp and clear understanding of their mechanisms exposes him or herself to losing much money.

John, a financial engineer initially trained as a mathematician, sets the problem of thinking financially along these lines[3]:

[I]n finance the type of math used is relatively varied, you can do everything with a nonstochastic[4] approach, there are a lot of people who do everything without knowing what a random variable is. They are satisfied with solving partial differential equations, and so many mathematicians have a profoundly nonrandom view of things. There are a lot of things in finance where, if you don't have an intuitive sense of probability it can be a problem.

. . .

[I]f you don't have a clear idea of odds you have difficulty in truly sensing things intuitively, which is a burden. There are many mathematicians who work in finance in a very plodding fashion, because they have no intuition. Sometimes it's because they are not at all probabilistic and because they do not envisage the possibilities and the weights and the events at all, so all they do is solve price equations. It is a problem because they have only a very small amount of intuition; they may perform satisfactorily, but they're plodding.

As we can see from John's descriptions, he likes to break down the ways of reasoning at work in finance in pairs: financial versus mathematical intuition, leading to stochastic versus nonstochastic. Yet, although he looks down upon quants approaching finance as nonstochastic processes, he reminds us of the rather heterogeneous form of engineering that needs to take place in the trading room for a successful operation. In that way, the intimate knowledge of existing financial products that quants can lean on when they devise a hedging scenario for the trader have similarities to the mode of reasoning that probability theorists adopt when they mobilize events and their odds of occurring. Just like the space of financial products, the space of events can be highly discontinuous and offer precious insights for understanding the dynamics of prices.

Two Ways of Engineering Finance

Operators can convey information about products to others in very different ways. The spaces in which financial conversations take place are scattered, and discussions almost never occur under ideal conditions wherein *all* properties of a given product are displayed before the eyes of an attentive interlocutor. The pressure surrounding financial conversation and the way work is organized on the trading floor make it difficult for any exchange to contain more than snippets of product presentations. Two areas of the desk offer two starkly opposite forms of conversation and illustrate the tension created by the encounter between scientific and commercial modes of inquiry: the quant's zone and the financial engineer's long desk.

The quant at General Bank and his assistant would spend most of the day working on simulations of prices and testing models' reactions to varied time series of underlyings. They were helped by a couple of interns from Parisian universities, but for lack of space on the desk, the interns were working two floors up and would have to come down to meet the quant. There was no uncertainty as to the currency in this small circle: finance was equated with price dynamics. The books at the desk were all related to physics or stochastic calculus, and the only journal was *Risk Magazine*, an industry reference that covered the "Who's Who" of quants. In spring 2000, the quant was working on implementing a new model in the traders' pricers and the discussion centered on the findings of an article in the *Review of Financial Studies* of 1993 that caught his attention. One of the puzzles of financial engineers and quants is the choice of volatility made to price contingent securities: volatility is the major factor of the prices of these financial instruments as they are insurance against price changes. A highly volatile underlying—with ups and downs of its price—increases the chance that the issuer will have to pay. What financial operators have discovered since they started trading derivatives and keeping track of their prices is a phenomenon passed on to posterity as the "smile" of the volatility: Contingent instruments that are either very valuable ("in-the-money") or worth nothing ("out-of-the-money") have a volatility higher than that of instruments that are just "at-the-money." Plotted as a curve, with X as the strike price and Y as implied volatility, it curves up as a smile. After observing this smiley trend in the volatility curve, quantitative finance scholars and quants in financial services firms started to model volatility as a random process with the curvy trend observed as the smile, but this decision carried a risk as the trend was not a market datum and could not be hedged by the trader. The quant had his group work on what they saw as a very promising way out of the risk of *stochastic volatility*: during four months, they dissected an article by Steven Heston (1993), a scholar and consultant for major banks, and implemented a new model that allowed traders to have a more realistic volatility—one that followed a random process—without adding risk to their portfolio. This interpretation of Heston's findings was even narrower than a discussion of the smile: it looked at the use of stochastic volatilities for instruments with very short maturities; that is, products that would come to term very soon.

Asked about the rhythms of his research and contribution to the pricing problems on the desk, the quant talked about waves of interest for certain hot questions—like the smile and the stochastic volatility—triggered by products invented by financial engineers. During these peaks of interest, the quantitative team would familiarize the trader with the formalisms and notions of a few articles or book chapters that they had dissected and tested. The traders coming to discuss their problems with the quant and his group would be presented a Microsoft Excel spreadsheet and a simulation of the volatility using Heston's model (1993) to convince them that the new plug-in would not add layers of complexity to their pricer. Once the problem was solved or sufficiently under control, traders would come less frequently—the notions borrowed from an article or another scholarly contribution would lose currency. The quant area would lose its polarizing quality until a new problem would make the quantitative team necessary for the traders.

Located at the other end of the desk, the financial engineers are a much more porous group. With the traders right behind them and the legal consultant of the desk nearby, financial engineers do not consume articles from the *Review of Financial Studies* when they work collectively around new products. Their collective, although located in one place, is indeed much looser than the group gathered by the quant on a regular basis. The resources they mobilize and their mode of collaboration reflects that disunity. Financial engineers see themselves as "sensors," as Pierre, one junior engineer, once told me with pride[5]:

> For us, it is simple, we have to be everywhere and know everything. . . . The job description was not very clear and it is still not clear today. They just want us to innovate and find new products that will make millions. And for that there is no recipe, I mean no clear recipe, otherwise we would not be here to work our ass off every day. We read and we talk to everybody, full stop. So yes, we are sponges and even if others see us chatting all day long, it is serious talk. Anyway, people in finance, that is what they do all the time. Take a salesperson . . . . what does he do? Always talking on the phone. Well, we talk to these guys, too [I understand the salesperson]. You can't be narrow-minded if you want to make money.

Unlike the quant who polarized traders around his monitor, financial engineers roamed the desk and, further away, the room in search of ideas for new products. For them, no wave system of interest—building up and slowly decaying—but a daily search for new ideas. More acute than for other operators, the imperative of finding a lunch partner who would provide the engineers with useful information kept them busy in the morning: not finding a lunch partner was a lost opportunity to learn about a market or sector. Lunches provided a setting for ideas to be floated around in terms general enough that they did not require a computer or a blackboard to be conveyed. The lunch itself was only one possibility of communication within the bank, however. Every occasion was seized by the financial engineers to squeeze out insights from any possible interlocutors.

This constant search for new ideas and new leads is exacerbated among the financial engineers on the desk, but, apart from the quant and his small group of specialists, all other operators face roughly the same imperative. Just like financial engineers, traders working the exotics desk are not specialists, and many are derided for their lack of thorough understanding of each of the Exchanges. They are seen by others as machine operators—the pricer—and as lacking the fine expertise of traders specialized in an Exchange rather than a customized service. Their exercise is made all the more uncomfortable as they coexist in the room with other traders who know much more.

The interstices of the trading room (figure 4) were the chosen places for these exchanges; here languages are implemented that can be characterized as *interstitial* with reference to the formalized codes. The spaces where this boundary language takes place are the wide aisles separating the rows of desks, the smoking area at one end of the floor, or around a coffee machine located outside the trading room—areas where people linger and in which people who do not usually work in the same location cross paths with one another.[6] The desks bring together operators likely to mobilize the same tools and who thus find themselves working with the same language, driven by the instruments at their disposal. When traders leave *their* spaces, they are likely to enter zones where they must deal with different approaches to prod-

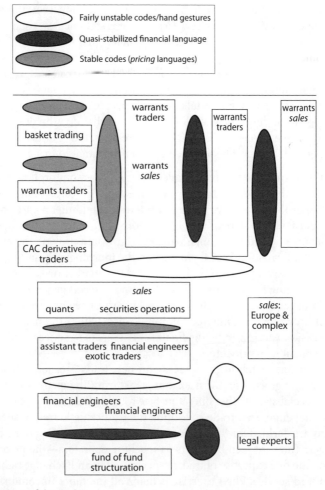

Figure 4. Map of the Codes

ucts, whether those of the salespeople or of traders working at other desks. In spaces where different players mix, though, matters of most importance to these specialists are not put on hold; quite the opposite occurs. Coffee breaks and strolls through the trading room become opportunities to obtain information on other markets, on other products, and in general on the inclinations of other players on the floor.[7]

The strategies traders need to apply to hedge the products in their portfolios are most frequently discussed during work breaks in these interstices. As we will see, hedging is a delicate operation because it stretches traders in a large number of markets.[8] They have to link the different operations while under pressure and without having the time to analyze the specificities of each one of these markets. Traders end up as heavy players in certain markets despite their inability to claim a thorough knowledge of these markets. The other traders on the floor are well aware of this lacuna affecting exotic derivative traders and, in fact, often make it the subject of mockery. Breaks are occasions to glean tips and pieces of information that only specialists have the time to accumulate. Which linguistic code to use in informal exchanges is critical because time is limited. breaks do not last more than ten or fifteen minutes, and it would be impossible to provide, in such a short period of time, a thorough definition of a product. Its characteristics must flow literally from a specialist to a less-specialized operator: the standardized code that reigns over the exotics desks generally gives way in these interstices to a characterization of the products in "natural language." It is important to clarify what this natural language represents in terms of its potential in the transfer of these products.

Lodging Products in Natural Language

Natural language refers to all of the modalities used to describe financial products—and all their associated characteristics, such as volatility, price, risk measurement, and so forth—that do not come from language created specifically to that end. In pragmatic terms, a natural language, from the point of view of these financial products and their models, can be thought of as a custom-made language from the perspective of another entity. The distinction between natural and engineered language aims to describe the variety of resources that are mobilized to deal with a new product that does not yet have a stabilized definition. From another more encompassing point of view, there is no such thing as a natural language. Idioms are always task-oriented. The common language used by traders and salespeople during casual financial conversations is natural compared with the computer languages they will use on the floor. They receive this language as is, without questioning its history or its potentialities because they experience it daily in a multiplicity of businesses. The artificial languages devised to respond to the problems raised by financial products detaches from this natural language core; their structures and what they afford are continuously invoked by those who use them, while those of natural language are never questioned. Nevertheless, those who communicate in this language when they linger in the trading-room interstices hone it, using the most efficient and expedient ways to express the relevant product properties. Although "natural," it is subject to the descriptions associated with products not at all natural, products originating from the imagination of engineers. Financial products literally force open the doors of this language: of course, these products can all be named *in* this language.

Consider an interaction between the quant and a salesperson taking place in the vacant space off their respective desks. The quant describes a "digital," a financial product with an "all or nothing" payoff. When the underlying reaches a threshold price px—which can be a floor or a cap—the bank pays 100 percent of the predetermined payoff. The abrupt payoff formula makes continuous hedging irrelevant.[9]

> When the market comes close to the strike, it [the product] is very unstable and the guy [the trader] will be very, very nervous . . . it is really not a continuous product [quant speaking to salesperson].[10]

"Unstable" and "continuous" are relatively precise terms in physics and mathematics. However, in this interaction, the quant refers as much to its mathematical meaning (continuity of the price function) as to the metaphorical implication of stability and continuity (should the investor decide to withdraw his or her money, he or she should not experience any negative surprises). The trading room, as an organization managing this particular product, is unstable, nervous, and chaotic. The relevant innuendo carried by each of these terms is respectively a descriptor of the product. In this case, one of the many meaningful elements in the definition of a "digital product" is the behavior of the traders when the price reaches the critical zone of the strike p_x (price level where the product becomes valuable). The numbers crunched by the pricer of a digital would not convey the same direct meaning as "unstable" or "continuous." But these natural language descriptors would also fall short of capturing the whole array of risks that a desk must tackle when the digital approaches its strike. No element of this dynamic definition takes precedence over the others: each casts light on the multiple implications of the product in the room.

Some innovations never require the engineering of a dedicated language. They can thrive through the mix of preexisting languages assigned to them by multiple communities. Financial innovations do that to a certain extent, until banks encounter situations where money is potentially lost by not standardizing a mode of description. Financial operators face the challenge of expressing what these products do and how they work in terms that are not trivial. The limits offered by the use of natural language stem from the fact that such language was not developed for describing products of this nature; it therefore elucidates products through determinants that are not useful to operators.

Operators are indeed searching for codes and codifications when they meet and discuss financial products and are unable to summon preformatted codes to their attention. These are the beginnings of codes, sketches, and rough outlines in the form of synecdoche. Products are designated according to specific traits operators are able to represent. Formalized codes do essentially the same thing, but they do it in a language that has already moved past the individual parties and almost everything else; these codes give operators durable tools and allow them to use longer-lasting and clearer expressions. Conversely, the codes of natural language are not likely to last. They must be redefined every time they are used.

Hands-on Finance

Moving ahead in this review of the informal codes expressed in financial conversations, what follows is a discussion of operators bodily performing the chaotic dynamic of prices of financial securities.[11] The material described here comes from several months of exposure to financial operators' daily handling of the products. Although I could not quantify the frequency of these practices, they were the lingua franca of the trading room. Figuring out the hedging puzzle and the price dynamics was in order whenever two operators with different backgrounds met. What follows is an analysis of the *phenomenality* of informal codifications through a description of operators struggling to simplify the dynamics of their formulas. The term, *informal codes*, easily reads as a contradiction. Codes entail controlled distance and secrecy. They carry with them monopoly and unequal access. Yet, they begin with gestures. Before they are codified firmly in an artificial language, products are coded by the operators in a more informal manner. Along with codes endowed with a syntactical structure, a dictionary, and compiler functionalities, operators develop in parallel other codes that allow them to gain a hold on these products. Although a code in C programming language[12] allows the computer program to execute operations on these products and to generate a valuation or an assessment of the risks involved, rudimentary and less-formalized codes that the operators use when they discuss their products offer similar leverage. The *incarnation* of financial ideas starts before the design of software; it starts where conversation originates, where mind and body are still struggling with unstable concepts, slowly bifurcating when hand gestures and conversations are seen searching for appropriate words. Operators perform in these many ways to define the qualities of these products and offer a view to what the future holds for the trader who will handle them.

Hand gestures are certainly one of the most striking aspects of financial conversations. Woven into the linguistic codes that are obviously present in these interactions are codes that involve the body in search of a missing grammar.[13] Communicating finance with one's hands come first in this list of codes because hand gestures stand as the site of germination of codes and models.[14] It is a practical site of investigation because engineers and traders illustrate—sometimes involuntarily—the challenge of creating a language of finance for these products. When operators use their bodies to flesh out ideas about future products, they use (and abuse) the ability of the body to patch absences in grammar by being physically present, dispensing from the constraints of the textual and sometimes verbal versions of products and models.

This mode of communication takes place between operators talking different languages: traders and engineers, salespeople and traders, and engineers and salespeople. The lack of a solid common language between interlocutors makes space for the handy resource of the hand. This method of translating a tentative sketch of the product from one operator to another was not marginal, in the context of the thousands of interactions that were taking place within the trading room when I was doing fieldwork there.[15] Banks, much like old-fashioned marketplaces, are collections of arms, hands, and fingers struggling to give form to products and figuring out how to get a strong hold on them. This formalization involves the entire body of its operators. Generally, the arms are used to *project* the products. The path adopted in approaching the body as a teaching tool consists of following its movements as it tries to make tangible and visible processes that are not easily drawn on a blackboard or that require the taking of several positions over time. The data at our disposal are not sufficient to let us establish a fully developed *hands-that-explain* grammar in the context of financial pedagogy. I only give two examples here of demonstration acted out using this manual language.[16]

To illustrate problems involving mathematical derivatives, the fingers of each hand come together, and the fingertips of one hand touch the fingertips of the other like two electric poles with the same charge, unable to make contact as a result. Hands thus held tense in the shape of a bird's beak place themselves one above the other and move along an imaginary plane following the movement of a curve. To express the option's attempt to replicate, to adapt, or to counter a product to be hedged, the grouped fingertips follow each other and are adjusted through little jolts. In all cases, the idea is to show how a well-designed mathematical tool can help to follow closely that which needs to be hedged at its junctures and specific articulations.

For loans, on both creditor and borrower sides, made at the same rate but changing over time, the person attempting to demonstrate uses the body to differentiate loans when referring to one (lending) then the other (borrowing) within the same sentence. Because an entire part of finance consists in showing how the balancing of all the variables through arbitrage[17] is achieved, the speaker has to describe numerous fictitious phases in which one borrows for the purpose of buying a security, on which one then earns a rate that is higher than what one had to sacrifice in order to take out the loan, and thus makes profit without risk. In these cases, the body opens up with one hand extended on each side, or else by placing the hands parallel to the body, at the level of the stomach and in opposite directions, with a space between them to show the gap between the loan given and the one taken; that is, the financial work separating the two rates. To show the difference in price between the borrowings and investments, arms strike different heights and move up or down as the rates are supposed to converge.

The body is also used in situations in which operators want to slow down and explicate steps that are taken for granted in finance manuals. The replication of a security's risk profile, for instance, is generally contained in a linear formula that does not adequately convey what the task of hedging entails (frequent calculations of the derivatives to follow the slopes, regular back-and-forth on the market). The explicit actions necessary for hedging are most often bypassed because they are not easily set down in formal financial terms. That is the advantage of the body: it is at once the site of tacit knowledge that evades a formal coding and also the most natural support to deploy the tacit and make it explicit.[18] The codes of the body language involved in this rough type of pedagogy thus play a dual role, which makes it possible to enliven the linearity of financial formulas. First, bodily movements pull apart phases that are otherwise collapsed together. The body achieves this objective by slowing down the narration of the financial arbitrage into parts whose temporality is not spoken of in finance textbooks. Second, and simultaneously, the body concentrates everything that must take place (purchase and sale, profile replication) into a single scene. It expands the time necessary to conduct the operation, and it concentrates the location of the actions by multiplying its dimensions with the help of these two-hand gestures. Derivative financial products require these dynamic embodiments because they regenerate themselves at great speed. One will not find a user's guide for the latest versions of these products in a manual, but the body can flesh them out and sketch the first codes for these manipulations.[19]

Varieties of Financial Intuitions

The financial engineers who develop products try to make them appealing to a large array of people while ensuring that they are as lucrative as possible for the bank. They are in direct contact with the salespeople who report the preferences of potential clients and who direct the design toward marketing niches that have been neglected by competitors.[20] They are aware of the latest trends in financial services and know the whole ecology of financial markets. They like to think of themselves as the creative unit, and also like to cast themselves against the other class of engineers in the trading room, the quants. Financial engineers at General Bank thought of quants as repressing their financial insights and submitting them to the cold discipline of risk valuation. Quants who create the valuation models of these products try to limit the risk undertaken by the bank by designing models. They think in terms of prices, whereas financial engineers think in terms of services. Prices are, of course, central features of these services and central to the financial engineers' understanding of these financial ecologies, but they do not reduce the import of other dimensions of services. Quite different from the attention paid to the gamut of financial services boasted by financial engineers, quants who take hold of a valuation and hedging problem do not need to know more than what the literal formula of the product provides. Financial and quantitative engineers may not communicate directly on a risk-hedging question. From this point of view, there are indeed two distinct sets of skills at work on the trading floor during the development of products. These two different functions must at some point come together as these models–products evolve to avoid a Tower of Babel cacophony.

John comments:

Q: So intuition does mean having quite a few mathematical rules in one's head?

A: Having laws in one's head, yes. But that is a first level of intuition—we can call it mathematical intuition. But, beyond that, there is financial intuition, which is different, which tells you what kind of financial product you will use, which makes you bring everything you understand back, not to rules, because that's obvious, but rather to products. This is the intuition that tells you which hedging product will allow you not to lose money if you sell a financial structure. So the problem is not so much that the probability that a given event will occur is 50%; the problem is rather which product will let me not lose money once I've established that probability. That is financial intuition: which product I will use so as to be able to calibrate this probability, that is, when I will hedge, what I will do to hold my price and to put in place a portfolio that I will manage in such a way as not to lose money. This is a financial problem; it deals with the reality of the operations you will perform with the money you have at the start. If you start with 10 francs, and the "I pay 100 francs" event occurs, the 10 francs have to have become 100 francs. The whole job is figuring out what the right product is, and so then the financial "thing" appears right away, and the problem for the mathematicians is to successfully mix a mathematical intuition with knowledge of the product. If you don't know the products, you're not doing finance. . . .

That is, you have to make use of all the products at your disposal, you have to discover the best and calibrate your price the most precisely possible given the product you are using. Where does intuition enter into it? Well, in the market, there will be many products which are associated with possible events and which will offer you solutions. It is up to you to find the different products that will effectively allow you to always maintain your inner balance. If you pick the wrong products, you will see variance, you might earn money but you could lose some, you do not control anything; from this point of view it's control, mathematically it's control theory.

John differentiates very clearly between this *mathematical intuition* and what he calls *financial intuition,* which relies on an intimate and thorough mastery of the financial assets going into the development of a given product—when the product is structured and connects different basic products—for the forecasting of its hedging methods. This area of expertise does not belong exclusively to financial engineers. The quant can enter this phase of the product configuration when faced with a hedging question that goes beyond the standard techniques, but such a situation is not common.

The challenge of addressing financial intuition is well captured by the distinction made by John. Financial modeling sits uncomfortably between a quickly growing ecology of products that need to be dissected and categorized in terms of their characteristics and, on the other side, families of mathematics or physics formalisms that address more stable entities. The universe may be growing, but the class of phenomena that physicists try to model does not expand as fast. Obviously, mathematicians and physicists relentlessly test new tools so that even if their study subjects do not expand, the ways of modeling them do. Yet, the proliferation of products in need of modeling far exceeds the pace of scientific innovation. If an operator (or for that matter a scholar modeling these products) is to develop an intuition for financial mechanisms, the two ends of these ecologies must be solidly held together. As a consequence, the financial engineer's intuitive sense must develop in a fairly heterogeneous world. The assimilation or fusion with the object that classical accounts of intuition often report does not suit the engineered nature of these financial montages. Evelyn Fox Keller's biography (1983) of Barbara McClintock offers a contrasting view of intuition within a much more homogeneous space: the genetics of maize is figured out in a quasi-unmediated way by the young McClintock in an episode that bears the stamp of a revelation. This direct contact was not available to operators in the trading room, as the folding and structuring of the contract achieved by its engineers twisted their mechanisms to the point of pushing them apart.

The financial engineer's particular skill does not exclusively come down to price modeling in the strict sense of the word. When a new product is created, one of the first concerns is to identify in the set of existing products—from all of the financial securities available in the market—the ones that should be used to hedge the position thus created. In products like the CGP, the hedge is done using the same products as the formula's basket of underlyings. What indices or stocks should be included in the basket? If the payoff depends on the correlation, financial engineers spend their early investigation of new products' designs upon simulating compositions on their computers. They have in mind the set of constraints that the bank sets out to comply with; they do not offer unrealistic plans, and they discipline themselves, even before the disciplining of the quant. One object of their enquiry regards the liquidity of the securities that are imagined as part of the basket. If the trader is not able to buy and sell Euro Stoxx 50 (an index of major companies' stocks from twelve European countries) futures without creating huge price variations, engineers know that hedging is compromised and that the maintenance downstream will be impossible. Yet, exploring the existing financial entities of the market is markedly different from what the quant does when reasoning exclusively *about* prices and *in terms of* prices. Financial exploration is spread over a richer space than that created by intersecting prices. The first kind of intuition—which he calls *mathematical*[21]—consists in developing one's thought processes in a "price space." This leaves open the properties of the space,[22] but limits its dimensions. In our description of the trading floor, this intuition is reserved almost exclusively to the quant and his team.

The chief quant was a physicist by training, a most unusual feature in the more typical French tradition of domination of mathematics over other sciences. Most major French banks usually hired young mathematicians to tackle the challenges of increasingly technical products. The quant was surrounded by some of these young mathematicians, who had all been trained in the Bourbaki tradition, which emphasizes rigor and denigrates fuzziness in mathematics.[23] When he arrived at General Bank a couple of years prior to my fieldwork, he tried to implement some changes in the way the models were written, attempting to emulate physical models and experiments rather than strict mathematical proofs. But he very soon experienced a divide between what he considered "good" models and what the rest of the quantitative team were familiar with. Not only did the mathematicians reject many of his assumptions, but they also carried something stronger than metaphysical certainty with their own mathematically grounded assumptions: the software helping them implement their models was written in a programming language that they cherished. They felt at home with this equipment in a way that no physicist could. This reified language helped them carry out many of the demonstrations that they would present to the quant.

Finding Finance in Mathematics

When trading floor engineers approach a modeling question, they either answer a demand by the operators (traders or salespeople) or they examine more deeply a question that has come to them from some other source (the reading of articles, attending colloquia, or the importation of formalisms that share a family resemblance to those used in their own work). These two stages of research coexist and sustain one another: pressing questions can raise larger questions; research with distant horizons can meet with the needs of the moment. This coexistence is made possible by the small material investment required for the engagement with a theoretical question, one that is detached from the demands of the moment. Getting involved in an ambitious question does not require endowing the desk with new equipment or machines. Quantitative engineers do equip themselves, but not through massive investments in hardware. They generally use software that facilitates their work and saves them from having to spend time on some of the elementary mathematics required to examine questions. It might be software aimed at the general public and relatively unspecific to mathematical exercises, such as Excel, or it might be more demanding in terms of the mathematical knowledge it requires, such as Mathematica or Scientific Workplace. The variety of the modeling experiments on these different types of software shows us the essential role played by the supports needed for trading-room modeling. This modeling will unfold according to different facets and traits, depending on those supports.

The discussions documented can be explained in the first place by the abundance of possible types of modeling that are available for each financial product. The absence of agreement between financial operators, as well as the strong incentives to outdo the dominant models, regularly bring onto the scene new models, which amend, to a greater or lesser extent, those that are currently in effect in the banks. Particular characteristics of products point the engineers toward the choice of particular models, but none of those that survived the market tests has thus far succeeded in imposing itself without being contested. The great innovation in products implemented by the banks feeds the race for models. Regularly, financial reviews set up testing benches for the different types of modeling. During these review sessions, models are tested on price dynamics that are, themselves, the outcome of very specific probability models.

Quants in charge of defining the model best suited to a given product are torn between two inclinations. On the one hand, by attaching models whose properties they are familiar with to products they are unfamiliar with, they can limit the uncertainty of a structure, which will be transmitted to the traders in charge of managing these products. On the other hand, by adapting a model to a product, the quants already know that the valuations that will emerge will not be optimal: noncustomized models will not fit perfectly with the joints of the product. This rough fit of an all-purpose model means that competitors could provide better fitting prices (possibly lower and thus more appealing to customers) for the same service. The security of having a robust model, but one that is not entirely adequate for the task, carries the risk of overbilling. The second inclination presents different dangers. By developing a custom-made model for a new product, engineers take on the risk associated with an innovation that has not yet been tested in the market and that entangles two sources of uncertainty. The product and the model combine their uncertainties and put traders in a completely uncharted situation. Traders who already know the models used to value a new product are more comfortable than those who are confronted with a new product and a new model. They know what the strengths and the weaknesses of a modelization are. We will later see how they can predict an excessive reaction in a model and correct it by hand when they have expert knowledge of their model–product–market trio. For an engineer trying to design a model, the temptation to fit it to a product short-circuits a detailed knowledge of the reactions of the model in a market. The hoped for outcome is an expert system that fits as closely as possible the structure of the product and allows management prices (hedging) to be lowered and the competition to be surpassed. Unfortunately, software designed to follow mathematical routines—such as expansions—leave quants with inarticulate results. As one quant reported, "Scientific Workplace could do the job, but it's too cumbersome, it does not produce summaries that would allow us to better understand what we're doing, it remains scattered" (quant, April 2000).

Figure 5 presents some of the steps—simplified here for the sake of a presentation—taken to extract finance from mathematics. The first decision to

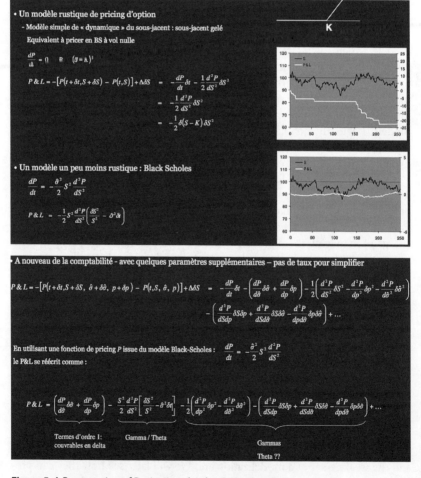

Figure 5. A Presentation of Derivations by the General Bank Quant

be made in choosing a model to dress a new product is the number of parameters that will be factored in. Derivatives are engineered products and
they can be tied to many sectors of the economy. Each design creates a list of
relevant variables—relevant, that is, but not necessarily tractable.

The trade-off starts in defining what can be left outside of the model and
what should be its included features. For correlation products such as CGPs,
the parameters that were taken into consideration were the market price, volatility, and dividend (or return) of the underlyings—the correlation between
the underlyings and the interest rate. Other parameters of the models were
also taken into consideration theoretically, but they were not directly factored
in. Practically, this distinction meant that the quant would keep an eye on
some of the correlations between the major parameters (above) while not integrating them up front. The exercise of accounting documented above starts
when the parameters have been set and when the model is chosen.[24] This
presentation is itself a pedagogical exercise and introduces its audience to the
variety of available models. These analytical derivations of the P&L formula
simulate what value variations take place when time passes

$$\left(\frac{dP}{dt}\right).$$

As each parameter is a function of time, the model derives the direct impact
that the parameters have on the P&L

$$\left(\frac{d^2P}{dS^2}\partial S^2\right)$$

but it also derives the interaction between parameters

$$\left(\frac{d^2P}{dSd\sigma}\partial S\partial\sigma\right).$$

These derivations are automatic: they simply follow the instructions coded
in the software when the number of parameters and structure of the model
makes them too difficult to derive by hand.

For the quant and his assistants,[25] after using software systems originally
developed for mathematical exercises, the next task consists of translating
calculations back to the framework of a financial interpretation, with its financial consequences. This translation takes on multiple forms, one of which
consists of *extracting* fragments of finance from all of the analytical results
generated by the software. When Scientific Workplace produces a result, it
generally takes the form of a series of mathematical terms that do not necessarily have a financial meaning. The preliminary investigation of models
carried out by the quant consists of discovering how the relevant variables of
a new product behave: prices, volatility, interest rates, risk indicators, reactions to shifts of other relevant market parameters. Each new product design
introduces new wrinkles in what the quant needs to be cautious of. Some-

times, new relevant dimensions are identified, such as when traders manage so many products in their portfolios that they are forced to hedge their portfolios as a whole and no longer just their products. Looking at aggregated products changed the risks that needed to be hedged: earlier concerns that were once central suddenly receded, and new problems came to the fore.[26]

Scientific Workplace software brings with it power and calculation speed, but it also operates with complete ignorance of what finance is and what the concerns of financial operators are. The software plunges into mathematical refinements without following the quant's investigative line. When it is done "churning," it delivers lines of equations, full of elements that are indeed of interest to financial devotees but in a disorder that—while respectful of mathematics—is blind to financial concerns. It is necessary to put order and financial meaning into these dispersed variables, and that is the job undertaken by the quant. However, this reordering necessitates combining multiple language games. For a while, the quant follows the software with a strictly mathematical language; then, he switches to another set of rules to interpret the initial results with an eye toward finance. When it comes to observing the reactions of a product price through a model, small price variations are usually assessed through partial derivatives (in the calculus sense of "derivative"). As these products carry several sources of risks, these partial derivatives address different dimensions of this risk, including the sensitivity of a product's price to changes in the interest rate, in the price and price volatility of the underlying stocks, and so on. But these derivatives follow strictly mathematical rules that are not necessarily relevant for financial questions. In figure 5, the translation from mathematics to finance happens in the last operation, down at the bottom, when the expansion of the multivariate function of P&L produces terms that can be clustered into financially relevant groups by using a pricing function à la Black–Scholes. Delta represents the sensitivity of the option's value to a change of its underlying, while gamma is a second-order measure of sensitivity to this change—measuring the speed of sensitivity in addition to its direction. Theta is the measure of time decay sensitivity. Each measure of sensitivity allows one to see through the expansion—and its proliferation of terms respecting the mathematical language game—and to make sense of the P&L function by decomposing and rearranging these terms.

Valuation models of exotic products have to borrow from the preexisting tools of mathematics and of mathematical software. This borrowing is obviously not purely fortuitous. The formulas that give the contracts their substance are written in mathematical language. They use the entire panoply of formalisms that allow simple calculations, but they organize underlying financial elements in an entirely new way. These borrowed clothes, in the form of software-embedded rules, are the very strength of mechanized processing, but they can lose the *spirit* of the contract formulas along the way. This spirit is not necessarily evident at first glance to someone unfamiliar with financial structures. As chapter 5 will document, the salesperson's job is primarily to convince the client of the desirability of financial services and cultivate his or her preferences. The financial engineers who develop products are, in contrast, very clear when they find themselves in front of the contract terms: they can visualize the probabilities of money flows that the formulas incubate in the language of salesmanship. They can give a detailed account of it, and indeed it is the only way they have of stating it explicitly. Using the language of finance—in terms of the amounts owed by the bank to its clients when the underlying securities evolve in one direction or another—they can paint a rough portrait of the product. But such portraits are just possible scenarios, and it is necessary to give numbers to these movements and directions. They must engage in assessments of these formulas. By relying on the mathematical sketches that mathematical software systems offer, quants adopt a different strategy and go in a direction opposite to that developed by the financial reports of the engineers and the salespeople. They no longer follow the slope of the financial report but rather grasp products by their mathematical formulas, dissecting them and subjecting them to the rules of mathematicians. By extracting products from finance and submerging them into mathematics, they bring out something different.

The tools they use tend to blur the simple formulas upon which these engineers can reflect. The operations they carry out to give ideas concrete form is threaded with an obvious tension. These products must be given transparent models, ones that do not upset either the literal aspects of the formula or the financial relationships that traders and, even more, salespeople, can master. Yet these products must also be *made to speak* by being passed through formalisms that bring out new relevant properties. A transparent model only reproduces the form of a product and does not bring out any additional information.[27] In contrast, articulating a product through a model may lessen the initial financial understanding and weaken the trader's abilities. This is the risk of articulation: it cannot take place without passing through this series of filters, which can increase intelligibility but may also undermine the immediate comprehension that was initially possible.

The Model in the Machine: The Pricer

Financial product valuation models take on a new, mechanical type of existence when they enter the trading room. This is different from their former identity as pieces of codes written as temporary programs, primarily meant for R&D. When the quant tested a product and model using Scientific Workplace, he was testing both models and products and was trying to sort out the model's effect from the product's effect. But these were still mostly experimental modes of exploration to find the association between the product and its model. Only the financial engineers, the quant, and his assistants could appreciate the simulation of new products and new models. This is only a tiny population of the desks. Traders do not enjoy the pleasure of fiddling with Scientific Workplace when they have to hedge their portfolios. They want to rely on a pricer that black-boxes some of the uncertainties experienced by engineers and streamlines the thought process from prices to action. Pricers must be able to work almost automatically and produce a price on demand. Once a contract is issued, traders need to manage it on a daily basis: the pricer becomes the answer to the puzzle of assessing the prices of products that, by design, blur their own rule of valuation. By looking at the role of pricers in the understanding of products by the room operators, I am not making the claim that models hold together by their logical coherence, whereas pricers hold together by their nuts, bolts, and squeaking joints. As we have seen, there is more than logical coherence at work in the choice of a model to price a product. There is also less to the extent that imperatives of coherence never precede the need for a familiar model. But the demand for instantaneous valuations addressed to pricers forces the model to adopt a new mode of existence and become more than a sketch activated intermittently for exploratory purposes. At any time, the pricer is on call and is expected to turn in a reliable price. To become such a reliable and commandable tool, the programs built in the wake of quants' ruminations incorporate materials other than those necessary for elaborations on paper or for the use of general mathematical software systems. These new demands immerse these models into a series of new constraints.

The modeling uncertainties that seized the quant operated, in some way, horizontally; the different actors choosing the models mobilized entities that were not compatible but could still coexist on the same level. Thus, there arose controversies between the supporters of Gaussian functions of price distribution and the defenders of the Levy[28] distribution. There, the plane of this controversy could be clearly defined by the opposing parties: nothing but mathematical functions and laws were called upon to settle the question of best modeling. The bone of contention was merely the trade-off between accurate price distributions and the tractability of functions.[29] Altogether different are the tensions between quantitative engineers and computer scientists who have to code a model into a pricer. When disagreements about price distributions are put aside and these entities take concrete shape, new conflicts arise that no longer involve simply competing grammars, but machine-like devices with no shared history.[30] When a pricer based on a model systematically fails to provide a price, the question that arises no longer regards the comparison of the mathematical laws as in the previous moment. The point of conflict has therefore indeed moved; we are no longer dealing with a discipline endowed with more or less explicit rules but rather a program that must find a solution so that its different components can be successfully woven together. The difficulty of incarnating a model resides in the act of bringing into coexistence this variety of elements. The coexistence that must be sustained, however, involves the contributions of professional bodies whose levels of understanding are even more varied than those that were required to sustain a paper model.

Understanding and Coding

I met Franck before starting the fieldwork at General Bank, at a time when I attended conferences in financial mathematics. He, too, attended this type of conference where finance professionals, researchers, and students all mixed. We stayed in touch for about two and a half years. He eventually joined the bank and worked there as a computer programmer in charge of writing pricer codes. But at the time we met, Franck worked for a finance software publisher that had developed a product called QUANTA. It was designed to help traders as well as middle-office and back-office personnel with their decisions. QUANTA was equipped with a series of complex pricing features. Depending on which products the traders held, it was possible either to use the pricers that were already present in the basic software package—those that made up the core of standard pricers—or to resort to more specific external modules. In rare cases, where a client's product could not be priced by existing algorithms, a new pricer module had to be developed by the R&D team for whom Franck worked.

Franck presents the path that leads to the decision for a new pricer in a fairly classical manner. In the beginning, an "academic"[31] writes an article on a nonstandard product, giving it a solution; that is, he attaches a value to this product. This article is read by professionals at the bank who are interested in its results and who wish to add it to the list of services they sell. If this bank does not have its own coding research department, it outsources the job of writing the program to a company such as the one for which Franck was working. Once the operation is completed, the new *pricing* module is added to the existing software system. Traders are then able to carry out pricing of this product at any time with the click of a mouse. Even though Franck's company did not do its own research in the field of quantitative finance, he needed to understand what the models he coded entailed. He could not stay completely at a distance from what he was asked to price. That was the role of the quantitative engineers:

[W]e are dependent on the understanding that the professional will have of the product, because he is the one who will undertake the initial research. He will examine the article with his research team. He will send us twenty pages or so after examining the model—a summary of sorts. He will meticulously go through the model from a purely functional point of view, he will tell you: "in the model there are such and such stages, a major stage of the model is this, and my understanding of the model is that. . . ." The mathematicians and engineers who are in charge of examining the model will not make any little additions to it, they will simply limit themselves to reducing and synthesizing. For example, when working on interest rate options, one can choose to approach the rate curve in various ways: The mathematician[32] makes this decision and passes it on to the computer engineer in charge of coding. . . . This transfer is not always easy. Sometimes the engineer receives something absolutely awful, that is, awful from his point of view, for what he's going to do. The mathematicians, on the other hand, do not see this aspect of implementation. Recently, we had to code a variant of the Hull–White model which uses a random process supposed to represent rates. The sensitive part of these models is calibrating[33] them on the interest rate curve. Which algorithm do we choose for this calibration? Hull and White do not say anything on this question. They consider it already a given, it hardly takes up three lines in the whole article. Whereas I find myself stuck on this question, and I even sent them a message asking for more information, but I imagine that it no longer interests them. They have a famous article; after that, implementation is just a lowly task. . . . This type of problem can definitely be good, we can give value-added to what we're doing by finding and proposing an algorithm that converges quickly . . . yes, trying to give back value-added to what you do, in a way to increase your credibility, as if to say "we're not just workhorses."

Later, Franck explains to me with amusement how implementation follows its course in the bank: "[T]he trader calls and says, 'I ran the module and, damn it, it's not working.'" He continues with an explanation of the reasons for failure:

[A]ll programs can fail. . . . Negative prices, or bad writing, or even a bad memory allocation. Next to the technical errors that can be corrected by any technician, there are errors where your reasoning is flawed [he means the reasoning of the programmer] and in that case it's much more difficult to correct the errors, because you have to understand the Hull–White model.

Mathematicians do not pay much attention to the coding techniques that make it possible to incarnate the model. They stay at an abstract level of the price, one that is just a solution to a system of equations or to an equally sanitized world of orderly simulations. Those who, like Franck, have to endow models with their coding forms are often perplexed by the small amount of attention given to this stage of modeling. The argument that runs through the interview with Franck points toward the *understanding* of models and toward the value-added of a smooth and successful transition into code. This came up again and again in the conversations I had with pricer programmers, typically in the form suggested by Franck when he evoked the workhorse image. He was well aware that clients were asking for pricing modules that were difficult to write. Indeed, he felt satisfaction within his team of developers: He was the only one to attend conferences at which he could communicate in both the language of the "academics" and that of coders.[34] Only he could penetrate both the financial technicality of the theoretical article and the organization of thousands of lines of code best suited to translate an idea from paper into a price-making machine. The conspicuous jubilation produced by the successful translation came from the cracking of a secret language that was not his—he enjoyed finance theory, but he did not have the mathematical expertise to engage Hull and White on their technical turf. He was only happy to grasp what was at stake. It also came from the recoding into another very articulate language: decoding and recoding, disclosing and enclosing, making public and keeping secret added to the excitement of working in finance, even though at its periphery. Writing codes entailed grasping the meaning of published articles that some of their authors could not even have envisioned. Devising appropriate outfits for schematic models allowed Franck to claim an understanding of the price—as technical achievement—that traders would not even need to have in mind when pressing the keys of their workstations. In these many ways, coding *above* the writings of scornful scholars and *below* the workstations of busy traders involved a kind of milieu trespassing for Franck.

Deforming the Models in the Code

One of the difficulties of implementation has to do with connecting two types of language that are not shaped by the same mold. The absence of a common form in these languages forces operators to use strategies to bring them closer as well as strategies to translate them. But what Franck describes refers directly to the distinction initially drawn between products and models. Coding exacerbates this distinction and shows how the incarnation of models is faced with the same problems as the transition from products to their models.

We should remember that the successful development of products requires a skill that John called "financial intuition." This is the term he used to designate the intimate and sometimes tacit knowledge of all the existing financial objects that could feature in the composition of the new product, and in the hedging strategies to be used. In his description of the creative process in finance, "mathematical intuition" was sitting on a different plane, made up exclusively of price coordinates. We can see how these two resources—indispensable to the development of a manageable[35] product—are also present in the construction of a pricer. A similar tension presides over the writing of a script and a product. Let us remember the complaint of the quant faced with the expansion rules of Scientific Workplace: The finance terms of the model are immediately returned to expansions that accurately respect mathematical rules. Prices are obviously central to these discussions but, at that stage, they are never produced by a pricer. They are the result of a deduction carried out by the math software, with a tranquility that is far removed from the pressures of the desk. When the quant's simulations fail, the failure becomes a subject of interest, but never does the performance of the program (whether Scientific Workplace or Mathematica) that carries out the simulation become a concern. On several occasions, the quant tried to code a little test model in C: for one tricky model, it took him more than a week to simply obtain a functional code. The code specialists were absent, the model did not lend itself easily to this codification, and he even had questions concerning how the traders could use it. But never did the difficulties of this model affect his work and his choice of models. That further step did not concern him and did not interfere with strictly theoretical elaborations.

Pricer codes are to models what financial intuition is to mathematical intuition. They force the broadening of the list of entities that need to be taken into consideration when a continuous, on-demand price is sought. Financial intuition opened up that list to the populations of securities that were likely to be featured in the hedging strategy that engineers and traders envisioned when they launched a new product. Pricer codes add a new set of constraints to the design of financial products. Their valuation models should be amenable to still another mode of existence. they need to be brought under the discipline of the traders' requirements and priced quasi-instantaneously. This requirement means that the price must now be produced by the trading room.[36] This environment must now simulate the other more common context of a price: that is, the transaction between two *or* more parties interested in trading. Absent this stage of the price as the outcome of a negotiation, a machine mimics it as best as possible. The room is forced to build a pricer to simulate a price without actual bids or offers because the products have no histories to which engineers can relate. They have no past or equivalent. Because CGPs defy possible comparisons, their value is dependent on the decisions made by the strings of engineers who collaborate around the models, from the quant to the computer engineer.

Conclusion

By relentlessly pushing financial structuring further, and by inventing new formulas intended to attract larger segments of a clientele that is being courted from all sides, engineers tend to heighten the uncertainty of these compositions. These uncertainties carry with them many possibilities: When the custom-made models fit well, the profits of the bank are level with the amounts invested by the clients. When the risky compositions of these new financial formulas are too chaotic to be controlled, they can harm the bank by locking it into a contract over many years. Faced with these uncertainties, financial operators can be tempted to increase the interpretative tools for these products. The lack of an ultimate model leads some to believe that it is within their free expression for these products to find the solution to their engineered opacity. The movement toward a proliferation of models/codes is perceptible among some trading-room operators: the fast-changing environment on which they draw their value, and the "massification" of the contracts, explains in part why there is more than one standard language. Growing portfolios of increasingly engineered products force traders to manage them "at a distance" by inventing codes to simplify them. The tension at work here is at the heart of the enterprise. The distance created by the codes—bear in mind the striking difference between the call option and its simplest Black–Scholes valuation model—produces a detour, but hopefully a loop that will eventually close and provide the trader with a price. Yet—and this is where the tension picks up—this loop slows down the very production of the price itself. Coding and modeling are conditions of intelligibility, but they take the entire trading room on a path that does not aim *directly* at the price. Without the coding, though, the room would be unable to even guess the value of all the traders' portfolios. This convoluted path is where the drama of "thinking financially" unfolds. The finance of the room's motto is itself such a motley group of product, model, and machine (itself another motley group of codes) that the object to think with or through is quite complex.

At this stage, when the financial formula[37] has given rise only to *formulations*, the opportunities of the operators to manipulate them are at their highest. These formulas stay in perpetual movement when they receive definitions from multiple filters. As a consequence, their direction is not firmly set. They move from one operator to another, shifting languages with each. By being bound to the more stable and standardized codes documented above, the speed of their circulation within the trading room declines. These codes impose the constraints of a language that cannot be changed without a cost, and they thus force operators to discipline themselves according to these rules for manipulation and description. The proliferation is reduced, and those who can take control of this financial formula clarified by a code become fewer, but this rarefaction also ensures simpler communication around the formula: the latter has lost its Brownian motion–like character to take on that of a more deterministic trajectory.

Yet, the operators of this market cannot be seeking the final and definitive stabilization of those codes. The eager inventiveness of engineers rules out such stabilization. Absolute stability would guarantee few risks but even fewer expectations of gain. Managing them would fall into a routine and prohibit the sudden short-circuits that created the unpredictable economics of these innovations. Setting up an industrial process for the handling of products made transparent has, needless to say, economic advantages. But at the modeling stage, setting up frameworks that would allow for more control in the daily exercise of product understanding would make the bank lose its monopoly over this understanding: these structures would bring into the modeling market, in transportable forms, that which the bank tries to safeguard.

The perilous exercise of an economy at the edge, threatened on the one hand by the chaos of multiple languages and, on the other hand, by the routine of standardized processes, guarantees short life-span species.

The risk associated with setting up routines is the risk of their uncontrolled diffusion through the movement of operators within a job market eager for smugglers and informants. But this mastery of *accurately modeled products* does not only depend on the spreading of appropriate codes. As the introduction pointed out, it is the fantasy of an abstract story of abstraction that locates formalisms in an ethereal world. The following chapters will reiterate a lesson learned by social scientists in their quest to pinpoint the site of scientific objectivity: formalisms wither when they are not pampered by careful operators. The strength of financial operators' articulation of products depends on the material felicity of financial gestures. Passing orders and managing purchases and sales on a daily basis do not require just a good grammar and a skillful coding; they also call for a balancing of the fragile trading-room ecology. From the price on paper to the complete transaction, the codes and models need to pass the test of the market.

CHAPTER 2

Hedging and Speculating with Portfolios

Speculation in Sociotechnical Networks

Securities are economic purifications (Latour, 1987) —vehicles that acquire a mobility and versatility not initially present in their underlyings. They capture nominal fractions of industries while protecting holders from some of the contingencies of these economies: with securities in hand, no manager is hassled. Here is the dream of capital made liquid and reversible for good: where wealthy investors are at long last protected from the future (they can sell whenever they anticipate a falling price) and from the spatial dispersion of industrial enterprises (they are worth their price through the Exchange, which is both central and detached from the space of the manufacture itself).[1] Yet, there is another story to finance besides that of sheer purification. This second feature, which we have called *interference*, drawing on the insights of historian of science Michel Serres (1980), is not quite specific to finance itself. Serres has been one of the most ardent proponents of a history of science that does not rely on fables of geniuses, rational methods, and simple linear progresses. Instead, he has relentlessly documented the complex and fragile fabric of scientific and engineering enterprises and their transformation through interferences and contaminations. Against the idea that sciences progress by purification, Serres has long insisted that they thrive only to the extent that they borrow from each other and create interferences between mutually foreign methods.

Applied to finance, interference is a vector orthogonal to purification in that it entails the combination of several purified securities into a new service. Unknowingly, General Bank engineers were implementing Serres's dream by designing CGPs with mutual interferences as the mechanisms of value along the lines of the correlation formula. This design exacerbates and displaces the ideal of securitization. CGPs contract the world economy (through the Exchange-traded indices of Japan, New York, and Paris) into a payoff formula and require their traders to hedge them on a daily basis by speculating on the upcoming price trends.

CGPs are useful experiments in financial engineering to the extent that they help us to see more clearly through the manufacture of profit by pushing purification and interference to the extreme. Here, they are combined in an explosive formula that seems to offer secure access to the world economy: guarantee and performance, insurance and investment. In practice, the design of too many interferences between too distant economic centers overwhelms the operators in charge of maintaining the product. The dream of finance collapses with an instrument that fails as much in its attempted contraction of the spaces of the economy as in its continuous grasp of prices. As it will turn out, this design is too daring and encounters finance's limits by pushing purification and interference too far. These limits question nothing less than the possibility of speculation.

Following Keynes's (1936) initial metaphor of the securities market as beauty contest, speculation has been studied mostly as a *social kind* problem (Barnes, 1983; Collins and Kush, 1999; MacKenzie et al., 2007): to speculate is to anticipate how other actors will act and react in the near future. As these reactions bring price changes, speculating is a way to position oneself to benefit from these shifts (buying low when anticipating a price rise and the reverse, short-selling in anticipation of a price decline). This quasi-exclusive focus on the interpersonal dynamic between actors has left aside the other maneuvering that takes place between the actors and the products upon which their strategies hinge. It is not difficult to imagine that speculating about a fully standardized commodity around which no quality uncertainty floats is not the same as speculating about a unique product whose qualities are partly unknown to interested parties. The recent financial crisis has offered some examples of that situation. Commentators have, with some sense of surprise, questioned the new nature of these financial services that seemed to escape both the issuers' and the clients' grasp, challenging the prior understandings of financial innovations based on the idea of asymmetry of information. Here, the problem is deeper, as there seems to be no "meter." Or rather, there are in fact too many competing "meters" fighting to become standards. What happens to speculation when an actor in the markets needs to keep one eye on the other actors' strategies and the other eye on the object of exchange itself (whether grain, commodities, or complex derivatives), so that one rarely enjoys the pleasure of looking straight? What happens to our understanding of finance if we see it through this lens and reopen the nature of speculation anew?

If speculation is more than the *common knowledge* (Lewis, 1969) thought experiment enjoyed by game theorists, new concepts are needed to crack open the operations of finance. Here, I use a common toolbox among practitioners of social studies of science. Following a movement that has changed significantly the way sociologists and historians of science and technology have approached their objects, I am interested in the generality of CGPs.[2] A fruitful wave of scholars writing in the wake of Thomas Kuhn (1962) have shown how the generality of science was a costly, delicate, and highly fragile achievement. Central to these accounts, the notion of "sociotechnical networks" (Galison, 1997; Hughes, 1987; Latour, 1987; Wise, 1995) casts light on the complex mix of institutions, disciplines, and material apparatuses necessary for science to perform as science. If generality is the main claim of science, it is not a lesser claim in economics in general, and in finance in particular (no puns intended here), as it engages precisely the way mainstream scholars of these disciplines have been thinking about the economy for at least a few decades. This mode of thinking sees the economy as competing sets of information around which agents struggle to extract as much value as possible. These sets look back to the past but they also look forward into the future. The investigation into the generality of economic goods only began in the 1970s when scholars started to complicate the narrative of economies as sets of information (Akerlof, 1970; Stiglitz and Weiss, 1981) by investigating the consequences of various formats of information (full, incomplete, asymmetric, and so forth). But, for all the progress achieved by the consideration of these formats, economic information is always the resource of these models, and the emergence of information is not questioned. The lesson learned from science studies scholars directs us to look upstream for understanding how goods can become information. These studies have shown that the generality of scientific entities is much more than mere play around sets of information: before goods can become unproblematic sets of information, they are part of long and sticky networks. It sometimes happens that they do not even make it to the level of "information" and linger in limbo, half brute matter, half coded pieces of economy.

This chapter looks at a financial service in such a state of limbo and questions the theory of speculation from the insights gained in a close study of its handling in the trading room. CGPs were quickly hailed by their engineers as sophisticated vehicles supported by a smart hedging mechanism. Yet, their very design also ruled out any speculation by the operators in charge of their supervision: traders were so overwhelmed by the designed complexity of CGPs that they had to lean on a script lodged in their computers rather than speculate on the underlying markets used to hedge. Although General Bank engineers had designed CGPs with the aim of exploiting information asymmetry between the desk and the clients, it turned out that they engineered a product that set the traders in a similarly difficult position.

From Scripts to Manipulations

The previous chapter covered ways in which models were brought into being through a series of mediators, who exerted powerful forces on the production of these models at the same time as they disguised some of the products' properties. The midwives for these difficult beginnings were principally financial engineers, quants, and pricer designers. The difficulty of understanding and controlling new products, however, does not end with these "secluded experimenters," but rather continues when products and models are passed over to the room's traders. Upon entering the market, these products take on a new mode of existence that tests the scripts of engineers: outside of the hands of their direct creators, new conditions await these laboratory creatures, and the trader is confronted with the task of reconciling engineers' purified scripts with the sometimes wild departures imposed by the market. Remember that this is not the first encounter between the engineering team and the traders. During the initial definition of products and the calibration of pricing software, the quant and the financial engineers solicited information from the traders about the *behaviors* of the securities they used in the hedging script. Yet in these exchanges, traders did not really contribute to the modeling discussion itself. They were mostly channels of information, and they typically reported on existing products and their price reactions to specific market configurations.

When traders enlist the products in their portfolios and start managing them, however, things change. They go back to school and find themselves struggling to make sense of their new ward. Indeed, in adopting a new product, they also adopt a new and particular model—a model whose features have played a role in the design of the product, one that is supposed to help the traders anticipate coming price changes. The model "anticipates," that is, but does not guarantee: for either the model is new—and thus is one more piece of the puzzle that traders need to fit in this new environment—or the model is old and familiar but of dubious utility for predicting the behavior of new products. Unlike the financial engineers and their ilk, the trader is not yet a specialist (at least not in the new product). He or she has to be very practical, and is judged on results, not on the promises of models. He or she lives in the worst of two worlds: no reliance on models is possible, and his or her experience is facilitated by attending to the beast's acclimation to its new market environment.

His workstation is therefore a site where a critical part of the information relative to the product is gathered: far from being the end point where models would simply be applied, it is instead a place where financial scenarios are produced and where analyses of products' reactions to the market are carried out. The quant describes the relationship with traders and the responsibility of model builders:

> If the model is finer, the trader has to be up to this level of refinement. It's not easy; this is where you can see how well a trading floor—and not only a model—is able to function. There has to be a symbiosis. Traders take it (the model) on their books: if you set a price, you have to be sure that it's a price they'll be able to hold. If they can't hold it, they can't put in place hedges with your price. You're now in a bad situation,

you're making them lose money. That's something that can be heatedly discussed with a trader, you set a price that's overadjusted, too hard, too tight, based on hypotheses that are too refined, and the trader can refuse to take it. That happened regularly. We had big problems with fixed incomes, there was a problem with skills, fixed income traders were not able to keep up; we found ourselves blocked from developing anything really refined.

The moment when a trader carries out an operation in the market marks the convergence of everything we have observed up until now. When an order is placed, the expert elaborations of products and models must take concrete shape through appropriate *commercial* actions. More than abstract manipulations, the temporal and spatial quality of traders' actions can make a deal collapse into a fiasco or ascend to notoriety through a successful bundling of flimsy opportunities. As with the more immediate commercial transactions known to anthropologists (Geertz, 1978), the deals involving novel products rely on gestures by traders. But global financial transactions problematize these gestures by the many layers of screens and the hundreds of kilometers of wires that disrupt the scene.[3] To be successful, these gestures need the collaboration of the highly technologically equipped world of the trading room. Precision and reaction must now be the quality of traders surrounded with tools that far exceed their technical knowledge and that are always on the brink of collapsing. This chapter looks at the conditions of possibility for such gestures, as we slow down and describe moments that are generally thought of as disconnected from the weight of the outside world. The simplistic picture of financial markets is one of purely *conditional gestures*, produced by operators able to make choices in an ethereal universe of possibilities devoid of asperity. The analysis put forth here will show that the possibility of placing an order that does not encounter obstacles from the thick architecture of the financial markets is very slim. Assembling the conditions of possibility for gestures that can enable the CGP turns out to be even more challenging. Attending to their complex agency leads to financial gestures that are encumbered, torn, and subject to the ordeals of a still scattered financial marketplace. The risks and strains of the globalization gamble are redistributed among operators who thought they could hold financial marketplaces in their hands through financial ingenuity—and who suddenly discover that their wager on the contraction and consolidation of economic activities scattered across the four corners of the world is doomed to failure.

CGPs are indeed heroic attempts at giving substance to the dream of financial integration, while also serving as its most striking counterexample by their continual asymmetry. They build on Exchanges and products in an original way: rather than keeping their distance from existing markets and assets by inventing products with radically new features, CGPs recombine existing products by bringing them together into a packaged service. Yet, this integration is more than just a simple collection of outstanding assets. There is a specific intensity to this process as the assets are bundled along the lines of a formula. A portfolio/collection of assets is also de facto an experiment with the interferences between underlyings—although it is one limited to the *arithmetical addition* of these assets. CGPs, in contrast, *bend* these interferences through their formulas. An infinite number of formulas can be designed; some quasi-transparent (think again of a portfolio with a simple arithmetical composition), and others with more tortuous terms. Yet, the bottom line for the trading room is that each design demands its proper maintenance. This design of financial assets has direct consequences on how they can be managed and, in particular, on how the risk associated with their issue can be controlled.

The composition of the portfolio—achieved by the direction imparted by the formula—exploits existing interferences between the underlying assets. But this mode of exploitation is, in Michel Serres's terms (1980), parasitic and, as a consequence, the trader who manages the portfolio pays the price of this derivative mode of value creation. The existing securities that CGPs combine and derive their value from have a life of their own, and the trader is dependent upon their continuity. They can disappear from the market when the company goes bankrupt; they split or aggregate when underlying companies merge. One easily figures out that designing a financial instrument from the combination of these uncontrollable securities is risky. The risk does not come so much from the recombinant form of innovation: that is all too common and could even be said to characterize all forms of innovation. Much trickier to manage for the trading room is the enduring life of the components of these new products. A quick thought experiment will convince the reader that a customized homemade car would be less than safe to drive should all the meticulously assembled parts—seemingly captured in the form of a vehicle—have a life of their own. Imagine a door changing shape and taking off without warning, a muffler losing its hard-fought compatibility with the rest of the engine, the windshield breaking apart while one drives. It turns out that this thought experiment was indeed a real experiment and not limited to the minds of engineers: a lucrative and risky experiment involving the trading room and the bank. General Bank purposefully designed the financial equivalent of such products, and the traders were forced to struggle to maintain them on a daily basis, much as would the driver of an experimental parasitic car, assembled with disparate, disobedient parts.

The trading room as a whole has to live up to this engineered curvature of the new financial service. By focusing the analysis on the hedging of CGPs, it is possible to show the tensions that products born of engineers' intelligence create for the work of a trader. The dispersion of the product puts the collection gesture of the trader at risk, as he or she attempts to hedge bets and offset the precariousness of his or her position. The trader finds him or herself at the intersection of two injunctions: wherever an underlying asset needs to be bought or sold, but also needing to attend to the curvature of the formula itself.

Hedging

I now look at the modes of risk exposure and risk protection in which the traders must engage once the client has given approval, the contract has been signed, and the bank has agreed to take on the product's risk. Given that the principle of CGPs is to guarantee capital and the formula-based performance to the client, the bank has to make sure it will be able to disburse what it owes by the end date. In the meantime, it must make this sum grow along the dictate of the formula. A close and slow reading at the CGP terms contained in Figure 1 will ground that imperative.[4]

The performance of the product will eventually depend on the value of a BKT, composed of three indices.[5] DJ Euro Stoxx 50, abbreviated STX, is itself a synthetic index reflecting the value of the fifty biggest European publicly traded companies.[6] S&P 500, abbreviated SP, covers the 500 largest U.S.-based publicly traded companies and, following the same logic, the Nikkei 225, abbreviated NIX, covers the 225 biggest Japanese publicly traded companies. The basket is equally weighted by each index, and variations in one index can offset variations in the others. BKT_t measures the collective performance of the three indices between the initial period (i) and quarter (t). The final measure BKT_m averages these performances over the 32 quarters and serves the client 120 percent of the greatest of the relative performance of the basket over 32 quarters. If over these 32 quarters the basket "underperformed," the guarantee kicks in and the initial capital is safe. The second chance offers the possibility of decoupling the indices from the negative basket. When the final averaged value of the portfolio is lower than its initial value ($BKT_m < BKT_i$), the client still receives 120 percent of the best performing index.

For the bank, the payoff dictated by the explicit formula creates a *mechanical tyranny*: whatever the indices do (moving up, down, or staying flat), the payoff has to be paid to the clients, and if ($BKT_m - 1$) is positive, the bank has to come up with money in addition to the nominal. During the 3, 5, or 10 years of the contract, the bank obviously has no control over the stocks or indices. From our example product, STX, SP, and NIX can move in any direction, with contrasting consequences for the final payoff. Let us review two polar situations.

For the bank, the ideal scenario is to return nothing but the principal, simply living up to the promise of a guarantee. This scenario would demand that the indices be inversely correlated, so that gains from one Exchange offset losses from another, which maintains the equally weighted basket performance around zero. If the basket does not gain value over the period, the bank repays nothing but the capital initially invested.

For a client, this scenario *ad minima* only appears advantageous when compared with a situation where the capital invested in regular stocks on the market was to lose its initial value. This guarantee could have indeed been a profitable service for investors who had assets in the market during the crash of spring 2000, not to mention the more recent financial collapse. The opposite possible outcome for the bank was to manage the nominal into a high profit when the indices of the formula turn out in such a combination as to dictate it. Consider three highly positively correlated indices and booming stock markets. In that case, the bank has to pay more than the nominal: [Max $(BKT_m - 1; 0)$] is positive, but it is compounded by a factor of 1.2 (120%). The problem in such market conditions is to find the money to cover not simply the guarantee but the basket's performance itself. Where should the bank invest the nominal to make it rise up to the letter of the formula? It cannot just invest the money in products replicating the performance of the indices—it has to do better and beat them by 20 percent.

That is the dilemma: the bank is entrusted with a large amount of money, and it has designed a financial service that necessitates management of the money at least as well as the *basket* boosted by a factor of 1.2. The choice of the formula itself and its components holds the secret for the bank's ability to survive the chaotic market and its uncertain course of action. This ability has a name in financial parlance: hedging. The more closely correlated the components of this formula, the more difficult it is for the bank to hedge and make money on it. Conversely, a highly uncorrelated set of securities make it easy for the bank to hedge and is also synonymous with a bad return for the client, with a depressed average basket. So the correlation of the set of elements was crucial in determining the money that General Bank would have to pay or make.

The hedging strategies implemented by the traders at the exotics desk bring us back to the models built by quants. For products where prices are not the outcome of a secondary market—with buyers and sellers confronting their bids and offers on an Exchange or through other mechanisms designed to match their needs—the models are the source of value.[7] With products held for a few years, quants use Exchange-based underlyings prices to simulate CGPs prices, but they never trade on these Exchanges. With traders becoming our primary interlocutors in this chapter, the conditions of financial experimentation change. When they morph from paper models to a pricer, the initial theoretical question of thinking financially meets its acid test. Can the models reach their condition of felicity and provide the traders in the room with a road map, charting risky strategies and paving the way for a smooth journey through the term of the contract? Can they help the trader who now faces "real" underlying prices, whereas engineers were playing with theoretical time series? Models also reach their potential for disaster if traders fail to see the products behind them. Thus, the traders' desk is the last test that models must pass to earn longevity in the bank.

Portfolio Structure

When a product is sold to a client, the amount of money cashed in by the bank is divided into two parts. The larger of these parts is invested in a zero-coupon bond. Zero-coupon bonds are financial products that do not make annual coupon payments: instead of receiving the interest for the money invested in the bond annually, the investor only gets the total interest at the end, along with the nominal. By investing in a zero-coupon bond, the bank ensures that it will hold the sum of the guarantee specified by the product sold to the client. If it has to guarantee a client an investment of €100 million in 10 years, it only needs to invest between 70 and 80 percent of it (€70 million to €80 million) in these bonds in order to cover itself. The rate of return on this investment—or, seen from the future, its discount—derives from the absence of coupons. At the term of the investment in zero-coupons, the €70 million is, in effect, worth €100 million. This investment is made when the product is launched, and the bank does not touch it until it has come to maturity. This portion of the client's investment is thus not really part of the trader's portfolio, and at this stage, the trader's work is not yet crucial to the fulfillment of the bank's commitment. It will become so with the active management of what was not invested in zero-coupon bonds.

The second portion of the client's investment—€20 million to €30 million if the bank receives €100 million—can thus be used to fulfill the second aspect of the contract: the performance of the baskets described in the formula. The structure of a trader's portfolio includes two types of financial support: the products issued by the bank (issue subportfolio) and the simplest derivative products, for example options (or futures) of sale or purchase (hedging subportfolio) of the assets on which the products are indexed. This structure theoretically allows the entire portfolio—made up of its two subportfolios—to be managed by continuously neutralizing the risk of variation of the products issued. It is important to underscore the theoretical script and the hypothesis of nonstop rebalancing at this stage. This will help clarify the constant gap traders will have to fill between the script and the hedging conditions in markets whose continuity is broken by the geographical dispersion of the products and the slowness of the operators.

When products are in the trader's portfolio, they are said to be *en pause*. The overall securities owned by the trader are called his or her *pause*. It includes both the products issued by the bank—such as the one illustrated in the introduction—and the securities acquired to hedge their risk. Several spellings of the term *pause* circulated, and some operators wrote it *pose*, which was used as a shortcut for position.[8] Their pose was their overall market position, the instruments they were long of and those they were short of. *En pause* could be translated as "on hold" but it also conveys the sense of *rest*, *recess*, and *break*, contained in the *pause* (versus *play*) of the music player. Either way, the term gives the perception that traders have of the market and the securities circulating around them. When securities are *en pause*, they are not floating around the market. They have settled in for a while: it could be a short while or it could last a few years. Their prices have been established during the purchase, and as long as they stay part of the pause, they have no resale price yet. However, their prices are still fluctuating. While *en pause*, these securities are actively traded by other traders and brokers, and General Bank's traders monitor them on a continuous basis. The pause is thus—contrary to its meaning of rest and recess—the riskiest of positions: it is that potentially treacherous moment when the portfolio's value can go up or down without any action from the trader. In that moment, profits and losses occur behind the backs of traders. Because traders strive to control their exposure to risks, the pause never lasts long.[9] It is more a perimeter term than a notion used to characterize the value of the portfolio.[10] Indeed, and as surprising as it may sound, the value of the portfolio is not the primary concern of traders. Traders work toward the formula and its moving target of client payoff, not toward the maximum performance of their investments. In a way, they are conservative, with their hands tied by the imperative of attending closely to the interference of the securities' move and the payoff requirement. In a nutshell, the goal is to repay the client the nominal and the performance of his contract, not to turn out millions. Even if the pause is relentless in its ups and downs, the prospect of action for traders is set by the term written in each contract. And if each variation in price of the assets in the basket changes what the bank has to pay the client if the product came to term at that given moment, the product issued by the bank will remain on hold for a long time in the portfolio of the trader, and this momentary shift in value may not have any direct effect on any final payments to the client. Remember that the money transferred to the client will depend eventually on an average of performance: big gains could offset prior big losses, and the bottom line will only be known when the last fixing is recorded.[11] That is the crucial feature of these products and the discipline they force onto traders. The part of their pause containing their issued products will only be cleared when the term puts an end to the contracts, but traders have to monitor them on a high-frequency basis while restraining themselves from making short-term profit. The desk has no use of cash in the short term and will only enjoy it when the relentless variations of prices of underlyings settle in the wake of the final fixing and the calculation of its payoff for the client. In the meantime, the money needs to stay in the market. Only there will it grow and will the trader be able to follow the dictate of the formula. This discipline has its rituals and its magic formulas: it is not easy keeping a trader from striving toward the industry goal (i.e., short-term profit). The environment of the trading room is geared toward that ultimate liquidity, but the hedging mechanism put in place by engineers tethers traders. The motto of the engineer-designed plans of action is, "You shall not gamble. Instead you shall follow closely the formula and aim to meet the client payoff." Adding to the pain of restraint in a universe where the deeply engrained ethos is toward risk-taking, the discipline of CGP traders requires that they visit all the Exchanges where the formula's underlyings are traded. Discipline and dispersion are not easy to reconcile.[12]

Hedging Several Places at Once

The formula products that derive their values from securities, bonds, and indices negotiated in Paris, New York, Chicago, and Tokyo have to be hedged in each of these places sequentially. Each new financial place added to the design of the formula through an index or a security needs to be visited at least daily. The time differences between these Exchanges break with the script of ideal continuity invented by the engineers of the trading room. These scripts disregard space and time and claim to invent global financial products, but the time-zone differences of these places remain tied to solar time. This geographic dispersion forces a trader to work with all locations when rebalancing a portfolio. A Parisian trader opens a portfolio when Tokyo is closing and finishes the day when the New York market is in full swing. He or she must constantly act with these staggered time zones in mind.

Prices have time patterns. During a trading day, there are peaks and troughs in trading intensity. Observing all the prices at 4:00 P.M. Paris time provides different information than does observing each price at the same time of day in different locations (4:00 P.M. in Paris for French products, 4:00 P.M. in Tokyo for Japanese products, 4:00 P.M. in New York for New York Stock Exchange–traded products). Four o'clock P.M. is not a random time: hedges are in full swing around that time, as this is the last moment traders can contemplate the Exchanges before picking a strategy. Traders are dependent on these differences when they assess the value and the risk exposure of their portfolios in order to balance them. This discrepancy of price maturities means that they conduct most of their reasoning with price volatilities that do not carry the same information. Traders who have to hedge products whose basket includes Asian stocks or indices must contact their local Asian brokers before the markets close there. This has to take place very early in the morning at a time when European Exchanges are just setting to open. Prices in Europe have yet to absorb the threads of information that trickled in during "their" nights: the American and Asian Exchanges have produced new data that are likely to bear on the traders' strategies that day. Remember that the correlation between underlying indices determines the product payoff and therefore the bank's liability. Any information that helps anticipate whether markets will go up or down goes a long way toward keeping the risk of correlation under control. Traders' pricing tools face the same problems because they process products that demand continuous hedging while being written on different regional Exchanges.

The source of troubles created by these multiple-time-zone products is also to be found in the organizational principles adopted by the bank. Many other operators have to deal with entities that span several time zones and require a collective rather than an individual for proper processing. A plane in flight is cared for by air controllers located along the arc of its journey, so that no one of the controllers is in charge of the whole flight (Mackay, Fayard, et al., 1998). A plane in flight has features similar to financial, as a controller has to adapt the plane's flight trajectory to the slice of airspace he or she monitors: redirecting the plane when the area is congested and offering the safest route in case of storm forecast. Traders do the same as they work at locating the path of least resistance (cost) for their hedging strategy. The only difference comes from the role of the correlation between the underlying securities in the value of CGPs. This feature, and the need to control it by hedging all underlyings, *simultaneously* turns a trader into a musical director of a multisited orchestra. When one considers the puzzle created by this multisitedness, it is legitimate to question the organizational choice of a trader acting as a musical director rather than by financial zone, as witnessed with air controllers. As we will observe soon, the distribution of tasks around the product is in place with the trader and his or her assistant working hand in hand at the crucial hedging moment when simulations of hedges and real orders overlap.

In Tokyo, the bank had a trader in charge of derivative products, but the division of labor was clearly skewed toward the Parisian traders. The portfolio was shared so that the Tokyo trader had the upper hand and some discretion during the day (night in France), but a series of trades that did not follow the plan of action of the French traders had significantly cooled the relations between the Paris and Tokyo trading rooms. The Parisian traders saw their colleagues in Tokyo as emergency operators, on-site and authorized to make decisions in case of abrupt price collapse—in theory, the (unlikely) catastrophe hitting Asia when French traders are not in command and calling for immediate action on the Tokyo Exchange. Apart from these moments, it was understood in Paris that a regular day—with moderate ups and downs of the Japanese index—would be better handled from Paris. In March 2000, when the Internet bubble started to falter, a series of decisions by the Tokyo trader infuriated the French desk as it went against the hedging strategies elaborated for such market configurations. In a week, the distribution of the hedging operations between Paris and Tokyo went by the wayside. From that moment on, the French traders only delegated the negotiation of the orders to the Tokyo trader. The hedging strategy was theirs and they lost the advantage of the multilocation of the trading room. De facto, they worked with the end-of-day prices of the Japanese Exchange.

At the same time as they complicate matters immeasurably, time variations in global markets lend traders an ability to anticipate upcoming variations from securities traded on downstream Exchanges. The notion of a "downstream" Exchange points to the temporal integration between Exchanges that successively open up and close in different time zones. A sudden shift of the European markets can be expected to impact the Asian markets when they reopen a few hours after London and Paris close. A trader knows this through the experience of the relative couplings of markets, but he or she cannot incorporate it concretely into a risk model or automate it into the code of the portfolio assessment software. This absence of codification forces the trader to perform a kind of balancing-cum-juggling act with numbers. NIX, SP, and STX indices at 4:00 P.M. Paris time are numbers that do not have the same meaning (maturity has its hourly pattern during the day): They are numbers that will impact other numbers; numbers that will enter into complex crosscombinations; and numbers that the trader will bring together in spite of their temporal disconnectedness. The semicontinuity and the semi-integration of these markets make this attempt to connect the indices from different Exchanges perilous. In financial terms, CGPs offer a *fake* financial integration. That is the wager of General Bank engineers: gathering indices already belonging to the same financial world would present little interest. Should they be replicas of each other—or variations around one unique financial theme—they would be redundant. The bold engineering move comes from bridging their distance and their difference. Jane Guyer's (2004) insightful study of Atlantic Africa trading brings to our attention the fact that traders are engaged in the business of bridging disjunctions. This notion is perfectly appropriate for our otherwise different case: the disjunctions between the financial worlds bridged by the formula are the source of its value for the clients, and also the origin of all worries for the traders. If CGPs are not yet global products, they become so and are made so by the incessant labor of its traders. They only owe their steadiness to the traders, who virtually move from one place to another and simulate the passing of time in New York to better hedge a product in Paris. The letter of the contract is global for the clients inasmuch as it gives them a flavor of the Japanese, the North American, and the extended European securities performance. The maintenance supplied by traders bridges the gap carefully picked by engineers and keeps afloat the product despite its stretching of existing securities ecologies.

A second effect might seem less problematic in strictly financial terms, but it is just as restrictive. Traders constantly check the day calendars of different Exchanges to make sure that they are open, and this activity is just as crucial as taking into account time-zone differences when they hedge the portfolios. These verifications are not only the business of traders; middle-office operators who monitor the calendars that figure into profit calculations use other information technology tools to mirror this part of the trader's work. Financial products that require only one reading of underlying instruments' values during their entire lifetime pose few problems. The contracting parties usually agree easily on the first and last date for rate verification. But when a product requires that the market value of securities be checked on numerous dates—sometimes more than thirty as was the case of the product we picked to illustrate CGP—there can be uncertainty concerning the dates farthest from the start. This uncertainty comes from the automatic generation of the schedule tables for the contract, regardless of the day of the week this date corresponds to. Yet, it is essential that the trader know precisely when to verify a date. The fixing, on the exact date, can determine how the contract is hedged; if the hedge concerns clusters of contracts, the value of the underlying securities are used by the *pricer* and the *risk-analysis software* in setting that hedge. Forgetting or miscapturing[13] the value of the underlying securities on the proper date can turn out to be costly.

The indication of the date can be explicit, in which case every date for fixing is recorded in the confirmation notice. It is usually implicit, in which case a rule (more or less clear) is adopted to determine the date. It is important that both the bank and its clients observe the fixing factored into the payoff formula on the same day and at the same hour. The series of fixings indicate how much money will eventually fly back into the client's pocket. Because the bank needs to pay out in the days following the last fixing date, any delay would put it in default with the client. However, more important than timeliness is precision.

Fixing verification can be problematic when the automatically generated days of observation fall when the Exchange is not open; that is, a weekend or a holiday. When that is the case, it becomes necessary to use a rule that generates an alternative date. There are three possibilities and two rules. The "PRE" rule (for *previous*) stipulates that the alternative date should be the day directly preceding the automatically generated day when the latter falls on a day when the market is closed. When the original date is a Sunday, then, going back one day, to Saturday, does not suffice. One must go further back, to Friday, in order to find Sunday's theoretical value. But it is possible that going back two days might mean a change of month, and that would not fall in line with a market verification schedule that is month-based. If, indeed, the rule calls for a verification every first of the month and April 1, 2002, was a Sunday, the simple rule of going back two days brings us to Friday, March 30, 2002. Both the client and the bank might wish for the fixing not to fall twice in one month. It then becomes necessary to apply another rule, the "PRE MOD" (*previous modified*) rule, which stipulates that the recording of economic data must necessarily be done during the theoretical month (April) and that the rule for looking backwards must be modified to become one of looking forward for the closest day when the market reopens. That is, from the theoretical Sunday we look at the upcoming Monday. Generally, the rule for adjusting payment schedules is indicated in the confirmation, but it does happen occasionally that it be omitted, in which case it is necessary to apply a bit of imagination and a lot of attention to put into place a rule that will hold for the entire life span of the product. Given that there is no automatic checking of the dates selected for fixing, it is not possible to generate a payment schedule without checking a calendar to make sure that the days chosen will indeed be workdays and that they will be suitable (that they will follow the rules that the bank follows). To help with this, the bank provides its employees with a calendar that covers about ten years and ten financial marketplaces while indicating each one's days of operation. This calendar was in the process of being installed on the software that brought together the front and back bases (the FED software, which I will come back to) when I arrived on the trading floor. The market kaleidoscope was on its way toward being discontinued, but it was still used as a security net for products over relatively long periods of time (some going up to fifteen years). The traders and middle-office people in charge of products involving fixing and hedging on more than one national market often called upon this paper calendar.

It is tempting to contrast the dispersion of the product, designed as a fragile collective of groups of securities and teams of traders located across the world, to the solid geographic location of the Exchanges, homes of these securities. This opposition is to a certain extent true, and General Bank capitalizes on this differential extension. CGPs appeal to clients in large part because they assemble species belonging to many spaces in one discrete space. Yet, this distinction between the trading room and the scattered Exchanges does not convey the elusive nature of prices found on these Exchanges. For traders, the burden of the CGP is not only in having to keep an eye on Exchanges, it is as much in finding the asset price *there*. The work of price collection, so aptly captured in the notion of the "fixing," is all but straightforward: much like entomologists' collecting of specimens, the traders collecting prices often must handle and preserve delicate organisms in unpredictable locales.

For any given product, the correlation between different indices had been an object of study for financial engineers for many months before they decided to launch their contract and committed to disciplining the trading room to the formula. The simulations used to study these correlations were based on public prices. Engineers play all the time with these big databases, and as cumbersome as they are to deal with, they have a comforting feature: prices are well behaved. They stay put and lend themselves to modeling and simulating. Well-behaved prices do not refer here to the more or less erratic patterns of their curve: extremely fast-changing prices are well behaved once they are caught on paper. When they are still fluctuating and still to be "fixed," the differential built upon by engineers is nowhere to be found. The trader is stuck *in* the Exchange and cannot retrieve the price up to the trading room and in a state that he or she knows how to work with. If prices are too elusive—if they cannot be grasped firmly and without contention by the parties—the product design simply collapses. It is premised on the existence of prices, as clear and clean information. Unfortunately, there are many ways for prices to remain elusive. One of the most common is through the lack of public data: although it is the business of the Exchange to release prices as they unfold between participants, it is also their prerogative to discontinue a price when conditions are deemed extraordinary enough that they would interfere with the natural forces of offer and demand and thereby hit inconsistent levels.[14] The bank uses a good amount of ink anticipating the possible

(b) If on the second Business Day at 11:00 a.m. (Paris time) preceding the Floating Premium Option Payment Date of a Calculation Period, INE (Instituto Nacional de Estadisticas) has published neither the definitive nor the provisional ICP_n, then the Calculation Agent shall determine a substitute ICP_n (the "Substitute ICP_n") used to determne the Floating Premium Option due in respect of such Calculatioin Period, as follows:

$$\text{Substitute } ICP_n = \frac{ICP_m}{ICP_0} \times \frac{12}{Nbm}$$

Where:

"ICP_m" means the latest ICP published by INE (Instituto Nacional de Estadisticas) in respect of a month prior the month of Mai in respect of which ICP_n didn not publish the ICP.

"Nb_m" means the number of months between the month of Mai of the preceding Calculation Period (such month of Mai included) and the month to which ICP_m relates (such month excluded).

(ii) If the ICP is no longer calculated or published by INE (Instituto Nacional de Estadisticas) but is calculated or published by a successor entity without any modification of the calculation formula, the ICP used for determination of the Floating Premium Option, shall be the ICP calculated or published by such successor.

(iii) If INE (Instituto Nacional de Estadisticas) decides to modify the year or month which was used as the "100 basis" and consequently adjust the ICP's (already published or to be published), thereafter the ICP_n and/or the ICP_0 used for the determination of the Floating Premium Option by the Calculation Agent, shall be the ICP_n as adjusted or calculated by INE (Instituto Nacional de Estadisticas) on the basis of the new "100 basis."

(iv) If INE (Instituto Nacional de Estadisticas) or its successor modifies the calculation formula of the ICP, the Calculation Agent shall determine in its sole discretion if it is posssible to establish a linking coefficient between the ICP calculated on the basis of the previous method and the ICP calclated on the basis of the new method, to preserve the economic situation of the parties hereunder. If the Calcualtion Agent determines that such linking coeffiecient can be established , then the Floating Premium Option shall be calculated by applying such linking coefficient.

If, in the determination of the Calculation Agent, it is not possible to establish a linking coefficient, then the Calculation Agent will notify the parties that an Additional Termination Event has occurred with the Floating Premium Option Payer as the Sole Affected Party.

Figure 6. A Confirmation Spelling What to Do When an Index is Not "There"
The deal was an inflation swap with a Spanish counterpart. The client would get a rate indexed on the Spanish inflation and would pay General Bank a market rate plus a spread agreed upon.[15]

disappearance of the underlying prices and inventing alternative means of collecting them. The contract confirmation documents some of the strategies used to remedy possible elusiveness.

Fortunately, and because the stakes and costs of elusive prices are too high for so many parties, a price is always reached in the end, but it can come late and can cost the bank a lot of energy to produce. This investment derails the sleek and fast script that engineers had in mind when they were thinking in terms of prices as information (their database of well-behaved prices) instead of prices as exploration. When it works smoothly, the Exchange streamlines this exploration but it does not guarantee a price under control. Disruptions to the engineers' script can come from that which had been kept at bay by the very project of finance: the industry and its vicissitudes.

Securities Operations

Attention to the calendar days and hours of operation in financial markets represents only the framework of a more general monitoring of traded securities (securities of the hedge portfolio) that must be instituted by the exotics desk so as to forecast securities operations. This procedure was put in place after an oversight that led to significant losses for the desk, which demonstrated how the growth of activity was putting the bank in danger. A product had been sold to a client; the hedge was going well until it was discovered that one of the securities entering into the formula had changed. The company's stock had undergone a split—x shares replaced y shares from before the split—which made it necessary to rebalance the basket of underlying securities according to a y/x ratio. The terms of the contract take into account this operation and others (for our concern here merging) that are quite common and without consequences for the bank or the client. Generally, the client is also told in advance of the planned modification of the product and has several days to make a decision. After this period has passed, the client must accept the substitution formula proposed by the bank. But in the case at hand, the trader continued to hedge his position, unaware of the change. Overnight, after a random check reported the split, he discovered that the bank would have to cover a bit more than ₣600,000 (slightly more than €90,000) for the stock split.

This situation exposed the flaws in the market monitoring system. The securities operations person (*operations sur titres* or OST in French) had not identified a tool that could have allowed him to detect the *split* immediately and just as immediately implement the change in the securities portfolio.[16] The manual market monitoring system presented a flaw. The monitoring of the companies whose listed securities the bank had used was rudimentary; it was one of the last activities on the floor that was still entirely manual. The person in charge could not anticipate the movements of company mergers, acquisitions, and bankruptcies. He could not contact companies directly to inquire about their status because the number of companies involved was beyond that allowed for active monitoring. But passive monitoring was risky; the desk could miss arbitrage opportunities during mergers.[17] Moreover, this passivity when pushed to its limits not only made for missed profit opportunities, but also caused significant losses.

Given the number of OSTs that influenced the hedging routines of the desk, the trader and the OST operator came to work closely together. Reopening what the engineers had black-boxed by assuming that prices and securities would not be ambiguous, was the price to pay for inventing financial services derived from practically all of the large financial marketplaces. It was no longer just the financial characteristics of those securities grouped into baskets that needed to be monitored; it was also the legal framework to which these securities belonged. While the division of labor gave traders the conditions for an activity geared entirely toward price forecasting, the disproportionate space taken up by the practical management of difficult financial products brought them back to questions of financial engineering. Focusing exclusively on the price was no longer possible, as back-office tasks seeped into front-office operations. The bank tried to solve the problem by insulating traders and charging the OST operators with the legal verifications and with the implementation of changes upon the portfolio of hedges. But delegating this activity could not completely block the interference of the changing legal envelope for the companies on prices. When a split occurred while I was present at the desk, the OST operator supposed to filter these interfering noises could not do so without the concrete involvement of the trader whose securities were undergoing a split. This trader had to be sure that the currency conversion of the securities in the hedging account worked well. Unable to perform the conversion for each transaction, he asked the OST operator to write up a macro in Excel in order to apply this conversion to the whole. But the operation proved to be long and problematic. The number of shares multiplied by two came with a change in the payment of dividends. The conversion could not be accomplished easily because scripts governing dividend payment did not transfer well.

The equipment necessary for the trader's management of products dispersed across many financial markets created some problems. The dream of purifying the economy into a collection of prices that could easily be manipulated without needing to reach out to the real economy with its endless legal complications was not easy to make come true. Traders wanted to deal with prices as theoretical entities, and they were constantly reminded that securities prices are solidly dependent on worldly companies that undergo all kinds of vicissitudes that challenge their contraction into prices. From price experts, traders were reduced to the status of bean counters by this excessive complexity.

Massive Hedging

The mass of products each trader handles makes the job of hedging complicated. Yet, the complications can possibly be handled through proper modeling. The real difficulty of trading CGPs en masse come from their challenge to the existing variables of hedging models, which prior to that were dealing with one product. The difficulty was compounded by the two sets of correlations realized by this massive aggregation: CGPs are correlation products by design; portfolios of CGPs create a correlation of correlations.

Hedging Scales

The traders of the exotics desk handle portfolios of up to five hundred products. In such a case, it is impossible to think of hedging the portfolio contract by contract. For each of them, one would need to visit all the Exchanges in which underlying securities are traded (Paris, New York, Tokyo, and so forth), adjust the hedge for that particular contract if needed, and repeat the operation . . . five hundred times. Having ruled out this option, traders solved the problem by hedging not at the level of individual products but rather at that of grouped products (portfolios). Thus, a *composite entity* becomes the base element for hedging, and its properties are calculated when deciding whether to buy or sell the underlying securities.

The new hold that traders wield over their shares through this assemblage has consequences due to the level of emerging complexity. Indeed, every class of products is tested over a long period during which engineers think up the most varied possible scenarios that might apply to these potential products. The trader is consulted whose portfolio is going to be receiving the products in question. Then the results of these simulations are presented to the trader, and he or she gives input. All of these testing procedures (simulation, back testing, etc.) aim at exhausting the types of price reactions that can be generated by products whose value depends on multiple underlying securities. The tests required by a single product are already complicated compared with simulations that "plain vanilla" products might require. They call for a cross-simulation of each underlying asset and are active in a much bigger space. But the complexity of the task is accentuated by the heterogeneity of product that each portfolio carries.

Although a class of products might be defined by the payment formula that the client will receive from the bank issuing the product, the elements making up this formula can vary greatly. Thus, as shall be seen, clients have a margin of flexibility when it comes to the definition of these components. They can choose their stock or index from a selection offered to them by the issuers; they can also bring into this basket stocks that had not been planned for by the issuers when the dissolution of a company begets securities operations. All of these events are liable to lead to unexpected and unpredictable variations in the financial securities prices that the issuing bank will need to manage over the course of a product's lifetime. Moreover, a class of products does not define a single horizon along which each product lives; each class belongs to a subclass that corresponds with successive dates of issue. From the point of view of the trader engaged in this task of portfolio valuation, different classes make for different maintenance techniques. Time is crucial to hedging transactions; a difference of one week in the issue date of a product changes its valuation and its hedging. Maturity and diversity are thus two elements that come to further complicate the work of a trader. But the complications are not over yet—they are in fact only just beginning, because each trader must handle more than one class of products. And each of these classes varies in terms of the maturity and diversity of its underlying securities.

To make their hedging task possible in one workday, traders hedge "by financial Exchange." In this way, the very notion of hedging undergoes an adjustment to stay within the realm of feasibility. This moment in the activity of a trader reveals the fracture that occurs between the theory and practice of derivative products in a universe that no longer reveals all the properties that models assume in order to reach certain results. Whereas risk-neutral management would require continuously rebalancing of the portfolio between positions on the underlying securities, the daily work of a trader does not allow for such continuity. There are several reasons for this limitation, showing how the management of polymorphic portfolios changes the understanding of markets.

The financial dimensions found in textbooks are what set products in motion when they are managed in a portfolio. With the advent of a system of management that no longer considers each product individually—as is generally the case in the demonstrations of hedging and of dynamic management found in textbooks—but rather by bundles, the relevant dimensions undergo a transformation. Theoretical product-by-product management makes some parameters seem relevant. But managing a large number of products at once, and on a portfolio-by-portfolio basis, brings about new parameters, especially because transaction costs[10] transform the perspective offered on hedging by finance textbooks. Parameters become relevant when their management conditions become possible: this is the one area where the business constraints that bear upon financial theories become obvious. The scientific parameters that catch engineers' attention are required to produce money. When managing only a single product on the market, an excessive level of refinement would not be desirable, for its profit difference would simply be eaten away by the costs involved in managing it. Even if the model's precision is down to quarters or cents, far higher costs of market intervention ruin these efforts. The pragmatic aspect of this method of management naturally sets limits to the possible modeling refinement. But as managers are carried more and more toward models that aggregate numerous units of individual products, and as the sums being negotiated on markets become more and more significant, the excessive refinements that were swallowed up by the high transaction costs involved in micromanaging individual products become more relevant; their excess comes to be within the realm of the *financially possible*. The infinitesimal differences that such modeling created for modest sums became more significant with increased differences on more consequential amounts. This represents an unexpected reversal that makes attention to details an effect of the massive broadening of the basis of products. Although we might have expected less attention to details and a cruder approach to hedging in the wake of product aggregation, it is in fact this very aggregation that renders the once negligible now relevant. Pulling into the picture previously neglected aspects of products points directly toward a choice of models.

Up until these products were designed, the dimensions taken into account did not bring product analysis beyond the first or second derivation of price dynamics. The payoff formula of CGPs makes them particularly sensitive to the correlation between their underlying components, so that the relative directions of these components become a major concern when hedging the products. Taking stochastic correlation matrices into account was made possible only recently with the development of the portfolio theory. Harry Markowitz, one of the American pioneers of quantitative financial economics, had encountered problems of this nature when he had attempted to solve optimal maximization of portfolio yield (Markowitz, 1959). The developments in probability theory in the 1970s helped the establishment of valuation models for products with multiple underlying securities and yields based on their correlation. The payoff formula of the product has made it necessary to embed advanced probability results into pricing software. Pricing models are thus dependent upon the form of the product and the success-induced "massification." Extracting those dimensions that were not previously relevant provides traders with new tools. These tools have effects that were noticed earlier when new products needed new models. They make traders temporarily lose sight of the financial intuition that allowed them to grasp products one by one. These dimensions are not part of traders' financial background: they are both too theoretical and generally sacrificed at the altar of transaction costs.

How does one become familiar with the theory in this level of financial relevance? What does this theory look like when the trader is sitting at a desk, seized with uncertainty over the best operation? Traders never contemplate the major academic pieces in finance theory. Their desks are not covered with these kinds of papers. Indeed, the desks are clear of nearly anything: only a couple of notepads and pens with which to formulate and clarify puzzling problems with passersby willing to help. The theories are *under the table*, in the computer he or she faces from 9:00 A.M. to 5:00 P.M. More precisely, the theories of price dynamics and hedging strategies are located in the software that traders use to assess how much to hedge a portfolio. Without these pricers, the thousands of products in a trader's portfolio would leave him or her staring blankly at their computer. In becoming animated through a pricer, financial theories lay the groundwork for a different style of interaction between the product, portfolio, and trader.

Pricer

Pricers are pieces of software that indicate these products' values and help traders run another decision-making machine, the risk-analysis software. Pricers are key tools of these markets, as Franck rightly suggested in the previous chapter: without them, processing the many operations necessary to hedge massive portfolios would be unthinkable. The pricer gives a price to these products, and this attribution must be understood in the strongest sense of the word. Without a pricer, the value of the securities in a portfolio would be indeterminate, which would force the trader to assign them one arbitrarily. With some luck, experienced traders could aim in the right direction, but they would always risk missing entirely the actual value of the contract. It is good to remember when considering closely the work of traders that these products do not have a market as such. No other financial institution provides clients with the exact same service, so there is no easy way of comparing the price offered by computer programs such as Franck's with a price coming out of a market transaction. If the product designed by the bank was nothing but a simple aggregation of securities (x shares of France Telecom, y shares of Microsoft), its value could easily be inferred from these components' price. This is what is usually done when casually assessing wealth: everything that is owned is added up and then a value estimate is determined for the scenario of an immediate sale.[19] CGPs defy this simple calculation by offering a service that bends the aggregation and always projects the trader into the future term of the contract. In tying the payoff to the twisted correlation between the components in a near future, the product leaves the ground of easy, quasi-mental calculation. It incorporates too many pieces of data to lend itself to noncomputerized value assessment.

Some financial products have both a market and a pricer that assigns them price and value. Warrants, close enough in style to CGPs, are much simpler. They can be bought, sold back on a secondary market, and their value can be assessed by a variety of pricers, some available on the Internet. The volumes of transactions taking place on warrants markets makes for a continuous animation of the price: people buy and sell, and prices and values constantly feed each other in recursive loops. When that is the case, the assumptions built into the pricer for anticipating the face-to-face price matching can be assessed against the series of transactions that continuously take place. CGPs depart twice from this competitive situation: they are only traded once under each of their forms, and they are so unique that the bank cannot confront its in-house pricer-produced value estimate against other pricers' estimates.[20]

Risk Analysis

The risk-analysis program comes into play after the work of the pricer. Risk analysis indicates the magnitude of selling or buying positions that should be taken on the various Exchanges to put a portfolio in a risk-neutral position; for instance, selling 1,200 IBM futures and buying 3,500 listed futures on Euro Stoxx 50. But as we have seen, the pricer applies the theory that has been coded, which does not show the same proficiency in financial markets as traders who are dedicated to these products do and does not take into account the imperfect nature of markets. The risk-analysis software that traders run is not endowed with the ability to choose a rule, any more than pricers are; it can only offer a set of steps that will minimize the exposure of the portfolio to the market risks. The trader, supplied with information obtained over time from the markets and from contacts, develops a hedging rule that incorporates these elements. At the time I was working in this department, the hedging rule was the following: the trader and the computer engineer who had coded the risk analysis had selected a hedging threshold. Below this threshold, they stopped hedging. By defining a priori an intervention threshold, those in charge took into account the transaction costs. But they also knew that fiddling with the theoretical hedging rule would weigh heavily in the balance of the hedging at the end of the day.

Each portfolio having been valued by the pricer and tested by risk analysis, the trader must choose to conduct a series of transactions among those recommended by risk analysis. By passing all the recommended orders, the hedging would be flawless, but the costs would skyrocket. Valuation models of derivative products have attempted to incorporate the costs of balancing a portfolio by including among their dependent variables the number of transactions needed to neutralize its risk. These models try to optimize the number of operations the trader performs while taking into account two constraints. First, they build upon financial theory, which shows how continuous hedging guarantees the neutralization of the option's risk. In such a context, there is a premium for a maximum number of portfolio rebalancings, and the trader should be concerned only with continually adjusting the hedges. Second, these models explicitly factor the costs of trade executions on an Exchange into the performance of a portfolio. In addition to the costs that a bad hedge can generate, this series of execution costs come to weigh on the trader's result. As such, rendering the transaction costs more explicitly allows the trader to limit somewhat the effort expended in evaluating the opportunity of an intervention (buying or selling) in the market. To put it another way, these models, by factoring in the cost of the trader's decision to hedge, encroach on the trader's domain of expertise by sensing how often and when to act. It is this ability to sense the *right moment* that will be described in the final portion of this analysis of hedging. But to emphasize the gap that separates this sense of quantities and timing that traders develop from the scripts that engineers supply, let us review the hedging script that the design of CGPs requires.

Hedging CGPs

A CGP issued on the exotics desk has a neutrality obligation regarding risk that is somewhat different from that of a single option. The sources of risk are increased by the number of underlying securities. For the bank, the risk comes from the prospect that none of the securities that make up the basket will collapse before the contract comes to maturity, thereby holding the bank to an excessive payout. But this is not a simple risk, as it is a correlation of as many risks as there are underlying securities. When a trader had to hedge a single option, only variations in the value of the underlying security mattered. Now all the variations count, but further, all the correlations taken two by two are of consequence. In the daily practice of hedging, this brings about a certain number of changes.

When a trader needs to hedge a product that points to an equally large range of first-order risks (variation of underlying securities) and of second-order risks (correlation between variations), he or she cannot take a position on one single underlying security.[21] The trader must take into account the possibility that each one of the underlying securities might become the least-performing underlying (*worst off*, in the scripts of traders). Every day, therefore, he or she takes up a position by buying a lot of the least-growing underlying security in his or her portfolio. But the trader also buys the second-least-growing security (i.e., the *second worst off*). Indeed, the trader takes a position on nearly all of the underlying securities. He or she may not buy the security that has grown best when believing that its probability of becoming the worst off is low, but in general he or she takes a position on most of the securities. As the performance of a security or an index rises, the trader sells some of these units and buys units of another security whose performance is relatively declining. The bank hedges through these daily balancings of the portfolio. This daily reallocation ensures that the number of securities that "perform" most poorly at any time can be increased. When the correlation between securities is very strong, few of them have price trajectories that cross each other, and the trader has few opportunities to increase significantly the number of securities held. These intersecting trajectories are indeed the condition of the structure's success. The ideal conditions, needless to say, come together when the underlying securities included in the basket are highly uncorrelated: when at least one of the securities collapses over the term of the contract, the capital placed in the other securities—and which in-
• creases in proportion to their performance—is more than sufficient to cover the amounts owed to the client. This series of steps forms the script written by the trading room's financial engineers. It sits on the desk as the risk analysis, locked in the computer of the trader and assistant. In practice, the trader remains distant from the script, as he or she is surrounded by a more messy financial market than that accounted for by the risk analysis.

Simulation

The trader's profile was typical—a student from Ecole Polytechnique with a master's degree in physics, who later turned to finance. The assistant was a young woman straight out of an elite French business school. She was trained in corporate finance and ended up interning at General Bank because she heard about the existence of the exotics desk and of the mix of finance and engineering that structured finance entailed. I interviewed her after having worked in her vicinity for a few months.[22] By that time, the markets were already contracting (April 2000), and the flourishing business of the desk was feeling the heat of weaker trends on most Exchanges.

The discipline that the trader and his assistant submitted to is worth close attention as it contains an inherent tension: sticking strictly to the script embedded in the risk analysis designed by the trading-room engineers would take too much time and cost too much money. In contrast, departing openly from the script or even discarding it entirely would expose the trader to uncontrolled risk. This tension was solved by simulating portfolio hedging. Simulations allowed the trader and his assistant to follow and test the script simultaneously, or nearly simultaneously. Thanks to simulations, the recursive distance the disciplining script enjoyed was offered by the overall goal of these exercises. For traders, the point was not to get disciplined but rather to compose the hedging portfolio in a manner that minimized their risk exposure overnight. Simulations were a way for the assistant to probe the markets and *test the water.* These experimental approaches to markets are nothing new among traders, who use a rich vocabulary for describing market qualities: resistant, deep, "not there," elusive. The uncertainty surrounding a market is particularly strong in the morning, when transactions resume after a night of financially loaded events. It is all the stronger when these events point to diverging interpretations by the community of traders. Then, absent a clear direction, traders wait for signs produced by the market. As in any strategic game, moving first is not always an advantage. Anthropologists of finance, such as Karin Knorr Cetina (2002) and Caitlin Zaloom (2006)—who have documented the nature of economic transactions occurring through complex layers of information technology apparatuses—have not missed the peculiar quality of these trials, meant to decipher the mood of the market more than engage in transactions per se. Traders accept losing money on small orders sent to the market with the expectation of a significant return of information. These orders are experiments on the market, but they are subsequently complemented by the flow of real orders meeting various resistances. Each transaction brings a set of fresh information that helps the trader adjust the next order. The goal of these probes is to unpack the market and *extract* the interests beneath the aggregate *bids* and *asks.* In markets populated by a few big players, the game is to anticipate how others will act. Anticipation necessitates knowing the entire structure of the participants' portfolios. The rationale for these small probes is that there cannot be simulations writ large. However a trader attempts to figure out what will happen in a market—whether by engaging complex thought experiments, counterfactuals, or by looking at past situations with similar overall economic conditions—there is no avoiding the actual test of the market. Only the transaction itself contains information: it may be valid only temporarily and be quickly wiped out by new pieces of information that set traders on other courses of action, but it is the only currency in situations of high uncertainty and much strategic concealment of plans.

The simulation that the assistant launches before trading takes an opposite track made necessary by the multi-Exchange hedging requirement. Here, the assistant is not a specialist of any one of the Exchanges she has to roam. She cannot probe these Exchanges one by one, and she has no time to collect subtle pieces of information; rather, she needs to visit them somewhat in a rush, and the simulation is the solution devised to avoid trading blindly. Her concern is no longer exclusively the depth of each market and the likely impact of her orders on the price she tries to clinch. It is now the consequences of multi-Exchange hedging on the exposure of her portfolio as a whole. Will her script produce what it is supposed to achieve? Will the portfolio react to a simultaneous hedge as anticipated? The locus of uncertainty has been displaced: it was once the market of one security with its chess player–like deep strategies, but is now the portfolio with its intricate correlation ties spun by the formula. It was once out there—distributed between traders and brokers in banks and firms located across the world—but is now nested in the database of the bank, distributed between the pieces of software and formulas of each product. The markets are still there, and assistants and traders hope to master each one of them as specialists do, but the imperative is elsewhere.

When the trader's assistant decides to take up a position, she first opens the simulation window in the risk-analysis software. This allows her to simulate a transaction and determine its impact on her portfolio as a whole before she decides to send the actual orders. The software loads the market data in order to simulate the effect of a portfolio modification. Loading can be slow from the financial market sense of time. It can take a few minutes, as several price sources are needed to calculate the level of exposure. It is only a simulation: there are no immediate consequences to these probes. It is a quasi-playful sequence in an otherwise stressful day, yet the playfulness is always threatened by the potential for consequences once the simulation is applied.[23]

Insulating the simulation from the flows of changes that relentlessly shape the market carves a space for experiments but, in such fast-moving markets, it also guarantees the obsolescence of its baseline. The sets of prices and variances loaded in the risk-analysis software no longer represent the market prices that traders had contemplated in their simulations. Simulations are executed under the pressure of price shifts, and because the simulation operates in isolation, the trader must keep an eye on the market to assess whether the experiment has become irrelevant. When the set of projected simulations take time, especially when the assistant tries one simulation at a time, the risk correlation can change quite seriously. One simulation at a time allows the operator to see more clearly what one Exchange hedging will cause on the whole portfolio: it limits the opacity that simultaneous simulations tend to create. Simulations that are able to determine multiple sources of risks at once and also save time for the assistant trader run the risk of forcing much more random trials. Faced with chaotic reactions from the portfolio exposure measured by the risk-analysis software, the trader tries random combinations of hedges and loses the sense of where the simulation is going. When the market is very active and many of the securities or indices at play undergo significant price changes, the assistant can reload the risk-analysis software with fresher market data. Yet, reloading only delays the actual passing of orders.

Simulating is torn between two antagonist imperatives: the trader needs to step away from the market in order to figure out which configurations are playing out therein. Yet, in doing so, the trader loses sight of its continual drifts and surprising shifts. Loading creates the peculiar quality of simulation as well as undermining its exercise. A solution to this tension was found by *socializing* the two gestures of simulation and market observation. The trader and his or her assistant would always conduct these two tasks together. Although each of them engages solitarily in the simulation of orders from the morning onward, they intensify these simulations as the hedging window comes to its end. The spatial distribution of traders and their assistants was unique to this desk. On other desks, the traders and their assistants would turn their backs to each other: each one faced one, two, or three rows of monitors, and they would talk as they were looking at these monitors, commenting on observed changes or directing each other (most often from the trader to his assistant) to search for information. That pair would unite for more intimate conversations and split by rolling their chairs forward and backward. On the exotics desk, the trader and his or her assistant faced each other, separated only by a double wall of back-to-back monitors. The communication literally took place *in the interstices* of the screens and wires. The division of labor was always the same, and the other trader–assistant pairs on the desk respected it as well: the trader kept an eye on the fluctuating prices while the assistant ran the loading and simulation. When the trading window of opportunity ended, they sat—one on each side of the wall—for the actual order. Talking in between the monitors, they moved sideways to find the few interstices that allowed them to make eye contact when the moment of passing orders came. Looking sequentially at their monitors and at their partners through the fence of monitors, the fine tuning of the hedge took place in a complex mix of interactions between the two operators facing each other, the simulated new pause/pose, and the fluctuating prices of underlyings. Let us return to the assistant to observe how she negotiated the tension created by these multiple sources of information.

She keys the order (buy or sell) into the risk-analysis software and reads the calculation of the new exposure of the portfolio. She takes into account this new threshold of risk and communicates it to the trader. And at times lengthy discussion ensues as they try to understand what accounts for the surprise, if anything, of the new figure of risk. During this discussion, the trader keeps an eye on the actual moving prices of the underlyings of interest. They then assess whether a second simulation is called for, if the initial effect is either too miniscule or too great. This phase is always something of a trial-and-error process, particularly because the assistant cannot anticipate the coupling between her action and the overall reduction in portfolio risk exposure. Because the aggregation of the portfolio does not follow the lines of product characteristics and does not simply pile up products of identical forms but, instead, a great variety of product structures, it is impossible to predict how a small variation of an underlying that impacts all the products will affect the portfolio as a whole. Thus, when an assistant decides to follow the risk-analysis software's advice about hedging and buys *futures* on Microsoft shares, every product whose value depends on the value of Microsoft's shares is *somewhat* hedged. But certain products demand the selling of Microsoft futures rather than their purchase; others, on the contrary, demand the buying of many of them because they are coming to term and the prospect of having to hand the clients a payoff indexed on Microsoft shares made it safe to acquire them. The assistant could not keep in mind all of the products that called for these portfolio modifications, and she could not have a clear mental image of each of these entities individually.

By trusting the risk-analysis software, she comes to apply a simplistic rule. Indeed, feeling her way toward a successful hedge, the assistant can hypothesize that the evolution of this impact is either increasing or decreasing, but never increasing and then decreasing. This monotone function of convergence ensures that she will find—through trial and error—the hedging point, but it says nothing about the speed at which she will reach it. It is possible that a small increase in the purchase of Microsoft futures might have a massive effect when she simulates at a particular moment *and* at a threshold of intervention. Thus, when she buys 100 futures, she actually covers a majority of the hedging needs. If she goes up to 110, she may then cover all needs but one. But at this point in the precarious procedure, she does not know any of this yet because she does not know which products have been hedged. So she continues to hedge, and here the effect becomes very significant because there is only one product left to hedge, and it goes beyond the portfolio's needs. While previously her hedging benefited all products by spreading itself among them, in this last move she hedges on a single product, and its effect is entirely for that product.

Things get complicated when she simulates not one but several operations on different underlyings at once. The hedging dynamic is chaotic because of the interaction between risks of underlyings. If these risks were orthogonal and the correlation close to zero, treating one security at a time would be legitimate. There would not be any effect of one on the other, and no uncontrolled feedback loops would be created. When she simulates multiple n sources of risk, she no longer controls $n - 1$ while testing 1. The correlation patterns between n sources can create many unexpected dynamics that look chaotic from her point of view. The controlled gesture, that was made possible when simulating one risk source against an otherwise stable portfolio, no longer works. The combination of simulated moves on each underlying market may either accelerate or slow down the pace toward the equilibrium that the assistant wants to reach.

This process of trial and error is a daily operation that they could not organize without simulating. They never carry the theoretical hedging through to the end because they cannot try to make the portfolio neutral vis-à-vis the risk on each of its underlyings. When asked about the cognitive resources mobilized during these few crucial minutes, the assistant said that she judges *by instinct* and, by following her experience of the market, she estimates how much she can diverge from a complete hedging.[24] The assistant operates in this way for all securities that she must buy, following her risk analysis. Often, she decides not to follow this advice at all and, instead, trusts completely her own sense of the market and knowledge of the trends she recognizes.

Treating Residues

After hedging the major stocks that have required action during the day—some securities may not call for any market intervention—the assistant relaunches the risk-analysis software one last time to take into account the fluctuations that have occurred since she last loaded a simulation.[25] As we have seen, making a decision takes time; it can span an afternoon and lead the assistant and the trader to work with prices that undergo massive jolts and that do not share the same maturity. Given that portfolios are hedged by Exchanges, the assistant usually conducts one final round. She brings together the scattered products that she has managed Exchange-by-Exchange: after having embraced products as portfolios, she has to consider them differently. She revisits each local financial marketplace to deal with components of these portfolios.

By turning to a financial instrument that bears a *family resemblance* to the portfolio, the assistant tries to bring her hedge to term. She generally concludes by taking position on the futures of the indices of the main markets (Paris's CAC 40 index, the NIX for the shares of Japanese companies, etc.).[26] She returns to her simulation/position-taking routine again, but she now simulates exclusively with these indices: a place-based risk is available on her risk-analysis software, which brings together the residual risks that were not covered when she was hedging security by security, each having an impact on a wide range of products. She now chooses a higher generality threshold by taking position on an index (its futures) that may be absent in the formulas of many products in the portfolio but that covers a number of such products through their underlying securities. Therefore, if the portfolio has a strong exposure on a couple dozen large French companies, whose market values weigh on the CAC 40, it is possible to take position in one move on this bundle of products through the composite index. This works through the miracle of the aggregation. The trader's portfolio piles together products that cannot be hedged individually by taking a position on the composite index but that bear a resemblance with this index when they are added up. The endless dispersion of the hedge finds a solution in these composite indices, thanks to the aggregation achieved by the portfolio.

But these composite products conceived to cover an entire financial market with a single order do not solve the problem posed by CGPs. Their formulas do bend the arithmetic composition of the Exchanges so that they are never simply models of these indexes. This is both their added value and their specific risk. They bet on the dispersion of a financial world not yet structured as an organized global Exchange, but they are also directly affected by this dispersion. This dispersion is felt broadly: the trader is no longer master of his or her own actions. Mobilized by the multiple financial places on which products must be hedged, the trader is often absorbed by the trading technologies and overwhelmed in the face of product reactions unforeseen by the models. Traders are torn between the relentless requirement to be attentive to the markets' shifts and the proclivity needed for deep understanding of the forces at play in their portfolio. This latter inclination is exacerbated by the exploratory mode in which they can easily indulge when they simulate their portfolio risk exposure. The engineered complexity of a multilayered portfolio creates an animation that repeated simulation calls can hope to decipher—but only at a cost, as each attempt to run simulations takes time and exacerbates the distance between the trader and the market value of products. Behind the trader's back, as simulation takes place, prices keep shifting. Another call interrupts this proclivity: the need to publicly account for the portfolio's value changes.

The Experimental Feedback of Nonexperts

In the trading room, our traders have to become CGP experts, as opposed to Exchange sportsmen or women, and they have to find ways to articulate the idiosyncratic risks generated by their portfolios. This is in sharp contrast with the usual expertise of other traders: they are experts of markets and typically specialize in cotton (Caliskan, 2010), telecommunication companies, or other sectors or regions. Sometimes, these markets are not located in one Exchange only. Such is the case of arbitrage traders who track the price discrepancy of standard goods on different Exchanges and make profit by buying low and selling high.[27] The notable difference between our traders and arbitrage traders comes from the length of investment and the variety of securities focused on. Arbitrageurs trade on elusive discrepancies, and they never keep securities in their portfolios for a long period of time. Such securities do not create puzzles, as they act the same on both the buying and the selling sides of the deal. CGP traders are much slower because they deal with different commodities.[28] The understanding imperative is higher here than in many other markets and is generated by the complexity more or less carefully controlled by the engineers. As a consequence, the image of forceful and blunt traders does not apply well here. In addition to dealing with Exchanges already opaque to most financial operators, the CGP traders face the source of risk generated by the aggregation of unlike products in the portfolio. The unpredictable animation of these portfolios is akin to dealing with wild organisms and, unsurprisingly, the term *beast* comes frequently to the forefront in the traders' conversations about their products. It makes them the people who look after the "beast" as much as the ones who determine how the financial experimentation unfolds beyond the scenarios imagined by engineers and quants. This articulation comes after the dispersion and must make sense of it.

In his description of the interactions between modelers and traders, John brings back one of the most common elements of the late-afternoon exchanges: traders know something that engineers do not—something worth imparting.[29] But what do they really know if they are neither experts of a security or sector, nor of a country? What level or layer of the financial reality do they engage uniquely? The success recipe of CGPs (bridging disjunct markets) is also their challenge to traders who can never be experts. CGPs force traders to operate on Exchanges and on underlying products of which they are not specialists, and they create trading situations that rule out any possible training on these Exchanges: ideal hedging scripts make transactions take place simultaneously on Exchanges that cannot be open simultaneously; they surround traders with pieces of software that take on some of the most important operations for traders to become well-acquainted with securities. In fact, it is common for engineers wishing to obtain fine-grained information on the product making up the basket (every index, every stock, or every national currency) to call up local traders who specialize in these basic products. So it is taken for granted that these traders are not market experts, as listed CAC 40 futures traders are. If there was a market, the trader would not need to rely exclusively on the model lodged in his or her computer to figure out the value of the products. That piece of information would be produced by the resolutions offered to the competing views of sellers and bidders. Absent this flow of transactions, however, the model and its actual form as a pricer and as risk-analysis script hold the secret value of the product.

Traders are not experts in any particular market, but they are experts in their portfolios. It is important to keep products separate from markets and realize that the organization of the trading room and the design principles adopted by engineers therein create the possibility to gain knowledge that is half-organization-based/half-market-based through the product and its aggregate form, the portfolio. The up-flow that the exotic traders perform aims at a level of product makeup that is not found elsewhere on the floor. The attempt to reduce both this intuition and idiosyncratic knowledge to an analysis of the basic components takes away the very specific nature of these skills. The decomposition that the trader operates when he or she hedges his or her products does not follow the structure of each of the products. Hedging by locations allows one to handle multiple elements joined together (for example, futures on CAC 40 indexes) from the whole portfolio. This disassembling makes it difficult to go from this group, put together for the purpose of speedy hedging, to the basic element underlying a particular type of product in order to elicit a typical reaction from it. The trader must necessarily become a specialist regarding each one of the markets in which he or she hedges these complex products, but none of the information gathered from initiating transactions on these Exchanges will allow the trader to characterize reactions that would be specific to the products he or she must handle. The trader cannot reconstruct, from this hedging by marketplace, the global reaction of the product. The particular activity of an exotic trader, forced to cover several Exchanges across the world in the course of any one day, brings out other relevant indicators. His or her activities arouse other constraints that are not the same as those that would be generated in the management of one single type of product and that could be hedged alone, without having to be joined with other operations with different profiles.

The discussion between the trader and his or her quant is thus biased by the type of feedback that the former can provide to the latter. The quant reasons in terms of product model; the trader hedges product pieces. The massive volume of products that are managed brings about these acrobatics that distort exchanges of information and makes it impossible to talk of the same unit. The trader reports back to the quant an assessment of each of his or her operations but, from this erratic and changing assessment, he or she must move to a valuation model. It is in these terms, of models of valuation—hedging—that the quant has always reasoned.

The design of CGPs creates an organizational puzzle. Instead of speculating on and with the market, traders speculate off the market and through the portfolio rather than through other relevant market competitors. The lack of competitors is an achievement for the engineers. They have sought and found a niche trod by no other financial firm, but at a high cost. The source of uncertainty is now by design, but it is not under control because the masses of products aggregated in portfolios blur the product-specific lines of articulation that engineers had imagined. Traders are left speculating "in vitro" so to speak, detached from the site of action and the origin of price changes. Indeed, if engineers have displaced the primary site of uncertainty from the Exchange to the local portfolio, they have not shut out the noise of the fluctuating prices.

PART II

Topography of a Secret Experiment

The peculiar assembly line called forth by the CGP has nontrivial consequences on the organization of the bank and on its spaces. Secrecy rules around these activities in the trading room. The mode of value creation exploited by CGP engineers cannot suffer too much publicity, and the business model adopted there is one of derivative finance, whereby profits are extracted quickly before competition catches up and undoes the expertise differential initially created. What comes out of the assembly line reaches the clients and, through them, possible competitors, but the formal mode of hedging and the local recipes invented by the traders and their assistants are never shared. Products circulate, but models in their various manifestations are meant to remain proprietary.

One of the consequences of the secrecy surrounding these products is the invention and design of the trading room itself. As we know by now, homogeneous activities are not contained therein. Multiple approaches coexist more or less peacefully, and lines of fractures emerge within the room, but, despite these tensions, what goes on in the room belongs to the bank. Traders, engineers, and computer scientists are General Bank's employees, as opposed to outside interlocutors such as clients and local Exchange brokers used in hedging. Still, this functional distinction between the inside and outside works against the quick and efficient business of the room. Orders have to be sent out on a continuous basis, and information coming in must be processed even more frequently and to such an extent that the room becomes an impediment to participation in the outside market. The room coalesces many bodies of expertise, but it also limits starkly the kinds of exposure these experts can get through this centralization. That is the difference between organizing a collective and roaming across collectives. The problem created by the design of the room around a secret product is made more severe by the mechanism of value underpinning such derivational services. If the channels of communication are too narrowly framed, the principles of derivation suffer, and the whole commercial architecture is in jeopardy. The architecture of the room is not a trivial one as it needs to take account of the product design. How should the room be organized around such hedging mechanisms? Can CGP's multisited requirements survive in a secluded environment?

The tension created by the confinement of research is a phenomenon well known to historians and sociologists of science that specialize in laboratory studies (Knorr Cetina, 1982; Kohler, 1994; Latour and Woolgar, 1979; Lynch, 1991). As documented by Steven Shapin and Simon Schaffer's 1985 study of the Boyle–Hobbes controversy, laboratories are inventions of modern science to control the process of ascertaining facts.[1] They are artifactual places where the audiences and methods of science are simultaneously constructed around experiments. Absent this carefully designed encounter between experiments and witnesses, facts are removed from control, and claims of all kinds can be made. The architecture of the laboratory is an unstable tension between complete porosity and full concealment. Shapin and Schaffer remind us how Hobbes relentlessly pointed to the lack of transparency of these sites of fact production and to the room for potential tyranny absent a public for checks and controls. Trading rooms are similarly torn by the dual imperatives of purification and confrontation. Purification entails a distance between the site of experimentation on the one hand and the fray of market transactions on the other. Quantitative engineers inhabit this confined space with their models and the formalisms borrowed from neighboring disciplines such as math or physics. Financial engineers throw at its envelope the rumble of relentlessly changing products on the markets. But traders are really the ones who puncture the room's wall and test its confined architecture against the demands of new products in the market. Thus, confrontation demands to take place in the market, which abolishes the distance and the seclusion created by the room.[2]

Laboratories and trading rooms share the mixed necessities of experimentation and control.[3] Ideally, they would be, in essence, inside out—in the field with their objects of study.[4] In practice, the field is noisy, and stabilizing facts requires generating data by means of the unique equipment of the laboratories and of the trading rooms. In both cases, the initial retreat can be lethal because it sets a distance between sites of experimentation and sites of development. Purification and distance come with risky instrumentation. Laboratory workers have to distort the signal of nature to make it speak. Trading-room operators have to dress the products with long chains of instruments (pricers, models) that can easily lose the signals of markets but without which operators are blind. The harsh criticisms of peers against artificial laboratory set-ups or straight fraud have the same consequence as the collapse of hypothetical performance lodged into product scenarios. Common to these criticisms is the lack of credit enjoyed by the sites of experimentation. In more metaphoric terms, the laboratories are operators of nature's projection onto instruments, just as the trading rooms are operators of market projections onto the formula and its instruments. These projections are the weak links of these purification designs. They require major investment by the laboratory and trading-room operators.

Topographies of financial institutions become relevant objects of investigation when the service projected outward is designed in opposition to the very idea of an organization. When CGPs strive to strip themselves of the materiality of the economy only to retain the purified principles of guarantee and performance, the sites of incarnation of such designs reveal insightful features. In the next two chapters, I launch my travels throughout the bank, slowly progressing outward and toward the markets only to discover that the markets are in the room and that the products can only survive outside of the room.

CHAPTER 3

The Trading Room as a Market

Currencies of the Room

Traders are central pieces of the puzzle created by this financial experiment; they sit at the nexus of the financial markets, where they collect information, and the trading room, where they trade it. This business thrives on several forms of information. Each of these milieus in which the trader operates has its own rules and its own economy: experimentation with products on the market (research insights made "in the field"); elaborations led by the quantitative engineers and financial engineers (and confined to the trading room) about the product, the internal labor market, and the external labor market. Mastering the scenarios designed by the room's engineers is an expertise that may not translate immediately into successful trading moves. Nor might know-how gained on these markets guarantee the full comprehension of complex models. These multiple and sometimes irreducible assets are the currencies that traders barter in and out of the room for promotion to higher positions, salary raises, and bonuses.

Trading rooms are literal rooms in which operators collaborate, with walls and partitions and an inherent opacity to the external world. But they are also rooms through which traders gain access to many markets and compete with one another over scarce information resources. The heads of the room have established specializations and have demarcated the perimeters of activity for each desk. The internal organization of the trading room outlines territories in the financial market, and it enforces a rule of nonaggression between the groups of the trading floor. Although each unit (desk) in the bank is in open competition with the desks and operators of other financial institutions that deal the same commodities, this competition gives way to a respect for status and hierarchy when it comes to relations between the various desks in the trading room within the bank. This hierarchy is not stable and is continually subject to review, fueled by the competing results of the different desks. The fragility of the discretionary division of the markets' territories is due in large part to the access to expertise allowed for by the models. They are the source of relentless questions concerning the intrinsic skills of the traders. Faced with the potential for huge profits[1] associated with territories of the market, the trading room is transformed into a vast market where operators show off their skills, protect their reserved domains, and put all of their resources to use so that they will be allocated the most lucrative products.

In this chapter, we have the opportunity to observe the *quasi-commercial* environment of the floor. This *quasi-market* is approached through two types of movement: that of people and that of models. After an initial stroll through the highly protected space of the room to get a sense of its physical space, the organization of trading spaces is described. This examination shows the layering of constraints created by the mobility of individuals within the trading room, the immobility of the trading equipment, and the need for operators to make themselves ubiquitous: available and alert everywhere and at all times. The chapter closes with an analysis of the complex economy involved in the movement of models and people.

Gates and Hurdles: Getting Used to the Room

The spaces where market operations take place are highly secure. The trading room[2] is a place where the bank takes risks and exposes itself and its capital. Because of this, multiple precautions are taken so that market operations are shielded from indiscreet eyes. At the level of the desk, privacy is the ultimate rule: the trader is the owner of his or her workstation, and protects the area surrounding this station.[3] But while work spaces must be partitioned, the imperative of information-sharing within the room forces some compromise in the "one station, one operator, one responsibility" equation. The pluralities of expertise needed to keep a given desk profitable demand a fluidity in the appropriation of stations and tasks. This tension between retention and dissemination is analyzed in greater detail later in this chapter, when the circulation of models is introduced. To familiarize the reader with the trading room, I invite you to follow me as I retrace the path I took when I first entered it myself.

A newcomer experiences a definite sense of surprise upon entering a trading room for the first time. But even before getting to the room itself, one has to penetrate the bank. To come into contact with finance, one must first be authorized to do so.[4] But at General Bank this *authorization* involves several levels that do not overlap or follow each other easily. Sixty feet beyond the entrance, a series of gates watched by highly competent guards indicates that the bank houses activities that are not to be accessed easily. In order to pass this first security point, you must identify yourself to a group of receptionists who then contact the operator who will be receiving you. Each floor of the bank's building is equipped with its own receptionist, in constant contact with the team of receptionists on the ground floor. The floors housing the trading rooms are subject to particular care because these are the places where the bank's capital is manipulated, where it is placed at the mercy of market fluctuations.

Access to the trading rooms requires a magnetized ID card, which can only be obtained with the signature of one of the room's authorities—that is, at least a desk head. Each trading room has two security vestibules equipped with a system of doors intended to prevent the entrance of more than one person at a time, a setup resembling that which can be found in retail banking outlets. But the heavy flow of bank employees makes it difficult for such a procedure to be followed in every case, and it is in fact possible to follow closely behind the person in front of you and to slip through to the second, more traditional door. I could not say whether this is an intentional form of flexibility, allowed by the technicians in order to facilitate the comings and goings during times of heavy traffic, or if it is simply a weakness with the potential to be exploited by the employees. In any case, a receptionist monitors the flow of operators and visitors toward the derivatives, equities, and indices trading room.

Compared with the other rooms of the bank I visited (using the trick of following closely behind someone and feigning a serious air when asking permission to enter), the derivatives, equities, and indices (*derives, actions, indices* in French) room is particularly crowded with computer equipment. It is inhabited by all of the fauna typical to trading rooms, although the nature of the products traded by the operators required an increased number of technicians and engineers who, otherwise, would have been in separate offices. The layout of the space was not specific to this room; rather, the room and others like it were designed to facilitate a potential migration of work spaces and the frequent reorganization of the clusters of offices within the bank. Over the course of my internship, I witnessed the move of a room whose activities were sold to another bank: all of the occupants of the emerging-markets room disappeared over a weekend and were replaced by operators from other surviving rooms that had become too cramped due to increased activity.[5] The imperative to be mobile, enforced by the bank's management, has noticeable effects on the organization of the work spaces. The room is set up as an open space, such that each person is under the eye of everyone else. The only blocking of this transparency came from the presence of computers inhabiting every desk in the room.

After a newcomer has been given clearance to enter the room, he or she is faced with additional obstacles. The room does not permit random wandering. It provides no privacy. Surrounded by screens and other operators, financial operators have nowhere to hide, no place to which they can withdraw. Surrounded by orders, called for by all the instruments in the room, one may be overwhelmed by the confusion of the market and the other operators on the floor who have already adapted to that universe. Newcomers may stumble or fall flat on their backs.[6]

In dealing with the spaces of finance in a bank, one must first understand the peculiar architecture of the transactions that take place within their walls—transactions that rely foremost on a market in which traders do not face other (banks') traders directly but almost always through the mediation[7] of equipment, which replaces the "marketplace" unity found in economic anthropology studies following Geertz's bazaar economy (Bestor, 2001, 2004; Geertz, 1978; Pradelle 2006). In this composite universe, operators deal with two types of movements: those within the room (a sequence of steps in a universe of chairs, screens, . . . and colleagues) and simultaneously those in the online[8] marketplace (a sequence of steps in a world of screens, computer networks, brokers and other traders, and indexes and rumors). These two spaces are linked in complex ways. The physical trading space is where the room operators stage competitions over their relative skill. They use the room as a theater stage, with all the drama that popular accounts of financial worlds have portrayed. But the floor is also the place from which operators place orders: they depend on an arsenal of equipment that makes networked markets possible. The physical[9] space is thus also set in motion by the operators' need for ubiquity on their online markets which makes them fill this online networked space in a starkly different way from that required by the "presentation of self" needed for competition in the room.[10]

Networks and Performance

The functions that are the least heavily equipped are the management's secretariat, the legal team, and the structuring teams.[11] These three groups work for the room, or—in the case of the legal team and the structuring teams—for certain desks in the room, but they are not, strictly speaking, "front office." Indeed, their identification as front or middle office has always been vigorously debated. One of the reasons they are located within the room is because the financial and legal structures that engineers elaborate with respect to equities and indices require constant interactions between these three entities. The other trading rooms[12] generally place these functions in remote locations, and this distance presents obstacles to achieving clarification in cases of ambiguities or disputes about a product. Being located within the room also has symbolic value. The room previously housed middle-office operators in charge of forging links between the front-office market operations and the back-office units in charge of accounting operations, but the growth of activity forced the personnel of the middle office to move up four floors. The reactions provoked by this relocation were quite negative; for the most part, the middle-office personnel saw it as a symbolic downgrading through a distancing from the most intense and lucrative activities of the bank. The personnel in charge of the structured operations and of the legal aspects are not in direct contact with clients or with the market. Their role is one of connecting the different strata of the bank, and in particular putting into circulation the information that needs to pass from the hands of front-office personnel into those, often described as *little hands*, of the middle and back offices.

The second-least-equipped groups are the salespeople. Although explicitly belonging to the front office, they do not *trade* as traders do. Salespeople have access to clients, but transactions always go one-way: clients always buy. As will subsequently become clearer,[13] the exposure of salespeople to the financial markets assumes primarily the form of a fat address book. The daily tracking of price changes of securities is not part of their concern. They need to have a precise knowledge of the bank offerings and to generate a panoptic understanding of product families in relation to the profiles of potential buyers. Their equipment goes beyond simply an address book, however, and includes the arsenal of instruments related to monitoring the market—the Bloomberg and Reuters screens providing information on the state of the markets and on the multiple operations. These screens provide information that can be followed in real time and are of direct concern to the maintenance of satisfied clients' portfolios, as salespeople match their clients to the trends and patterns of products. But those are still relatively rudimentary visualization devices, and although the monitoring services of Bloomberg or Reuters offer small modules of standard calculation beyond pure and simple monitoring, salespeople hardly use them. At this level of instrumentation, desks are filled with a row of single screens; sometimes a screen is positioned above the first row, but this is rare.

Traders, whom we started to observe in the previous chapter, use the greatest number and the most sophisticated of market transaction instruments. They typically have two rows of two or three screens, stacked up on their desks; on average, five or six screens literally wall up their work area. On the best-equipped desks, a third row of screens is placed on top of the second; traders must stand on the tips of their toes in order to see the elements on these screens. Under such conditions, the open office space becomes further defined by these multiple rows that split up the room and delineate zones that correspond, more or less precisely, with the divisions that the trading room heads have decreed.

Employees are grouped in various ways: by type of product, by professional activity, or by the geographic areas of their Exchanges (for salespeople). Their clustering within the room is critically important, and the ways in which the room is split up into small units is the work of the room management. This disintegration of the room is both functional and arbitrary. Managers are adamant about the efficiency[14] of the division of labor and the need for desks to specialize in a very few number of products. However, the training regimes of traders located at different desks do not show much variation. Neither does the allocation of market segments seem to depend on prior scholarly achievements.[15] The managers of the room decide who will get the better slice of the cake. Although it calls for especially careful attention and forces traders to take uncharted risks, obtaining a choice piece of the market is desirable because it is a source of considerable additional revenue in the form of bonuses. A desk that gains and controls access to a market segment of new financial products forges a monopoly for itself in the room through the principle of specialization that reigns there. As a consequence of this mode of allocation, a struggle takes place between desks for the capture of these segments of the economy. This internal contest sometimes takes precedence over the competition with other banks and creates tension between the desks in the room. It turns the trading room into a site of interest studied with a view to understanding the dynamics of multiple metrics of performance at play there: narrowly defined economic performance is one dimension, but because P&L is subject to competing interpretations, other varieties of performance are also heavily invested by traders and salespeople.

Two Extended Bodies in the Room

Actions in the dual space of the room and the online market create a series of puzzles for traders. They have to negotiate two different landscapes that cannot easily be mapped one onto the other. Despite the homology between the organization of desks along product lines or geographies, traders face different constraints here, at the bank, and there, in the specific locations of world markets. The site and the tool of the negotiations demanded by these unreconciled spaces is *here*, and it has effects and consequences *there*. The success and felicity of traders is thus a function of their *extended bodies*, built with the many resources at their disposal. This extended body is tested *here* (as a trader strives to use all of the knowledge and technological augmentation at his or her disposal to occupy the room's space appropriately) and *there* (as the trader struggles to hit the price of the script received by engineers).

Bodies are more than human bodies in the trading room. The primary and most obvious reason why these have no preeminence comes from the highly technical environment of the room. Traders enclosed by their computer screens are also thoroughly connected to the outer world in ways that are emulated by few other operators.[16] The trader's extended body is highly fluctuating with a composition that is not stable, which makes integration problematic. The operators—if we take them in their regular outfit—are only parts of this larger and extended body. Left to their fleshly envelopes and disconnected from other operators and markets, they would lose their grasp on the economy. Taken alone, they are not able to operate as efficiently as they do when equipped with the proper market prostheses. The success of these prostheses leans heavily on the subtle and fragile alignment of these heterogeneous parts. They act as an extended network, every segment lending as much weakness to the whole architecture as it does strength in creating sources of additional empowerment. An adequate desk, a well-designed room allowing for quick communication between traders of different desks who need to negotiate together—all are conditions that promote the extension of the reach, the contraction of the space, and the control of the temporality of the market. Because deals—and the money they turn in for the bank—are dependent on very short time spans, traders' extended bodies scattered around the world can easily get swept away by the speed of buy and sell orders largely automated through scripts that are not affected by trader hesitation or overwhelmed by a sudden spike of information along one of their networks. The actual extension of the body complicates significantly the problem of the timeliness of the financial action. Appropriate actions are usually defined as the felicitous integration of the environment and the specific temporality of the gesture itself, as in the Greek notion of *kairos*, which includes both notions of time and space through the idea of adequacy.[17] With a body pulsating simultaneously in Tokyo, Paris, and Chicago, the environment—the place—is no longer unitary, and its sense of adequacy struggles with too many inputs.

Remuneration and Manipulation

Despite the networked configuration of extended bodies, they are tested in two different arenas with criteria of success that do not necessarily match. To understand how these seemingly disparate criteria can work together, let us clarify these two bodies.[18] The first is the remuneration body.[19] The problem for traders can be stated quite simply: someone higher up in the hierarchy decides what their remuneration will be.[20] This remuneration has two components: their base salary negotiated through the human resources department, and their bonus. A bonus can amount to several times—sometimes ten, twenty, or thirty times—the fixed salary of a financial operator. How does an operator such as a trader maximize his or her bonus? In the environment discussed here, remuneration works through successive divisions of the bank-wide bonus down to the trading room on the basis of its results. It is parceled out to the desks, then subdivided to workstations, with the final allocation going to the operators. Bonuses thus constitute a strong incentive for employees to maximize the capital of the bank. With this procedure of bonus distribution, it is in the operators' interest to increase not only the overall amount (from which they will earn their part) but also the fraction of the whole that they will personally take in. These two goals are not always reconcilable because the former suggests a strategy of teamwork in maximizing the overall amount of the team's bonus, whereas the latter fosters working for oneself in the hope that the increase of one's personal fraction will compensate for the decrease in the collective result generated by an absence of close cooperation. Collaboration and opportunism thus each exert a pull on the body of trading-room operators. At each stage, the decision to allocate portions of the overall bonus to trader X or trader Y is based on a complex series of factors. As mentioned above, the monetary results—the overall take—of the unit under consideration features prominently in the amount of its bonus.

However, the allocation does not follow a formula, let alone a public formula that would produce the bonus out of the P&L. In addition to maximizing the results of one's unit, one also must take into account the more arbitrary dimensions of the decision.

Remuneration and the enticement of personal gain require that one be active and make oneself visible both on the trading room floor and in the market. Due to the limited size of the labor pool of financial operators, reputations on and off the trading floor become entrenched very quickly. Information moves fast in a small community of self-centered individuals eager to build personal cache. Events occurring outside of the trading area can play as important a role when it comes to an operator's reputation as those that occur inside the trading area. Networking, for example, is commonly practiced by those in search of recognition, salary, and increased status. Networking in this sense involves making oneself known to those who decide bonus allocation and who can provide access to better and more prominent positions. From this point of view, performing with one's body—taking the room as a stage and the other operators as audience—is in no way an exceptional part of the job. Rather, networking is in some sense a question of putting in place a hyperprofessional body.[21] This trader's body must no longer present itself as it would in the extended online space of the securities market, in the form of a more or less well-known avatar lacking any physical qualities. Rather, it operates in the space of the floor, on the internal labor market with its many bridges to the external labor market, where reputations are attached to the physical composure of the operators as much as to the results they produce. More standardized securities' markets evoke scenes of traders yelling at each other in pits—when they are still active sites of transactions—or over the phone, whereas the demeanor of the CGP desk is different. Traders aim for a sense of composure and engage in quiet and polite conversation with their assistants and with the quant. Self-control and academic-style interaction are the qualities they pursue when performing for the room. At the same time, when they buy or sell or when they engage in a technical conversation with the quant, they are simultaneously absorbed by the imperative to accumulate as much information as possible. In these instances, the manipulation body (covered below) takes precedence. These two dimensions are in constant interaction: an operator who would try to make either his or her professional or manipulation body prevail at the other's expense would run the risk of being disqualified by those casually but intently assessing his or her reputation as too superficial in one case, or not diplomatic or social enough in the other.

This second body—the manipulation body—is absorbed by the usage and handling of the trading and information collection equipment. It requires subtle movements within the online space of the securities market and quasi-symbiotic relationships with the many tools that accommodate the passage into this online space, all taking place in the small area of the desk. The success of such a subtle operation requires sustained attention to market signals, memory of similar past events, and expert use of the available instruments. When all of these factors are coordinated, the body of the operator becomes one with the securities market—the trading infrastructure becomes no more than a long extension of the traders' able hands.[22] When a plan of action does not yield results, the fragile balance of the body struggling to hold together and align the long network of electronic markets is broken. It is important to note that a complicated buy or sell order (itself composed of several orders passed along in a fixed sequence and rhythm) can fail for various reasons, not all of which are attributable to the deficiencies in skills of the traders. Success requires that the entire network—in which traders are but one in a series of links—must hold up.

It sometimes happens that the success of an operation stems more from the others in the chain than from the skills of the trader. When conditions are propitious, a mediocre trader might rip the low-hanging fruit from a market full of opportunities. The success of manipulation is coextensive to the many components of the network that the trader attempts to bring together, even if temporarily, for the short duration of an order. The strain put on the bodies of traders who take great care in the quality of their orders does not necessarily translate into profit. A very ably executed move may fail because of a small shift in the market price or because of another element beyond a trader's control. An elegant and well-thought-out move has its own intrinsic merit and success, independent of the financial gain of the trader, but qualifying such merit is not easy. A financial engineer, Paul, recalls a trader colleague for whom he was working on hedging models who was obsessed by the aesthetic of the "adequate gesture" in the case of multiple trades to be carried out simultaneously[23]:

> He was an outstanding trader. Really the kind of trader with whom you can have deep discussions about trading on such markets. He had developed such a deep understanding of the architecture of his markets that he could tell you exactly what the conditions needed to be for a move to be successful. All the conditions. . . . This may not sound like much, but the guy was never surprised by an unexpected feedback from the market. All his moves [in French *coups*, which can carry connotations of cunning and slyness as well as the more obvious behavioral description of a discrete action] went through as planned. When you think about it, it is quite an achievement. The downside of such abilities was the very low frequency of his trades. He would prepare and think about his strategies for ages, he was hibernating or sort of . . . and then all of a sudden he would do it. But you had to be with him to understand that it was done . . . it was so sudden and so quiet that he could as well have just checked a few e-mails, but there he was putting in place a heavy hedge for a 10 million francs deal. He really liked it this way, clean and quick, no hesitations, no external sign of fear. He joked about the

art of trading and compared it to the art of the *samurai* whose sword could cut through flesh and bones without resistance. (December 1999)

There is a certain texture of action that comes about under the perfect coordination of the moves involved in the execution of an order, the conception and sequencing of moves, and perhaps even the grace of the accomplishment. This assessment takes place at a level different from the performance that radiates in the room and is meant to impress colleagues and management. Yelling at the vicissitudes of the online market or posing for the online market does not improve a trader's strategy. Online, other currencies are to be mobilized, and they are of a much more technical nature. Although the trader praised by Paul for his understanding of markets might be present in person, he is absent socially from the room as he works the sequence of quick moves that will take his portfolio from one position/risk to another.

However, traders face both environments. This diffraction is not exclusively a source of schizophrenia that they must learn to control; it is also a resource to the extent that the room is more than a mere stage where roles are played and performances assessed as such. Those who deal with different products on different exchanges know things that their colleagues at adjacent desks do not. They are engaged in other online worlds whose data are not always perfectly rendered by numbers on a screen. The states and qualities of other markets can, however, be gleaned through the grapevines of informal conversation in the room. Moving from one form of information to the other is risky and can fail if the imperatives of each body do not overlap. In each case, traders struggle to achieve poise, but that achieved *in* and *for* the room may conflict with the poise achieved in the manipulation of the online market sociotechnical network.

Reconciling Use and Projection of Self

The two bodies can mingle and unite when the two spaces line up and allow for one behavior to feature imperceptibly in both. Thus, when a negotiation by phone is not carried out according to the codes of the profession, or when either the trader or the salesperson finds fault with something, one or the other may stage a performance for the benefit of the floor *and* for the interlocutors in the online market—a performance that serves the trader's strategies in both of these spheres. For example, in the trading rooms, young and impetuous men and women may shout into microphones and successively address, with great vehemence, the market floor (their colleagues/competitors and bosses) and their distant interlocutors. When asked about these exchanges, the people with whom I worked provided me with an interpretation that pointed to a "strategic" staging of the simultaneous performance in the two spaces. Given that the operators' skills are, according to the operators themselves, underutilized, and given that there are no accurate means for determining the efforts of each of the rings in the profit chain, those wishing to distinguish themselves constantly show their active involvement by increasing the signs of activity. Such demonstrations of commercial vigor are clearly produced for the benefit of the trading room, and the specificity of each contribution cannot always be maintained: namely, the manipulation and the remuneration requirements. The remuneration body can easily interfere with the manipulation body and disrupt its course of action because the stages required of the two bodies do not necessarily meet anywhere in the trading room. For the performance to be effective, manipulations must allow elements of the remuneration body to slip into the trading operation with the distant operator while allowing the show and its effects on colleagues and managers to go on undisrupted. The performance is tricky to orchestrate because it entails deploying one's body in two worlds, at least enough so that observers (in the room) and auditors (online) do not interpret it exclusively as a show. Given these constraints, the remuneration body cannot detach itself too much from manipulation and from its use of the trading-room equipment. Only this connectedness to the market through the mediating equipment legitimizes the staging of such a scene. It gives birth to unexpected *slow-motion* exercises where the gestures of a public outburst must be made visible, but as if frozen in midcourse (when the trade cannot follow its normal course or when its critical moments are exacerbated and almost typified). The problem is that the two bodies' pace of gestures do not easily match. The gesture of the remuneration body cannot be fully carried out in the space of the online market because the act of gathering, contracting, and accelerating necessary for sending an order by computer or by telephone, or accelerating a verbal exchange to seize an opportunity, has constraints of its own that are not easily compatible with the scenes staged by the remuneration body. The two bodies of the operator both performing for his peers[24] and elaborating a subtle price strategy, is constantly torn by these two different sets of requirements.

When an order must be sent, the trader in the online or phone market must be tuned in to the corresponding market in the outside world. During these moments, he or she cannot take on multiple roles. Thus, when the market becomes *agitated*, it is necessary to raise one's voice to be heard by the market's intermediaries. In contrast, when the market is very sensitive, the interventions are implemented tentatively and more gently, so as to not "make waves" in the market and so that the orders do not alarm operators trying to decipher strategies pursued by others.[25] In each case, it is necessary to bring the gesture together and define it sharply after a sequence of relevant information is collected. After having opened up one's body to the greatest number of market impressions, it is important to hit the market sparingly and not to disperse one's energy by revealing particular interests to one's adversaries.[26] The remuneration body needs to place the trading room above the market, and it must display classic sales or trade figures, which do not easily emulate the accepted forms of interaction in the market.

For the two trading strategies—compensation (putting on a show) and manipulation (taking financial positions)—the immediate surroundings of the body are crucial. In both cases, being an active operator in the trading room and the market implies carrying out one's actions with the help of numerous supporting tools. These systems make the strategy of following prices on multiple and disconnected markets possible: dilating and contracting, multiplying and becoming omnipresent, and then disappearing into the anonymity of an order. These supporting tools deserve a thorough description.[27]

The Commons in the Room

The sharing policy in the organization of the floor is visible in the impersonal nature of the available computing and telecommunications equipment. Thus, when traders from the same desk move from one workstation to another (within this same desk) to search for information, they may use a station that is not *theirs* when pursuing their research. I observed that this was all the more true when traders were supplied with additional equipment and when one moved from "listed products" traders to traders of "complex products." However, I never saw the legal consultant or personnel from the financial engineering section yield their stations to others. It is mostly the functionalities of market monitoring that are shared. The manipulation of the Bloomberg and Reuters services, while requiring a good amount of knowledge of the keyboard shortcuts that give access to different markets, does not jeopardize the trading activities of a station or a desk. Indeed, on the exotics desks, traders often move from one station to another, and even from their stations to those of their assistants or colleagues, to perform optimization calculations or to analyze their positions and buying or selling decisions.

Arbitration may be necessary when the line is blurred between appropriating equipment and sharing it. When traders are involved in sending an order, available equipment can quickly become a source of conflict, as an order's success depends on simultaneously occupying and absorbing the market information. It depends on an omnipresence—which can be silent if satisfied principally by the gathering of information—that is indeed very similar to the efforts of the remuneration body when it goes through the room in a display of advantageously staged scenes. Traders need to occupy the market, and this requires support from the equipment of the room. It is not only a question of reputation or of technical access to the market. It is a matter of maintaining an adequate and controlled presence, one that can be achieved only with the proper tools dedicated to capturing information and to transmitting orders. A trader's performance in sending orders therefore puts him or her into competition with the other traders around the trading tools. It is not that one needs to mobilize all of the trading stations, but the moments immediately preceding an order are marked by the scattering of pieces of information and advice, and mobilizing those elements helps to make the operation success-ful. A trader who is "on the verge of" a trade is like a spoiled and demanding child who needs constant attention and all his or her toys within close reach. After the snippets of information coming over the wires are assembled and put into the trade, the situation normalizes. The stations are deserted for a few minutes, and conversation regains its usual rhythm. To occupy the space of the market in ideal conditions, traders would need to be divinely ubiquitous, but even though the appropriation of desk stations is not as stringent as other properties of the room—like the salary and bonus—traders are still attached to a place that is equipped with tools that can uniquely capture the market data onto a screen.

Marking One's Chair

All the desks are equipped with standard roller chairs. Although not luxurious chairs, they seat their occupants amidst a full range of possible adjustments. They allow operators to move about smoothly from one group of screens to another, to concentrate on their screens during phases of sustained attention, and to rest between these phases. But there are only a few chairs because they can clutter the aisles and upset the equilibrium of a trading room—conceived as a market in which everything, information and operators, must circulate freely and rapidly. Market operators try to claim a seat by writing his or her name in marker on the chair's armrests. When new operators enter the room, it becomes necessary to increase the supply of chairs, but in order to do so, it is necessary to contact the furniture department. This organization is quite rigid, but one that has the advantage in this configuration of allowing each employee to have a chair at his or her station. Foldable chairs would be a solution to the space limitation: they could be unfolded when traders had temporary visitors. But folding chairs would not offer the same qualities as roller chairs, being essentially static. Roller chairs, in contrast, dilate the body of operators, create fluidity between workstations, and connect operators to sources of information.

One can distinguish several types of movement in the room, depending on whether one is entering the room from the outside, moving alongside the desks, or strolling down the aisles from one desk to another. Having these rolling chairs in the room guarantees traders easy movement alongside the desks and allows for access to all of the instruments that bring them into contact with the online market. They play the role of a lubricating agent for the market by serving as support for a body that must move around quickly within the geometric space of the room and, as a result, in the dilated physical space of the online market. The collection of tools that have to be utilized is too large and too spread out to be at the trader's fingertips—his or her body cannot be at the center of this collection of elements at all times. Isn't a rolling chair that adequately extends the body of the trader the first condition of a well-equipped and delocalized market? The minute a chair gets stuck, the felicitous body of the trader who had managed to live up to the dream of ubiquity falls back into its original slowness, and all fluidity of movement is impaired.[28] The trader has to stand up to reach for equipment and to come close enough to the screens to assess price curves or data tables. The trader also has to step up from his or her dysfunctional chair and join his or her assistant to communicate the next order strategy. At such times, at least one of them must abandon the screens and leave them unsupervised. Once the conversation has ended, each one returns to his or her station and takes hold once again on his or her little parcel of the economy. But these gatherings of operators rarely last very long, precisely because the fluidity of the room envisioned by the engineers did not make provisions for such a manifold and shapeless body between the desks. When they do come together, one of them must be standing up, awkward and as though deprived of his or her agility. When the conversation does not require viewing a screen to comment on it, the trader and assistant can sit on the desk, facing the interlocutor and turning his or her back to the screens. But most of the time, the screen is the source of discussion (a volatility curve, a history of rates). The visitor must therefore face the screen by bending down slightly and stepping back so as not to have a distorted view. In this position, his or her body ends up pulled back, away from the desk, and almost in the middle of the aisle that separates two desks: it gets in the way of the movement of other traders who wish to circulate, either on their chairs or by foot. Chairs, these agents of fluidity in the trajectory of the trader in his or her market, are also significant obstacles to the freedom of movement within the room. The desk space was designed without taking into account the necessary moments of detachment from screens and market that traders go through, and without reflecting the necessary extension and contraction phases of their market body.

The Pocket Calculator and the Contraction of Financial Gestures

The sharing of calculators, very much standard instruments, is problematic and often provides the opportunity for small crises on the desks. Unlike the pricers that outfit the workstations, a personal calculator can be removed. It thus enters into the master program of detachment/circulation in the room. Its ownership comes into play when small groups form around a workstation to discuss a price or another market measure (volatility, maturity, etc.). In these cases, the calculator passes successively into the hands of the various parties involved, without them needing to look at the computer screen. Each person receives the information, looks at it, and can redo a calculation of the same order. Calculations using this instrument can be carried to the work space of another trader/salesperson. It is in such cases that marks of ownership appear, often taking the form of the user's name, either carved into the surface or written on a strip of tape stuck to the back of the calculator.

Places of calculation—especially those in which the sharing of calculations is imperative, such as General Bank—require these personalized and easily appropriated tools. This notion of appropriation shows all the ambiguity of its semantic duplicity.[29] It refers back to the trader who holds the calculator and who has *appropriated it,* but it is also the most *appropriate* tool for these calculations. The ecology of the room forces traders to appropriate the tool in both ways. First, showing oneself (off) demands locations—areas of one's own, beats that will not be challenged by others. The discretionary and sometimes arbitrary allocation of bonuses makes these performances central in the strategies of traders: because the room result will be parsed all the way down to the trader's bonus without a fixed or public formula of allocation, displays of active presence can only weigh in positively. Such mundane items as chairs and calculators establish a trader as inhabiting the place. However, this property is trader-centered. It is a Lockean understanding of "property" premised on a fully equipped individual.[30] Traders in the room are not such citizens/merchants. Their understanding of markets and, even more, their manipulation of markets hinges on more than ownership of equipment. The appropriate tool destabilizes this Lockean "proprietor." It encroaches on the trader's alleged unity but extends him or her to tasks unimaginable so far. The clean and stiff figure of the proprietor undergoes some subversion in the process as the tool forces the trader to bend and bow in front of the screen, to forget the stage of the room for a while in order to better fold him or herself into the online trade. The calculator is unique in this respect.[31] Whereas most of the tools are fixed and command the traders to move around them when they are not gathered sufficiently, the calculator offers a most needed mobility to the operators. The calculator is adequate to these precise calculations that are carried out in this universe of shared tasks, but it is also the most appropriate tool to follow through with these calculations. It allows the necessary dispersion of traders to come to an end and yield a single figure, which can be used in the market with the required speed and without going through a formal collaboration with other traders.

Bringing in profit to the trading room—claiming the money that is in limbo in the market and that can be brought into the portfolio of that trader who is able to predict its movements—would not be possible without the appropriate gesture and without the operators' extended bodies blending in with the ecology of the room. In many circumstances, a retention strategy is not viable. Except for the few elements that accompany the operators in their movements within the trading room (calculators, chairs), the trading equipment must be shared. To resist sharing would minimize the operators' surfaces of exposure to the market and rumple the extended body's fragile fabric. Traders recognize this and they have gotten into the habit, over time, of ridding themselves of an attachment to *their own* equipment.

Cooperation is a way of ensuring the continued expansion of traders' bodies; it is not a limit but an investment by which they fill their spaces, in the room and online. The models used to evaluate price and risk and the tools used to act on the market—such as chairs and calculators—belong to the same set of *equipment* that allows products to move from one area to another, from the trading room and one set of operators' hands to the market and other operators' hands. The need to understand these products calls upon all the traders' senses—their presence and their prescience. Models offer resources in mental agility, and chairs follow suit in physical agility. When the integration of these heterogeneous resources in the room turns felicitous, products multiply and occupy many places at once. They are projected by a model onto traders' screens as scripts for hedging; from there, these strategies are implemented into buy and sell decisions.

It is the wager of CGPs that they create niches and exploit them before competition catches up. Yet, *niche* is as misleading a term as one can find. It hints at a single site—out of the way, unexplored—whereas the wager is about connecting to this point in a series of disconnected sites, and nothing about bridging these sites is trivial. The product design hubris of engineers, who pay little attention to the conditions of market operations, resonates painfully in the room because the room is organized on the physical premise of more one-dimensional transactions. CGPs test the ability of the room to accommodate their eccentricities without too many glitches showing up in the script. It is expected by room designers that the organization of the room will catch up with the tortured product design, and traders will rearrange the desks to foster the needed collaboration, only to be challenged by other designs, calling for other organizations. Successive waves of novel products come with an uncanny ability to disturb such organizational structures. The call of the online world is not to be ignored for fear that a fleeting business opportunity might be missed. As a consequence, these outside voices prompting quick reactions relentlessly disrupt the internal life of the organization.

Circulation and Retention in the Room

The expert manipulation of models and the access that this expertise offers to sectors of the market are critical elements in the (local) economy of the room. As a consequence of this centrality, a complex dialectic of the retention and the dissemination of specific assets emerges in a context in which the room is itself turned into a market, not only through the competition around fruitful sectors of the market but also through the noisy presence of competitors who are ready to lure away those operators unsatisfied with their lot in the bank. The financial risk expertise accumulated by the room operators is in great demand among other financial actors and regulatory bodies. This is because the industry as a whole is involved in disseminating models that capture actual risks and that provide accurate information to the main players in these sparingly risky exchanges.

As we have seen, desks are assigned sectors of the market. The management of the trading room makes these decisions and creates clusters of products, people, and valuation models that have direct competitors in other financial firms (e.g., banks and hedge funds). But the bank itself is a place of strong competition: within its walls, traders compete to obtain the most lucrative market sectors. The significant growth of activity of the exotics desk—with profits considerably exceeding those of most other desks—raised questions about the reasons for its success. To what and to whom did it owe its unprecedented results? The skill of its operators? The accuracy of its models?

The unification of the terms used to describe financial products is a crucial component in the development of this activity. Early on, the bank's operators perceived unification as an issue at stake in the control of these products. But although the multiplication of descriptions was stigmatized as a significant factor of risk through the creation of groups with separate languages, sometimes unable to communicate with one another, it nevertheless also became clear that models and codes were only one component of a larger "risk of dissemination" facing the bank. For all their partiality, these product perspectives contained precious information, but the actual vectors of dissemination were the operators themselves.[32] They could leave the bank by the side door, join a competitor, and leak methods and models learned at General Bank. Starting as a question pertaining primarily to the organization of research and the command of modeling activities, the dissemination of models must also be examined in the context of the movements of people within internal and external labor markets.

Internal Markets of Models

Innovative models move around when people move as much as they spread outward from official pedagogic places like universities, where they are taught to students. Financial operators moving from one bank to another carry with them the information produced in the initial bank.[33] The efforts invested by banks to keep their formulas secret and to capitalize on the leverage they offer against harsh competition give us an idea of the expectations attached to these financial codes. The emphasis on confidentiality—the heads of trading rooms continually instruct the bank's employees to never divulge any confidential information they may be entrusted with—may lead one to conclude that the product–model duo alone creates the bank's success. The bank develops a cult with its precious formulas and builds its commercial strategy on the differences these formulas bring into the competitive world of banking services. For an observer not privy to the background work invested in maintaining these formulas, the mystery surrounding formal models evokes magic spells more than engineering enterprises. Just as with magic, there are those with the gift and those who can only watch it operate; there is much energy spent in securing the monopoly of the magic formula.[34] This focus on *the* formulas as the operators of profit has some direct consequences on the economy of the room's population.[35] The glory of portable formulas and fear of uncontrolled disclosure translates into the sharing of information within the room itself: developments carried out on a desk are usually not passed on to the rest of the room. This compartmentalization of research is particularly noticeable on the exotics desk.

The exotic products desk features all the characteristics that generate a climate of retention. In this emerging sector of financial markets, a considerable amount of dissemination and spreading of models occurs as a result of turnover. The economy of these complex products' handling is asymmetric: training operators is expensive for the bank, and their departure is perilous for the portfolios, but the attachment the bank has toward these operators is not necessarily reciprocated. Traders are not committed to the banks in the same way that the banks are committed to the traders. On the one hand, trading more standard products (equities, bonds) tightens operators' ties to specific markets and classes of products and focuses their expertise. On the other hand, trading complex products requires of its operators a multifaceted set of skills. Operators must use diverse strategies in different markets, and although they may not claim such intimate knowledge as that of traders who deal with fewer products, they maintain a versatility[36] with and a wider perspective on financial markets. For these traders, the call from the *outside* is heard all the more clearly when expectations are not met and bonuses decrease. If they are unable to bring with them a model to sell as is, they can nevertheless circulate bits of techniques and little tricks that facilitate *pricing*. These techniques are most vulnerable because they can easily be transferred elsewhere when the knowledge is not idiosyncratic. It is therefore at this desk that the need for comparisons of methods is strong enough for the bank to benefit from the local knowledge germinated within its walls. It is also here, ironically, that it is least put into action.

The room goes through moments of sharing, when models are compared and traders are summoned to explain the strategies on which their scenarios are based. The risk department orchestrates this liquidity. It has the task of collecting information on trading strategies, preventing undesirable bottlenecks, and leveling the field of risk management. In theory, the risk department should organize the circulation of information pertaining to risk models in the room. In practice, it rarely reached this objective because of the expertise gap between the risk department and the trading room operators.

The risk department was located in a building adjacent to the main General Bank building—a much smaller building and not easy to find at first. Its physical separation from the front-office fray could have been read as a sign of autonomy and independence, but the reality was much grimmer for those working there. Controlling risk was a secondary task in the bank's priorities. Those who were to control risk were not even situated close to the site of the very operations that needed supervision. Relegated to the periphery, the risk operators delegated much to the expertise of the traders and the engineers. The quant, for example, presented the risk department team with valuation models used on the desk, including the hedging models and the risk analyses specific to the desk. As the head[37] of the risk department confessed during an interview, it is the theory and the kind of monitoring that regulators expect from good internal risk surveillance. But he recognized immediately that applying these models to ameliorating risk was difficult. To explain this difficulty, he invoked "an inescapable reality of the banking industry": front-office operators move faster than the risk officers in charge of monitoring them. They are constantly attuned to markets they observe closely and on a daily basis. The engineers of the risk department watch these bold developments unfold with envy and delayed reaction. As a consequence of this differential of perspective and reaction, recruiting for this department is complicated. All engineers want to go "on the market." By working for the risk department, they may have the feeling that although they help the bank avoid losing money, they are deprived of the fast-paced glamour associated with market operations. In 2002, the market for financial engineers was strong; the risk department would regularly lose people, who were lured away by offers from other banks seeking financial engineers. These rapid shifts in personnel led to additional problems for the daily functioning of the unit. Recruits generally arrived less qualified than their interlocutors from the front office, and they could not be trained to understand the relevant models in time to be of much use. The head of risk assessment attempted to hold onto the engineers in his unit, but he did not have the budget to pay them on par with the trading-room's remuneration. A deeply rooted interest in auditing procedures was the only means for these young engineers to remain in place. But this was unlikely, and each new resignation confirmed it. More exciting employment venues were pulling them away from the poorly paid area of internal auditing.

The fast pace of modeling in the front office did not allow for any slowing down in the face of audits. The trading room quant was aware of this weakness in the procedures of surveillance: it was not uncommon for auditors to come and ask him for advice on the best way to assess the risk of the products he had just presented. This dysfunction illustrates the proportional discrepancy of the exotics desk and the absence of the controls necessary for its durability. Thus, the exotics desk remained the single master onboard, for better (by instantaneously seizing on market opportunities) and for worse (by never having its models compared with other forms of assessment and risk measurement). But the monopoly boasted by the quant did not exclude only the risk department. Indeed, monopoly was the last of the exotics desk's concern as the expertise gap between the desk and the risk surveillance unit was so conspicuous. The real competition took place between desks that could claim to deal the exotic derivatives by stealing one another's expertise in these lucrative products.

The R&D team (computer developers, financial engineers, and quantitative researchers) that I was able to follow over several months, made up the largest group[38] within the trading room, and they formed a resource that all other desks endeavored to enroll for themselves. The R&D group was divided into two subgroups. The computing engineers worked for the entire room, and would intervene on all pricing problems arising at the desks. Most of the time they answered software questions and were not expected to devise innovative pricing model solutions for the traders of the room. When they needed to solve problems akin to Franck's—such as translating a model into an algorithm that provided a price—such a task was the intellectual feast of their day. The regular calls were less exciting, and most often they did not have access to the pricing formulas that traders relied on. The other group, made up of the financial and quantitative engineers, was, by mandate, not available to the whole room, and all other desks in the room understood that they were exclusively the exotics desk's pricing support team. Requests coming from other desks were rejected. The presentations given by the quant to the exotics desk's traders were never passed onto others, the slides[39] used were not distributed, and all the results were reserved for the exclusive use of the desk engineers and traders. The intellectual elaborations around the pricing formulas were restricted to a group within the room, and although most operators in the room were aware of the literal expression of the product formula (as seen in figure 1), such was the limit of their knowledge. Should they have been in charge of managing these formulas overnight, they would have found it difficult to do so.

This retention policy had its limits. Exotics desk traders needed to contact traders from other desks when they hedged their portfolios with products or on markets that the traders from other desks understood better. To articulate the problems they encountered, they needed to elicit some indications of the hedging techniques they were using. It was difficult for them not to reveal the hedging strategy that the desk's management was trying to protect. They would manage that secrecy by discussing only one side of the formulas. Cutting into only one of its components, sometimes even just one of its underlyings, kept the whole structure literally transparent but financially beyond interpretation.

The reasons behind this protection of research findings originate in the organization of the room and in the remuneration mechanisms of room operators, whose bonuses hinge directly on the results of the desk. Remember that the bank is subject to a dual constraint: the need for all-round competition on the one hand and the need to maintain the unity of its rooms on the other.[40] It develops structures that promote successful competition—forms of compensation, organization of activity—but, at the same time, it must control what is produced within its confines, because the results of those experiments expose its wealth and its credibility. However, retention of this knowledge is not easy. No matter how many metal-detection gates the bank installs or written pledges of confidentiality and loyalty its operators sign, bits of knowledge are treated as assets by everyone and circulate unbeknownst to the head of the trading room, inside as well as outside the bank. The deeply embodied nature of skills, and their elusive articulation by traders, goes a long way toward explaining the limitations of confidentiality incentives.[41] This control is made more difficult because the models nurtured in these spaces are often not formalized and not easily traceable. The trader's assistant had her own recipes, developed after many trials and errors through close interactions with the pricer: against the full script passed down by engineers, she could only complete her hedges within her workday by inventing shortcuts and by tweaking the system whenever her nose told her to do so. The bank can never prevent two traders from communicating and from developing similar *personal* models of the values of their assets. When this happens though, the bank loses its grip on this precious intelligence. These exit strategies greatly worried the management of the trading room.[42] They reinforced the need for supervision of the knowledge acquired by operators.

At the same time, the antagonistic nature of the relationships in the room does little to facilitate the movement of information, and this carries with it an obvious risk: traders from the desk may leave the bank, taking with them the expertise they have developed. This knowledge is, in turn, highly valued on the open labor market.[43] That is, traders can leave the bank, taking with them techniques, methods, and know-how that are less explicitly recognized as what the bank can legitimately cover by confidentiality agreements. The prospect of turnover therefore forces the bank to supervise its traders as much for the results they produce as for the errors or offenses they may commit.[44] It was not uncommon for good traders, aware of the sums they brought into the bank and not satisfied with their remuneration, to decide to leave their jobs in order to start up a private endeavor using their own assets or by raising funds from contacts they developed during their employment at the bank. The bank may thus witness the departure of those who had worked in a relatively isolated way from the rest of the bank, and who had not shared with their employer and colleagues the "profitable tricks" they had discovered. Salespeople carry with them, in the form of an address book, their networks of clients and acquaintances, the best of which are obligatory points of passage for markets that are still composed of few institutions. Their affiliation is all the less important when the breadth of their networks and the personalization they have established are coupled with a skill that is highly regarded and quite personal. The bank's clients in most cases will willingly detach themselves from an institution's name if they can hold onto the individual skill—and thus, profit generation—it harbored.

The story of my access to the trading room is in itself an illustration of this mobility of front-office operators at a time of high confidence in the market economy, a confidence itself boosted by what looked like the new economic regime ushered in by the "dot com" business. After spending two months working for the research department of the fixed income trading room, I heard about a front office vacancy needing to be filled immediately. Within an hour, I was interviewed by an agitated operator, who quickly asked what I knew about exotic derivatives and whether I would be ready to help his desk rationalize the process (the rationalization I describe in chapter 4). After fifteen minutes of conversation, I understood that I was talking to the operator who was leaving the trading room and had been asked to find a replacement for the job he was deemed unworthy of holding. Once this strange situation had been made clear, the conversation turned into a rant about the rest of the desk and the lack of consideration and reward for what he had done. Frustrated by a dismal bonus earlier that year, he had decided to leave General Bank and attack their monopoly-based business by creating a clearing platform for products similar to CGP. On that platform, other banks offering like services and clients interested in allowing competition to lower the fees associated with such services would be able to expand their businesses. Key to his strategy were his relationships formed with other operators in similar banks who had looked with envy at General Bank's near monopoly on exotic financial products. When he recruited me, he was in the process of contacting the Commission des Operations Boursieres (COB, the French SEC) to clear some of the regulatory hurdles. After he left the bank, I never heard again of his grandiose and vindictive project and it seems it was abandoned. Still, the move and the belief that he could, by himself, and without the backing of any other major financial institution, create a viable alternative to a long-honed expertise cultivated by General Bank's exotics desk is symptomatic of a vision of the economy nearly exclusively centered around the skills of operators. This individualistic understanding of the economy was obviously nurtured by the dot com bubble, on its way to reaching historic highs in the months following the capricious decision by an operator who was, like everyone else in this industry and at that time, confused about the sources of value.

Less Don Quixotesque than my elusive employer, the end of the 1990s saw an explosion in the financial services offered by ex–bank employees, dissatisfied with their low participation in the rapid return growth of the trading rooms to which they once belonged. The growth of hedge funds in these years can be explained by a great variety of causes, but it is important to note that these funds[45] were opening themselves up to alternative investments and to increasingly complex products. Products that had been limited to large banking institutions now floated to smaller institutions geared toward portfolio management of wealthy individuals. The spreading of this expertise owes much to the dissemination of skills and knowledge associated with mobile individuals.

The risk posed by the possible defection of operators brings about a dilemma for the bank. The ability to measure its risks safely is the basis of the bank's business and builds client and shareholder credibility. But by choosing to retain exclusively its models of assessment/risk, it exposes itself to the looting of its operators by its direct competitors. It is not only financial products competition, therefore, but also competition on the job market for front-office financial operators that subverts its work organization from the inside. In these circumstances, is the knowledge retention of these learned but volatile formulas the right strategy? Does the nature of financial exchanges and commitments instead require models to become standards quickly? We must temporarily leave the trading room to understand the dynamics between the retention and dissemination of models.

Spreading Models Outward: When Leakages Are Beneficial

The felicity of research in quantitative finance is subject to the stability of the financial sphere.[46] One could argue that finance is not the unique domain where cooperation is the prerequisite to competition, but it is certainly a domain where lack of cooperation very quickly destabilizes the very world around which competition takes place. It is in the interest of most major players to see to it that the financial architecture be resilient.[47] A bank's model can only pass a market test if financial conversations persevere and are able to hold out against the wariness awakened by excessive speculative refinement. Trust in the bank's risk models is crucial to this persistence. The most refined models—when existing on their own and unable to influence other players of the accuracy of their predictions—can do nothing in a market that suddenly collapses, as was the case with the 1987 crashes and more recently when the subprime mortgages revealed the weakness of their structures to growing customers' credit defaults from 2007 on.

A bank cannot hope to orchestrate the establishment of a market on its own; it must release the models' retention and let the results filter out through its walls. Without this dissemination, the bank lacks counterparts with whom it can build deals—in this sense, security closes a market before even creating it. Models represent a specific example of an economy of standards. By imposing a standard on a market (whatever that market might be: personal typewriter, personal computer, or pricing models that set the market price of financial services), it is possible to channel competitors to adopt a class of products. Once in place, these standards stabilize the conversations that market operators can have when they assess the value of a product. Some parameters are central, while others are peripheral: the standard promoter can set the tone of the conversation. The industry as a whole benefits from the decrease in uncertainty associated with the standard dissemination. A quasi-market, emerging without any authority to enforce a standard, may never be able to consolidate sufficiently the expectations of its different players.

Yet, the situation is more complex with standard models of finance. Unlike computer keyboards, sizes of car tires, or frequencies of an electromagnetic network, finance models are also price and "risk-producer" instruments.

With a keyboard, the standard dictates all characteristics except price; with financial products, a standard model dictates all characteristics including the product's price. Remember that the price is produced by the room and its model: it is not the outcome of a face-to-face transaction between market agents pondering preferences against the price that their counterpart is willing to concede. Models are central to the cognitive equipment of all bank operators, and if there is a market, it survives through these little prostheses. Take the models away, and chances are the orderliness of the clean market will also go away. When the QWERTY and AZERTY keyboard standards gained control over their rivals, users could appraise their characteristics by themselves: it was handier, faster, more convenient, and so forth. Despite the numerous mediations that stand between the typists and the machine (the training of professional typists; the marketing that boasts the ergonomics involved in the layout of the keys), the keyboard can still be assessed by every user.[48] Financial products like the CGP, with a long life span and customized terms, cannot. When they are designed to meet the special needs of a client, they have no secondary market—hence no price—so that the bank is left on its own to figure out what its value and risks are. The voices of like competitors and industry associations are equally lost by the engineered complexity of these services. The standard adds to the room and its operators the stable chorus of the industry association.

If standardized models disseminated in the industry solve so many of the uncertainty problems that plague financial markets, why are they not adopted more thoroughly? We can better understand the reticence in allowing a standard model to circulate if we keep in mind the nature of these engineered products. They thrive on an asymmetry that dissemination threatens. As a model is disseminated, it limits the relative profit that the bank might anticipate by taking advantage of its comparative advantage. When all participants of a market line up according to this model, the possibility for discussion is at its peak and financial conversation is in full swing, but no one particular bank stands out.[49] The choice between dissemination and retention holds to two imperatives: establishing a common language that can allow for the spreading of products with a family resemblance, and securing a comparative advantage. But because these models have very real effects on the economies of the financial institutions that use them, they play yet another role, absent in the QWERTY/AZERTY–style economics of standards. By offering banks control over the risks they may take, these models limit the risky strategies of competitors who could pull the market into a downfall.

The Dilemma between Science and Finance

The models developed in the trading rooms attempt to win out over other competing models, but they contribute, as do all models, to the establishment of the level of risk to which the banks are subject. As banks develop more refined models that monitor risks more accurately, they can indulge in tighter hedging policies. Instead of hedging in an approximate way, without regard for the actual risks on the market, banks use models to limit as much as possible their inactive capital.[50] Every euro cent that is freed from the hedging of market activities can thus be reinvested in a potentially lucrative activity. A very dependable model, but one that requires excessive provisioning with regard to the actual risks, forces the bank to withdraw capital from the economic machine. In contrast, a model that underestimates the risk might force the bank to spend, ultimately, more money than what a healthy provisioning would have required. In this way, models have an impact on the bank's bottom line.

This "race to the bottom" helps more conservative banks working with more accurate models to resist the turbulences of markets. However, models protect them only marginally and over a length of time that does not suit the far-reaching horizons of banks. When more than one large bank collapses, the entire banking industry is in danger. The unpleasant aftertaste left by the recent spate of crises is evidence of the consequences of the modeling hubris of a few investment bankers—convinced that they could beat the market and escape unscathed before its collapse.[51] The inadequacy of models is a considerable source of risk for all the actors on the market. Bound by the need to cooperate as much as by the aspiration to yield the highest performance, valuation models are chained together in a complex network. The developers of models themselves build the world in which they seek a specific advantage; they are interested in the behavior of this industry but want to dominate it.

The researchers from the Parisian group, Science & Finance (S&F), have a policy of releasing their findings, which sets them apart in this market for models. The S&F group focuses on one particular segment of the market for models: models of risk associated with market fluctuations. These are not models dedicated to a certain type of product but rather to the overall commercial position of an institution. Used at an aggregate level, these models are regularly consulted to evaluate the global risk taken by the bank on the markets. Although this group is primarily dedicated to research, its policy of revealing its models seems to point to a growing concern among financial market participants. A new consciousness of the risks brought about by new products not yet well controlled by the majority of financial intermediaries, orients many major actors in these markets toward an open access policy, quite against the grain of the received views of finance.

Q: How does the question of confidentiality play out, considering your nature as an integrated scientific structure[52] and your policy of releasing findings?

A: [W]e do not publish everything; in general we publish everything that has to do with risk control without any problem, because if our competitors monitor their risk well, it helps us, it does not bother us in the least, because it helps keep the industry in order if everyone controls their risks. . . . In one specific case, linked to risk-control, on a way of pricing exotic objects, and which is potentially sellable as a research contract, we decided to publish the article, maybe not giving all the details concerning the implementation of the model. We expected that a serious bank interested in the model would have two choices: it could either give it to its research team for it to study it, or it could approach us and ask us to put it into place, and that's precisely what happened.[53]

"Cleansing up the industry" is a motive behind the dissemination of models that could otherwise be held and sold. S&F has a contract with a large Swiss investment bank that chooses to double-check the risk analyses carried out by its own services (traders, engineers, and the risk-analysis department) against those of outside experts. The terms of the contract binding S&F and the bank take us back to the multiple dimensions that need to be controlled to produce a model. The "published" and public model—much like the recalcitrant Hull–White model that Franck struggled with—maintains certain elements of mystery that the researchers from S&F can quickly lift at the request of a client showing interest.

Thus, models have a paradoxical economy. They are valuation tools that help to beat the competition, but they also guarantee this competition and affect the financial industry as a whole, preventing minor players from defaulting in the game. Because the face-to-face production of a price is not possible for classes of products like CGPs that are not traded on Exchanges and have no real markets, the trader-to-model appraisal of risk is the only possibility offered to the bank. The risk that everyone is wrong in their chosen ways of modeling financial products has some clear contemporary resonances. The blind trust that most actors granted risk models in the recent subprime crisis reminds us that there is no clear solution out of the conventional assessment. Relying on models that are freely available on the market exposes them to systemic risk, which is fueled by the creation of shared patterns of hedging. Developing one's own risk model against the conventions followed by the crowd exposes the institution to another risk for its willingness to bet on its superior grasp of markets dynamic. Isolation and disconnection looms large for lone institutions. The painful experience of French physicists entering the field of quantitative finance late in its development is evidence that the market for financial models is structured along layers of taken-for-granted assumptions, solidly cemented in batteries of instruments that cannot be challenged so easily.[54] The specific tension that animates the dilemma between competition/retention and cooperation/dissemination is due to the nature of financial services. More than any other good or service, their survival hinges on consensus. As immediately as this fragile agreement disappears, financial products are nothing more than a few lines of code and the vivid memory of great promises. Arguably, all traded goods and services share this instability of some of their properties. In a matter of seconds, a car once praised for its minimal environmental footprint can become a lethal weapon if one of its mechanisms fails to operate properly. Originating as a good, the car becomes a liability and a real nightmare through a quick requalification. Scholars of science and technology studies (Beck, 1992, 1996) have richly documented the oscillation of engineered goods and the strain generated on collectives faced with such reversals. Financial products exacerbate this characteristic, as they are easily revisable properties. Toyota can recall its hybrid cars en masse and fix their brakes when it discovers a defect in the braking systems it has produced; when a market collapses and trust has dried up all around, no recall is possible.

Conclusion

The trading floor is a market. This trivial observation becomes insightful if one is careful to describe the currency of this unique market. Expertise on the financial positions and mastery of models goes hand-in-hand with famil-iarity with the equipment that makes up the complex ecology of the room. Without housing the principles of market activity (most of the time in the form of models) in an environment that gives them support to lean on, finan-cial scripts miss their goal. The temptation to be self-sufficient, to go it alone, is constant for financial operators: the rumors of gigantic profits circulating in the room make newcomers dream of the good times to come, and embit-ter those who are still awaiting their finest hour. But these temptations doom operators to failure, whether they be caused by an excess of confidence in the models available, a mistrust of the cooperation forced by a continued pres-ence on the market, or even an exercise in order-sending that is not mediated by all of the pieces of equipment that ensure the integration of the room to the outside market.

The trading room establishes—and requires—the cohabitation of different types. As a space that holds the key to the bank's internal market, it is closed on the outside, and efforts are made to minimize the possibilities for information retention that might give operators a piece of knowledge too easily negotiable on the job market. On a larger scale, a financial actor who generally withholds his or her models may let them circulate freely once his or her knowledge depends on that of competitors. This collaboration—forced by the nature of a financial market that can topple all participants as easily as one entity—is typical among the operators in the room. The mobility that calls for being constantly prepared for the lurches of the market brings traders to suspend, in clearly defined conditions, an exclusive claim on their workstations. But this loosening immediately meets its limits, and the implementing of financial strategies, and particularly the sending of orders, calls for a financial operator who is "collected," equipped with all of his or her tools and in tight control.

Being here and there is the perfect dream of General Bank engineers. The script of CGP capitalizes on the dispersion of Exchanges and on their lack of financial integration so far. This is the wager of these products: they expect their traders to beat the weak integration of distant Exchanges by using the channels of this integration. This only works if these channels are not yet heavily trod and if the technical integration achieved by the wires linking General Bank to the Exchanges does not hold the key to the financial integration. Strategies need to be designed, and hedging rules need to be followed cautiously. That is where the operator achieves (or does not achieve) the derivation of value, by sitting at the edge of the bank—an eye on one Exchange; another on the other Exchanges that he or she needs to match and hedge—and with the formula in hand. The tortured design breeds a tortured body for which collaboration with fellow traders and brokers and with familiar pieces of equipment populating his or her desk, is dictated by the upheavals of the Exchanges.

CHAPTER 4

The Memory of Banking

In this chapter, we travel to the bank's back office to observe how products are stored.[1] From the perspective of the back office—not dissimilar to that of the front office—CGPs are disruptive: they impose themselves on a bank's conservation methods and demand new rules. The challenge for the bank comes from its complex topography—its *invagination*, to borrow a physiology term used by the philosopher and historian of medicine, François Dagognet—as contacts with the outside world morph from being driven by the front office (salespeople, traders, engineers) to being the realm of the back-office managers.[2] This reversed topography is the consequence of products that can only be counted, maintained, and hedged if they are simultaneously in several of the bank's sites *and* in contact with outside Exchanges. Just like human bodies need membranes that allow the passage of oxygen from the outside world— the air we breathe—to the blood circulating in our veins and ultimately to the organs, efficient bank operations are dependent on a similar structure, which accommodates a circuit for the products designed in-house while maintaining both the products' unity and the identity of the bank. The dilemma is simply phrased: the value of CGPs for the bank comes from the ability of traders to hedge them properly while under the constraint of inconstant clients allowed the luxury of revising them. Hedging products with payoffs contingent upon minute changes in underlyings requires a close monitoring of the Exchanges listing such underlyings. One way or another, operators need to transport themselves outside of the bank or get these prices inside the bank. From the point of view of the bank's general topography, it means one and the same thing. The walls of the bank must let information in and out. Yet, the very object commanding such attention outward is also an unstable entity that allows clients to step into the bank, demanding to be heard on aspects of the product design. The center of gravity of the bank seems to spiral outward, quite consistently with the ideal of a derivative mode of operation seeking value by mobility and versatility rather than by investment and stability.

Yet, this decentered mode of operation entails risk when the bank multiplies membranes and apertures and finds itself no longer in control of its treasured products' unity. With blurred boundaries and the even more blurry products, who knows what is to be hedged?

Topography of the Counting Places

Portfolios are traders' companions. Despite the omnipresence of "products" in the conversations between engineers, salespeople, and around the trading room, portfolios are the tangible and manipulable presence on the desk— they are the single points of stability onto which traders can cling over the stormy life of a contract. There is an arc of transformation between the design, issuance, and term of a product/contract. Organized around products in the beginning, the contract shifts to an aggregate version of the portfolio when traders are in charge, only to veer back to a contract-centered discussion when the bank settles its obligations with its clients. Whereas new products are designed on a quasi-continuous basis and contracts issued as frequently, portfolios seem immune to the day-to-day changes that rock other principle points in the contract. They have a momentum and continuity that conceals the incoming and outgoing flows of products. Yet, portfolios are only one of three versions of the product with which traders must contend. As the contract is worked through its cycle of transformation, it goes through three phases: the imminent contract, the portfolio (aggregated contract), and the ending contract.

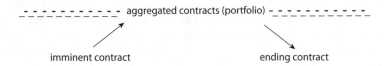

Figure 7. Aggregation and Disaggregation, from Contract to Portfolio to Contract

These transformations—from imminent contract to portfolio, and from portfolio to ending contract—are relevant in that they expose the folded organization of the bank vis-à-vis products that challenge a linear conceptualization. Still, despite its broken trajectory, this chronology conveys only partially the transformations of the products through the apparent continuity of the portfolio. The customization enjoyed by General Bank's clients allowed them to transform their products—thereby issuing a new contract—as often as they would see fit, within bounds set in the initial contractual agreement. The transformations undergone by the product follow a pattern that repeats the previous sequence—captured in figure 7—many times.

Figure 8. From Contract to Portfolio to Contract . . . Ad Infinitum

With hedging calculations focused on the portfolios (i.e., the aggregation of up to 500 contracts), and with ending contracts exiting the steady stream of the portfolio to reclaim their individuality one last time, how does the trader keep track of the successive versions of the initial contract? His or her assigned job is to take care of the portfolio and to attend to its fluctuations so that the bank does not lose money. The attention required for such a task is not like that of a collector keeping track of the minutest details of each specimen. It is more that of a one-person air traffic control center, where the operator is in charge of keeping an eye on dozens—perhaps hundreds—of moving targets, all at once. In other words, it is a sort of attention that requires quick reactions. The portfolio has no other identity than that of an aggregate. It does not need a memory of its own turbulent ins and outs. Whether the portfolio contains 500 or 478 contracts changes the trader's engagement very little. It is still a portfolio with a fluctuating value and a series of risk indicators as attributes. Contracts, in contrast, are clearly identified. They have precise terms, are attached to well-known clients, and have clear nominal amounts: in a nutshell, a defined identity. Yet, traders also know that clients can tweak contracts and alter their identities. The attention required by the unique properties of these moving contracts is different in nature from that of monitoring of the portfolio. The trader sits uneasily between these two different tasks, and with him or her, the tension of issuing and managing innovative and customizable products becomes visible.

The problem created by the imperative of holding onto a contract's memory becomes clear when the sheer variety of contracts illuminates the diverse array of operators working to build such a memory. If the trader is always part of a conversation with salespeople and engineers when the decision to offer a new product is made, he or she becomes part of a chorus when the contract is issued. In addition to the front-office discussion, with its preparations for the long and tortuous hedging period ahead, the room's back office also takes notice of the issuance and creates its record of the contract. This chorus only chants in unison when no glitches disrupt the issuance itself. When the relationship with the client is not as smooth, the chorus can turn into a scrum, with each client's interlocutor pulling the product onto his or her turf, with little consideration for the others' needs. The back-office operators have no business whatsoever with the portfolio as such, that is, as a fiction designed to rationalize the maintenance of hundreds of contracts and as a construct that has a reality nowhere other than the trader's workstation.

contract 1(a) issued ⟶ contract 1(a) canceled and contract 1(b) issued ⟶
contract 1(b) canceled and contract 1(c) issued ⟶ contract 1(n) canceled and
contract 1(n+1) issued ⟶ contract 1(n+1) ending

Figure 9. Back Office Perspective of Contract Versions

Their contacts with the trading room are necessitated through the contracts themselves, and to add to the misery of a function already looked down upon by the front-office operators—the curse of versatility—these contracts undergo multiple versions. If one were to represent this succession in diagram form, see figure 9.

With several versions of contracts and several memories of their transformations, where have the products gone? It seems obvious that the products are in the bank, somewhere between the trader's desk and the back office, but even these two locations do not exhaust the possibilities and risks attached to such instability. Complicating further the bank's organizational diffraction is the client's demands for new contracts. With their unpredictable presence, the topography of the bank changes.

The problem of counting contracts—"How many contracts do we have in a portfolio," as opposed to the pricing concern, "What is the value of a contract"—arises when customization starts to be carried out on an industrial scale. In such cases, the operators are not able to remember offhand all the products they are dealing with, and have to acquire the appropriate equipment to manage these large bundles of products on a daily basis. Their preoccupations change, as their job is no longer simply assessing the value of a single product but also knowing how many products have to be assessed. Sometimes it is simply a matter of knowing what the bank's commitments are, how many products have to be hedged, and on which markets. The trading room therefore has to build up a memory of all the products. The massive scale on which this banking activity is now carried out requires an army of back-office *little hands* devoted to these tasks, behind the scenes of the trading activities examined thus far.[3] These little hands feature prominently in this chapter, which will set the record straight as to their actual work: far from using their hands exclusively, back-office personnel also spend most of their days struggling to penetrate the opaque terms of the contracts. They get little credit, unlike the traders and engineers who have fathered such puzzles and pushed them into the bank.

This distance between the trader's computer, from which orders are passed and a portfolio's value is cared for, and the bank's safe, where versions of contracts are stored and updated, presents problems of day-to-day management. The products that are now managed in large quantities exist in multiple databases that have to be compared and reconciled. That is, the information on products in one database must be corroborated with another, because the databases can be so out of synch that there is uncertainty around the actual

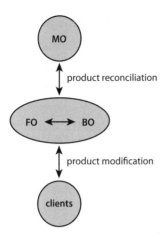

Figure 10. New Topography of the Bank under Product Modification

terms of the deal. "Reconciliation"—one of the terms most frequently used in the discussions of operators— indicates that the location and structure of the databases is a point of concern for the bank. By analyzing these databases, we can shed light on the nature of products that *(a)* have to be exposed to other financial markets on a daily basis for hedging operations, *(b)* lend themselves to customization upon customers' demand, and *(c)* must nevertheless, for all of their different versions and iterations, be identical in all the databases where they exist through the course of their protean lives.

The disappearance of the contract's spatial unity—with several versions in several databases—is both a condition and an obstacle to the operation of counting. If the products are put aside and protected from market fluctuations, their value is not clear. If they are never removed from the portfolio, they lack the identity needed for counting. The bank that wants to count its assets (how many, and how much each one is worth) must diffract itself in order to be in contact with the market to generate value while also maintaining a hard core, immune from market fluctuations: literally, a safe. At any time, the two modes of existence of the contract—diffuse entity bouncing on hedging exchanges and hard local core resting in safes—need to match, lest traders lose track of their hedging. This diffraction under the constraint of unity brings new bank functions to the fore. The maintenance of financial operations necessitates new operators on the scene.

I was fortunate to witness and participate in the reorganization of databases and the remodeling of products. Reorganization and remodeling were necessary for the success of this financial undertaking. Autonomy in designing its *value at risk*—or VaR more commonly—came with more scrutiny of a bank's organization by the national regulator. The bank was consequently summoned to "clean up" its databases and to standardize its modeling of the products therein. Because General Bank was handling products with unusual characteristics, it could use its own metric of risk only if those doing the valuation could show that they knew what they were measuring. The consequences of this local metric of risk granted to the bank were pervasive. The transformations of the databases consisted first in reconciling them to make sure they were consistent and that the different modes of a product's existence (in the front, middle and back offices) were compatible. This overhaul created an ideal situation to observe the tension generated by the design of products forced to be many things at once: a price, an aggregation of prices to be hedged daily, a model, a paper document, and a legal contract.

An Ecology of Documents in the Room

What is the final form of a financial contract? What does it look like, and what is it made of in a place like General Bank? These questions might seem off topic as we easily imagine that a contract is a modern digital "thing." It has to be advanced, transparent, and flexible, lending itself to coding and recoding upon request. With the click of a mouse, the contract is in place. Another click and its characteristics change. All of these iterations can be stored in a computer, easily accessible should the need arise. In reality, it turns out a contract has much more exciting modes of existence—a double life, of sorts, as it is both paper and digital through its multiple versions. To understand why the task of keeping track of contracts across many offices was so problematic for General Bank, it is helpful to look first at two paper versions of a contract.

A Ticket; Not Quite a Contract

In the beginning, a ticket is issued by the trader in charge of a new contract. It lists the characteristics of this new contract, yet in sketchy ways. More to the point, it lists just enough of the contract properties so that the trader can enter it into his or her pricer and personal database. For each change brought to the contract, a new ticket needs to be issued. The information needed to write up a contract—a legal and binding document—go beyond this sketch. The trader does not spend time collecting that kind of information: he or she summarizes the few pieces of information needed to do what he or she does best, which is to assess the contract's value and hedge it. Yet, for all its sketchiness, the ticket is one of the most central documents in the life of a deal. It is the first in a series of other documents that give shape to the deal and without which there would be no such deal. The convention that forces the room to issue a new ticket for each amendment to the deal reasserts the role of the trader. Without his or her approval, the action in the room stops.

The kind of information production that will eventually yield a contract takes place along parallel channels of communication set between the client and the back office of the bank. In this division of labor, the salesperson does

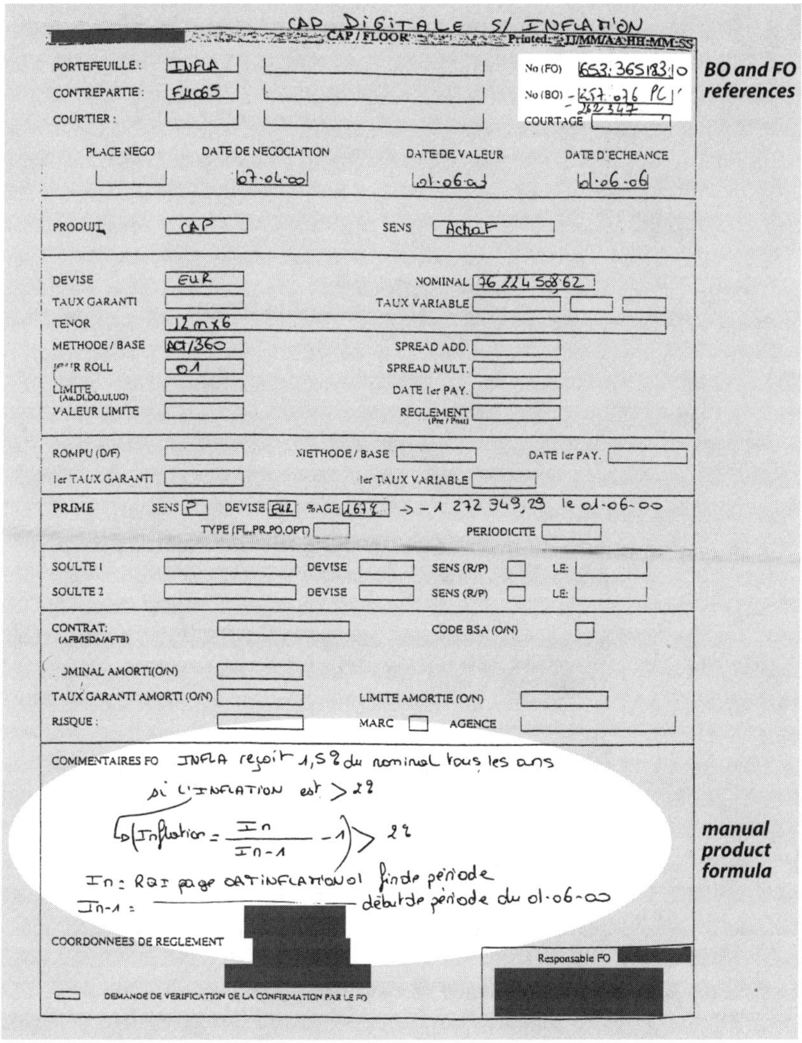

Figure 11. A Trader's Ticket

play a central role, as we have seen, but he or she quickly recedes to backstage. He or she will rarely step forward into the fray; even when the client decides to push for contract changes, engineers and traders handle the case on their own. Actually, they do not handle it completely on their own, as the back office becomes part of the dance around the contract's precious features. These additional pieces of information are collected by the back-office manager, who eventually writes up the contract.

BO references and name of the BO manager in charge

271039
PiGu
+

Back office
■RUE MARBOEUF
75008 PARIS
FRANCE

Paris, the 29/09/2000

BO references and other related products

RE   : SWAP TRANSACTION

Our Ref   : TAU-271039 (TAU0271036 – TAU0271030)
                    To be specified in every document exchanged between you and us.
Your Ref   : (to be specified in your confirmation and mentioned in every document
                    exchanged between you and us)

Dear Sir,

The purpose of this agreement is to confirm the terms and conditions of the Transaction entered into between ▮▮▮▮▮▮▮▮▮▮▮ and ▮▮▮▮▮▮▮▮▮▮▮ on the Trade Date specified below (The ' Transaction'). This agreement constitutes a 'Confirmation' as referred to in the Master Agreement specified below.

The definitions and provisions contained in the 1991 ISDA Definitions (as supplemented by the 1998 Supplement, as amended and supplemented by the 1998 ISDA Euro Definitions), as published by the International Swap Dealers Association, Inc., without regard to any subsequent amendment or revisions thereto, are incorporated into this Confirmation. In the event of any inconsistency between those definitions and provisions and this Confirmation, this Confirmation will govern.

Until you and we execute and deliver a master agreement, this Confirmation will be subject to the Master Agreement in the form published by ISDA, as if you and we had executed that Agreement (but without any schedule thereto) on the Trade Date of this Confirmation. Although the schedule has not yet been signed, which schedule will be substantially in the form set out in the Master Agreement published by ISDA, with such modifications as we may on good faith agree, this Confirmation, together with any other Confirmation(s) of Transaction(s) previously entered into between us and with the terms of the Master Agreement published by ISDA, evidences a complete, single and binding agreement between you and us.

Figure 12. First Page of a Confirmation

A Confirmation: A Contract

In bank parlance, a contract is a confirmation. Unlike the sketchy ticket, it covers most aspects of the deal. The confirmation is written using the ticket as a guideline—which is to say, under the tacit supervision of the trader—but the trader rarely revises a confirmation. Instead it goes to the counsel of the exotics desk, who checks with the back-office manager that the confirmation does not make the bank responsible for honoring unreasonable commitments. The confirmation follows a circuit different from that of the ticket. It never spends much time on the trader's desk. Sometimes it even does not stop on his or her desk, but flies immediately into a binder of utmost importance (that will be discussed later). The interaction of the counsel and the back-office manager can also be minimal because the counsel reviews only the most standard portions of the confirmation's terms. The perimeter of the underlyings' basket and the formula as such is usually left to the engineers and traders to verify. The legal dimension of the contract is procedural in nature. Of interest at this phase of vetting the confirmation are things like, the modality of fixing and quasi-fixing when an index is not available on a fixing day. With the ticket having precedence over the confirmation, of course, each new ticket entails a new confirmation. Unlike tickets, however, confirmations are contractually binding. Whether a new confirmation is issued on January 24 or January 25, 2002, could have nontrivial consequences for both parties to the deal.

Long neglected by social scientists for their supposed lack of insights, documents have recently been given their due place in such investigations (Riles, 2006).[4] Indices of memorial practices as well as central tools in the process of proof administration in scientific and legal arenas, documents have caught the attention of scholars for their ability to help to collect the past and project the future. In keeping with the Garfinkelian lesson (Garfinkel, 1967), scholars of various stripes have seized on documents as ways to capture the issue of intelligibility of actions in large organizations. Sociologists of medicine, for example, have turned their attention to the complex role of medical records in the functioning of institutions such as hospitals and HMOs (Berg, 1997; Heimer, 2006; Meehan, 1997), and documents have also featured centrally in studies of large financial organizations (Harper, 1998). These scholarly works exploit the few instances of documents' mutability or the coexistence of multiple documents produced by one institution to question the nature of organizations. These approaches resonate with a Weberian tradition that looks at organizations through the prism of the rationality/formality couple. In the case at hand, however, the documents that give shape to CGPs are unstable by design: contracts can be changed, and clients do not shy away from exploiting this clause. The question raised here is thus slightly different from the question tackled by previous scholarly accounts of documents in circulation: what characteristics of documents allow transformation *and* identity across the recursive assembly line of the bank?

Disjointed Memories of the Contracts

Even though each financial product can be presented very simply as a contract with a terminal contingent monetary flow, the management of this type of product requires the development of complex modeling tools. As complex and multilayered as they seem, prices are only the tip of the iceberg of a larger modeling challenge posed by structured products when they are managed in bulk. Pricing models that we studied to this point were needed because of the lack of a market, with similar services priced through the encounter with other financial firms and clients: modeling was a necessary evil when evaluating customized and unique goods. Allowing the entry of outside conversations when focusing on a greater number of standard products would have alleviated the burden of the room—by letting in external insights about the values of its products, albeit at the risk of divulging lucrative secrets. The pricing model was a consequence of the isolation of the bank from other sources of information. Although cut from other markets, these unique contracts filled the trading room. Unable to hear the whisper of prices coming from these markets, the survival of the bank demanded that the loud and conflicting conversations seizing the room be channeled. Faced with the risk of having too many modes of apprehension for too many contracts, a model is once again needed, albeit not for pricing but for mass management. Value is no longer at stake here; rather, operators now query their contracts database to know which particular products have a given characteristic.

The products designed and issued by the bank are likely to be kept for long terms in a trader's portfolio. The traders have clients as interlocutors who can decide to modify the design of these products whenever the product's basket of underlyings undergoes changes. This customization creates problems: each one offers a unique profile that resists a simple categorization. CGPs are obviously "exotic products," but that simplistic categorization does not offer much to the operator in the way of control. So varied a group of products falls under the rubric of "exotic" that such a classification affords little clarification. Modeling becomes imperative at this crucial transition, when mass customization leads to uncertainty in the characteristics of the diverse products that have been issued. Insofar as the bank has to find solutions for handling products that by nature circulate across various milieus, it needs models. In this instance, modeling no longer concerns each of the products taken separately but rather the whole mass of products that have to be formatted so that they can be managed as a single product. Their description once again proves to be their Achilles' heel, yet it does not cross the limits of the room itself. The description stays local, and given the relatively low number of products involved when the desk started operating, no infrastructure was built yet to make space for a description that would be readable by other operators not present on the trading floor. These operators also want to look at products, often as intensely as traders do, but they wish to see them along different lines.

They need to model these masses of products, just as traders do. Each office (front, middle, back) that processes financial products has its own enduring product management system. Each of these systems categorizes its own operations, which correspond to how operators input its main operations. Thus, the front, middle, and back office each map their operations in a way specific to their needs. This poses an additional risk for the bank because these competing models of contracts may well never point to the same product.

Modeling against Fraud

The expansion of activity on the exotics desk called for order in the databases, which required the definition of norms—something of an anathema to products defined as "exotic." Thereafter, modeling was no longer assumed to afford the leeway and creativity that traders had previously exploited. The lack of a standard way of modeling across the front, middle, and back offices had produced some abuses that the middle-office operators had failed to pick up on. One of these abuses exposes what the overly open modeling allowed when it was used for dishonest purposes.

At the time when only traders had the right to inspect models of contracts, a trader manipulated the value of the contracts in his or her portfolio several times (and the remodeling work attested to this as many times).[5] Proprietary trading frauds were the most blatant cases exposed after General Bank reviewed the coherence between front- and back-office records. This sort of fraud does not entail direct theft, exactly; rather, it involves an operator indirectly capturing a larger share of the annual bonus than would ordinarily be his or hers by artificially beefing up results.[6] To put it another way, the scheme did not play with the actual capital of the bank; it only depressed it initially to boost it up later. This is how it works: By applying a "negative additive spread" to the contract, the trader would magnify his or her own hedging abilities.[7] By altering the operation from the *keying* stage, the trader thus included a contract valued less than it actually should have been in his or her portfolio, were it not depressed by the negative spread. Thus, an operation with a market value of F350,000 would only show F300,000 on the trader's portfolio account after being trimmed down by F50,000. The trader then managed and hedged his or her operation in the usual way. Before its term, the trader changed it by removing the "negative additive spread," thereby restoring its initial characteristics. By making the negative spread disappear, the F50,000 were restored to the operation, and the trader appeared to be F50,000 more savvy than he or she actually was. The trick was completely reliant on the model: it consisted simply in never modeling the product with its real characteristics, but instead in artificially reducing it from the outset and then boosting it toward the end. Through clever modeling rather than clever trading, a trader's remuneration, indexed on performance, was thus increased by a few points.

Such a scheme was also found among some of the exotics desk's portfolios when the nature of the products permitted it. This trickery worked well only on products that generated a cash flow at their term. The trader was then free to manipulate his or her entries at will. Detecting the trickery would have entailed deconstructing the modeling of the operation and matching the front- and back-office records. Several pages of the software code had to be open, and only an expert eye could pick up the irregularity. In cases of products that produced continuous payoff flows while held in a portfolio, the forced interaction between traders and back-office managers would have rendered entries that were intentionally wrong more difficult. Surprisingly, in some rare cases, even this natural affinity between the two groups did not rule out such frauds. The absence of communication between the two sites of data entry was a real problem. Each of the two databases recorded the amounts paid (for the back database) or payable (for the front database); however, there was no link for putting these two flows in parallel. The two formulas could thus remain divergent for a long time without the data coming to the attention of anyone. The risks[8] that the bank took by not controlling the traders were by no means devoid of consequences and justified a heavy reconciliation program. The term "reconciliation" itself speaks loudly about the two cultures ruling at two opposite ends of the bank. In many ways, customization exacerbated the problem of making these cultures coexist. It forced them to interact on a much higher frequency than more standard products had so far.

The Two Cultures of the Bank

The front office must be reactive to changes in the value of these operations. Traders have to know their portfolio's state (value) at almost any time of the day. *Pricing* organizes the choice of the financial modeling system. General Bank developed an in-house[9] approach to its pricing software. The software created for this purpose—TRADE—was designed to solve all the problems that the management determined would occur in a rapidly growing database. It was simultaneously a pricer and a front-office repository (TRADE-Management that provided the traders with the IDs of all the products) keeping track of the current version of products. In theory, its database reconciled the different sets of demands that the front and back offices would have. It allowed traders to assess prices and back-office managers to keep track of the many products. The manager of this project explained to me the reasons for this pharaonic project:

> What I tried to do with TRADE is to separate clearly two things which are usually mixed in people's minds, let alone in the code of products; I tried to differentiate clearly between the *definition* of a financial contract, what it is, and its *pricing*, what it is worth [his emphasis]. These

are two things most people confuse. . . . This is very important, all the finance textbooks start with "a market, let's assume n assets written n_1, n_2 . . . following an integrable submartingale" . . . but this does not matter, it comes afterwards; they should tell me first what a financial contract is. And then, comes the definition of a call, and it is Max $(0, S - K)$. . . .[10] It is extremely difficult to formalize the notion of a contract independently of its pricing, and in most finance textbooks the contract and the pricing are being confused but these are two different things.

This is a very algebraic approach; this is a language. I work on a language with a rigorous semantics. A language that distinguishes between a *contract* semantics and a *pricing* semantics [his emphasis]. At the end of the day, in the bank we all agree that we write contracts that are vouched for by the market department lawyers. It is very unusual for a lawyer to understand what a Brownian motion is or what a complex pricing means. And yet, they can tell you whether the contract is good or not, and that shows that there are different semantic levels. We must be able to manipulate the notion of "contract" regardless of the notion of "pricing." That is the idea, "if you do X, then Y . . . ," but to be able to express this kind of events, we must adopt a very clear formalism that takes into account the passing of time. . . . Take for example three-month LIBOR.[11] Ask someone from the front office what it is and you will get the following answer: it is the ratio of two zero-coupons . . . that is what a mathematician will tell you. The back office tells you, "for me a three-month LIBOR, this is a market datum, there is a fixing every night and I must be careful to check the accurate data and to input it in the historical database." You have two completely different approaches, but the problem with the mathematician's solution is that it already contains a model, it is already a pricing of three-month LIBOR. When you say "a LIBOR is the relation of two zero-coupons," it is immediately a no-arbitrage reasoning.[12] What you say with this definition is that if you have a [no-arbitrage] model of the dynamics of interest rates, then three-month LIBOR is necessarily equal to this formula. That is true, but this is not a definition of LIBOR. . . . Everybody dreams of the long-searched-for front [office]–back [office] integration but nobody asks the good question, "What do I need, what description do I need in order to achieve this result?"

In this software, the basic modeling element is the *TRADE object*. Each contract was comprised of an aggregation of these objects, literally a series of rows in a window on a computer screen with the contract front-office reference as a name. Each row could be expanded, creating an embedded window with the characteristics of the object. These objects varied greatly, covering the whole gamut of existing basic financial products as well as connectors between products. Once aggregated in the main window, a local compiler would check the coherence of the composition and prompt for changes when it was faulty. The whole modeling experience was intended to be intuitive so that traders could quickly price any product by dragging characteristics from a rich library of base elements—such as plain vanilla options and futures—and dropping them in the contract window. It is no coincidence that this choice was adopted in the early 1990s when object-oriented computer languages were in full expansion, but it also reflected the pride of its designer, who thought all and any financial transactions could be reduced to a few elementary units. These units, once combined, exhausted the possible invention of financial engineers. They traced, in a practical manner, the perimeter of finance: beyond these limits, contracts would be suicidal, and no party would want to be on the wrong side.

In practice, for a trader working on a TRADE window at his or her workstation, the products are presented in *legs*, which do not correspond with the elementary flow units. Not each flow has its own leg, its TRADE object. A *logical aggregation* of flows is performed, which in the software architecture mirrors one of the formulas in the contract. Consider an *inflation swap* linking the bank to its client for a three-year period. The bank pays a sum (the *soulte*) for the launching of the operation and every six months receives a sum defined by the first *swap* formula. The counterpart will therefore credit the bank with six payments. On the same dates, the bank also pays a sum to its counterpart, according to the second swap formula. Hence, there are six new flows to the counterpart's credit and, all in all, thirteen flows will circulate between the two contracting parties. It would have been possible to model this operation with thirteen objects, but TRADE groups them together according to two main criteria.

The first criterion is the direction of the flow. A single TRADE object cannot contain flows going in different directions because this overrides a dimension of primary concern to the staff working with it: who pays what to whom. Parsing objects according to flow directions was a compromise made by the front office to the back-office operators. This method separates what is to be paid from what is to be received—even though, in practice, two equal sums would cancel each other out, and no two back offices would respect the letter of the TRADE modeling; that is, no money would actually be exchanged.

The second criterion is the nature of the financial operation upon which the flow is contingent. If a formula applies to the entire period of the contract, it has to be modeled in the form of a single TRADE object. But it may actually contain financial elements of very different natures. This is a new modality in the modeling of a financial contract into TRADE objects that we see at play: the nature of a financial flow, should this nature be entangled with others in a formula in the contract. The partitioning by natures operates by distinguishing deterministic and contingent flows. A formula that contains both deterministic elements and random elements (*Bank receives LIBOR + 3 points*) can thus be broken down in the form of two legs, one random (*Bank receives*

LIBOR), the other deterministic (*Bank receives 3 points*). The possibility of a more detailed breakdown of the contract formulas is potentially endless. The driver of this fragmentation of flows can change by offering ever-finer categories. We can see that by switching from a rough input that discontinues its investigation of the nature of finance at the "direction of flows" to a finer input that considers the *nature* of the flows (contingent or deterministic), the qualification of the contract changes considerably.

The hubris of the TRADE project was twofold. It first tried to solve a problem endemic to financial institutions by inventing a model of all possible financial transactions that would meet the needs of front- as well as back-office operators. The standardization was a concession made by traders to post-market operators, who could thus monitor the contract after its kick-off and, so to speak, from its guts. As we are about to see, allowing someone to peek into the trader's own way of modeling financial transactions was a serious compromise, as it represented a breach of their privileged turf. Yet, they were offered a compensation for this major intrusion. TRADE empowered traders in a way that no other pricer had, so far. Starting from any contract—the confirmation exchanged and signed by the parties—traders could build its model by combining elementary units available in libraries of the pricer. They would pick a few of these building blocks, assign them the characteristics set by the contract (the dates, the spread if needed, the underlyings), and get a price. From that standpoint, TRADE encouraged fluidity and versatility in traders. They could try different models, testing possibilities without needing to delegate much. This system gave them added fluidity and autonomy on the one hand, while it took away the privacy of their choices on the other. The compromises (bringing traders and back-office managers closer) and the radical ambitions (empowering both of these populations by making the former more autonomous and the latter more knowledgeable) were one and the same problem. They tried to leverage technology to solve a tension that existed between starkly different communities.

This grand project of unifying the different sites for processing products, using a descriptive language promoted by the front office, turned out to be a mixed success. The dream of integrating the organization through a single tool foundered because of persistent friction between the processing centers. Parallel to the development of this allegedly revolutionary tool, the trading room's information system continued to function as before. Each center carried on using its own local database. Despite the compromises accepted by traders, back-office managers were still unsatisfied, as the database side of TRADE did not meet their expectations: the pricer, with its value assessment imperative, continued to set the pace of TRADE, against the meticulous and slow requirements of a deal repository. The age-old precedence of market operations on back-office–monitoring operations had taught the back office to be wary of the lack of attention paid to their concerns for contract details. They knew that the constraints under which they had to work would not be central to the workings of the tool. Between the slow introduction of the TRADE system (1995–1997) and the year 2000, a back-office–only database was the touchstone when past relationships with clients had to be checked.

Historically, back-office operators have not been constrained by the near-instantaneous value assessment so familiar to traders. Their primary function was to ensure that the contingent monetary flows defined by contracts were paid and/or received properly by the bank once their calculation was complete. The back-office database was entirely devoted to the sound completion of transactions. Nothing was worse for these operators than deals that lingered in the limbo of everlasting negotiations between the engineers/traders and their clients. A good deal was a done deal. So, CGPs and their changing perimeters were a nightmare from the perspective of the back office. They would hold the future open and force operators to keep track of each contract. This added workload was a by-product of the two cultures splitting the bank: customization alone without memory would work fine; meticulous record keeping of standard contracts would work equally well, but their coexistence was a problem, FIX was the name of the back-office[13] database. Each operation keyed into this database had a six-digit code; such as FIX-XXX XXX. Upon pulling up a contract, the first screen provided users with the general characteristics of an operation. They could then click on links to open other windows affording access to more valuable information on elements of the operation. For instance, the schedule gave the dates to be observed for fixing prices and the dates of payment of the flows thus calculated. A second schedule indicated the value of past flows and what the bank and the counterpart had exchanged. A series of requests was possible through this interface that allowed searching for packets of operations on the basis of fairly strictly defined criteria.

Designed in a way that made local manipulations by an isolated operator impossible, the FIX database prohibited fraud.[14] The underlying data tables were linked by codes that precluded any inconsistencies in inputs. Each inconsistency identified by the software would immediately trigger an alarm and block further changes to the operation. On the days of price fixings, there were also warnings that prompted the operators to "collect" the market value from the relevant underlying. As much as possible, the execution of financial contracts had been automated to ensure that the front-office operator's creativity would be kept at bay. As a result, no operation could ever be canceled. Instead, it was stored in the database and simply deactivated (the operators "terminated" it, as they put it). When the operation underwent changes, the primary characteristics window of all deactivated contracts would refer to the immediate next version. FIX was all about keeping a clean record of each contract oscillation. Memory was its business, so that at every point of the contract's trajectory, its past was easy to retrieve through the trail of successive FIX codes.

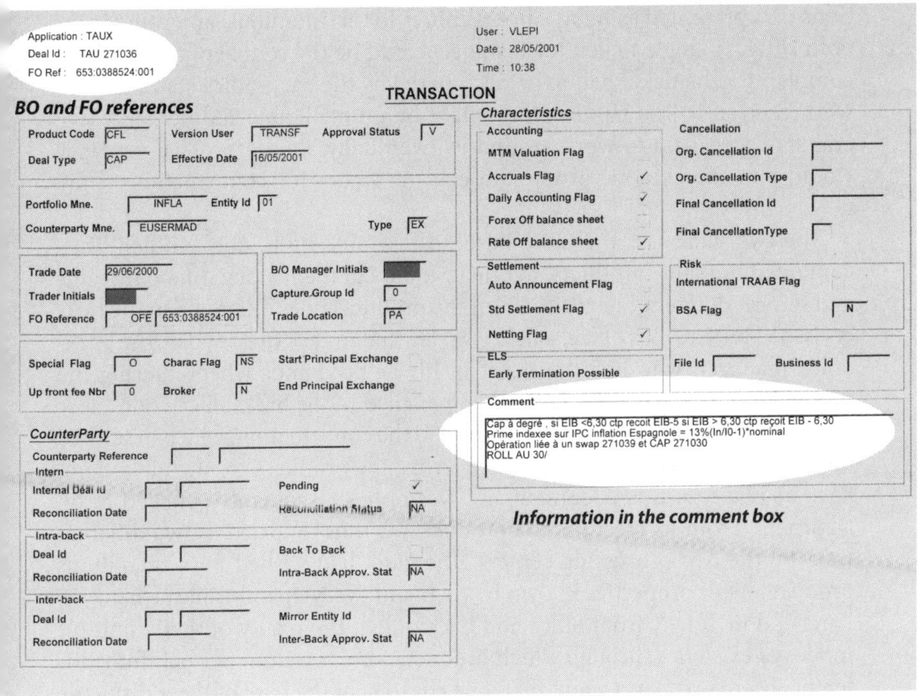

Figure 13. FIX's Transaction Page with the Payoff Formula Written as a Comment

The organization of the back offices followed the seams of the trading room. The equity trading room had its own back office; the fixed income room also had its exclusive back office with dedicated operators. These "silos" could be designed as Russian dolls with sub-silos and sub-databases having their own operators. The exotics desk had grown big enough that a group of back-office operators was working exclusively at smoothing the relationship between creative trading-room engineers and clients hungry for impeccable services. This group was managed by someone who supervised all the transactions and was also the mediator between his staff and traders. It was not uncommon for members of one group to become irritated with those in the other group, stoking tensions between the offices. Traders, for instance, would stigmatize the back office as slow, and in these situations, everybody understood "slow" as more than just a behavioral qualification. Back-office staff, for their part, would point to the lack of organization among traders, which they felt led to traders misunderstanding the organizational depth of their own financial transactions. These tensions were nearly as numerous as the flow of documents that ran from the front to the back office after every contract change. Every new ticket issued was followed by a series of interactions that presented as many opportunities for acrimonious lamenting from both sides. A single ticket, for instance, could be the source of a cascade of complaints. The ticket had to be deciphered by the back-office staff member who received it. The handwriting might be unintelligible and demand several staff members to work around it. Eventually, the back-office manager would join the exegetic group and call the trader for confirmation of the new terms.

The two databases therefore bore no resemblance to one another. They contained the same products, but they would cut them along different seams and rely on different categories. Even the product codes differed. On the tickets issued by the front office, a field was devoted to the "front code." The back-office manager, who had the ticket in his or her hands when entering the product into his or her database, then penciled in the back-office code, close to the preceding fields. The same applied to the confirmation, which described the operation in typically back-office terms; the product's front code did not have its place on this document and was only subsequently penciled in on a corner.[15] From its creation, the product was thus modeled in two different ways by the two processing centers. The bank had wished for a ubiquitous product—with properties known by each and every operator in the bank, in Paris and in Tokyo, front office and back office. The reality of these multiple modes of existence through which products were traveling was painfully different. There was never more than one contract at the base of these disparate local expressions, but because its unique animation came from the various descriptions attached to it by operators in each milieu, there was no possibility of finding a single, secure perspective from which to settle disputes over characterizations and descriptions of contracts. Operators could not bypass these partial expressions to look the product *in the eye*, having instead to deal with all of a contract's incarnations.

Transfer and Reconciliation

During my work in the back office, the complications generated by the two simultaneous modes of existence for contracts were the bread and butter of the staff. The one fear common among back-office managers was the disappearance of contracts and the possibility that traders would either intentionally wrongfully manipulate them or simply change them without the back office knowing. Modifying a contract was a perilous exercise to the extent that half of the bank's personnel would be forced to coordinate closely in updating their records. The disconnect between FIX and TRADE entailed a human coordination and sometimes a face-to-face interaction to verify the identity of the product across its front- and back-office expressions. One such case illustrates the choreography around this moment.

During the cleaning and verification of the database, it appeared that one contract had been keyed in by the *wrong* back-office manager. The contract was supposed to be internal—a deal between two desks in the bank—and it had been wrongly keyed in as a deal with an outside party. Different desks in the bank can strike deals with one another on a formal basis—at least, formal enough so that the transaction is recorded in the front- and back-office databases. But the formality demanded by that kind of transaction is also challenging for the bank inasmuch as the same operation shows up twice in the bank's accounts. Internal deals create "twin deals" in the back office, which the operators call "mirrors." Each desk carries a deal in terms that are strictly opposite to those of the other desk: one paid what the other one received and vice versa. For many reasons, not least the protection of shareholders' good judgment against artificial market operations, the bank needs to cope with what is simply a budgeting trick.[16] The problem could seem to be artificial, but it creates puzzles for the accountants as it questions the nature of a transaction that was deemed worth documenting. Is this one transaction or two transactions? From the viewpoint of the shareholder, it looks irrelevant, as it simply distributes money within the bank, yet it can have economic consequences. Internal swaps can trigger external deals by releasing pressure on a local desk and creating opportunities where there were none before. The bank had devised a solution to this puzzle by keeping its internal interactions in a separate database. The contract that was initially entered into the back-office's external deals database had to be moved to that for the internal deals.

The transfer had to be done simultaneously. One contract had to be killed as another one had to be created. It was an operation of identity creation. In the bank, identity takes on a simple form: a product code. But once again, this identity is problematic. Even though each office (back, middle, and front) has its own product code, changing a code is taboo—a technical taboo. Products are indexed in multiple tables, interconnected by ODBC links and called by SQL requests.[17] Modification of a contract code would cause bugs through these computer links. To solve these problems, an engineer would have to work on this transfer, perhaps for several hours. The database administrators recommended canceling the transferred operation and immediately afterwards re-creating the same one again. For some time, the back-office staff flatly refused to do so. Leaning on the formal procedure of deal creation, they argued that only a new ticket could require the creation of a new operation and the front office would not want to redo the same ticket for nothing.

The existence of the contract was dependent on its presence in one of the databases, but moving it would suspend this solid existence. Detaching it would cause it to disappear momentarily from the bank's archives. Despite the brevity of this disappearance, the operation was considered risky enough for a transfer protocol to be decreed to limit the risk of the operation. A deal missing from the trader database would mean no hedging and no provisioning in view of the final settlement with the client. However, because it was an internal deal, it was slight in material terms. In fact, it was even incomplete because its initial ticket was missing. Only subsequent tickets issued by a trader when the terms of the deal had changed were included in the file, and they were handwritten. Without an official confirmation signed by the two parties, it was difficult to read what was marked on the tickets; only the computer entry of the operation could be relied on. Thus, the fuzziness of the internal deal procedures[18] precluded the verification of digital entries, which was the aim throughout this operation.

The high premium on continuity must be understood in the context of previous chapters. The composite and structured nature of these products forces traders to rely on the pricing apparatus to assess their value. Absent this umbilical cord, traders are left blind and deaf to the market changes. The sequences of hedging showed the conundrum of simulations. They severed the precious link to the fluctuating market and forced traders to rush their hedges for fear of making decisions on the basis of outdated prices. Without this bond, contracts' values are indeterminate, but another bond is just as crucial to their survival. A disruption of the bank's information technology infrastructure suspends the life of these contracts. These products dance clumsily on two legs—the front office's and the back office's—to such a point that their chaotic animation activated by the clients and the traders has made the question, "Where are the contracts?" as difficult to answer as the other taboo question, "What is their value?"

The Modalities of Reconciliation

The reconciliation of the two databases lasted for more than three years. It kept the "fixed income" middle office busy throughout that period. It also brought into the bank a cohort of consultants who shouldered the General Bank operators through the many reconciliation problems. These turned out to be troubled times for the front office as the past modeling practices were reviewed and a more *rational* modeling formalism was enforced. "Rational" was a much-debated term during these times, as it basically came down to finding the one modeling system that would tie in the front- and back-office databases and rule out future disjunctures between products' expressions *here* and *there*. Rational specifically meant setting the rule for future front-office behavior, as it quickly became clear that the back office would not be remodeled. Traders would keep their authority through the ticket-based modifications mechanism, but they would also behave.

A former trader, Guillaume, orchestrated the wholesale remodeling that the bank launched with the reconciliation. Everyone talked of him as the specialist in TRADE, the pricing software. Guillaume had arrived at this desk at

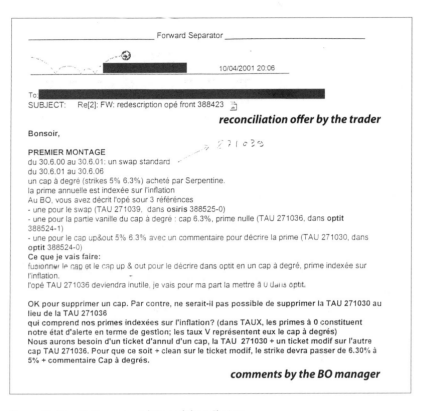

_____ Forward Separator _____

10/04/2001 20:06

To:
SUBJECT: Re[2]: FW: redescription opé front 388423

reconciliation offer by the trader

Bonsoir,

PREMIER MONTAGE
du 30.6.00 au 30.6.01: un swap standard
du 30.6.01 au 30.6.06
un cap à degré (strikes 5% 6.3%) acheté par Serpentine.
la prime annuelle est indexée sur l'inflation
Au BO, vous avez décrit l'opé sour 3 références
- une pour le swap (TAU 271039, dans osiris 388525-0)
- une pour la partie vanille du cap à degré : cap 6.3%, prime nulle (TAU 271036, dans optit 388524-1)
- une pour le cap up&out 5% 6.3% avec un commentaire pour décrire la prime (TAU 271030, dans optit 388524-0)
Ce que je vais faire:
fusionner le cap et le cap up & out pour le décrire dans optit en un cap à degré, prime indexée sur l'inflation.
l'opé TAU 271036 deviendra inutile, je vais pour ma part la mettre à 0 dans optit.

OK pour supprimer un cap. Par contre, ne serait-il pas possible de supprimer la TAU 271030 au lieu de la TAU 271036
qui comprend nos primes indexées sur l'inflation? (dans TAUX, les primes à 0 constituent notre état d'alerte en terme de gestion; les taux V représentent eux le cap à degrés)
Nous aurons besoin d'un ticket d'annul d'un cap, la TAU 271030 + un ticket modif sur l'autre cap TAU 271036. Pour que ce soit + clean sur le ticket modif, le strike devra passer de 6.30% à 5% + commentaire Cap à degrés.

comments by the BO manager

Figure 14. Negotiations around Remodeling Choices

its inception, in the mid-1990s and he immediately familiarized himself with TRADE. The high level of turnover of traders and engineers left him stranded as the only one able to implement and run a remodeling operation of this size. At the beginning of my field research, he had already remodeled a large number of the desk's 1,300 operations. Remodeling aimed to make possible the daily and automatic reconciliation of the back- and front-office databases. Reconciliation was thus a post-TRADE project—a pragmatic exercise rather than the ideal, foundational change envisioned by TRADE. Rather than an entirely new way of thinking about linking two offices, reconciliation was designed as another layer of code connecting the two culturally conflicting databases.

When reconciliation was settled upon, the front- and back-office databases were not prepared for this additional layer of code. Their interfaces were not designed to become feeders to still another database. Tying the databases thus exposed the depth of financial transactions kept in databases for several years. Contracts represented prices, but they were also hundreds of interconnected code modules. Redesigning not only involved questions of financial engineering but also shook the computing sides of these contracts. The prerequisite of remodeling was reviewing: all the operations once modeled in TRADE had to be analyzed, and standard models had to be designed along the lines of large product families. Previous traders had sometimes keyed in operations quite randomly, without sticking to one particular modeling convention. This desk's orientation toward "complex products" tended to favor *inspired* and *artistic* modeling. Each contract would be modeled as unique, regardless of its family resemblance with contracts already modeled in the database. Things were easier for the back-office operators called upon to rationalize and standardize their databases: creativity and inspiration had never been highly prized values there. The back office was rigidly organized as a matter of course; the standardization was established and the plug-in made easily. The back-office staff's habits and interaction with the accountants made them willing to accept the minor changes entailed by the reconciliation. The front-office's database was not as easy to integrate into the reconciliation. From financial operations worded on confirmations to TRADE objects populating the base, there was no "one best way." One and the same contract produced multiple TRADE compositions. Extracting contract information from the front-office's modeling database was as difficult as the keying was loose in its approach. The reconciliation thus brought far greater upheavals for the front-office staff.

The software launched to operate the reconciliation of the databases was called the Federating Tool (FED for short, from which the term to "FEDize" was derived, meaning to run an operation in the Federating Tool software). Its function was to link up data inputs from the back- and front-office databases. Each of the operations that had to be reconciled also had to be fully integrated into the new FED database. Inventing this new software and its associated databases had consequences in terms of the trading-room organization. Reconciliation gave status to the middle office. In many trading rooms, the middle-office function was and still is hardly formalized in the bank's organization. Here, its recognition by the head of the trading room was such that it was located in the room itself, next to the traders but with an additional constraint. Sited in between front- and back-office staff, they had to master the modeling of each of the information systems to be able to carry out successfully the "reconciliation" operations of each database.

Regarding the internal deals between desks in the bank, although this operation had to be keyed in twice in two different places, the middle-office staff in charge of the reconciliation re-did the operations in identical form but on yet another database. After confirmation by means of the paper document, the new database could be compared with the FIX and TRADE databases. A series of functionalities in the FED software served to launch the reconciliation check as such. This fastidious work of negotiation between the two groups of operators could take several weeks. The delays and refusals in making alterations to the existing versions of contracts kept by these groups made the reconciliation a long process. After the parties had agreed on the final form of these operations, the databases were monitored daily to ensure their stability and the absence of any one-sided change to the contracts' terms. The trader's monopoly on modeling was not terminated, but it became public information, shared with the other offices and checked by their operators.

The reconciliation exercise was tricky because it required remodeling contracts while they were already in portfolio. The amount of contracts that would come to terms in more than five to seven years was such that the decision was taken to not wait for their initial modeling to phase out. For most of the contracts, the switch was straightforward, if costly. The consultants who were hired by the bank to speed up the conversion had started with these products. The value of the portfolio did not move during the contracts' conversion. These were the relatively easy operations, but they were followed by fewer contracts that were so unique in their terms that they had to be remodeled one by one. Because they were one of a kind contracts—sometimes belonging to a family of only a few contracts—their value was nothing but their *current-model* value. No benchmark would correct that model by offering a competing value by a similar contract. In such cases, TRADE objects and their chosen combination were not only an organizational and categorization concern, they were also the only source of value of the contract. With the margins of action left to the trader who remodeled these exotic contracts, the value before conversion became one touchstone of the quality of the new model chosen. A huge shift following the conversion would hint at a problem with the modeling decision just made. It could indicate that the new form given to the products did not correspond financially to what the contract meant and what the previous version of the model had translated. The remodeling thus had to be done along the way, in phase with long market trends and short shifts. The market value of the products thus took on two dimensions: fluctuating with the market, it also served as a fixed point for the remodeling operation.

Changes in data entry that Guillaume devised could not be implemented *outside* the market, withdrawn from the traders' portfolios. Each conversion of an exotic contract became a quasi-experiment monitored locally by the middle office, much like financial products are observed in the market by the trader when he or she is not busy remodeling. The spread between the initial model and the new model's value was the key variable, and the middle office's close scrutiny was intended to discern the distinct causes underlying the divergence between old and new models. Even when the modeling is stable, this task is not easy. The underlying markets driving the value of these products keep moving as the conversion is activated. Unlike the simulation conducted by the trader's assistant, the conversion is quicker, but market shifts can be faster still, and the formula of these exotic products can magnify small shifts into big payoff gains or losses. During the conversion, the middle-office operators became metatraders, hedging between changes made on the TRADE contracts' architectures, the minute details prized by the back office, and shifts in the market outside of the bank. The full completion of reconciliation demanded several iterations, whereby pairs of coherent categorizations would be obtained (TRADE-FED, FED-FIX), and the stability of the price would be reached. This point of equilibrium could take several rounds.

The exotics desk, literally by the very design of products, was rife with daily *chaos*. This chaos was caused by the changes that the parties to this financial dance afforded themselves. Remodeling added to this blurring. By suspending even momentarily the form of contracts, it masked—except to the modelers—the value of the contracts. This confusion presented an opportunity for traders to reassert their monopoly of competencies on the TRADE software, which is what gave Guillaume a considerable degree of freedom. He was the only one in this phase of reformatting to really master the TRADE grammar and to understand how the objects had to be linked up in order to describe a product. This privilege was also a mixed blessing because he became the sole target of a large population of middle-office operators, who spent their days stalking changes to the portfolio of products. Against his monopoly and the custom-made application that allowed him to implement the massive reconciliation process, the middle-office operators developed a cult status of the *original* document—the immaculate contract. They sided, strategically, with the back-office managers in their mistrust of the swift and sometimes hasty manipulation of the traders.

The reconciliation operations involved a return to the paper form of the contract. It was necessary to go back to the origins of contracts to clean up and consolidate the databases into a single reliable one. But where could these paper contracts be found? In the bank, the products were archived for years, yet they underwent modifications. Was the original one the first, immaculate version of the confirmation or was the last one (literally and figuratively) the ultimate contract? Was the original document the client's version or one of the in-house versions? To the imperative of nurturing an agreement between in-house centers having conflicting cultures, the bank added another—the need for a parallel agreement with the inconstant client, who was quick to take advantage of his or her status as a quasi-engineer. With unscheduled sequences of transformations and a moving referent, things were tricky.

Memorizing Changing Products

The search for the appropriate model is associated with another problem: financial documents must be saved. Even though financial operations are expressed in multiple ways (from the ticket to the confirmation, from the front-office database to the back-office database), contact must also be kept with the client's version that sits outside the bank. Traders and clients have to be able to compare the data on their confirmation sheets. Nothing is easier if they have the *same* confirmation. But due to the reframing of its terms, not one but a series of confirmations are issued. Often, more than ten confirmations are exchanged by post, fax, or email over the lifetime of a transaction. Despite the back office's long digital memory, every ticket and confirmation is kept until the term of the contract. However, the accumulation of these documents on the bank's back-office shelves raises several problems. Where should they be stored if they are to meet two demands: as immaculate reference, and as accessible documents to operators located two floors apart?

First, this accumulation slows verifications. When contacted by a customer, the back-office manager must fetch the relevant file from the cabinet in which all the operations under his or her responsibility are stored. Upon opening the file, *all* the versions of the confirmation are investigated. They are all there, each one bearing the "final version" stamp, shedding little light on their current validity. The file also contains all of the documents that the back-office manager has considered useful to keep—which facilitate an understanding of the operation. These consist of e-mail exchanges between the trader, the middle-office staff in charge of this type of operation, and a person from the back-office team who guarantees the contact with the client. The complexity and time span of certain operations contribute to the substantial thickness of the memory files.

The elements pertaining to the deals in the trader's possession (the initial ticket) are no longer valid and have to be aligned with whatever is mentioned on the confirmations. A client will not trust a trader waving his or her ticket with illegible scribbles; she or he will not agree to enter into the middle of an internal bank investigation. The only valid document is the confirmation. The different states of this document can only inform one of the changes that it has undergone during its successive versions. In any case—and unlike the cognitive profusion observed earlier with the products' models—this profusion of versions is a hindrance rather than an asset. It cannot put an end to the quarrels that erupt between front office, back office, and the client from disagreements concerning the amounts that need to be paid off. The confirmation thus acquires a particular status. It becomes the only document that can protect the bank in case of an erroneous reading by the client, whether deliberate or not, and it is the only document reaching the client's treasury. The weight on this single document stems from a combination of factors:

- the confusion that the multiplication of underlyings causes, particularly with the launching of the product and its input into management databases;
- the regular changes affecting customized products under pressure from clients who want customized services;

- the high turnover of the bank's staff, which makes it impossible to rely on live operators' memory;
- the strong exposure of product files to the pace and chaotic circulation of the trading rooms.

In this context, a confirmation file's disappearance is dreaded. This eventuality has led the back-office managers to consider two solutions for safeguarding these archives: (1) holding them in a vault, off the *market* movements, impersonated by the front office's speedy and casual manners; and (2) making them ubiquitous across the bank's multiple centers through a platform with digital versions.

Finance in a File

Until the decision to switch from paper to digital documents, records of product versions were stored in thick and heavy file binders in the trading room, within the reach of traders' assistants.[19] Each binder contained from twenty to forty files, sorted by chronological order of issuance. Each file was kept together in a transparent sleeve, which could get quite thick as new tickets and confirmations were added. These sleeves, although detachable from the binder, were to stay inside it: a binder was big enough that it would be easy to spot when misplaced, whereas a transparent sleeve could easily be mistaken for still another stack of discarded printouts. Consultation of an operation file necessarily entailed moving the entire binder, displacing it with all the other operations stored in it from the shelf. Regularly, a trader's assistant, busy checking the terms of an operation, temporarily placed the binder on a shelf situated between two computer monitors or above them. As waves of inquiries required mobilizing them, the contracts within the folders would be moved around. Often, binders went missing or operation files were removed from them despite the rule, long established, that bulky binders were the safest containers of files.

Back-office managers did not check these front-office files. A second version of the binders, identical to that of the front office, was located in the back-office manager's area, a few stories up in the same building.[20] Situated in two places, the materiality of these documents was perceived as their main weakness.[21] The binder structure that was arbitrarily used to attach operations files together was pointed out as a flaw. Because files should not be taken off the binder, everything had to circulate together. Yet, despite the rule, losses occurred. The disappearance of one of the binders was a traumatic moment in this changeover from paper records to digital records. A popular anecdote about how the bank had lost a huge amount of money when a binder had gone missing circulated among the back-office staff. The back-office manager and the trader had accepted changes to a contract, but the trader had not immediately updated it into his pricer. The ticket had been added to the front-office binder file, but thereafter, nobody could find the file. The trader had been hedging an outdated version of the product, as if nothing had changed. When eventually the difference between the back office's version, the client's version, and the trader's version was exposed, the trader was forced to pay off much more than he had calculated from the previous state.

The Safe

Against the risk of exposing the archives to the rhythm of markets, the bank had first opted for the duplication solution. By putting aside an unalterable version of confirmations, in another part of the bank and under the responsibility of other people, the contracts existed in the same paper formats as in the front and back offices but were no longer handled by the traders or the back-office managers. There, confirmations could finally live without negligent treatment. But this protection against the whirl of updatings triggered by clients' hesitation had its limits. The guardians of these archives were taking too literally their role: "hands off" was their paradoxical understanding of maintenance. Even their own hands were kept at a distance. As a consequence, this archive was not regularly updated for fear of disrupting its purity. Often, it was not updated at all, so that one would find only the initial confirmations in their original state in the files.

This retreat off the "market" (from regular consultations) could be read in the absence of financial expertise from the people who were responsible for maintaining this archive. During my observations—between 2000 and 2001—these operators had been placed in this position a couple of years before they were expected to retire. Three women were in charge of these files. One of them was on a prolonged maternity leave for at least half of the time I

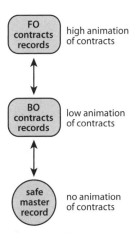

Figure 15. Withdrawing Products away from the Front Office, into a Safe

was present. The other two had been sent on other missions during that period. None of the three were familiar with the content of the files. On several occasions, operations that were supposed to be in these files were said to be "missing" when they could not be found in the back-office manager's database. They were simply unknown to the guardians of this valuable collection. The motivation among back-office staff in contact with clients was absent in the archiving operations. By keeping these files separate and protecting them, the bank could easily lose sight of them. Thus, when these contract documents were laid to rest, they gradually became buried. Never consulted, poorly archived, and moreover virtually unknown, these files were often unusable. It was as if the solicitations of the market were no longer felt by these financial products. Operations within the archive department—not least of all the staff's low competencies and their imminent retirement—contributed toward slowing down the market.

The speed of the transactions under the salesperson's influence—relayed by the traders, and taken up by the back-office managers—irreversibly ran out of steam when they reached the safe. The imperative for a sure database, a place away from the hectic rhythms and vicissitudes of the market, immediately subjected the archive to an equally threatening disconnect between its movements and those of the market. Counting transactions could not take place anywhere else but *in* the transaction itself. The constant animation of these contracts challenged the strategy of a gradient of stability achieved through this remote safe far removed from the front office.

Changing the Nature of the Medium

The second solution to the loss of memory incurred by these highly animated contracts was to orient the management of documents in an entirely different direction: a switch to digital archives.[22] Unlike the previous solution—reconciliation—that had been enforced bank-wide, this second solution was meant to be local, tailored to the constraints posed by the class of products managed there. The fear of seeing paper documents turn to dust or get lost was decisive in this choice. But the required change had other functions: it was not only for the protection of the data that generated wealth for the bank; it was also a way of taking over client relations from the middle-office and back-office operators (by a more expert hand, it was said). The slowness of operators too distant from the clients would be bypassed by giving the staff in the front office all the documents they needed to control the operations.[23] By thus shifting the memory of the products (i.e., the product management base) from the back to the front office, the delegation of power downstream from the initial client relationship was reduced to a strict minimum.

The perimeter of access to the tool gave the head of the desk a greater supervisory capacity.[24] The head of the desk's watchword had been to eliminate "paper," throughout a phase of consultation with the operators involved in the use of this database. But the real aim, acknowledged privately, was to tighten control over the traders' assistants and a few casual traders. Without this common database, each of the operators involved had developed one unique to their own base. Traders' assistants created personal databases, usually using an Excel spreadsheet, that enabled them to communicate with their trader, the salespeople whose contracts they managed, as well as the back- and middle-office staff. These databases were fragmented and failed to integrate and document the changes made directly by e-mail with the clients. Because email was used in many of the data exchanges between the back office and the assistant traders, it was necessary to link these email documents describing the different phases of the product to others. The Excel database thus contained a file in its Lotus Notes mail software. But as it was out of the question to create a file for each deal, the Lotus Notes files would cover not one product but families of products. This high level of aggregation made it impossible to link e-mails explicitly to data relevant to the operation.

An exclusively digital mode of existence for the contracts was to change the bank's topography once again by locating the innermost memory of the bank into a continuous, if folded, interface. Under these conditions, the back-office staff was simply left to validate transactions and inform the bank treasurer of the amounts to be paid to customers' accounts. A digital database with scanned copies of the variety of documents constituting the contract made the idea of a back office obsolete. Yet, empowering the front office against the back-office intrusion into deals brought to light and exacerbated tensions among front-office staff.

The first point of divergence involved consultation. It was necessary to define a hierarchy within the trading room, both in the management of tasks and in terms of handling client relations. There were two contrasting points of view. The first was that the software should be open to each and every trading-room operator, salesperson, legal advisor, financial engineer, trader, and assistant trader. In this scenario, everyone would be able to open the program from their computers and consult the history of an operation. This solution left open the question of data and attachments input (feeding the database). The possibility of input by anyone, without restriction, was quickly excluded as it could jeopardize the credibility of the database for its most demanding users: the traders. Traders insisted that operators who were not in charge of the management of the contracts would have weaker incentives to feed the database in a clean manner. The adopted solution allowed only some of the staff members (the traders and their assistants) to write data and granted reading access to all in the room. The traceability of successive changes to contracts and their related documents was, in turn, an incentive for the traders and their assistants to add data cautiously.

When the perimeter of operators allowed to write was determined, the question of consultation became even more acute. Prohibiting the other operators in the trading room from consulting the database, once the data keyed in were accurate and the base reliable, became untenable. Among these operators were the salespeople. They had initially not been informed of the project. Their deliberate exclusion was justified by the traders, pointing to the conflicts existing between the two groups. Their relations with the clients were polarized in different ways. The salespeople were aware that their bonuses were derived from the number and volume of contracts that they brought to the bank. The traders were aware that they, themselves, had to manage these contracts and to guarantee the bank's solvency by ensuring that, at their terms, the operations would not cause the desk to lose money. Traders' work, therefore, effectively started when salespeople's work ended. This asymmetry of the two functions in the trading room was the origin of many conflicts. Salespeople regularly urged the traders to take on riskier positions to generate volume and to get clients to stay with the bank. To attract new clients, traders and engineers were forced to propose very low prices. The salespeople were sufficiently well acquainted with the engineers to be able to negotiate with them. By encroaching on their field of expertise and invoking another, more concrete type of expertise, the salespeople constantly called into question a well-established division of tasks. The initiators of the digitization project wanted to avoid these very conflicts and quarrels over commercial expertise. Their main concern was to not give salespeople too much of the engineers' information, to avoid enabling the former to bypass the latter. A trader assistant who was deeply involved in this project related the following anecdote:

> Yuri, I know for sure, has already given his client a price. He had the engineer spreadsheet and his simulation of possible baskets and he gave that away to the client without asking anybody anything. Because that was his client and he did not want to look bad and just a middleman. It was a done deal when he came to us.

The sharing of information on *pricing stricto sensu* thus housed the risk of a reversal in the sharing of tasks. In the end, only traders and their assistants had access to the tools. Consultation was controlled, and data input as well as the attachment of documents to operations was traceable. In the final version of the software delivered to the desk, all the deals were managed by an explorer and by an interface of queries. They were stored in a database according to the operation's main characteristics. Each of these operations was represented on a line, along with its characteristics. By clicking on one of these lines, the user accessed a window that grouped together links that had been attached to this operation: the various confirmations, the initial ticket, the subsequent tickets, the e-mails exchanged by the actors involved. By clicking on these links, the documents that had been attached to the operation were retrieved.[25]

Folding the Organization

This software addresses the memory of financial transactions in a way different from that proposed by the physical duplication of documents. It solves the time–space problem of the instantaneous updating of the documents that storage within the safe prevented. But more important to our analysis, it also relocates the place of the counting. The safe is not a solution for contracts that have to beat in synch with their commercial rhythms. Put aside, they decay— unlike gold and some other mediums of exchange, whose immutable compositions are impervious to the daily ups and downs of the market.[26] An ounce of gold will always be an ounce of gold; only the price per ounce counts. Although CGPs may be advertised as better than gold, they have starkly different characteristics: they change as the market fluctuates; they are indexed to securities that disappear and have to be replaced; and they use original payoff formulas that require the collaboration of multiple parts of the bank and a sound understanding of the client. Because of these numerous links that tie these products to the underlying markets from which they acquire their value, they cannot be detached too much or for too long.

Digitizing documents that until then existed only on paper, and networking the various electronic documents in a heterogeneous database, produced a major change in the topography of bank operations. By redrawing the boundaries by which people understood who had the authority to design and update contracts and to state their numbers and natures, the adopted solution represented an attempt by the bank to redefine the hierarchies in this branch. The salespeople, always eager to supersede their prerogatives and encroach on traders' turf, were kept at a distance by traders and their assistants. The collaboration was not broken off; on the contrary, it became more fluid. It was

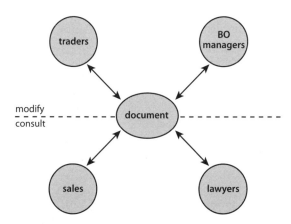

Figure 16. Putting the Digital Product in between Operators

nevertheless framed by an information tool that gave access to products that were clearly both delimited and delimiting. Likewise, the middle and back offices were short-circuited, and any intelligence on the products was *gathered* toward the front office. Using an image that is dear to topologists, the fabric of the organization was folded toward the front office, and relieved the back-office staff of a whole range of tasks. The distances between the points of this new surface were altered significantly: the traders and their assistants worked in closer collaboration, and the information usually handled by the back office was "moved closer" to the heads of the desk, whose supervisory role was enhanced. The formerly conflicted relations with postmarket operators grew more amicable, and the assistant traders' responsibility grew.

These conflicts, the primary subject of most interactions between the back-office members, also revealed one aspect of product management in these databases. As the traders were gradually pushed toward the back office, from front applications to back applications, the flexibility of use decreased markedly. The traders' breaches of good use and compliance were ruled out by the applications. From this point of view, the fact of the trading-room staff taking a hand in producing the product records marked a turning point. The adoption of a constraining software architecture that broke away from the front-office tradition of inspired modeling introduced into the room an attentiveness to the conservation and care of the material *forms* of the operations that, until then, were the business of the back-office staff. It also indicated that the commercial nature of these products was taken into account, even after their sale, which required them to be left in a place of maximum exposure to the rhythms of market fluctuations.

Hedge on the Edge

The perennial question of the topology of the firm is reactivated on a regular basis by economists and organizational theorists. What should go on inside? What is the core of a firm? Firms are indeed so distributed that their topography can trick observers into seeing nothing but networks of ties where there are crucial differences between modules with more or less control.[27] We will see the political turn taken by the dilemma over the best topography of General Bank in chapter 7, when operators actively manipulate the integration of the room's parts to strengthen its unity. Here, the issue of the bank's best organization is raised by the daring design of a product. Not yet a strategy, the topography is an outcome of a commercial service that challenges the very existence of the bank's boundaries.

What happens to an organization that deals in products whose form requires the end of the organization itself? These financial products have an unusual characteristic: their value is known if and only if they are exposed to their constitutive markets. Respecting their spirit and controlling their risk requires that they be held in an unstable equilibrium on the edge of the bank. Other types of products could be treated less chaotically, but the formulas for CGPs preclude these products from lying dormant in a safe. Their necessary vibration is no longer guaranteed if they are relegated to the dusty shelves of a remote stronghold. This chapter illustrates the reversal of the banking topography produced by products that demand to be both protected at the core and exposed on the periphery, here and there, in the hands of both the salesperson and the client, while remaining within reach of the trader's assistant. The bank is a fine example of a Deleuzian body without organs (Deleuze, 1987): CGPs push it from the inside, expose its entrails at the surface, and question the attempts at grading that the various processing centers try to set up.

What these products enable us to see has particular relevance for understanding organizations. To clearly understand the functioning of human entities embedded in lasting arrangements (technologies and rules), it is essential to follow the flows circulating at the heart of these unstable constructions. But more than the trails of these flows, the properties of these circulating products inform us about the organization. The upheaval these new financial services cause, and the care they require, highlight their boundaries with precision. The questions surrounding the conservation of the bank's operations show how the choice of customization and the complexity of financial formulas affect its organization. In respect for the spirit of these products, conservation is trumped if it means having to withdraw them from the market. But that is not their only requirement, for another risk emerges on the horizon: unbridled management in which financial operations are allowed to circulate too freely. Although their complexity demands the maximum of contact points, the products are averse to a dispersion that overlooks the strict adherence to the letter of the contracts. The client is omnipresent, and behind this client are other shareholders who demand from the bank a solidity that an overly whimsical management would not provide.

PART III

Porous Banking: Clients and Investors in Search of Accounts

If the trading room mimics a laboratory by strictly controlling all the trans actions taking place at its margins, the financial experiment still owes some of its features to outside factors. The last part of *Codes of Finance* pays attention to the interferences created by outside forces in this quasi-laboratory. The open communication required of the bank so far occurred exclusively through two channels: first, through the job market pumping new operators in and out, and second, through the Exchanges on which traders and their assistants would carry out hedging in the afternoon. But neither the job market nor the Exchanges demanded special negotiations. They did not modify the perimeter of the firm either.[1]

Yet, General Bank was at the intersection of more than two transaction spaces. Its business was primarily designing and commercializing CGPs to clients, and, in order to achieve that task, getting access to sources of fresh capital was a necessity. The Exchanges were not only sites for hedging; they were also sites for financing. There, the bank would raise money by issuing its debt or by increasing its equity. Investors in search of the most lucrative investment assessed General Bank shares on the Exchanges against other publicly traded companies, financial and others. General Bank subjected itself to other forms of calculation that it did not control on the Exchanges. Sophisticated models, such as those described earlier, were applied to probe the bank's overall value. Although this position offered more autonomy to the bank inasmuch as it was designing the product and choosing its most appropriate financial structure, it turned out that the privilege of invention took a toll on the real autonomy of its operators. In addition to keeping an eye on the competition waged by other finance firms, the bank had to be attentive to clients buying the CGPs and to investors[2] buying its property titles. These two constituencies reciprocated generously, scrutinizing the bank's activities, invading its space, and challenging its monopoly of expertise.[3] Existing at this intersection surely thins the boundaries of the bank, and the two new actors who most contributed to this porosity are the new main characters covered in our travel through the bank.

The clients and investors of a bank challenge the bank operators not only because they expect the operators to foresee what the next market convulsions will be but also, and more radically, because they claim participation in the bank's decision-making process. Instead of salaried workers bargaining for better remunerations, clients and investors demand to be heard regarding the design of the products and the overall organization of the company. With these compromises, bank operators are no longer solely in control. Control was the traders' and engineers' key word when they were launching their new products, but when traders were hedging, the constraints and hurdles they faced to keep their portfolios afloat stood outside. Those problems were difficult to steer through, but they did not make claims on the right to dictate the bank's strategies. With the advent of the CGP, clients and investors can instill their views on the bank operators, and what was formerly a self-contained entity suddenly looks more like a hub than like a company making its decisions autonomously.[4]

To understand the presence of clients and investors, it is once again useful to reinvestigate the unique combination of transparency and secrecy built into the CGP business. The modus operandi of the product—what we have called the general economic gesture of derivation—creates a new security by recombining existing underlyings. This process does not black-box the product. Rather, it opens up its machinery to the curious gaze of the client.[5] Remember the prospectus: everything seems transparent and open to discussion. Why this underlying rather than another one? Why 120 percent and not 130 percent? It is all there, open to scrutiny. This transparency has been

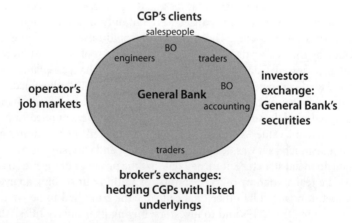

Figure 17. The Porosity of General Bank

taken to its ultimate consequences by the desk: clients are given the opportunity to customize the service.[6] Clients have their say, not only up front, when the characteristics of the product are initially defined, but also whenever a relevant event in the market gives him or her cause to request a product change. Yet, the bank attempts to keep control of the product design. As a consequence of these contradictory pulls, the stabilization of the product into a contract can take time, sometimes as long as the product is held by the bank. The combination of complex design and authorized hesitation set the stage for long transactions. Unlike transactions around unproblematic goods or services—such as the exchange-based underlyings and futures—that close instantly, CGP negotiations are never on solid ground because even if the payoff formula is literal and alluringly transparent, nothing else is clear in these products. Unlike cycles of gifts (Mauss, 1924) that recur over time with a frequency and timing as crucial to their efficacy as the amount of goods returned, the interactions between the clients and the bank have no predefined schedule. As a result, they leave open the transactions to potential further requests and additional negotiations. Once the clients are working within the bank and challenging the engineers on their turf, no one knows how the transaction will end up.

Yet, the attention to high-maintenance clients does not mark the end of the toll taken by innovative finance. At the other end of the bank, on the highly standardized securities market, investors deploy treasures of ingenuity to anticipate the future returns and decide whether to buy a bank's equity. These investors are General Bank's peers, sometimes its partners on other deals, and they submit the deal to the same techniques that the local engineers apply to the products' underlyings. Yet, when they consider the bank as a security and not as a financial service provider, the nature of transactions changes, and the expectations shift to another register. The unique structuring offered by the CGP is no longer sought here because General Bank shares are in an absolute performance race with a host of other publicly traded companies. Unlike the many services offered by its star product, the bank can do only one thing for its shareholders: rise high and rise fast. Compared with the pampered designs offered to the client, the investor wants very little of design when it comes to foreseeing future results—a figure and no design.

Ironically, the investor's tragedy is orchestrated by this frivolous client, but indirectly. The client's relentless inquiry of the bank is exacerbated by the lack of accounting transparency for the structured contracts delivered to the clients. The exact opposite of the apparent clarity of the prospectus, the production of the yearly profit/cost of the CGP follows tortuous and winding roads that demand expert eyes to decipher. The customization of products, their long duration, and their increasing structural entanglement place them at odds with accounting imperatives. At the same time that they have won the praise of their peers, General Bank's exotic derivatives activities have raised the concerns of its owners and of the regulatory agencies monitoring financial firms. The accounting puzzle created by the CGPs is not limited to the exercise of financial accounting per se. The question of costs concerns the bank before even the disciplinary contortions often generated by products that are bound to the off-balance-sheet zone.[7] In the first part of this book, the hedging prowess of the traders dealt with the prices of CGPs, and infinite caution was taken to save pennies for the bank. But no one was concerned with costs. This was the repressed unconscious of fetishized products. The trading room did not question the wealth of support at the disposal of the traders' unique activity: hedging properly priced products. Yet, this sole activity contained a cost for the bank. Actually, it was more than just a cost. A cost would have been easy, but instead of a unique figure, the bank had difficulties circumscribing the limits of these many costs that unexpectedly plagued the general economy of CGPs. This budgeting opacity could not have zero consequences on accounting proper, and soon calls for transparency propagated by the regulatory agency resounded in General Bank.

CHAPTER 5

❙

Selling Finance and the Promise of Contingency

❚ **A New Actor in the Landscape of the Bank**

From the complex topography of the bank observed in chapters 3 and 4, it became clear that salespeople were standing at a crucial juncture for the business of secrecy. Moving back and forth between clients and engineers, salespeople straddle an expensive borderland between that which is inside the bank and that which is outside. The main problem facing them as they shuttle back and forth between these two areas is therefore one of border control. As we have seen, even within its confines the bank is not unitary, and selling these complex products forces salespeople to negotiate the small but entrenched communities within the bank whose jobs revolve around defining the product. Traders, engineers, and lawyers all have legitimate opinions as to the development of a product, but salespeople have an even more legitimate opinion in a context where clients are the ultimate short-term[1] arbiters of a new product's success. As such, salespeople are central agents in making the skin of the institution grow thinner to allow for passage between its outside (the client) and its inside (the front office).

Yet, this ability to settle bank disputes by invoking the clients' needs or whims is complicated by the fact that clients are nominal placeholders. Clients are not yet there. From the perspective of groups and individuals involved with developing and marketing novel financial products, clients are both notional and actual—they exist as agents in their own right and also serve as placeholders in the development of products. Their chief characteristic is to have preferences, which is also the most problematic of their properties, as this chapter will make clear. Clients of innovative financial services do not know what their preferences are. On the one hand, this lacuna can translate into flexibility for the salesperson and make innovation possible—leaving maneuvering room upstream in the client's decision-making process wherein the salesperson can "educate" the client. On the other hand, this process of shaping the client's preferences also brings them dangerously close to the inner circle of product development and establishes an intimacy that subverts the distinction between the service provider and the service customer.

Who are the clients who purchase these expensive products? General Bank catered to two classes of clients that marketing studies have tended to separate neatly: individual clients and corporate clients. These two types of clients are brought to the desk by two different General Bank arms. Individuals are brought to the exotics desk by an arm aptly named, "private banking."[2] Private banking is a form of retail banking for high net worth individuals (HNWIs), wealthy clients with special needs that demand more than the standard retail banking set of services.[3] This population has increased very quickly over the past thirty years with the polarization of wealth: more capital in the hands of a few individuals and increases in poverty-level families. Like retail banking, private banking is organized around a network of outlets, but in the case of private banking, these outlets are both more centralized and more internationally distributed. HNWIs cannot be pampered simply in the ways extended to ordinary clients. They are treated to meetings in the bank's cozy headquarters in Paris and at high-end restaurants where deals are gently discussed, among other appropriate topics.[4] As private banking intends to be a uniquely customized set of services, all aspects of wealth management are considered (legal, fiscal, and financial).[5] Yet, for all its alluring properties, Paris is too limited a center to capture much of the worldwide wealth, and General Bank private banking is also organized as a network of international representatives who seek out wealth wherever its global services (through General Bank SG Private Banking) to HNWIs are offered. Although private bankers conduct thorough analyses of the market products available and best suited to their clients, they naturally push General Bank's in-house services and their asset management arm.

In contrast with individual clients, the corporate and investment banking arm of General Bank is responsible for bringing companies to the desk. Much as wealthy individuals struggle to figure out what to do with their assets, these companies are in search of ways to invest their cash that are more liquid than investment in industrial enterprises. General Bank provides these companies with fully integrated suites of services covering tax and accounting issues and also provides a direct channel of product updates for treasurers who do not wish to spend all their time browsing for the latest financial innovations. If HNWIs and corporate treasurers needed a standard service, they would not contact a salesperson working for the exotics desk. At the same time, this contact does not necessarily mean they know precisely what they want. Sometimes, they simply reach out in an open and vague manner. Nor do they always know where they stand in terms of risk exposure. As such, salespeople at General Bank in large part served as navigators for their clients. By exposing them to a new class of products that offered two seemingly contradictory profiles—investment and insurance—they planted the seeds of confusion.

CGPs shake the existing markets through their new properties and are disruptive of the existing order. This disruption is both an asset and a risk. It is the only way to displace existing preferences and to substitute the new formula—combining investment and insurance—for established financial services that only offer one or the other. However, driving a wedge into the preferences of prospective clients can destabilize them and force the bank's salespeople to rebuild a fragile client who has lost the solid ground of his or her previous routines. Destabilization, however, does not necessarily mean falling prey to the latest marketing campaign—the bank could just as easily create more confusion. Controlling the risk of an even more confused client entails teaching the client what his or her preferences should be: once the client's previous views are shattered, the marketing department must assist in their reconstruction. This new role brings new risks for the trading room. If a client whose preferences can be shaped is a precious resource for the bank, it is also a mixed blessing because it forces salespeople and engineers to imagine themselves *as* clients. Doing so further destabilizes the role that each group strives to impose in the cacophonic trading room. "If I were a client, what would I need, what would I buy, and what would be my limits?": these questions preoccupy the salespeople, who do not hesitate to pass them on to the other relevant actors of the room. These moments during which sales-people and engineers imagine what reactions their products will elicit are not specific to new financial services: whenever new products are designed, a designer must destabilize his own personal identity in order to simulate the viewpoints of potential consumers. What is unique in the case of General Bank Private Banking's novel financial products is the capacity of clients to cross the divide in the other direction, inviting themselves into the trading room to discuss products on a par with engineers, salespeople, and traders. The possibility of the client negotiating the design of a product with the engineers destabilizes the already fractious coalitions of the room. If the client really does not know what he or she wants, painfully established routines in the room are slowed down and divisions of labor instituted therein are derailed.

What has become of a bank whose salespeople have to reinvent themselves as teachers for clients who do not hesitate to step into the room and dictate their taste to engineers? It seems that all bets are off and identities are up for redefinition when so much can be decided during the transaction. It is a zone of risk richly documented by anthropologists: whether the entity in circulation is a good, a person, or a performance, its transitional state raises many questions for the parties involved in an exchange. This is all the more true when the distance between the object of the transaction and those affecting the exchange is not well under control (Thomas, 1991; Weiner, 1992). When that which circulates reshapes significantly the identities of the parties, the moment of transaction is loaded with risk. The transferring of CGPs falls into that category of risk due to the series of conditions that make the alien nature of the service less than clear.

The identity crisis experienced during the transaction by the client and trading room occupants can linger much longer than the moment of trade—a property of the transaction that can be traced to the characteristics of the service itself.[6] It is paradoxically the service that reveals the closest resemblance[7] between the literal description (the formula) and the ultimate delivery (the amount of money) through a transparent contract, but it is also the one that tells least about what the actual amount will be. The value of the contract reveals itself only a posteriori. When the contract binds the two parties, each one can assess the prospect of making or losing money, but the conditionality of the payoff on the final state of the markets spreads the transaction over the term of the contract (which is more or less long). Even if salespeople wanted to reduce their transactions to the minimum amount of time necessary—a quick and momentary contact between the room and the client—the design of the product rules out such limited contact and opens the door for multiple interactions between the two parties. That is the danger of these products: they blur identities and force promiscuity upon individuals who pride them selves on exploiting the world economy from the pinnacle of a formula. The dream of a financial instrument that would do away with the industrial world and seamlessly navigate through a purely formulaic existence is put to a stop by a service laden with too many overlapping mediations.

Salespeople's Stories

A former financial engineer, who had worked in a bank where the R&D team collaborated closely with the marketing department, told me how they would develop products for the clients[8]:

> [T]he whole job was to know that there were banks which were in touch with corporate treasurers, and that we knew these corporations. We would anticipate their needs, and so we would speak with the bankers, telling them, "Say, aren't you looking for financing for such and such, and don't you think we could do this or that?" So, then, the banker would say, "Why not?" and we would give them ideas on how to guarantee their corporate clients something more advantageous than what they had planned. Generally, they ended up saying "We can't manage it" and so we would say "That's okay, we'll handle it." And so we were the providers of services, and the marketing was very much akin to a method of generating ideas for engineers, but *we* were not necessarily in direct contact with corporate. Michel,[9] on the other hand, knew many corporate people. He spoke with them over the phone very regularly, but it was rather in a friendly tone, where he would ask them where things stood regarding their portfolio, their risks, the type of structure. . . . so much so that we were aware of a lot of things. And because

we were aware of a lot of things, we could make attractive proposals to the intermediaries whom we needed in order to put things into place with the corporates.

We scrutinized *Les Échos* every morning. We would identify needs. That's what we would do. For example, we knew that they need to allocate their liquidity and that they make profits when such stock goes up. So we would look at how their stock correlated to the market, and we would offer to index the payment on an indicator matching more or less their gross income, that kind of thing. Then we would try to formalize this in the form of a product: we would define a particular product, and Michel would tell me: "There, now go get its price" and I would go and make a price. I would ask the traders how much the stocks were worth, I would make a price with a wide margin just to see, and then I would discuss the margin with Michel. Generally, he would say "Oh!! But he won't accept that!" because he had an idea of what was acceptable and what wasn't. He knew the proper way of packaging things, and as a result we tried to find ideas which made the thing appealing and fair, and which brought in large margins, and when, after all was said and done, we would find the margin, . . . it was a whole discovery process . . . , at a given time we would find out the margin, and, well, that was really the shining moment. Then, the difficult part was to get into contact with people, to meet them, to submit proposals, to change the product, to redesign the pricing program; a continuous back and forth, until the project was finally realized. That moment certainly brings about great excitement.

You're engaging in *haute couture* when you spend a lot of time with a client because he is not, himself, able to formalize his product, so you create the product for him, you do everything. It's really interesting; it truly becomes *haute couture*, in the sense that you spend months and months and months with the person. There was a large deal which we worked on for more than six months—and in the end we didn't get it; we often worked at a loss. Often, in such cases, if you work with someone on something very complicated and in the end it doesn't come to fruition, which is very, very frequent, in fact the majority of the times, he'll return the favor and put you to work on something else, maybe on a silly thing, but where he won't be looking too closely at the margin.

The most striking feature of this introduction into a salesperson's task is the dance around the client himself. Clearly, the bank cannot sell just any product to anybody, and attention needs to be paid to the economic particularities of a given situation. Information exudes from the companies or from the accounts that clients are ready to give. This work largely bypasses the actual articulation of the client. Thus, faced with a given budget structure or in anticipation of future cash flows, the salesperson imagines a product that offers a previously unavailable answer. Indices of preferences are collected through a general financial publication such as *Les Échos*, but it is also through the financial intermediaries of these *corporate* clients that salespeople make themselves indispensable.[10] This initial framing replaces face-to-face contact between banks and clients with a side/peripheral approach. Penetrating the client's economic psychology occurs through the capture of one expression: the client's needs are formulated and articulated only through one of his or her *satellites*—financial advisors or bankers. Elements of the client's life that slip into the general financial press are better indications of his or her potential preferences at this stage[11] than face-to-face meetings. Everything becomes relevant in this space because it is a clue to the client's possible needs.

The approach that Michel, head of marketing, was able to turn into an art form worked by tracking the difficulties of companies and individuals as they unfolded. Each new financial incident plaguing a potential client was an opportunity to inform salespeople and engineers about the risks the client faced and thereby opened up the potential to offer the client solutions to fend these risks off. There was a drawback to this method, however, it was dependent on the particularity of the occasion and on the freshness of the traces. General Bank implemented an alternative strategy. In order to not have to track so carefully the ups and downs of companies, salespeople would anticipate the needs of clients. They would draw up outlines of stable preferences for them, setting up concise economic fictions involving preferences and characteristics of products. Instead of hoping to derive needs from vicissitudes relayed by word-of-mouth or specialized press, the room systematized the study of preferences. The client—now an ideal client—lost in colorfulness but gained in proximity as he or she was simulated and rehearsed by the trading-room salespeople.

Sketching the Clients through the Product

I describe the process of stabilizing a notional client's preferences in this section, through two case studies. The first is a classic case from the finance literature of the 1980s, at a time when derivative products—which have since become quite standard—still needed to be accompanied by explanations in order for clients to understand and accept them. The second is taken from my fieldwork in the bank. They are both instances of financial pedagogy taking place in the room and directly influencing the client and his or her preferences. The pedagogy documented in chapter 1 did not mobilize the client: it was primarily an exercise of a product's characteristics explored between operators in search of the most appropriate code. These two cases characterize a dual movement in the qualification of products: that is, through composition and then reduction, and through opening and then closing. This rhythmic pattern has a particular affinity with the type of derivation performed by financial products. The opening/closing rhythm in the language of salespeople bears witness to the derivation of the economy that finance struggles to achieve.

Portfolio Insurance

The work of anchoring preferences (clients) to characteristics (products) is not limited to the rare instances of formal pedagogy taking place in the bank. Academics also apply much energy to the elaboration of a joint mapping of products and financial agents.[12] To illustrate how this *extraction of preferences* is the result of economic and finance theory, it is worth looking back at an important example: portfolio insurance. The practical[13] aims of these "academic" exercises are not in question here: Hayne Leland, the professor we are about to meet, was directly involved in the management of portfolio insurance. But the description of financial innovation that he targeted brings out certain elements that are only potentially in the bank's pedagogy.

Leland's article, entitled "Who Should Buy Portfolio Insurance," published in 1980, is particularly relevant to this study of the articulation of new product properties.[14] It describes the population likely to benefit from the purchase of portfolio insurance at a time when the concept was still new.[15] The CGPs that are the focus of the current study were at a slightly more mature stage in 2001, but still at a time when their principles were not yet well known by investors. A client investing in equities must immobilize amounts that will either bring him or her a profit or a loss: the client's profit is measured in the form of a relationship between this immobilization and its yield. Insurance breaks the proportionality between the portfolio's profit and the growth of securities by creating thresholds that are both downward (guarantee and insurance) and upward (by dampening the impact of the growth of securities on the portfolio or by asking for a price with allocated insurance). Portfolio insurance, anticipating CGPs, offered a solution to this dilemma between risk and return. In both cases, an investor suffers a variation in the value of his or her portfolio that is nonlinear and nonproportional to the variation of the underlying securities. The mechanism of this clever financial structure is presented in the following way, in the opening pages of the article:

> The existence of options markets can generate new opportunities for portfolio management. As Ross [1976] has shown, a complete set of options markets on a reference stock or portfolio will enable investors to achieve any desired pattern of return conditional on the terminal value of the referent asset. While "buy-and-hold" equity strategies allow investors to achieve returns *proportional* to the terminal value of a reference portfolio, buy-and-hold option strategies permit *nonproportional* returns to be achieved. A *nonproportional* return of particular interest to some investors is that which provides portfolio insurance. Equiva-

lent to a put option on the reference portfolio, portfolio insurance enables an investor to avoid losses, but capture gains, at the cost of a fixed "premium." Unfortunately, options markets do not currently exist for portfolios of securities and a portfolio of options is not equivalent to an option on a portfolio. Even when options markets do not exist, however, investors may be able to achieve *nonproportional* returns on terminal asset values by following dynamic investment strategies. . . . While the theory of option pricing suggests how to value options, and therefore how to value portfolio insurance, it does not suggest the nature of investors who would benefit from purchasing options or insurance. Unlike traditional insurance, in which everyone can benefit from a pooling of independent risks, portfolio insurance involves hedging against a common (market) risk. For every investors buying portfolio insurance, some other investors must be selling it, either by writing the appropriate put option, or by following the inverse dynamic trading strategy. Who should buy, and who should sell? In this paper, we provide a characterization of investors who will benefit from purchasing portfolio insurance. (Leland 1980, 581)

A close reading of this passage illuminates a scheme that speaks to the art of marketing in general and to the articulation of finance, in particular, as a way of bending the economy of underlyings. The presentation of portfolio insurance follows a dual motion of *opening up* and *contraction*. The *opening up* is represented by the opportunity of producing "any desired pattern of return" through the existence of option markets and the possibility of dynamic management. Whatever the structure of the client's needs, there will be a strategy that will guarantee his or her initial capital. These strategies come at a price, but the argument's strength originates from showing how it is possible to cover oneself from risk and to show the potentialities of financial engineering. What comes out from the glance at cost and risk is that the former is known, whereas the latter involves the investor in the unknown and in wagering. The *contraction* movement comes into play later, when showing differences in the universe of possibilities and connecting characteristics of financial services with those of clients. Beginning in the very introduction of the article—and developed more formally later—clients' preferences are clearly outlined. It is a clever strategy that describes a whole family of insurance services in the initial momentum of a promising market, and specifies immediately thereafter how the services will suit the preferences of certain investors. This movement is so pervasive that it is possible to lose sight of it as a technology of demonstration. The formula of portfolio insurance does not meet existing preferences of investors: it creates, on the contrary, a population within this group of investors through the mobilization of their preferences. But who has preferences? Who has ever had preferences that existed prior to the products and services preferred? The product is simply the opportunity for categorizing investors according to *their* preferences, but by preempting the question of the origin of these preferences, it sets a precedent that will make this division a lasting one.[16] The strength of this characterization resides in the fact that the product as such (a guaranteed portfolio) is cloaked by its derivative: the preferences (and the ensuing differentiation of investors) remain both the stable element in this whole story and the critical outcome of the article.

The rest of the article develops the notion of "portfolio convexity."[17] This refers to the profile of a group of securities plotted on a space linking the performance of an underlying security (x axis) and the return of the option issued on the security (y axis). According to the characteristics of the option, and depending on the number of options—with different strike prices—that a client holds for a single underlying security, it is possible to tinker with return profiles. What this article achieves is a grammar of the convexity—the definition, within one single theoretical gesture—of the categories of investors and the categories of products matching their needs. Convexity is a clever solution and one that is indeed useful in this exercise in defining an order of preferences. In its favor, it has the neatness of mathematical functions: it lends itself to representations in a two-dimensional space, which strikes a clear pedagogical note and seems remarkable for its simplicity. By immediately moving up to a higher level of generality and by imposing a language that does not admit any hesitations, the article enforces a clear image both of the investor and to the investor. This diagram has a strong ally: it involves the products that can speak its particular language. Options have a certain family resemblance with convexity, because they can fix a profile (by straightening it out) that might not otherwise suit the investor.

Preferences and convexities are in no way notions invented by portfolio insurance or CGPs. These two families of products inherit a battery of financial notions (return, risk, convexity of profiles . . .) already in use. At the same time, they reactivate and reinforce the meanings of these notions by illuminating them through a formula of products previously unknown. However, the availability of these notions must not mislead us about their genesis. Their stabilization hinges on the regular evocation of their definitions through a series of fictionalized scenes such as the one invented in the article: portfolio insurance in the 1980s, as the CGP later in the 1990s, reiterates the existence both of preferences in clients and convexity as preferences sets. Remove the central characters of these economic fictions, and the preferences/convexities disappear instantly.[18]

Training Salespeople to Think Financially

It was during an informal conversation that I learned that the object of my investigation was the subject of a course offered to the trading-room operators. A professor in financial mathematics who taught at a Paris university and at one of the area's business schools, taught this course once a week. The principles of exotic financial products were explained to bank employees—mostly salespeople—in a fairly nontechnical way. Some of the young lawyers and assistant traders attended the classes, too, as well as the middle-office personnel most interested in their task. What was taught was not marketing as such, but rather the logic of clients' preferences that they were supposed to service. The emphasis was on the principles governing how the products in which the bank had specialized worked, but the instructor made sure that the technical aspects of *pricing* never gained the upper hand over the general understanding of these products. It was an ideal situation for me: it gave me access to the marketing policies of the trading room and to the first intrusion of the clients into the room, albeit in the form of a set of simple mechanisms said to animate them.

This training described "clients' need scenarios." Considering the variety of financial products, the course inevitably ran the risk of losing participants among all the esoteric terms, without ever truly penetrating the financial architecture of products. The instructor reminded us of this more than once, emphasizing the need to understand the *economic rationales* underlying these products. The rich ecology of products was matched by a rich ecology of needs that the course attempted to list. Despite this effort to anchor particular products in particular needs, some participants were nonetheless surprised by the complicated formulas designed by the bank and voiced their concerns that they were "losing touch with the economy." To calm down the apprentices' revolt, the instructor would engage in a series of fictions meant to flesh out the use of these "monstrous" products. Indeed, fabricating scenarios for the economic uses of products took up much of his teaching. He operated by developing little hypothetical situations involving an investor faced with a treasury problem (unexpected cash surplus, for example, or a need for financing, or a desire to get around regulations and tax rules). Several products reappeared under different names such as "digitals," which could also be defined as "barriers" or "activating barriers" to figure out their mechanisms.[19] These presentations of the product fauna—the instructor called them "critters," *bestioles* in French—were marked by a tension between the exhibition of all the possible qualifiers, on the one hand, and the folding in of these products onto universal needs, on the other.

In the first of these two stages of presentation, the instructor would display a variety of qualifications, each expressing one aspect of the product. This applied to the "digital," which was firmly positioned on the side of speculation and wager because of the hedging difficulties it raised. As it was difficult to find a clear economic situation where it could be used as a hedging tool, emphasis was put on its speculative nature by excavating the deep meaning of its name. The instructor reminded his audience that digitals should make them think of "0" and "1," just as in heads or tails and other games where only two outcomes were possible. He insisted that financial products have much in common with games: there are few limits to imagining new ones. The only limit was indeed the imagination of engineers. The drawback of this way of thinking resided in the limitless apology of financial creativity: practical economic needs were quickly lost in this celebration of creativity. The various classes of products examined made up the core of this initial approach: the client and her or his preferences receded to a secondary feature, subsumed by these infinite combinatory possibilities.

The second way of thinking went in a direction that was practically opposite to the first. Instead of presenting each item as an original and irreducible expression of financial ingenuity, it brought the structures of these products back to universal principles of economic activity. It undid the combination of particulars that characterized the first approach to understanding novel financial products. This would generally take the form of catchwords, such as *managing interest rate risk* (for the presentation of swaps) and *managing currency risk* (for those swaps involving currencies). This second phase of the rhythm would witness the rattling comeback of the client. It would solidly root the client's preferences in either those needs whose stability made it possible to call them "universal" or in positions motivated by private information and by idiosyncratic preference systems.

With the Client Around

The preparatory exercises of the pedagogy set the stage for a felicitous encounter between the bank—primarily its salespeople and engineers—and the potential client. They empower the bank's marketing by drawing the limits of otherwise unanticipated clients, and they simplify the market exploration into which clients would otherwise launch aimlessly. Yet, these exercises also blur the limits of the bank. The uncertainty faced by clients confronted with new products forces trading-room operators to engage in imagining how to best sell that which has no market. Unlike the clarification that the portfolio insurance article attempts to achieve, the room does not have one unique product[20] for all of its potential clients. Consequently, it does not sally forth to meet them with a clear identity and a straightforward process. As for the clients, their hesitations and uncertainties resonate in the multiple paths that the commercial encounter can take. From the bank's perspective, preparing for this contact entails making space for this amorphous client early on—and as we will later document, these paths can mobilize different groups in the room. This preparation—and the other preparation that the initial description of the client capture mentioned—complicate the perimeter of the bank when it opens up to clients. The intermediaries that Michel would call in order to subtly offer services for clients with preferences exceeding their traditional bankers' expertise, also reset the perimeter of the bank. As salespeople attempt to get closer to the clients to better manipulate them, they are also invaded from within by acting as Trojan horses by bringing the enemy into the bank.

The process of generating the client's interest operates from an assumption that the client's preferences are more or less stable. Without stability, it is difficult to make a client feel the "custom-tailoring" effort, as hesitation makes it impossible to speak to *one* client. In contrast, when the client is quite sure of his or her needs, the work of shaping his or her interest is not necessary: the client wants a product, and the salesperson takes pains to satisfy those preferences. The magnitude of the instability in a client's preferences determines the kind of dance that clients and salespeople enjoy.

One anecdote told ad nauseam by salespeople on the desk insisted on the malleability of clients with a mix of malice and pride. A ski resort hotel owner in the French Alps had contacted General Bank for advice on ways to hedge his exposure to risk of currency fluctuations and national economies. The hotel had a clientele primarily from Germany, Switzerland, Italy, and England, as well as some American customers, and the owner tried to control the ups and downs of these customers' national economies because he had noticed that they were responsive to currency fluctuations. After a few meetings, the owner walked away with a weather derivative, protecting his revenues from the vicissitudes of inclement conditions—lack of snow or warm temperatures. The scenario was perfect as the client walked in with what looked like a clear idea and walked out with another very clear service in hand, although they were not one and the same. The salespeople's pride stemmed from the clean redirection given to, and accepted by, the client. Nothing had disrupted the relationship that the salespeople had envisioned with the client: the client had not only purchased a derivative, but the waltz with the engineers and salespeople had itself been a derivation. A core mechanism demanded by the client had been respected by the bank (it was still a flow of money conditional on a state of nature), but the engineers had managed to talk him into reading his past business exercises in a new way and accepting a new source of risk (from the inflation in Germany to the snow accumulation in the French Alps). The quasi-mythical status garnered by this client transformation indicated the rarity of such smooth interactions.

Emotions of Negotiations: Slowness and Tilting

The length of the negotiation phase was the topic most frequently addressed in the comments salespeople made when asked to describe their work. The pace in the clients' decision-making depends largely on the market, of which the salesperson is in charge. Thus, teams from the Benelux and France zones have shorter negotiation phases than the teams working on countries located in the Persian Gulf and the Middle East. According to salespeople in these zones, this difference is due to the number and frequency of contracts. Some particularly talented salespeople can brag about having very short wait times for client decisions and very short negotiation phases, but all emphasize that selling these innovative products requires working directly with the client in a way standard products do not necessitate. This close contact with clients deserves scrutiny.

The particular financial emotions triggered by these deals come from the apparent lack of proportion between two series of elements: the intelligence of a structured product and its return. The disproportionate amount of money involved in the contracts and the sudden tilting of the negotiation, after hesitant framings, destabilize and thrill salespeople and engineers. The joy associated with a deal that has gone through is proportional to the level of seduction necessary in getting close enough to the client to convince him or her of the product's worthiness. Reaching a firm agreement is like making it to the other side of a hill; it is the compensation for the effort made in an arduous climb. Of course, satisfaction also depends on the amount of money in play, but the appreciation of the sheer "figure" is also colored by the intellectual content of the financial contract that initiates it. Financial operators include a variety of elements under the rubric of "intellectual content," ranging from new methods for hedging options that help shrink the price, to new formulas spanning new Exchanges. Even though the content itself shows variety, it must be distinguished from the emotion tied to the sheer "figure."

These products are uniquely situated in the gamut of commercial services inasmuch as they are tested several times. They are sold and the amount of money they return is a first test, but they also have a life beyond the sheer return. They develop associated tools (pricers primarily) that also have lives of their own. The multiple trajectories of these bundled services—some of which make it to the clients, others of which enrich the pool of tools subsequently used to price and manage similar products—belong to a complex economy in which rhythms are set by the big figures that clients agree to pay. If the contents and the big-figure returns are distinguishable in theory, they are not always distinguished in the heat of the transaction. An engineer, whom I asked about these moments of jubilation, expressed his bewilderment to me:

I: [I]t often happens all at once. You know the clients, you've learned to know what might work. It's a long process and when it pays off it's very satisfying.

Q: [T]he payoff is satisfying?

I: [I]t is also having succeeded in bringing the project to completion, which is rare; it is also what that brings with it. The client had been leading you by the nose, you had been there just following him in all of his demands, and then, all of a sudden, he pays you; it sort of turns things around. It is quite a binary progression. You're killing yourself, you're obeying, and then suddenly the money's flowing and the client is a partner with whom you're working hand-in-hand; but it's true that when you redo the calculation and see how you sold the deal to them, it's pretty satisfying.

Q: [A]t that point does the elegance of the structure fall into second place?

I: [L]et's just say that the creation of a clever structure is a pleasure that spreads itself out, that takes time; there are many involved in the project, it's a shared satisfaction. A bit at every stage, you appreciate what you're in the process of doing. The moment in which a transaction becomes certain, now that's different. First of all, you know really what the deal will bring in, whereas when you're thinking of a structure, you just have a general idea. Once it's definite, everything becomes crystallized, the price and then the structure that is agreed upon.

The flurry of emotions that accompanies the final stretch of the transaction and the end of the client's indecisiveness is a mixed bag. Even if a project submitted to the client is seen as very clever, it may be forgotten if the market does not bite. Even if a failed structure had displayed promising attributes and clever subtleties, it was not followed through on. The moment of agreement is, therefore, indeed still crucial, even if what is invested in the negotiation has its intrinsic value—and labor value, quite independent of the success. The work of the engineer—and even more that of the salesperson—is marred by these experiences of failure and of aborted collaboration. Ingenuity is only measured concretely when it comes from a product that the bank has sold to a client, who has been stabilized by attaching a contract to him or her.

The various populations of the trading floor do not all see this achievement in the same fashion: salespeople are those for whom the moment of transaction marks a successful conclusion. Of course, they know that selling has a counterpart, but they do not experience it directly. For a smooth-talking salesperson, a "prospectus" can well be traded for €1, €2, €10, or €15 million. For traders and engineers, the product continues to exist and to require attention even after the transaction negotiation has passed. Furthermore, the engineer who designed the product knows better than the salesperson just how much selling such products commits the bank over a number of years. If one further broadens the range of operators to the middle and back offices, selling a product becomes more and more a "mixed blessing." Because the middle- and back-office operators benefit less from the effects of a transaction—their livelihoods depend much less on bonuses, unlike salespeople for whom bonuses can make up more than 80 percent of their annual remuneration—what comes to their mind is the length of time during which a product is maintained, and the possible complications that long-term commitments of customized contracts carry. These operators never experience the euphoria of the transaction; they do not get a taste of the client's hesitation and the outcome of negotiations. They know that the transaction does not conclude with the confirmation signature; for them it is rather the beginning of a not-so-glamorous journey. That is the burden of custom-made products that can be modified by the clients. For a back-office operator, the bank never walks "hand-in-hand" with the client.

Shifting Alliances

Salespeople straddle the bank's confines. They are connected to the room, but as they reach out for new clients they also sometimes loosen their allegiance to the bank. To characterize this reconfiguring[21] of alliances around the room, I use a conversation between a salesperson and a client. It took place in April 2000, at a time when stock markets were reaching their tipping point and when salespeople[22] were doing their utmost to hold onto their clients and to convince them not to rush toward more liquid instruments. The conversation has the drawback of being one-sided. I did not have access to the clients, and on the rare occasions when salespeople would turn on their speaker phones, the conversation would lose all interest for me, as it generally meant that the deal was on the verge of being canceled and that the personal contact was going out the door. After having tried at length to foster this fragile link, the salesperson generally staged the failure, blaming it on his client's cold feet.

> Stockholm is very good stock, but, if you'd like, we can change, we can put something less aggressive . . . if we look at the period up until now, it has never crashed, and the vol[23] is low . . . you have to look at today's market; who is offering this product today? [probably a query from the client aiming at a modification] . . . but you have to tell me quickly so that I can negotiate with the engineers [from the salesperson to his client after the engineer has given some information on possible modifications].

In this brief exchange, a recurring trait stands out. One of the resources regularly used by salespeople when they approach a client works by undoing the salesperson–client opposition and subtly replacing it with a salesperson–client collaboration. This strategy would backfire on slow engineers and even slower back offices. By distancing himself from the other functions of the trading floor, the salesperson defuses the possible suspicions of opacity of the calculations being carried out on the floor. The collaboration that he initiates by mentioning *his* negotiations with the engineer on behalf of *his* client is corroborated by the purposefully nontechnical language he uses to initially describe the security he wishes to add to the product. The price loses some of its opacity when it is so presented (i.e., as the object of a *negotiation* of its components). It is no longer a price that imposes itself bluntly, as is generally the case for standard goods, about which negotiation is rendered impossible by the distinction between the producer and the salesperson. Bringing in the engineers who model products—and, to a certain extent from the point of view of salespeople and clients, who *produce* them—and the salespeople who propose these products to clients, concretizes the *feeling* of a relative malleability of prices. As will appear clearly, it is more a malleability in the perimeter of securities, prices still being held a step back from negotiations. Whereas the client may have the right to express him or herself and make choices when it comes to the structure of his or her basket, the client is not equipped to battle on the price front. The client can negotiate the composition of the basket and subsequently observe its price change, but the pricing mechanism is still a black box to him or her. And engineers never surrender their pricing secrets.

Salespeople regularly play on this dialectic of the financially "tailor-made": products are conceived for each client, and, as such, they are custom-fitted; but finance has its constraints represented by the securities markets. Volatility comes along when evoking the hard rules of finance and the realism that must be adopted when designing a formula. Salespeople dissociate the price of the service from the risk that the client might take on by selecting a basket of securities in a rash manner. Of course, this dissociation is somewhat deceptive: the price billed by the bank is directly linked to the basket's structure and to the correlation among the securities. Yet, focusing on risk allows the negotiation stage to last. Everything happens as though the price was outside of this picture, fixed in advance by the engineers. By telling the story in such a way, the salespeople can entice the client with a custom configuration. Nonetheless, the limits that engineers give to the flexibility in their scenarios reminds us that price is not a "flat rate"; it is directly linked to the possibilities offered to clients for structuring their products. This does not mean that the flexibility granted is completely deceptive, or that the choice does not have any impact on the ultimate nature of the service. Clients can have needs dictated by their other investments—these investments being only one component of a portfolio that is unknown by engineers. Clients can thus distinguish between securities that engineers do not distinguish from the point of view of the price they make. Each party to the transaction has a preexisting structure of risks and searches a common ground with the other party. The heterogeneity of the clients' needs and the assessments of securities make it possible to reshuffle the cards in the securities portfolios to the advantage of the client and the bank.

The cooperative effort during the framing of the product redraws the boundaries of the bank by bringing salespeople and clients closer in the face of the implacable reality of finance, which is embodied by the engineer. This passing alliance between clients and salespeople leads to a larger concern: these products are sold, but they are also managed by the bank and can be modified by clients. Their transition from the bank to the client is never complete, and commercial ties remain. The service will only definitively take on a shape when the contract ends, when the nominal (through the effect of the guarantee) and the performance of the underlying (through the work of the formula) are returned. In the meantime, and before the products speak the clear language of the payoff, how should they be spoken about?

| Articulating Products: Giving Shape or Giving Time to Products?

It is appropriate to step back momentarily from our close description of the client's slow incarnation to reiterate the question at stake. Transactions are risky moments, regardless of the nature of the commodity being circulated. Whether they are verbal transactions creating the possibility of misunderstandings or the circulation of goods and tribe members meant to rule out possibilities of war, much is at stake when individuals or groups open themselves to let assets or expressions come or go. Commercial transactions add a layer of risk to the structural danger of transacting: a price crowns the exchange and summarizes the flow of goods. With a price, no uncertainty is admitted and the transaction has a beginning and an end, bracketing the range of interactions that this transaction has generated. CGPs challenge that concision by authorizing reshufflings of the formula's components and de facto opening the design to the client. Customization crowds a conversation around the product that was already torn between multiple points of view, as the trader, the engineer, and the salesperson had legitimate claims on the design. Yet, customization is not the whole story, and to make things even more complex, the nature of the product undercuts the very notion of an interaction *around* the design of the product. The problem is easy to state but difficult to solve: If salespeople, engineers, and clients want to gather around the product and bargain over its properties, what should they look at? What is the stuff of finance that can be discussed for so long and so fiercely? A formula seems to speak for itself. Indeed, banks selling formula products are adamant that nothing is hidden by the very nature of the service and that, consequently, any payoff surprises have to be imputed to the erratic moves of the market and not to the product's design. Transparency rubs against the grain of marketing, inasmuch as marketing banks on maximum opacity. Where, then, are the resources of this marketing exercise found, and how do salespeople invent an absent good to advertise?

Classical studies of the marketplace by economic anthropologists have shown how central the involvement of the body is in commercial transaction (Cochoy, 2002; Clark and Pinch, 1995; De la Pradelle, 1996; Miller, 1998). The mobilization of all the resources of the *remuneration body*—to bring to life instantaneously the qualities of the item for sale and the potential that a standard usage could draw from it—demonstrates the reciprocal support between the salespeoples' bodies, the settings, and the goods.[24] When a street vendor has to convince someone of the great powers[25] of his magical vegetable-peeler, he projects the miraculous tool in time, intensifying into just a few seconds that which would be spread over days, weeks, and probably months on an amateur chef's table. But this contraction also happens through a slowing down of the gestures that make the tool work: a firm grip, the correct angle, and the steady flexibility of the gesture. Nothing must openly deceive. The use of the tool must be easily accessible to the potential buyer: anything too fancy and the demonstration will be seen to showcase the expert rather than the tool.

Is there an equivalent to these expert demonstrations in the case of our financial products? Where do we see what these financial services do? They are obviously different from kitchen utensils. In the first place—and to pay a little respect to an old distinction wielded by classical economists—financial products are not, strictly speaking, going to be *used*. We call them financial "services" or "products," indiscriminately, but one would be hard pressed to find a more disincarnate service. There may be much to discuss in the design of the product, and there are definitely many characteristics to be chosen during the negotiation, but ultimately what the product *does* come down to is greater or fewer euros, served at the term of the contract. Such products are not designed for exchange: the products are customized for the client's needs and they cannot be transferred to a third party. They can only be "returned" to the bank with a penalty (95 percent of the nominal is guaranteed in early terminations). Neither use-value based nor exchange-value priced, these products escape an easy definition that would make their commercial promotion straightforward. One sure thing is their deployment in time. What lies in the future—yield and potential of resale to the issuer—is both the only promise of the product and the most uncertain outcome. There is nothing more in a financial product than its promise; nothing to offer other than what is to come in a distant future—quite unlike the fruit in the marketplace that the client touches and pokes, smells and scrutinizes, when wanting to assessing what he gets for his money.

For those who wish to understand the transfer of products to the client, it is just as important to understand these promises as it is to describe their conditions of production.[26] The promises that woo the CGP's clients have yet to be defined in narrower terms, even negative terms. They are promissory inasmuch as they have nothing to offer in the present but an ink and paper mode of existence that has no quality in common with the money turned in when the term of the product comes. These are not the objects typical of what the anthropologists of *material cultures* chose as objects of their studies (Appadurai, 1986; Kopitoff, 1986; Miller, 1998). The products covered by these anthropologists had pasts that traced a path toward the future. Our financial products do not have a past; they only have conditions of production, but their future financial outcomes are quite insulated from the sheer production conditions.[27] They have "protographies" rather than biographies. They are entirely aimed toward the future, and operators anticipate their results in the form of scripts and expected bottom lines. The simulations used by engineers and traders are also refined forms of protographies: their theories do not come out of thin air and the scenarios for these products are not invented from scratch, but the resources they use to offer a sense of how products will behave over the course of time are distilled and preserve only a reduced number of dimensions. These are not traces that are proper to each product and that guide the investigator down new paths each time.[28] Nor are they the successions of relevant events so characteristic of the biographical genre. The protographies reduce much further the resources drawn from the past: they do not command solely the shape of this report (forward looking, discounting the past); they *strip down* all financial events and bring them back to preexisting dimensions. The future draws all the inscriptions[29] that go along with the birth of these financial innovations. If it is true that many innovations are by definition forward-looking, derivative products have the further peculiarity[30] of being independent of the past and almost of the present. The forward-looking design of these products exacerbates the burden weighing on financial protographies at the very moment when it deprives the salesperson of a relevant past for these products.

Articulation from Liquidity

The slowness of the transaction comes primarily from the fact that the custom design approach forces salespeople to tailor their pitches to fit as closely as possible to their client's profile. The task is to sell a financial service that will materialize in the form of cash flow (payoff). This materiality of the service constitutes a departure point for the contact between clients and sales. Nothing is better shared, it would seem, than money that circulates among the partners to a deal. Liquidity is the baseline and the background from which all these financial innovations depart. It is the neutral medium that cannot be articulated as such. This common ground allows for a relationship between salespeople and their clients. But framing the nature of the transaction in terms of liquidity can quickly derail the trade. Although liquidity in and of itself may not pose a problem—and indeed forms the background of all monetary transactions[31]—the specificity of one service rather than another is not easy to demonstrate if all its dimensions are constantly cast in terms of the future liquidity to be enjoyed by the client. Selling money (beyond the sheer absurdity of this formulation if it were to mean selling it here and now) can only be imagined if that substratum comes with qualities that give it appealing traits. Thus, this common language must be clearly specified and articulated; it must demonstrate advantages that liquidity does not have. But how does one specify this substratum without losing the qualities of the common language? How can liquidity be maintained despite the twists and turns of the formula?

The work of the salespeople occurs at this juncture, when financial innovations work their own spin on the classical language of advertising to give it a new twist, compatible with the imperative of liquidity. Because in the end, the CGP performance—or lack thereof—will be spoken of in monetary terms. Consider the difference between investing one's liquidity in CGP and investing it in the shares of a company whose activity can be described in economic terms. France Telecom was one of the most traded companies at the time of the fieldwork. Its appeal was threefold: It combined the appeal of a French "too big to fail" company with major public participation and capital share, with the appeal of a multinational company investing in almost all corners of the world, with the appeal of a new economy investment fund with interests in most cutting-edge start-ups in Europe. Even if the ultimate goal of France Telecom investors is to make profit, the rich range of activities engaged in by the company exist as many possibilities for the salesperson to weave a marketing narrative. Tying the expected performance of France Telecom shares to economic scenarios is easier than giving a sense of the potentialities of performance of a formula as convoluted as the double guarantee mechanism. The challenge comes from the twist introduced by the formula: whereas salespeople of France Telecom shares could ground stories of the company business plan by resorting to sharing clients' experience of the economy, how can one convey such a sense of the mechanism at play when the formula concatenates *mins, maxs,* and *averages* of already composite indices? The narrative pitched by the salespeople may be more "misleading" than the bare reiteration of the formula components. Reiterating the formula is always correct but it does not excite clients. The sheer mechanical articulation of the mathematical operators at work in the formula does not get to the point where the CGP derives from the economy because the derivation is engineered in such a way that no one client can see through the structure: it is the combination of indices (themselves summaries of national economies) through the mathematical operators that are derivations.[32]

The tension between these two approaches to wealth (liquidity and articulation) is often mitigated by mobilizing entities with enough flexibility in their usage to immerse them both into the world of liquidity and into that of specialized language. The work of salespeople is punctuated by these efforts to transform financial idioms and sometimes even technical terms designating the properties of these formalisms into common language terms. The existence of a solid base of mediating terms common to clients and salespeople does part of the work. The popularization of formalisms and the technicalization of language do not have to be undertaken from scratch. But even if these transactions work on the common ground of past financial innovations that are common knowledge, they do not have any less need to detach themselves from this foundation to mark a new difference. The problem we glimpsed earlier is displaced: the vocabulary available is already too heavily weighted to the side of the shared language to make any notable difference.

Once the product is in the hands of the client, the parabolic narratives that salespeople like to tell are replaced by the actual reactions of the specimen.

Although the transfer is not final—as the client can still hope to negotiate the perimeter of his service—it is a great leap toward the completion of the service transaction. No longer uniquely a contract in paper form, it is also a series of flows of money that will now come due in one way or another. The promise becomes reality, often with some nontrivial adjustments to the otherwise exceptional prospectus.

The Qualities of Finance

If it is accurate to define the financial innovation of CGPs as a process of increasing derivation of underlying economies, marketing that derivation is not easy because it must navigate the passage from existing forms of economy—the underlyings of our CGP—to the new vehicles. The process entails a series of reductions of the qualities of the patches of economy under consideration: from a national economy to an index of top-forty company public shares; from a company to its transferable securities, debt, or stocks; from the underlyings to the payoff. The performance of companies or the construct of the "national economy" are not necessarily present in these accounts. Salespeople do not necessarily cover the whole chain of derivation when they sell a product indexed on Exxon Mobil, which itself is several steps removed from the sweat and pain felt by salaried workers in South America. It is indeed clever of them to glorify the trend of the stock price over the past fifteen years rather than to elaborate upon the labor conditions of the gas company workers. The problem facing them is to flesh out the terms of the formula and give a taste of the economy behind it, even if the economy is only a temporary still image in a cascade of derivations. This cascading move, however, impoverishes the qualities and limits the number of characteristics and qualities available to salespeople. Marketing the new security is only possible in the terms of existing securities: salespeople talk of CGP as a better investment vehicle than the more mundane shares or bonds of a pool of companies. Their language leans on notions that are already in circulation and out of which they combine increasingly innovative services.

The risk is for the combinations to lose touch with the economy as it is experienced by clients. At the end of a chain of derived economic purification, these financial products cannot appeal to clients with the full range of qualities that make other, less purified goods appealing. Think of a fancy car sold by an upscale car manufacturer. The variety of qualities available to cars since they started selling is much greater than those attached to the securities representing the manufacturer. This variety grows by the day as other goods become compatible with the car and lead to enriched descriptions. Cars that offer audio systems, TV systems, and Internet connections are feasts for salespeople. However securities for such cars are sold, the gamut of qualities is more limited, and the combinations salespeople enjoy are finite. Packaging plays a role, too, but within a more limited array of possibilities: risk and return profiles are repackaged, but a shiny and colorful prospectus, although crucial to catching clients' attention and convincing them of the bank's trustworthiness, will not tilt their hesitation toward buying alone. Hence, more than any other innovation, financial innovations oscillate between the two poles of extreme reduction (consider the problem however you want; it is all about risk and return) and the wide range of possibilities created by combining existing securities into new services (risks and return as unitary notions recede, leaving the stage to as many measures of risks and returns as one can imagine).

Cannibal Finance

How varied are the descriptive terms that can be used when "talking finance"? This apparently inconsequential question contains, in reality, interesting lessons. We have already seen how two opposite forces (opening/closure) set a tension between the advertising of products and their grounding into preferences. This rhythmic movement shapes finance between the noisy and tottering economy of industries—with the vicissitudes of risk that industrial investments create—and the purification of pure price exercises dreamt of by the mathematicians and physicists who model these products. This tension and its resolution has been given a name: derivation. It represents a simplification and purification of the economy, and, as a result, limits the variety of qualifiers that can be attached to it. Of the thousands of relationships taking place in a publicly traded company—each of which is articulated in numerous and rich ways by its employees—the language of finance only saves one or two indicators. Each of these relationships can have effects on the value of these indicators, but they will be filtered and in a way stripped so as to fit with the grammar of the indicators.[33] How strong are these purified ties created between the clients and the products?

As soon as a client takes possession of a financial product, the conditions for criticism are put into play because the properties of finance are generic. These properties inaugurate a space—with some dimensions well known to us by now, such as return and risk. This space sets the stage for other products to potentially challenge and displace the original product. Therein lies the paradox of financial products: the attempt to create an advantage by generating a new product opens up a space that will endanger that very product and institute competition. Thus, a product can boast a particular return for the year, but in so doing it creates the *return dimension* and opens the way to criticism that would pit another product against it, only with a return just higher up. Such a dimension inaugurated by a product helps to immediately mark its obsolescence because the potential for its being surpassed by another financial product candidate is increased. The product moves within a multidimensional space whose crucial feature for our analysis here, however, is its ordinal nature. Its specificity is not intrinsic: it is a dimension/property that is never guaranteed preeminence over other financial entities.

The tragedy of finance comes from the centrality of prices and the difficulty of singularizing products. If the crimson red fabric of an elegant dress is incommensurable, it is because small variations in color cause an immediate shift in the qualities' space inhabited by the product. The crimson of this cloth carves out its preference by eliminating possible competition. To stick with geometric terms, the red color was an extraspatial point, and no other point could surpass it. To weaken the incandescence of this particular red and, thus, its commercial success, any competing color would need to dethrone that point and to impose ex nihilo another point in the space of the client's preferences. The quality of a financial product can always be surpassed by a product that positions itself in its immediate vicinity, only slightly above it. That is both the great weakness and strength of these products: they can be defined in common terms and continuous measures, but they precipitate their own fall. They invent too much by opening up dimensions instead of drawing up dimensionless points. A commercial entity that is nothing but a set of points, outside any axis system—that would bring it back into the realm of the commensurable—is less fearful of competition. It struggles to impose itself because it cannot latch onto the dimensions preexisting its advent— it does not use the existing language of (+) and (–). But, once it is in place, it imposes a language that does not allow any approximation. How does one describe this unique, unequaled, incomparable crimson red? One uses comparisons, but only comparisons with other objects that are not immediately related to it, that are indeed so distant from it that the comparison is metaphorical: a comparison that does not threaten but rather strengthens by tying the crimson dress to other universes. The other elements brought into the picture to qualify the dress are not potential enemies; rather, they are allies. If I praise the color of the dress for reminding me of a red I had once seen on a rose in a Japanese garden, the rose enriches the dress' features by one element. Conversely, if I associate this red with a negative event (this dress looks like a bloody Sunday outfit), I do not threaten it from the *red dimension*. The experience of the sublime and the difficulty of putting it into words must be kept in mind as a thought experiment describing what financial products will never be. Sublime objects are not easily expressed in words, but they force one to burst apart language and to invent new formulations for it.

As a consequence, this continuous space grants financial products more flexibility vis-à-vis their definition, all the while remaining financial products. Inventing or jury-rigging dimensions rather than spaceless points creates a risk to the survival of products, but it also makes possible a discussion. If products do not fulfill the clients' expectations, they remain in their own space: they still have a yield (weaker than expected, but a yield nonetheless) and variability (higher than expected, but measurable). Raising criticism against this class of commercial products is not easy. They can dodge questions about their performance thanks to the existence of a continuous space. They can escape along this dimension but, at the same time, any other financial product can ride the dimension and dethrone the product. Finance creates the conditions for a narrow but never-ending commercial conversation, one that concerns only a very small number of qualities but which is intense.

When Products become Nothing But Liquidity

When clients and banks part ways in the middle of a deal (i.e., when a deal goes sour), the long and convoluted transaction orchestrated by the salespeople comes to an end. In another reversal of the bank topography, the very talkative salespeople disappear from the conversation and an agreement over the product's value—the product is being returned to the bank, so to speak—must be found. As we now know, nothing is really being returned to the bank. Updates to contracts are signed again, early end-of-term agreements are also signed, but the bank does not come out much better off with these new documents to store. It was managing a large amount of capital, but has to return it promptly. On the other side of the deal, things are slightly different. The client gets his or her share of contract updates to store somewhere new, but of much greater importance is the money that is returned. This moment is of particular importance as it marks another reversal. This time it is not only a reversal of spatial distribution among the experts working in the room but also a reversal of preferences for the parties. Whereas the initial appeal of the bank came from its ability to customize products for clients with treasury needs not matched by more standard products, when the contractual relation breaks off, things change. The client no longer looks at her or his personalized products for their unique features; these now only have appeal for their worth in liquid terms, here and now.

The switch—and it is a sudden switch—needs to be dissected for the way in which it focuses attention on the changing characteristics of the product. Because no other offer was available when the client was on the lookout for a one-of-a-kind service, the price could not be a priority. There was no easy comparison, at least no term-by-term comparison given the customization offered by the bank. The client could also have other financial deals with the provider, and would therefore look at a more global relationship with the provider: the overall and consolidated services and prices were the client's bottom line, not each one of them taken individually. What prevailed and ranked highest in the client's preferences during this first phase of the transaction, were all the other characteristics of the product. These characteristics vanish when the client decides to pull out of a deal and to retrieve his or her capital—or, more precisely, when the client decides to turn his or her capital-as-investment into capital-as-liquidity. All of a sudden, the price that remained only a fleeting characteristic becomes again the primary motive of the client. Until then the price could not easily be equated to liquidity, because the combined weight of other aspects of the service (such as the ability to modify the product during its life without incurring fees) prevented it, as did the distance and uncertainty coating the liquidity to be achieved in the future. Because it was in the future, the capital that the client expected was mostly seen through the formula: still a quite indirect liquidity, so not quite liquidity. With the termination of the product, the price that the bank attaches to the services for the client is now the amount of money about to be repaid. If it were a natural termination, the liquidity reclaimed by the client would be dictated simply by the formula. Back-office operators would do the math, collect all the fixing values, average them, and turn back in the nominal and the performance of the basket of indices:

Nominal × 100%

Nominal × {100% + 120% × [Max(BKT$_m$ – 1;0)]}.

An early termination makes the client disregard the formula and its unique way of articulating the basket of indices. Its promise recedes backstage, and the actuality of liquidity takes over the client's order of priorities. The monetary here and now—without any further conditions attached to it—is demanded. In other investment circumstances,[35] when markets are bullish and when clients do not have unexpected losses incurred from other financial adventures, the conversion from the formula to liquidity can even be bypassed altogether and formula performances seamlessly morphed into nominal.

This market for products—which we now understand is not really a market in the same sense as the one in which we buy our fruits and vegetables—has an extraordinary feature. It promises money, but it does not match it with a price. In fact, the promise is conditional, and the money in question is not truly liquid money anymore. Money without a price seems irresistible—but what is money if not its own price? But money comes in various guises, and by giving bizarre forms and pace to the transfer of money, what is traded already loses the simplicity of liquidity. Even if it is not industrial capital embedded in questions of use-value and even if it shows all the features of liquidity a posteriori, it is still not close enough to liquidity to allow a client to attach a price as he or she pleases. It is money in the last resort and at the end of the game, but in the meantime it assumes tortured formulations. Prices, which are usually derided for reducing the rich and multiple dimensions of goods, are now unable to perform this violence. They cannot do violence to the complex elaboration of preferences undertaken by the salesperson and the client together. They are stuck in the labyrinth of the complex formula, once ravishing everyone, now embarrassing all. And, yet, it is at the moment when the price is most docile that the client wishes for its natural violence: to escape the web of complex tailored needs and come back to a simple price, one that announces a liquid capital and erases a cumbersome investment.

CHAPTER 6

|

The Costs of Price

| One-Figure Reduction

The claim trumpeted by CGP salespeople is appealing to clients. It offers access to the worldwide economy through a payoff formula and—it seems—nothing more than a payoff formula. Farewell dusty and noisy economies. Farewell manufacturing plants and their recalcitrant workers. Enter the agile vehicle of modern capitalism: clean profit and controlled risks. Yet, this shift from physical capital to payoff is only one of the operations taking place in the bank. Accounting takes place simultaneously, and that other reduction is the direct consequence of the legal status of the bank, whose activities must be made public on a regular basis. Investors are entitled to these regular snapshots of the bank so that they can make informed decisions when allocating their resources. The sophistication of financial engineering activities documented so far must give way to straightforward accounting disclosure and standardized financial statements. In opposition to the claims made that the world economy can be reduced to a formula, this second type of reduction has already been standardized as a matter of common practice. The bank does not have to invent the methods of public disclosure and the techniques by which to reduce their financial activities to a single figure. To serve their standardization purpose, these methods are similar across the board, and no one company gets to fiddle with the disclosure rules. In theory that is true, at least, as the discipline of financial reporting has recently shown to be a creative field (Veron, 2006).

The preexistence of this disclosure framework turns out to be more of a hindrance than a resource for the bank. Salespeople had to painstakingly invent a language by which they could articulate what engineers were crafting in the room. But that challenge was also the main resource of the front office, allowing them a hand in designing the product *and* its description. This flexible coupling is no longer a possibility when the language of financial statements is forced onto the bank. The engineers' creativity needs to accom-

Financial statements

CONSOLIDATED BALANCE SHEET AT JUNE 30, 2001
Assets
(in millions of euros)

	June 30 2001	June 30 2000	December 31 2000
Cash, due from central banks and post office accounts	4,867	6,074	3,276
Due from banks (Note 2)	58,491	56,978	54,174
Customer loans (Note 3)	178,954	155,113	163,119
Lease financing and similar agreements (Note 4)	16,952	11,425	12,153
Treasury notes and similar securities (Note 5)	39,963	31,039	27,657
Bonds and other debt securities (Note 5)	57,687	49,177	51,568
Shares and other equity securities (Note 5)	45,719	40,880	41,994
Investments of insurance companies (Note 6)	34,091	31,251	32,618
Affiliates and other long term securities (Note 7)	6,297	5,648	6,291
Investments in subsidaries and affiliates accounted for by the equity method	693	332	837
Tangible and intangible fixed assets	4,086	4,034	3,769
Goodwill (Note 8)	806	456	400
Accruals, other accounts receivable and other assets (Note 9)	53,762	66,699	58,025
Total	502,368	459,106	455,881

Off-balance sheet items

Loan commitments granted	99,999	89,989	98,519
Guarantee commitments granted	35,722	35,966	38,282
Commitments made on securities	18,940	19,642	11,649
Foreign exchange transactions (Note 16)	382,716	313,313	289,063
Forward financial instrument commitments (Note 17)	5,744,162	5,384,524	4,999,529
Commitments made on insurance	380	331	356

(The accompanying notes are an integral part of the consolidated financial statements)

Figure 18. General Bank's June 30, 2001 (second quarter) Balance Sheet: The assets

modate a call for transparency now. A population we have not yet met thrusts this imperative upon engineers—the bank's accountants. They produce the bank's financial statements four times per year (one per quarter) in what is hailed as the most transparent presentation of its otherwise secret activities.[1]

The financial statement presented in figure 18 contains a very dense summary of the bank's assets as of the end of June 2001. Of interest in this document are the "off–balance sheet items" at the bottom of the page. It contains the most important subcategory, outweighing by far all the other items of the off-balance category: the "forward financial instruments commitments" weighs fifteen times as much as all the consolidated assets of the balance sheet above. A note explains this huge commitment.

Although these items are not part of the balance sheet, they weigh as much—per euro—as the official and accounted items of the asset section of the sheet. Should these forward commitments cost money to the bank,

NOTE 17
Forward financial instrument commitments
(in millions of euros)

	Trading transactions	Hedging transactions	Total June 30 2001	Total 2000	Total December 31 2000
Firm transactions					
Transactions on organized markets					
– interest rate futures	461,206	11,160	472,366	360,576	328,179
– foreign exchange futures	366	1,405	1,771	1,306	2,613
– other forward contracts	92,246	365	92,611	60,641	81,914
OTC agreements					
– interest rate swaps	2,671,767	65,570	2,737,337	2,609,125	2,611,064
– currency financing swaps	76,848	3,996	80,844	54,299	68,750
– Forward Rate Agreements (FRA)	278,393	1,317	279,710	412,684	262,491
– other	14,923	396	15,319	8,655	18,557
Options					
– interest rate options	940,711	1,408	942,119	857,523	797,585
– foreign exchange options	69,821	187	70,008	57,722	86,057
– options on stock exchange indices and equities	724,695	264,490	989,185	907,498	683,466
– other	62,892	–	62,892	54,495	58,853
Total	**5,393,868**	**350,294**	**5,744,162**	**5,384,524**	**4,999,529**

Credit risk equivalent (in millions of euros)
The credit risk equivalent on these transactions determined in accordance with the methods recommended by the Basle Committee for the calculation of the international solvency rations, stands at:

	June 30 2001	2000	December 31 2000
– OECD member governments and central banks	325	230	338
– OECD member banks and local authorities	15,897	14,354	14,991
– Customers	8,846	7,111	7,653
– Non-OECD member banks and central banks	504	368	411
Total (including netting agreements)	**25,572**	**22,063**	**23,393**

Bilateral netting agreements reduced the credit risk equivalent by 46,869 millions of euros at June 30, 2001.

Figure 19. The Riskier, the More Buried in the (Foot) Notes

the investor owning General Bank shares would feel the same financial pain, measured in lower dividends served annually. Yet, for the bank willing to present a clean balance sheet and glorious indicators of economic success, moving most of the items that would otherwise feature as debt off its balance sheet is, naturally, appealing. The drive for financial innovations and tortured engineering has come in no little measure from the accounting incentives of contracts, which can creatively lend themselves to advantageous qualification. The opacity of engineered derivation worked in favor of the bank in its relationship with clients but it was also exploited in its relation with shareholders and prospective investors. Designing financial services like CGPs, that sit uneasily in financial statements, was not a mistake made by some wild financial engineers unaware of accounting procedures or of unintended consequences. From their first sketches to their complete contractual version, these products respond to existing regulation, in a move that has been hailed as the ultimate manifestation of entrepreneurial spirit by Merton Miller—as well as the rationale for calling an end to regulation.

Financial statements do not easily accommodate CGPs because they are conditional claims. Unlike deposits or loans, CGPs are not clearly a transfer of money from one party to the other. The bank only enjoys and manages the nominal for a limited number of years and will have to return it and its formula-driven performance at the term of the contract. It is thus only a temporary transfer with an uncertain payoff for the client. Under these conditions, where should the bank keep track of its value? How should it be made public? The contention here is the elusive nature of the value itself and the attendant role played by the operators of this disclosure, the accountant. Well before CGPs were designed in General Bank, the tension between engineering and accounting had fuelled the critique of finance operations as artificial. The alleged artifice is that of the presentation of a company's business activities that distorts its real state. Necessary to this critique[2] is a solid definition of real economic activities, as a way to contrast the real from the artificial, in the usual terms "the mirror from the smoke" (Veron 2006): in a nutshell, nothing less than an ontology of value. And indeed, who could deny a ground to these critiques of infamous Enron book cooking and other accounting manipulations? Who would defend rogue accountants who fully exploit the gray zone of creative accounting to show up their company to shareholders too happy to be told of the mysteries of the legal and financial ingenuity? There seems to be no possible discussion on these matters as the investor is tricked and the blame can fall nowhere but on the accountant, whether in-house or in breach of a fiduciary duty when employed by an external consulting firm. Yet, as we have started to understand from the close examination of financial engineering and the puzzle created by hedging, this consensus hinges on the problematic notion of the real economy. What the angry critics of rogue capitalism are demanding is simply the economy, clean and dry. No distortion, no manipulation, simply the facts and nothing but the facts.

Still, it is not clear that we can ever look in the eyes the real economy and get rid of artifices, as the difference between artificial and real is not ontological but technical, and that is the irony of this otherwise legitimate anger. Technologies of monitoring and tracking are supposed to help us navigate these economic forms and parse the real/good from the artificial/bad. If the goal of these criticisms against partial and distorted representations was for direct, face-to-face interaction with the economy, it is not clear that additional layers of technologies will offer that. The case of our contracts, sitting off the balance sheet, can only be solved and made more transparent—bringing the contracts back in the space of the calculation and as contributors to the economic indicators of the firm—by providing them with a monetary value. Yet, with a term far in the future, nothing less than a model will provide the investors and shareholders with that desired value. We wanted facts; we are given models of facts and the doubts over the artificiality of their results are no less torturing as the recent controversy over the use of Fair Value has illustrated.[3] Which model should accountants use to convey the reality of contracts due to unwind five to ten years in the future?

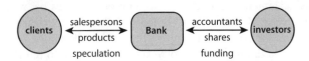

Figure 20. The Two Reductions: Their Operators, Supports, and Motives

Accountants are second only to salespeople in the degree to which their work, by necessity, breaches the confines of the bank. As such, they have one foot inside and one outside the bank: they keep crossing its porous surface, enforcing outside regulations internally and disseminating financial statements outward. Despite these similarities with salespeople, accountants interact with the other end of the bank. Accountants report to current and prospective shareholders rather than interact with clients. Another difference with salespeople comes from the relative lack of flexibility given to accountants. The stringent standardization of the norms of disclosure stands in stark contrast with the organized multiplicity of codes that the front office works with. We now have to revisit the scenes described in parts 1 and 2 in order to understand the proliferation of counting methods in the context of this accounting framework.

The standardization that accountants try to achieve is put to a difficult test by the opposing efforts of the salespeople and engineers, on the lookout for new forms of contracts that could appeal to elusive clients. The variety of the information systems forged to multiply the possible interpretations of its products forces the bank to develop intricate operations to reconcile the different modeling sites. Indeed, as we now know, calculations originate from different sites within the bank, have different functions, and are produced by different methods. The bank is thus a collection of islets, each one wedded to its own methods and tenuously linked to others for which its calculations are accountable. Against the Weberian (1904–1976) view that capitalism marked the rise of a unifying mode of calculation that fenced off the once-rich variety of approaches, actions at the bank—the most intense site of economic calculations—are proof to the contrary. Calculation is plural—a flourishing ecology of methods broken up into a number of approaches by operators who are often unaware of the other methods used by neighboring centers.[4] The exigencies of keeping ahead of the competition produce calculations that are multiple and adrift.

What Bottom Line?

Despite using economic metaphors reminiscent of Bruno Latour's "centers of calculation" (1987) such as *profit centers* or *cost centers*, the exotic products desk at General Bank never abides by the rules of accumulation and standardization. It ended up accumulating much, probably beyond its wildest capitalist dreams, but never through a process of economies of scale, as those economies were made impossible by the quasi-artisanal organization of product design. The notion of centers of calculation describes a world in which scientific facts are agreed-upon through the stabilization of chains of reference and from the circulation of immutable inscriptions. In this sense, matters of international credit and matters of fact are not so dissimilar. However, the imperatives of replicability and accountability that structure scientific communities only affected the bank through its shareholders.[5] The products' innovation, driven by ever-hungrier clients, does not set out its course with that constraint. If anything, it drifts away from this constraint and thrives by inventing processes and methods that are not immediately transparent, even to their authors. This scattering must, however, be controlled in order for the bank to be accountable for the activities carried out over the year by its trading rooms, operators, and products. Yet, the uncertainty over the value of these products starts at a level much more basic than the sophisticated calculations of the front office. What do CGPs cost?

There is a thick layering of costs for new products issued by a bank, a phenomenon not fully rendered by the mathematical finance literature concerned with pricing. The pricing found in textbooks deals only with market costs. It gives rise to demonstrations of formal subtleties that lack the analysis of the *overall cost* of these operations. Pricing may be of concern to meticulous investors who would want to know whether the bank miscalculates its risk. Yet, product pricing accuracy accounts only minimally for overall costs, and investors' return depends on that final figure. The profit of a transaction, after all the costs incurred along the way are factored in, is no longer of the same order as that which is counted in textbooks. There, finance is almost always captured in the form of costs and returns accrued during hedging procedures on the securities market, as if their wider organizational and economic dimension did not count. In reality, the incarnation of financial ideas carries along with it numerous costs that add up as products are modified. The very notion of "overall cost" is awkward when it comes to describing the adventures of innovations—with long life spans, and created by financial institutions with long-term views. In the near future, complex derivatives of CGP flavors may be described as having done considerable damage to economies, and as one keeps playing up or down the perimeter of calculation, the final tally on these products will vary. It is not the aim of this book to settle once and for all the real cost of these products. The task at hand is more modest and very different in spirit. It aims only to point to the transformative effects of the CGP in the bank and highlight some of the costs that were hidden behind a discourse too busy chanting the praises of risk-free financial innovations.

Miscalculating the Costs

Whereas the operators working in the centers of financial product pricing easily get intoxicated by the constant innovation of language needed to work with these products, shareholders, for their part, expect different sorts of thrills. When they calculate the bank's business prospects, the plethora of figures and measures produced internally by the bank must give way to a stable measure. The investor may, in turn, indulge in the multiplication of technologies of interpretation of the bank by diffracting the figure supplied by the quarterly report into many figures, but that is his or her decision. Upstream, the investor needs a figure to start playing with. This tension between the profusion of calculations within the bank and the necessity for a single, clean, and dry figure released outside its walls is resolved by the bank's accounting system.

Two dimensions of accounting exercises point to the same difficulties encountered in producing the final figure. First, there is the difficulty of capturing the associated costs of an operation. Put as simply as possible, it is not easy to calculate all the costs attached to the complex products managed by the trading room. Determining costs is relegated to second place—far behind the priority on calculating market costs—and does not benefit from the sophisticated techniques used by the front office for pricing their products. Most centrally, the costs of execution are burdened by the portfolio of employees managed by the human resources department. As a portfolio, it cannot be hedged as easily as the front-office securities portfolios. An additional snag casts a shadow over investors' efforts to predict the activities/results of the bank: the accounting system itself offers some flexibility in the way in which it qualifies financial operations.[6] No financial product can claim one single accounting method. Even products that have been traded for a long time still exhibit varying valuation methods among investors. When products have no history, an adequate method is even less clearly defined. The distortions operators introduce into the methods of calculation (of cost, profitability, etc.) rattle the bank, which loses its points of reference, as well as the investors, who look into their portofolios and find entities that no longer fold themselves as easily to their old valuation routines.

The Costs of Customization

The circulation of these products through various quarters of the bank makes their economic assessment difficult. If one operator was in charge of a product, from its initial design to its term, it would be simpler to compare the cost and the profit, but the convoluted and recursive assembly line that carries such customized products rules out a one-to-one comparison. Many operators work with these products—from issuance to maintenance—at times on a continuous basis, such as when a trader hedges one product on a daily basis, but at other times several operators work simultaneously but irregularly. Assigning the success of a contract to a person or to a group of persons is made difficult by this layered and folded organization. The postissuance processing can be chaotic. One has to recall the initial contract sequels enjoyed by the client and the difficulties they create for the trader and the back-office managers in figuring out the possible magnitudes of such changes on sequences of intervention around portfolios. The jolts that come about at this stage often cause an increase in the overall issuing costs. But, whereas the reactions of the new products to their hedging markets are meticulously monitored by engineers and traders, their vicissitudes in the subsequent processing chains of the bank are most often neglected by the bank's managers and economists. Just as it is possible to follow the effects of market prices on the value of a security, one could expect that the organizational costs of a financial operation would be a concern to the bank. But they are removed from any front-office tracking tools, and are simply considered the fixed costs of postmarket processing.

The reasoning goes as follows: some operators are already dedicated to the task of processing these products, but these operators are not used to their fullest capacities. It is possible to use them more efficiently by issuing new products without raising the existing fixed costs. It would seem that the scheme is a sensible one. In reality, taking advantage of fixed costs to achieve economies of scale holds only at the margin and is true for standard products whose processing does not require particular attention from operators. As soon as the number of additional intellectually challenging operations soaks up the unused capacities, it becomes necessary to hire new operators. But the unit cost has taken a significant jump, and the principle of the economy of scale will only work again if a sufficiently high number of operations are taken into a portfolio by this larger team of operators.

This mechanism is valid for any industrial organization, and the bank is no exception. But CGP customized services upset the industrial process and the application of the principle of economies of scale. Custom operations belong to a craftsman's logic. Now, the slow waltz between the client and salesperson can cast serious doubt upon the logic of standard goods and economies of scale. Rather than production efficiencies accumulating over the long run, in the logic of this tailored economy, tasks can last as long as it takes for clients to be both taught and listened to. The client, once entitled to have his or her say, does not hesitate to keep the line of negotiation open well after the deal has been signed. Salespeople are no longer the client's exclusive interlocutors: back-office managers must be mobilized, too.[7] The subtleties of the operations conceived of in the front office by engineers, salespeople, and traders require the disentanglement of the multiple conditions laid out in the contracts. The need to mobilize people simultaneously from the front, middle, and back offices weakens the application of economies of scale. The work required by these operations from the postmarket operators goes beyond what was imagined by the engineer, who formulated the product by keeping in mind the subtlety of the legal and financial structure but forgetting the weight of the later processing.

These difficulties of anticipating the full chain of costs was pointed out to me in a conversation with the person who invented TRADE. The ambitions of this technological development went far beyond the sheer question of modeling. This software reflected an overall policy of the bank, an economy of the bank's management choices.

Q: Do new products accentuate the problems related to the circulation of information?

A: It's always the same story: in a large institution like ours, between 90 and 95 percent of products are processed more or less correctly; they are entered into a catalogue of ten standard products, and the necessary investments are made once and for all to correctly deal with those products. So that is the industrial aspect. But there is always that little margin, those products springing from the engineers' creativity, and they represent 5 percent for us. But when we look at the numbers, we realize that this costs half of the back office, whereas, in terms of volume, it's relatively insignificant. Yet, it's very important for the reputation of the house, for the sense of innovation that people get. And for that, colossal sums will be invested, and that's where the whole problem lies: in managing these products before their quantities become sufficiently significant to justify an investment that is, quote unquote, industrial in scale. . . . The development of a new product today does not really take into account the cost of executing the contract, and that is a huge problem. You have a department that optimizes something, that is, the three products it thinks it will be able to sell to clients for the most, and that in the end does not include in its economic calculations another factor. And so we have, on occasion, discovered that a large part of the marvelous margin we thought was being made on a product was, in fact, pared down by management costs.

During my stay in the trading room, I crossed paths with some rare individuals who shared my interest for the discrepancy between the cost and price treatments of products. I asked myself a simple question: namely, whether the refinements and subtleties of the structured products were endangered by the growing costs that overly recursive assembly lines would beget. This question had come to me almost naturally while working with hordes of people who spent their days simply trying to understand what the engineers had developed, oblivious to the costs they generated in "intelligibility time"—that is, the hours they invested in trying to comprehend the new products in order to maintain them. The quick *hurrahs* of the front-office personnel were in sharp contrast with these slow back-office struggles. The embarrassment that this question provoked was not only the discomfort of an expert confronted with a naive outsider's question. It was also a deeper discomfort rooted in the tensions that ran alongside the front, middle, and back-office divisions of the bank. The front-office operators would complain of the slowness of "post-market" employees, by emphasizing the inordinate costs they imposed on the aggregate costs of these products. The "small hands" of the middle and back offices would turn this criticism around and fault the absence of an overall calculation for the impact of these innovations. Over the course of these disputes about the origins of profit and the means by which it could be wasted, coded expressions were developed that pointed clearly to where money came in and where it went out. The front office was the *profit center*; the back office was the *cost center*. This expression was mobilized as a mantra, and to my ears, as a way to repress the possibility that these products were not so lucrative after all. Nested into this conflict over the responsibility of uncontrolled costs was the incentive system that banks have relied on to foster more efficient commitments from its traders. Traders were judged on the basis of the performance of their portfolios, while the notion of costs floated around the bank without a stable referent or metric. The P&L measure already observed in previous chapters captures an ambiguous part of the total work invested in these products: although traders are clearly in charge of their contracts, the background work in preparing a contract's virtuoso exercises is not singled out in the same manner. Back-office managers also have a mirror portfolio of contracts, but as their operations are more scattered, they cannot claim the same paternity as traders. The differential of memory inscribed to the front- and back-office databases is another clue to the two cultures' unequal access to paternity/responsibility. The lack of memory of TRADE removes from the front office the hesitations and recursivity of the act of caring for a product. The traders represent themselves there as continuous operators, supervising the infinite speed of products. In stark contrast, the back office's quasi-obsessive memory of the minutest changes brought to contracts documents the trader's numerous interventions. In and of themselves, these two repositories of interventions do not carry any meaning, either positive or negative, but the front-office operators frame them by default as either speeding up or slowing down. In this worldview, documents represent a drag on an otherwise streamlined process, and the back office is pictured as the relentless hindrance on what could have been a perfect deal.

Calculating a Margin

In 1999, a new product was launched. Early plans counted on a limited number of high-volume transactions. But the appeal of the product to many more clients than initially expected forced the bank to respond to the greater demand—and what turned out to be a lasting one. Faced with this unexpectedly high interest, the tools used for the projection of costs proved simplistic.[8] Simplicity was sought by the managers and heads of desks: it could allow them to approach products, having various shapes and involving equally varied bank personnel, with one unique method. Simplicity made it possible to handle operations belonging to different classes of products without having to custom-design calculation methods. But this simple tool also proved rudimentary. It had been conceived around the Excel application, with the development of a macro. The program fed the expected costs of operations into a formula that did not allow for the incidence of external events. The moment of comparison between anticipated costs and real costs did not make it possible to easily identify the *failure* of the projection formula.

In general, operators are in charge of products from a variety of classes. When the new product was introduced in the processing system of the trading room, the other products continued to be processed just as they had been up to that point. The overlapping of these different generations of operations prevented operators from measuring the effects of each product on the trading room's costs without further action. Such simplicity held up well until the issuance of the new products. The effects of such massive growth of issuances had never been experienced on this scale, so that the ensuing costs had always been held at negligible levels. The sudden influx of products revealed the "simplicity" in the bank's quotidian calculation software. The problems exposed by this simplicity were explained during a discussion addressing the economy of complex products. For the first time, I received an account of the policy of products' issuance that was in sharp contrast to the absolute confidence of some and the obvious disinterest of others.

> We are trying to put in place another system because for the past year we have been overwhelmed by what has been happening. . . . I don't think it's rocket science; it is just personnel costs, processing costs. It's fairly simple budgetary calculation. But there is something to be said in our defense: the personnel moves around a lot. We have to play it by ear. . . . Above all there is a problem of information flow. People leave from one day to the next; we don't get any warning, and we can't hold them back. But you don't find a specialist in this kind of product every day. In addition, we are not just losing a person; it's almost like losing an entire team, because let's not kid ourselves on the way the whole thing works: all the information passes through the person who knows how the product functions. Training is not easily passed on, and I doubt they really want to transmit their knowledge; they understand how things work. There wouldn't be much in it for them if just anyone could take their place (June 2000).

The human resources manager had made similar comments several weeks earlier. She emphasized a growing concern among heads of postmarket operations (back and middle offices) regarding the resignation of operators who had been trained during the boom-years of activity. One case had stood out particularly for these managers and foreshadowed the end of an era when personnel management was still possible. A young manager, just out of the Ecole Centrale de Paris—one of the feeder Grandes Ecoles for General Bank—had been recruited to supervise the risk analysis of complex derivative products, such as CGPs for the fixed-income trading room. He had to develop risk models that would instruct the heads of desks about their exposure to market reversals brought on by the new products. He did not work on the floor with traders but with the middle-office personnel. After a few months, he declared that the working conditions he was offered were not competitive considering his qualifications. In support of his claim, he pointed to the positions occupied by former classmates and asked to be transferred to the front office. After numerous negotiations[9] that challenged the heads of the bank's various departments contacted by the operator, he decided to leave the firm and join a competitor. The story created a big stir in the human resources department, which criticized the trading-room heads for their inability to hold onto management personnel, who were harder and harder to come by in a job market dominated by American investment banks. This case illustrates how the appearance of very lucrative products can disrupt the routines of the bank. These products impose new methods for the management of employees who have become volatile and demanding, fully exploiting the lively competition between banks to attract skilled personnel. The skewed distribution of bonuses created by the exotics desk success story quickly belittled other bank activities: upon hearing of the seven-digit bonuses earned by front-office managers, new operators looked down upon less glamorous jobs and turned personnel management into a nightmare.

The "unification" operation I started documenting in chapter 4 provides another example of the inability to manage the portfolio of operators mobilized around the products. The release of a large number of tailored products since the end of the 1990s made the unification of the various databases challenging and time-consuming. After the request of the Commission Bancaire that General Bank should modernize and rationalize its product management system to be granted its own risk metrics, the floor managers reluctantly agreed to the plan of an additional piece of software designed to meet this transparency requirement. To speed up this task and introduce a competitive spur into a trading room that was increasingly resting on its laurels, the head of the market division decided that a consulting firm would be hired to implement this unification. A permanent team of eight to ten young consultants from Deloitte & Touche was allocated and distributed between the middle and front offices. They would be shuffled and reorganized in small teams to best meet the needs of each day. Two or three senior consultants would spend three days per week ensuring that the operation was running smoothly. This collaboration was supervised by several individuals in the trading room—working for the front and middle offices—in a cacophony that seemed to satisfy everyone, starting with the consultants who were given the opportunity to assert themselves as rational and efficient managers that were dearly needed in an inefficient universe. But they found further satisfaction in the billing system used by their employer. I was not given the exact figures associated with this operation, which lasted close to twenty months. But the junior consultants were paid F4000 (€600) per day, and the amount paid to senior consultants was double this figure. The quick response requested by the Com-

mission Bancaire was just one of the many demands for general accelera-
tion and increased transparency in the management methods for derivative
products. But to bring these activities up to the same speed as the other, more
classical financial securities that had been transferred quickly into the new
system, it was necessary to employ an outside force. The complex derivative
products, "genetically" slow, thus called for the bank to spend a huge amount
of energy to endow the process with the necessary speed. The consultants
brought in were the ready-made vectors of this force: they would constantly
claim a separate status within the bank and emphasize their ability to take
charge of and resolve the difficulties created by the multilayered organization
of the bank. Available on demand for any troubleshooting task and proud of
their status as middle-office "Bohemians,"[10] they carried these products with
them through the conflicted bank offices in a movement that soothed the
Commission Bancaire and the investors, but that burdened the bank with unexpected costs in the short term. The bank was doubly the victim of its own
success: first, the unexpected demand for treasured knowledge had agitated
its volatile workforce; next, these successful products had forced the bank to
undertake colossal investments meant to make the organization more transparent to investors. Further challenging the autonomy of native operators,
the consultants were outsiders straddling the confines of the bank, in this case
to bring in a new piece of software that was supposed to allow more direct
and informed control by the shareholders and prospective investors.

To grasp fully the scope of consequences incurred by the bank's inability
to understand and control its costs, it is necessary to document the reactions
that such a fast but uncontrolled growth triggered among the regulatory authorities. With blatant lack of controls over its costs, renewed monitoring had
become even more of a concern for the market authorities. The Commission
Bancaire's push for a more transparent and better-controlled circuit of financial products was a quid pro quo response to a larger movement initiated
by the Bank of International Settlements. Banks operating within specialized
niches would be given the autonomy of risk calculation, yet they had to show
impeccable control of their operations internally.

The Mixed Blessing of Customization: The Burden of In-House Value at Risk

In the face of costs not always measured well by the banks themselves, the
regulators of financial markets from the Bank of International Settlements
(BIS, otherwise called the Basel Committee) have enforced rules for the provisioning of capital. The regulatory authorities have gained an awareness of
the entanglement of new risks that these products have brought to the financial industry. They have come to realize the multiple effects generated by
these innovations on the level of operational risks as well as on the relatively

better understood problem of market risks. Faced with new risk exposure configurations (organizational, commercial, etc.), they have defined rules for placing a portion of the capital in *reserve* for any potential cases of failure. The value at risk (VaR) dictates the extent of these reserves.

The first installment of the VaR proposed by the BIS did not take into consideration credit risks. This absence soon appeared to affect the need for a more conservative stance in terms of capital requirement: the magnitude of banks' trading activities had to be taken into consideration. During the 1990s, a series of consultations between the government and major financial industry players led to the adoption of a framework that mandated the assessment of market risks for financial institutions and the translation of this measured risk into a capital charge. After the BIS initially proposed a standard VaR model in 1993, it subsequently (1995) opened the door to customized VaR, under the pressures of financial industry leaders. Only big players were affected by this decision: their trading volume had to be either $1 billion or 10 percent of their assets—whichever was lower—to be entitled to an in-house VaR. The BIS and the local regulator in charge of applying the capital charge rules (in our case, the Commission Bancaire) designed an incentive for adopting the standard, rather than the in-house VaR, by creating a system of penalties for institutions whose local VaRs underestimated the risk they faced. When the BIS accepted a compromise on its initial framework of a standard VaR, it made sure to set a caveat to the deregulation of risk assessment. The local regulator would have to approve the internal VaR.[11]

General Bank applied for a customized VaR to better meet the risk structure of its new products. This attempt to benefit from the specificity of their risks reinforced the interest of regulators for the organization of the bank. As we saw in chapter 4, the reorganization carried out with the aim of obtaining a personal VaR has an important impact on the processing of products and on their circulation within the bank. The Commission Bancaire—and, higher up, the BIS—present these transformations as a step toward greater transparency, but they also have a major economic impact. The rules imposed by the regulatory bodies of the financial markets are not just aimed at the visibility of procedures and the control of their risks by floor managers and heads of operations. Behind the bank risk operators, the profile of the investor lurks—and behind the sketchy figure of the investor, the stability of the whole financial market.

For a long time, discrepancies between the three products management bases (back, middle, front) had been haunting the trading-room managers. It had been sparked by numerous mismatches in the previous months. By requesting its own internal VaR accreditation from the Commission Bancaire, General Bank had to show the impeccable procedures of its trading rooms and its market operations management services. The Commission Bancaire's watchwords were *transparency* in the market activities and the *integration of risk-management procedures*. The specifications went into great detail in listing the elements to be implemented to ensure these conditions: it was an organizational blueprint for the bank's risk management as well as a method for monitoring its market positions. The goal of this improved transparency was summarized just as clearly by the Commission Bancaire in the words "risk-control."

Establishing an internal VaR was crucial for General Bank. At stake was the pursuit of its most lucrative activities and the international status it sought. To get the accreditation, it was necessary to show that volume and specialization had not derailed a good command of the bank over its internal development. In other words, it was necessary to show that the demand of shareholders and supervising authorities for a *unique* figure was indeed going to produce an *accurate* figure. Granting a bank its in-house risk metric was itself a risk for the regulatory authority: a local exception ruled out an easy comparison and could mislead shareholders and the regulatory body itself. The bank was already a specialist at proliferating calculations of all kinds. Clients knew that presenting ever more sophisticated formulas was a skill long-honed by the marketing department. The expectations attached to creating a local VaR were different. Commission Bancaire wanted to guarantee that the product specificity and its associated calculations did not generate too arcane an organization that would rule out standard assessment. This was the cost associated with this accreditation: the ordering of the bank and the accountability of its local practices into standardized procedures, if they had to work on custom operations, and thus utterly unprecedented. Put more simply, the specifications associated with the local VaR tried to guarantee the commensurability of General Bank with its interlocutors. The "local" metric had to live up to two requirements: on the one hand, inventing a method of calculation that would respect the specificity of the ingenious financial structures designed by the engineers; on the other hand, modifying its internal organization and shaping it according to a program imposed from the outside. What was the payoff of such a conversion? It is not clear that the bank gained autonomy through this local accreditation. It primarily redistributed its exchanges with the outside. The autonomy granted with the in-house VaR allowed the bank to adjust the capital charge to the risks as they were measured by the risk department of the bank. Yet, it came with a stringent program of rationalization that offset the autonomy of the metric. Accreditation comes at a cost. Although it can carry with it the hope of limiting the share of provisioned capital, it does not, however, limit the intrusion of a foreign body into the bank. If secrecy was the motto of trading-room activities, here it was truly put to the test.

Accounting: Modeling, Organization, and Communication

The third stage of this conversation between the bank and its current and prospective shareholder takes us back to the accounting operation per se. It is time to elucidate how another aspect of the work of the bank's accountants is complicated by the tension it must overcome between the proliferation of value calculations in the front office and the need to produce a single figure as evidence of the activities of the bank for the benefit of investors. The front-office operators try to give themselves as many indicators as possible to penetrate the secrets of their operations. At the other end of the circulation chain of products, investors have a different ambition: not the multiplication of perspectives on one product, but one single perspective on a great number of products. Being able to put into competition financial securities *standing for* varied sectors of the economy demands standard account presentations: accountants perform the transition from many calculations to one figure.

Three Configurations of Accounting

To penetrate the accounting puzzle created by complex products, it is helpful to present examples of three accounting procedures triggered by three different types of products.

(1) The products I describe as *simple* follow an accounting procedure that was stabilized some years ago. These standard operations only require the intervention of the bank operators at two points during their lifetime—when they are launched and when they are closed. They can be thoroughly described in the back-office database. Their value is assessed in this database thanks to an embedded back-office pricer. As a consequence, the information (characteristics and price) contained in the database does not need to be complemented by any other elements from the middle or front office. The front-office interventions and the accounting calculations are sealed off from one another so that accountants do not need to rely on the skill of traders. The flows of payments are automatically brought up to the accounting department, which is nothing but an extension of the back office. The indus-

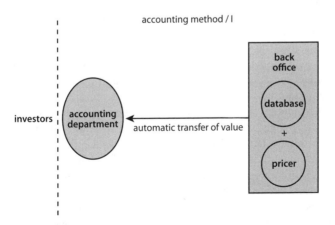

Figure 21. Simple Accounting

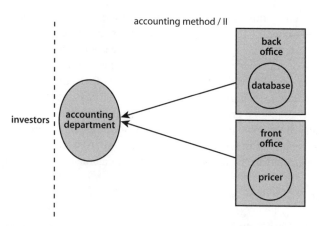

Figure 22. Partial Accounting

trial organization designed around these products limits contact between the employees of the middle and back offices. The valuation automatically performed by the database can be consulted on demand by all. This first category of accounting procedure depends primarily on computer technicians. Accounting work is conducted through the happy integration of management systems. The second and third categories of accounting are closer to the concerns raised by the CGP. They are the ones in which new financial products reshape accounting.

(2) The second accounting procedure can be seen as a response to products that are only partially represented in the back-office database. The schematic and sketchy keying of the financially relevant characteristics of these operations breaks the well-integrated industrial system of the first category. Besides, pricing is no longer performed by a piece of software integrated into the back-office database. The patchy information stored in the database makes it impossible to call forth the value of a product from this digital identity. The task of assessing the values of these types of operations falls to an outside pricer. As such, traders reenter the scene, and with them come possible conflicts. Traders come forward from backstage in particular when choices must be made pertaining to the value of market indicators that are necessary to assess these operations. When some products are present in small numbers in the bank's management databases, certain market indicators necessary to pricing are not available[12] to the back office. The back-office operators and the accountants must then turn to the traders, who have this information.

(3) The third category of accounting is activated when operations have so many new properties that they cannot even schematically be keyed into the database of the back office. In this situation, the operation is reduced to a simplified ID featuring its transaction number, the client's name, and a few other pieces of information (currency of the transaction, nominal, launching

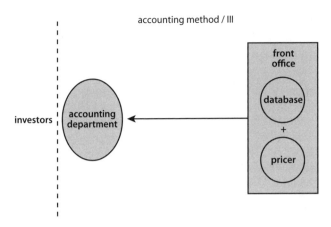

accounting method / III

Figure 23. Accounting as Front-Office Prerogatives

and closing dates), none of which touch the payoff. The pricing data have gone out the window. Our formula finds no place of inscription in what has become an outdated database.

This third type of operation reverses the roles and reasserts the monopoly of traders. The back office still checks and controls important information, but the information is incomplete. Pricing is beyond its reach. The back-office operator must return to the confirmation to know what the product looks like. But even digging out the paper version of the product does not always give access to its value. Only the trader can now rule on what it is worth. This third category is thus a complicated job for the accountant, as he or she must delegate almost everything. While the accountant could passively observe the different threads of calculation collapsing into a single figure as if by magic for the first kind of products, he or she must now rely on the front office for valuation (i.e., the trader). But it is also in the context of renewed abrasive contacts with traders that the accountant will once again be involved in a job of "accounting," that is, not hesitating to set him or herself to taking the work of the floor to account.

Organizing the Reduction to One Figure

The accountants must have the last word in the dispute concerning calculations because they are the ones who produce the figure served up to investors and financial analysts. Working at this reconciliation occupies an entire team from the "complex derivative back office" (CDBO), which, for this reason, was nicknamed "method gap bridging." The method gap is acknowledged and accepted and provides work to a horde of operators in the bank. The complexity of the tasks at hand has triggered a new organization: accounting is now split into two subgroups that together produce the unique figure.

Preaccounting

A preaccounting unit overseeing the smooth connection between accounting and the front office was created within the complex derivative back office. Its purpose was fairly vague because it overlapped with both the accounting and the back-office operators. Its location in the back of the area occupied by the CDBO was evidence of its subordinate role: it was only to be mobilized in special cases. They were contacted by their colleagues because they understood what was needed and took a quasi-forensic joy at fitting rare and tortured products into accounting reports. A classic intervention will detail the nature of their involvement. During the remodeling of an *equity-linked swap*[13] into a *swap*, one of the back-office managers working on the transformation consulted the preaccounting unit to check that the calculation methods attached to the two products were not incompatible and that it was possible to switch from one to the other without rewriting all of the (past and current) flows that had to be keyed into the database. What was carefully checked during the consultation period was the way in which what was paid out and received was communicated to the accounting department. If the two products had different channels of communication to accounting, there could be a problem. When equity-linked swap information was sent up to accounting at the beginning of the fiscal year (during the observation of the fixing used to define the flows of capital in or outward), and when swap information was sent up at the end of the period, switching from one model to the other could cause the accounting department to record the same flow twice. The preaccounting unit had become a specialist in the arcane rules that governed each new product. This expertise came as much from good knowledge of the local uses (what to do, whom to contact) as from accurate and up-to-date information from the Commission Bancaire.

The Footbridge

Every day, the back office takes in cash flows from clients. They are taken into account—literally—by the preaccounting department that channels them up to accounting. But this outward circulation of the figure toward the surface (in this case, the investors) of the bank is jerky and marked by a series of checks and controls exacted by an organ that was created when customized derivative products that raised problems of interpretation started piling up in the processing trays of the accounting department. This organ was called the "footbridge" (in French *passerelle*)—an appropriate name judging by the number of translocations its employees had to make during a given day. Situated between the front and back offices, the footbridge was in charge of checking the compatibility of figures produced by the two. As it dealt with products whose values were not produced automatically by the back-office database, it was necessary for the accounting department to supply itself with the ID of the products while using the front-office pricers. The accounting department strives to stay neutral in relation to the competing versions that the back and front offices provide it with. It maintains this neutrality in part by not obtaining all of its information from one source. However, this neutrality works strangely: lacking the authorization to come up with its own pricing,[14] the accounting department draws information pertaining to a contract from here and there: from the front office's future-oriented pricing, and from the back office's past payment flows. This is the exercise performed by the footbridge every day—literally to amalgamate past and future into the practical, manipulable present. A second example of the mistakes the footbridge tracked will clarify the management of the different calculation spaces. A product is in its portfolio from January 1, 2001, to January 1, 2002. It is characterized by a series of flows every three months. The back office receives a cash flow from the client on June 30, 2001, and communicates this flow to accounting. Accounting must assess the full value of the contract that yielded this flow of money at its halfway point, but it cannot turn back to the back office for this. It must turn to the trader, as the full value of the contract lies at least partially in the future. The original valuation of the front office counted this future flow and takes it into account in its valuation. If accounting prices this product by adding the flows that have already been served and the valuation by the pricer over the remaining period, it will count one flow too many and will overvalue the portfolio. The two calculation spaces, not reconciled until the involvement of accounting, blend into a single calculation. But this fusion requires accountants to check the terms of the contract and more precisely the date of the cash flow deposit.[15]

These new products have planted the seeds of a new organization that stretches and thickens the accounting zone considerably. Now involved with the front and back offices, new specialists have emerged in the periphery of the bank who listen to regulators and clients as carefully as they do employees of the bank. Unlike clients who come into the bank—first in the guise of the individual that the marketing department strives to anticipate and decipher, subsequently in the persona of a codesigner of their tailored financial product—current and prospective investors struggle to control General Bank from further afield. For all of this distance, however, these interferences are not felt less intrusively. They lean on more disruptive tools than simply the whims of a few demanding clients. The disclosure requirements and the accounting disciplines forced onto the bank's organization reduce the discretionary space of the bank's operators.

Recursive Calculation

From being a calculating entity, the bank finds itself subjected to calculation. The bank's complete submission to the pressing demands of investors would work if the valuation timings of these two sides of the bank (the calculating front office and the calculated results produced by the accounting department) were the same. The slower pace of the bank, holding these strategic external calculations at bay—through a carefully engineered inability to value its products in a manner that satisfies the desires of shareholders—introduces a structural discrepancy. Yet, the relative opacity of a growing number of structured financial instruments has influenced the regulators to devise ways of categorizing them so that they could be made more legible to investors and to the local bank accountants in charge of assigning their value to standard reports in financial statements. This endeavor is meant to minimize the number of financial instruments categorized as too unruly to figure on the balance sheet. In looking at the three accounting models, one can clearly see the trend followed by ever-more innovative instruments. By challenging the existing categories and by blurring the classes to which they should be assigned, engineers withdraw these products from public scrutiny. When the products are off–balance sheet, the bank can be held accountable by the investors, but only when the contracts are being unwound. Thrown into a catch-all accounting category, these innovative products survive under the radar until their formulas fall under scrutiny and its parts are broken down.

A classical argument that runs from Weber (1976) to Sombart (1953) sees the development of double-entry bookkeeping as one of the major steps in the development of economic rationality.[16] These calculation systems have indeed to do with the command of time and space and with the creation of tools fit to transform the variety of economic activities into figures, commensurable and manipulable on a sheet of paper. The drawback of this pervasive story of accounting and rationality comes from the lack of consideration for the intense creativity of accounting itself. Rather than giving form to an ethereal and eternal rationality, accounting systems select paths of development for modes of accounts. They can certainly be described as adaptation of means to ends, but this vocabulary is misleading by its extreme generality, as we have seen repeatedly that the end (making profit) is many-faced. Innovations in accounting do far more than simply wed means to ends. They do not apply the script of a preexisting system of rationality but rather invent one by drawing new horizons for it. Customized financial products provide an excellent field of observation for this generation of new accounting frameworks. They show that such rationality is open and changing, and that its fate is in the hands of the actors who succeed in imposing their views.

The bank is torn between two temptations, and this tension transpires in its costs' calculation and its overall organization. First, front-office operators pull toward devising ever-more sophisticated cost calculations to capture financial transactions. This gives carte blanche to the free imagination of engineers and salespeople and attaches the bank's entire accounting architecture to their chaotic trajectories. In contrast, the operators in charge of calculating costs, who have in mind the need to produce a figure summarizing all activities on a regular basis, try to overturn the sometimes wild profit-making mentality of market operators.

The difficulty to offer a bottom line of this activity to shareholders and prospective investors mirrors the difficulty to describe the relevant features of the CGP to its clients. In some instances, salespeople have intentionally hidden risks created by the design; similarly, accountants have knowingly qualified products in ways that mask their ultimate cost to the company. So, in what looks like a common sense diagnosis, they have used artifices to distort the risk of the products and its manufacture. Yet, this is too simple a diagnosis, as it implies that somewhere and at some time during the design and management of CGPs—and most complex derivatives—someone knew of the exact magnitude of risks taken by the clients, the bank, and its owners. What the current voyage into General Bank shows is that there was no such privileged site of comfortable exploitation. There was indeed the exploitation of gullible clients and investors who were happy to be told stories of genius quants and infallible traders, but there was as much self-deception. This is the most crucial finding of this travel into quantitative finance: opacity of financial designs does not produce asymmetry so easily and naturally that it would give the bank engineers and traders a solid and lasting edge. There are obviously some differences between clients and engineers, and the lack of an existing "market" allows fat commercial margins, but it also leaves the bank alone, without the solid ground of a market price acting as a referent. Speculation and simulation, the two resources for asymmetrical control and foresight, would require a less tortured design of CGPs, which would immediately level the playing field between the client and the bank.

CHAPTER 7

|

Reverse Finance

In this chapter, I come back to the question of the nature of a financial firm and the strains generated therein by the design of financial products. Trapped between offering ever-innovative services through a chaotic and hardly accountable organization on the one hand, while on the other hand simultaneously delivering itself as a publicly traded company under the mode of securities, the bank tries to accommodate two incompatible gestures. The first imperative privileges the client to the extent that he or she does not need to worry too much about the process used by the engineers and traders. A client is given a say as to the product's literal expression—the prospectus detailed in the introduction, with its embedded formulas and the perimeter of its basket of underlyings. Although this focus on the contract and the client's ability to revise it before it comes to term is separate from the more secretive hedging process, it still complicates it, as every detail of the prospectus has its corresponding sequence in the trader's activity. Investors who own General Bank equities may not have much interest in the process, but they care about the possibility that their money invested in the bank's equities might not yield as much as it could, or even worse, might disappear entirely if the bank manages its operation poorly and wastes the client's capital (which would force the bank to draw on its own capital to repay the nominal and the performance of the basket). Investors have a procedural definition of responsibility. They want the creative and somewhat unruly gestures of the front-office operators to stick to a script that can be subjected to surveillance. This move, radicalizing a trend long stigmatized by early scholars of publicly traded corporations,[1] amounts to questioning the firm as an autonomous entity. Going beyond the request that management rules be made public, shareholders who intrude into the bank demand that banks be run as portfolios of securities are handled. They demand that the firm be nothing but a bundle of cleanly priced activities on a par with, and comparable with, securities.

Examining the tension between organizing through rules and transacting through prices is nothing new. Economists in particular have produced prolific studies on the *nature of the firm*—to borrow one seminal formulation of the problem offered by Ronald Coase in 1937. Even a minimal definition of the firm as an organization of agents grouped around a common goal immediately poses the question of the mechanism designed to allow such a grouping. A quick glance back to chapter 3 and the competition in the room reminds us of the risk of chaos facing financial firms channeling such huge amounts of money: all operators want the biggest share of the profit for themselves so much so that left alone to the wild competition of a market, the firm would implode from the agonistic relations that set in. Another quick glance back to chapter 4 reminds us that rules of access to clients' deals are constantly bent by operators attempting to act ahead of their colleagues in the firm. The bank seems to offer an appropriate case to test the nature of the firm: the problem of trust is compounded by a situation of unequal information distribution by surrounding operators with the potential for easy money. An appropriate case indeed, only made richer thanks to the actors' accounts of an innovation that sharpens the rules to be followed and the prices to be paid.

If we keep in mind what we have learned of the design of financial products by traveling from front to back office, there is a thicker and richer story to be told than what transaction-cost economists might tell us. Their framing of the agency question is mostly detached from precisely the level of sociotechnical description adopted in *Codes of Finance*: how can firms that are a highly complex patchwork of operators, products, instruments—each with their own temporality and rhythm—hold together? There is obviously a way in which characterizing firms through such formulas as *profit maximization* and *incentives mechanisms* is correct and, indeed, the agency framing of firms sets the description to that level of generality. Yet, such a framing device disregards the nature of the profit and the incentives at stake. The lessons of previous chapters need to accompany us as we move to our final investigation of the trading room. There is a genuine uncertainty over the adequate measure of profit. Behind the motto/mantra of profit maximization, operators and investors are offered a great deal of latitude in defining their own metric of profit. The horizon of maximization is up for grabs, and each constituent within the bank and at its fringes pushes for his or her own metric to rule the game of investment. So, yes—the name of the game is still profit maximization; but which profit and how to maximize?

Parallel to the uncertainty over profit is the uncertainty over the limits of the crucial actors of General Bank: the bank itself and its units, the product. Tracing neat boundaries around these actors is made problematic by the design of CGPs. Sitting here and there *in* the bank, valued now and in the future, they defeat the simple alternative offered by the economists who have framed the question of the firm as either a whole or a finite series of units.

Yet, going beyond that alternative is not only a matter of finding a common ground between organizations with their hierarchical rules and markets and their elusive prices. The blurry boundaries of CGPs and their operators' units fit *neither markets nor organizations*—to paraphrase sociologist Walter Powell (1990) and his solution out of the economist trap—as the puzzle created by the elusive products come from the lack of either clear rules or clear prices. What should we call the quality of organizations that host products like CGPs?

A solid stream of scholars of large organizations (Nohria and Eccles, 1992; Powell, 1990) have long contended that there is nothing more to organizations than networks and that the search for the substance of organization is a chimera.[2] This lesson has not been lost on investors, who are avid readers of organization theorists. In particular, one aspect of this ontological lesson has struck a sensible chord: if organizations are nothing but networks, then the basic unit of value may have to be revised from the company to its networks. It may be these constituent networks alone that account for the quality of a company and the desirability of its equities. This new perspective on organizations has serious consequences for investors and operators. If the relevant value unit is no longer the company as such but its constitutive networks, its liquidity changes: it is no longer a single piece, but rather a composition of elements that only coexist momentarily and can be moved around in the future. What is the consequence of such a shift in focus and scale on investment behaviors? If operators belong to networks and no longer to indivisible companies, how do they relate to their surrounding environment? In practice, in a globalized bank such as General Bank—selling CGPs and in a continuous state of crisis from the forceful innovation promoted there—how does the Coasian *nature-of-the-firm* question become an issue to people in the bank?

In this chapter, I look at a reaction that took place within the bank—against its intense financialization and I extend the notion of network to encompass sociotechnical networks. The operators behind this reaction resorted to a strategy of high technological integration that could aptly be named "reverse finance." If finance is indeed a trend that generates "simplifications" of existing economic units and invents stages wherein such vehicles can be traded, some operators at General Bank endeavored to engineer an area of the firm that did not easily lend itself to such derivations. They did not design a firm that resisted securitization[3]: after their "reverse finance" reaction and the sociotechnical scheme that they brought to life, investors were as able as before to acquire nominal portions of the firm. Instead, their resistance strategy protected the implicit contract of the securitization gesture. In addition to reasserting the autonomy of the exotics desk by integrating it more strongly to the rest of the bank, they also reiterate the distinction between the firm as a composition of production factors and the property rights standing for the performance of the firm. They fight back against the view that liquidity is not only a quality of property rights vehicles on the securities market but also of the firm itself on the market of the firms' units of value. The resistance strategy of "reverse finance" insists that the firm has to be seen as a whole and not as a collection of temporarily and exclusively legally bound pieces. Ultimately, "reverse finance" relies on engineering a "round" firm—one that lacks the sorts of modularity that would have weakened its integrity.

The Business of Selling Businesses

The success of the exotics desk was accompanied by hosts of complications. Increased scrutiny from regulators and investors was only one dimension of the unease triggered by a story too good to be true. In a company increasingly managed as a portfolio of relatively autonomous businesses, being an exception in the bank became a mixed blessing. It detached the desk and its wunderkind operators from the bank's local activities—and recent events had signaled that being detached could also be seen as being fungible.

A Room Disappears

During my first year of studying the bank, I witnessed the *disappearance* (April 2000) of one of its trading rooms. Disappearance is the way in which those operators not working in the room described the transformation that took place in their landscape (the sudden disappearance of people with whom they had maintained trade relations or had taken cigarette breaks). This disappearance had not, in fact, eliminated this small community from the financial market: it still existed, but it no longer worked for General Bank. The "emerging markets" room, which had not proved to be efficient enough and which no longer fit into the plans of the bank's upper management, had been sold to another bank and left the premises of its previous owner. The collection of people along with their equipment disappeared from the bank within the space of a weekend. The room remained, of course, but was empty of its occupants and equipment. The operators most critical of this disappearance described it using the terms of a "sale" while emphasizing the monstrousness of an operation that swallowed up—seemingly without care—people, contractual relationships, techniques, and everything that keeps a trading room running. Nor was the simple loss of people and equipment the only disturbing element of this disappearance. The rapidity of the move contributed to the apparent savagery of this detachment, not least of all because it showed that the seeming *physical integration* of the room in the wider ecosystem of the bank could be disposed of at the whim of the upper management, without any serious resistance on the part of the operators. The emerging markets room had not been able to protect itself against this fragmentation. For many operators, this sudden change in their professional surrounding was a shock. For the operators of our desk, it was less surprising as they already considered

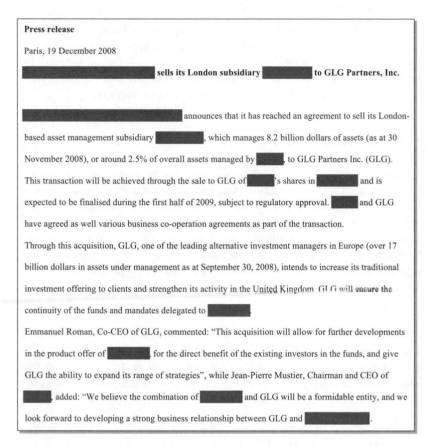

Press release

Paris, 19 December 2008

███████████████████████ **sells its London subsidiary** ████████████ **to GLG Partners, Inc.**

████████████████████████████████ announces that it has reached an agreement to sell its London-based asset management subsidiary ██████████, which manages 8.2 billion dollars of assets (as at 30 November 2008), or around 2.5% of overall assets managed by ████████, to GLG Partners Inc. (GLG). This transaction will be achieved through the sale to GLG of ████████'s shares in ██████████ and is expected to be finalised during the first half of 2009, subject to regulatory approval. ████████ and GLG have agreed as well various business co-operation agreements as part of the transaction.

Through this acquisition, GLG, one of the leading alternative investment managers in Europe (over 17 billion dollars in assets under management as at September 30, 2008), intends to increase its traditional investment offering to clients and strengthen its activity in the United Kingdom. GLG will ensure the continuity of the funds and mandates delegated to ██████████.

Emmanuel Roman, Co-CEO of GLG, commented: "This acquisition will allow for further developments in the product offer of ██████████, for the direct benefit of the existing investors in the funds, and give GLG the ability to expand its range of strategies", while Jean-Pierre Mustier, Chairman and CEO of ████████, added: "We believe the combination of ██████████ and GLG will be a formidable entity, and we look forward to developing a strong business relationship between GLG and ██████████.

Figure 24. Other Rooms moving around in a Major French Bank

ways of controlling how their own activities could be protected from such a fate. They had figured out that the resistance to this commoditization of the bank's units (trading rooms, whole portions of the market division's activities) could not exclusively rely on alliances of operators: ultimately, they knew they would not be able to talk on an equal footing with their CEO or CFO.

The alternate strategy of these operators drew on a first-hand understanding of the kind of commodities into which that banks' units could potentially be transformed. The rooms are organized according to different modules, each having a relative autonomy vis-à-vis the bank. They have their respective markets, operators, and techniques, and this independence is specifically cultivated by the owners of the bank to allow units to be displaced over short time periods. This movement involves whole sections of activity: operators with their techniques in hand; vendors together with their address books; traders along with their parcels of the market. Modularization of the organization involves much more than a simple spatial division of the room. The success of units' commoditization requires the unit to become part of the transaction—needing to find a buyer, another company ready to absorb it. It must be both autonomous—with respect to its initial home company—and compatible with the future home company. The understanding of these restrictions bearing on the commoditization of bank units grew also out of a precedent in recent financial history. The stripping down of companies, victims of the *raiders* of the deregulated finance milieu of the 1980, served as an example for the operators who resisted. The problem of this understanding was that it came about in a context that weakened it: the increased importance of activities on complex derivative products helped instill commercial relations both within and between the bank's different trading rooms. All factors contributed to the growing trend against which our operators were struggling.

The Domestic Economy

The success of the exotics desk's activities had a great impact on the unity of the trading room. Foremost, it affected the relationships among the desks in the trading room. The culprit of these changes was in part the relentless growth of the volume of products handled by the exotics desk. This growth transformed relations within the trading room by instilling market transactions where there were once hierarchical distributions of roles. The culprit for this dramatic change was the derivative-based activity of the room. The uncontrolled swelling of the hedging account on the exotics desk slowly displaced the roles assigned so far to the desks within the room, and even to the room in the market division at General Bank. After having achieved such prominence among its bank partners, this provocative desk unleashed more market-based interactions with its newly found competitors. This change in scope turned out to be one of the unexpected consequences of the desk's success: the swelling wealth ushered in profit maximization, no longer only among competitors outside of the bank but also between different specialties within the bank.

The weight of the exotics desk's capital was a product of the underlying securities held as part of the hedging scheme. As part of hedging strategies, these securities were inactive. Sitting in the bank as it were, they were not immersed in the greater economy as part of investments. They were kept, as a hedging reserve, but there was no legal obligation for the bank to hold onto them. Even though this practice resembles the mandatory capital adequacy requirements imposed by the Basel Committee rules, it was essentially meant to respect the more informal rules of efficient hedging. The bank could choose not to hedge and just bet on the zero-coupon to cover the performance owed to the client, but it would pay a high price should the wager ever fail. Although the mandatory capital reserves must be held at a distance from the market and pulled aside from its risky fluctuations, the hedging portfolio reserves accumulated by the desk can *legally* be reintroduced into the economy. The trading-room managers, torn between the imperative of smooth hedging accumulation and the other imperative of profit, created a mechanism meant to reconcile profit and safety, guaranteeing against the risk of default of the other party—in other words, they created the *hedging reserve*. This reserve was not, strictly speaking, completely static: trading-room managers instituted local loans of these securities to other desks of the room or of the bank. For example, when the exotics desk held a large number of France Telecom futures (at the time, the most weighty security of the hedging portfolio) and knew that it would need to keep a large portion of them for a long period, it had the opportunity to loan them to a nearby desk in need of these securities. Because the corporate identity of the lender and the borrower were one and the same (both belonged to General Bank trading rooms), the usual borrower default possibility—the fact that borrowers sometimes do not return what they have been lent—was ruled out. The terms of the loan were also simplified; these desks were situated either as literal neighbors sharing a floor or, at worst, on different floors but in constant contact. Therefore, the transaction would simply be recorded as tickets kept by traders. Moreover, these loans, although local, bore interest for the exotics desk. There were no small gains.

The domestic character of this exchange mechanism seems to point initially to a strengthened set of bonds between different parts of the bank: these flows of money are like many ties between otherwise unrelated desks, each dealing with a specialized territory on the broader market. This simple procedure can also be read as a genuine domestic mode of exchange: stripped of the formality of contracts between parties unknown to each other, the loans have the misleading flavor of the domestic-ties-binding economy. Yet, if such transactions look domestic, they only appear so in the sense of economist Gary Becker's domestic ties: that is, profit-driven interactions in domains that were thought to be immune from these price mechanisms. If anything, these local loans corroded the rules of organization within the bank and instilled price as a coordination mechanism.

By instituting this lending practice between a bank's units of operation, the heads of the trading rooms introduced an element of division in the bank. They put these units in competition with one another, thus challenging the bank's ostensible unity. The local loans tended to be made at conventional rates, but these were rates that the exotics desk could choose to later revise.[4] When the lending rate is set once and for all, independently of the market rates, this relation can be seen as commercial, albeit conducted under the aegis of the necessary legal cohesion of the bank's many centers of operation. When the rate becomes negotiable and aligns (within minimal variations) with the market rate, the inside/outside difference disappears: legal unity remains, but economic unity gives way to competition. While enjoying the successes of their activity and taking advantage of the trick of risk-free loans among their compatriots, a general awareness grew among the exotics desk operators that the unique characteristics of their operation also made them ideal candidates to be traded during merger talks—especially at a time when such talks were taking place among all major French banks.

The Jewel of the French Banking Industry

The transformations of the financial organization of the bank set off by the successes of its main activity had been preceded by discrete nudges from a crucial player in this story. This drive toward an increased competition both inside and outside the bank, as observed on the floor, had been orchestrated on a different scale by the French government.[5] After the 1980s—having felt the effects of financial deregulation initiated in England and the United States—French banks were forced to compete with their European and American counterparts. The French government had a long tradition of intervention, and as it braced for the increased exposure of French banks to the competition brought on by European counterparts, it started looking closely at General Bank and the handful of international-size banks with a set of principles similar to the modularity principles in action in the bank.

The French government delegates the enforcement of the proper market rules (client and investor protection) to its national regulatory bodies (observed in chapter 6), but historically it has not limited its action to this role.[6] Guaranteeing transparency of the French marketplace in order to attract investors and clients from around the world is only the most visible part of the State's involvement: behind the scenes, the organization of the French financial industry remains a State priority that is not delegated to any other authority. The run on the European market accentuated the pressure on the French State to organize—once and for all—French companies before intrusions by the national authorities would be criminalized under the newly empowered European Union commission. The 1990s witnessed the preparation of the European banking industry leading up to the establishment of a single market and to the unification that would later come into play. Faced with the harsh competition of powerful financial services partners, the State set to work figuring out the best possible institutional architecture with which to equip the few banks that would come out on top of the increased competition of this unified economic space. In facing Germany, England, and to a lesser extent Italy, the governments that came to power from the end of the 1980s through the middle of the 1990s reasserted a typically French capitalism by emphasizing the role of the State in large industrial groups and tight networks of cross-participation. What was at stake here—and what would again come into question a few years later during the various attempts at merging two of the three banks, Banque Nationale de Paris (BNP) and Paribas—and Société

Générale, and with the Crédit Agricole and Crédit Lyonnais merger—was a question of national (economic) independence. The maintenance of a national economic integrity was heralded through the participation or the full ownership of major industrial groups by the State or by *reliable* institutional French investors, thereby making it unlikely to fall into the hands of foreign groups. The metaphor most used at the time to describe a capitalism that would be able to hold up against both deregulation (in the United States and Britain) and super-regulation (through the emerging European Union) was that of "solid cores"[7]: concentration of companies' property titles in the hands of a few trusted investors, who are able to resist the lure of over-priced takeover bids by competitors trying to buy their way into the capital of French companies. This "solid cores" scheme was supposed to be resistant to competition while not excluding hybridization of industrial strategies. The solid cores had to guarantee that the majority of property titles would remain in the bosom of the State or of its loyal groups. The solid cores would only be viable if efficiency was achieved. Successful protection was to begin with the industrial cohesion of the groups that would come out of this reshaping of French banks. By endowing these new banking institutions with sound prospects and by equipping them with the necessary tools to face the future, the risks that a majority of shareholders might be lured by a generous takeover bid were minimized. What ultimately resulted was a traditional French recipe for economic policy: a mix of industrialist beliefs and State intervention going back to an entrenched *saint-simonisme* shared by most high-ranking French civil servants.[8]

Throughout the 1980s and 1990s, the State increasingly made its presence felt around General Bank. The outstanding results of the market division made it an ideal candidate to spearhead an innovative investment bank focused on institutional clients. The bank found itself at the intersection of a historical drive toward competition orchestrated by the unprecedented experiment of the European Union; of a tradition of State intervention that ran counter to the liberal agenda of the European Union; and of a new market niche that generated considerable profit. Under these combined forces, it was difficult not to feel the threat of dismemberment. That was the unexpected effect of success and its usual burden: success aroused envy and brought about scrutiny. The logic of government intervention was similar to that of the head of markets activities: the State looked at banks as bundles of value creation units and sought to combine the most compatible of them in creating efficient and resistant blocks. The level of financial organization for an actor such as the State was not the bank itself but its divisions and units: focusing on coherence and performance at the company level did not rule out redundancy between French banks. The looming competition with major German and British banks—sure to be harsh—set the level of organizational scrutiny one flight up. That is, in the view of the State, a country like France could not afford too many dispersed and uncoordinated banks undermining one another; in keeping with an entrenched mercantilist view, then, the nation became the relevant focal point of analysis. For the banks that found themselves in the State's line of sight, the strengths and weaknesses of their various specialties became pieces of a complex puzzle.

The omnipresence of investors, through the regulators—and of the State, through pressing concerns of rationalization of the national financial sector—triggered strong reactions among the architects of the exotic derivatives desk. Faced with endless demands for instantaneous assessments and the flexibility of production structures, some raised their voices in defense of the rights and specificities of their particular financial activity. There is an irony in the interventions of the French State in the banking industry. The operators who realized that the jewel in their crown was under attack—by the combined modularization of the bank's business units and by the pressing interest of the State for their particular modular units—engaged in a strategy of resistance to preserve the unity of their business and their integration to the bank as a whole. But this counterattack operated on grounds similar to those of the ministry of the economy that struggled to find the proper equation that would protect French banking assets against European competitors, eager to engage in merger acquisition to brace themselves for the European financial fray.

Technology of Resistance

From Securities to Physical Capital

The main problem with publicly traded companies originates with the "public." Once the company's equity is up for grabs and its possession decided on the basis of the bids and offers matched on an anonymous market, no one knows—let alone controls—who owns what. Exchanges and regulatory authorities have set limits on anonymous takeovers and "friendly" acquisitions that would destabilize companies. Yet, even if publicly traded companies can protect themselves against aggressive strategies, the equities they possess are outstanding and sensitive to prices. If the distinction between the nominal capital (property titles) and the actual capital (buildings, machines, etc.) was safe, operators of publicly traded companies could also feel safe. They would obviously feel the need to please investors should they need to tap into their assets to raise further capital, but their decision would be relatively insulated from the tumultuous world of the securities exchange. There is indeed a limit to the representation of securities as mirroring that of the actual companies. The shareholding composition (either divided into an infinite number of small investors or composed of solid cores working together) determines the sort of latitude that the management has. When shareholders reach a majority and when they start stepping into the realm of management, ownership becomes management. Shareholders can indeed *almost* pass seamlessly from *nominal property* to *real property*. Once this threshold is broken, what are the terms of negotiation between two groups that were not supposed to tread the same field? Shareholders get a new lever by disrupting the division of labor settled by securitization. In many ways, they can talk on an equal footing with managers. How do these embattled managers reinvent a space of autonomy against this intrusion? They know from a long history of bank mergers and acquisitions that movements affecting the nominal side of capital (the securities' side) can entail related movements on their side of capital (the underlyings' side).

In the context of increasing tensions between French banks over the looming unification of the European financial market, the development of an in-house information system held off more or less explicit plans for collaborations, mergers, and acquisitions. The managers of the room, who had been at the forefront of the exotic derivatives activity in the late 1980s, fought the prospect of being disassembled, detached from their current host, and merged with another financial institution looking to strengthen its financial engineering services. To that end, they pushed for an integrated information system, strongly tying front, middle, and back offices. We have covered this system, TRADE, in passing descriptions within previous chapters of this book. We discover it now as a "political" tool meant to serve a function of integration and forced *decommoditization* of the bank's units. *Decommoditization*, in addition to being an unpleasant neologism, is also probably misleading. The units—the desk and its development in other rooms of the bank—had not yet been commoditized to begin with. The resistance strategy preemptively launched by the founding fathers of the exotic derivatives group was meant to prevent commoditization before the fact. Commoditization and modularity would have required standardization and compatibility: in contrast, resistance to these moves took the path of singularity and entanglement. By developing such a strategically entangled system and promoting it as the panacea to all the bank divisions' concerns, well beyond the exotics desk, the plan of the desk's managers was to attach the parts of this financial institution in such a way that the modular approach could not disassemble them.

The first hours of this activity were exhilarating moments. Operators who were part of the initial team and were still on the desk at the time of my fieldwork had a mix of a few vivid memories and many canned stories about harsh beginnings and a swift takeoff. This choice of modulars was made by the market division of the General Bank early on, when it addressed the question of the best processing systems for derivative operations at the beginning of the 1990s. The bank's front-runner position on a segment of the market that was then not very developed partly prevented it from seeking resources outside its own internal teams. No other bank had a comparable degree of development of this activity and, as a result, using subcontractor services was not a conceivable option. Comparable services available to the large French banks entering this new market were not yet fully developed, but several strategies were open to those in charge of equity derivatives activities. Outsourcing to pricer developers could have been one solution, but the relative novelty of exotic derivatives and the banking industry's low demand for front-to-back integration services for exotic products ruled it out. A second consideration concerned not the lack of existing available offers but the effects that an in-house system of product management might have on the future of the bank. The development of a system within the bank allowed it to remain a step ahead in the management of such products and to put forward a technology so far restricted to the simplest of financial products: front-to-back integration and modeling standardization were intended to convince potential clients interested in these innovative products.

Some of the most outspoken opponents of this strategy stigmatized it because they saw the economic calculation of this choice being contaminated by considerations of prestige. They insisted that such a system could not meet the specific needs of each desk and that it was bound to become one giant system, useless because homogeneous and expensive to maintain. While recollections of the argument over the "system" were repeated to me many times, they were not always configured as criticisms, and even less so as criticisms of the disproportionate visions of the managers who had ultimately made that decision. Choosing to follow an approach that emphasized the unified specificity of the bank was seen, by some, in a positive light and was even defended by many heads of desks in the trading room. This defense recalled the need for the bank to have full command over its internal development and strategic choices: by adopting a technology that would force it to outsource each new addition to the functionalities of the management software, the bank would lose its edge. It would very quickly make public the updates that would have allowed it to have a leg up on its competitors.

It was difficult to track how the decision to invest in that in-house system had been made. In conversations with historic members of the exotics desk, most operators downplayed the resistance strategy when my questions got more precise. When I asked the head of the market division about the choice of this system, he replied in vague terms claiming that this was a level decision, the kind "not strategic enough" for shareholders to look into seriously.[9] He remembered that this decision did not even trickle up to the CEO or board of directors. When I submitted the possibility of a technological resistance to competition waged at the level of technical compatibility, he replied that the number of problems to tackle during a merger-acquisition operation was such that calculations of these sorts were de facto ruled out. According to him, bidders know they cannot exhaust all the sources of additional costs incurred during a merger of two different productive systems, but they count on the law of large numbers and the balancing of surprises, good and bad ones. Notably, the head of the market division was not part of the desk during early hours. Slightly older than the desk members, he was hierarchically above them, but his bonus could be below that of the exotics desk traders.

This resistance was a subtle technological version of a well-known phenomenon of off-price competition. This form of competition retreats from the field of price and deploys its assets elsewhere, principally in the qualities of the good/service. Prices are bypassed and made irrelevant by throwing light on their other characteristics, a move familiar to the historic operators of the desk, who were doing just that by crafting unique services. The significant difference stemmed from what was to be pulled out of the competition. The desk itself, composed of a unique combination of personnel and projects, had become the asset to be rendered unique and incompatible. In the uncertain context when the bank's survival was not guaranteed and where important decisions were being made outside its walls, the response brought by second-ranking managers was to construct the information technology system of the bank in such a way as to make it less vulnerable to takeover. The risk of disassembly was limited by the bank's configuration as an *indivisible* unit. Insofar as merger strategies were designed in terms of anticipated yields of several targets, engineering the bank as an irreducible form was a direct response to the prospect of being disassembled. This was also—and maybe primarily—an act of resistance against a distortion and subversion of the principle of publicly traded capital. The distortion came from the confusion between management and ownership that was being staged by the corporate governance revolution in full swing in Anglo-Saxon countries.

Ironically, the managers of this trading room achieved through information technology what finance achieved through the invention of securities. Securities—that is, shares of the bank—stand as identical placeholders for the various and heterogeneous activities making up the company. They are a highly refined version of the company as we know it, but they retain all its features: each security, one might say, holds the DNA of the company. When an investor buys a share of General Bank, he or she is getting a portion of all the bank's activities—the high-performance ones as well as those of lesser importance. The managers' plot was geared toward a similar end, albeit through technological integration: by constructing a bank-wide system, they hoped to retain all the details of the bank's activity, keeping its memory intact and not compromising it by other activities that did not come from the same bright minds. Yet, investors wanted all that, not only in securities, which lacked the distinctive stamp of personal enterprise, but in their workplace through the very technology that made this activity so successful. The point was to turn the desk and its activities into something so unique and attached to General Bank that transferring them to another bank would become impossible. This calculation performed by the managers—who came to act, in effect, as "owners"—was concerned with the maximization of their territory's durability. Ironically enough, it was also a calculation about the best information system vehicle that would make further calculations of the desk as a tradable unit impossible. It bet on the excessive costs required to either adopt another information system for General Bank or to reform another bank into adopting General Bank's. The strategy was one of incompatibility and the only solution for a merger was to throw the baby out with the bath water.

Through the very definition of a publicly traded company, the bank's property titles do not interfere with its production tools. More shares issued provide the bank with more capital, but the secondary circulation of securities does not alter the core of the bank: securities are exchanged, underlying assets remain. This fact of operation is true up to a certain point. When the movements of securities create a majority shareholder, this shareholder can demand that the core of the bank undergo modifications, and the link between the bank's security and its physical body becomes clear. Above a certain volume, the security—a share *in* the bank, a share *of* the bank's being—is held not only for the strategic ends of a financial portfolio with a return, thanks to dividends and value increase, but also because it affords a lever into the politics of a company's capital. When an investor owns a fairly insignificant portion of a company's capital, he or she is subject to the strategic choices of the management. An investor can vote, but the weight pulled is too light to guarantee that her or his voice will be heard and that changes will ensue. Under these circumstances, the security, its evolution, and the risks it entails are all elements imposed on the investor. Not having direct access to them, not being able to act on the dynamics as matters unfold through the production tool and its strategies, the investor simply endures. Things change when the weight an investor carries in the overall equities increases. There comes a point when the holding of property titles allows one to bring one's weight down upon that underlying. It is no longer simply a question of randomly falling dividends that marks this property; physical capital and the company's assets are in the hands of the investor. At this point, the fate of the company can indeed fall into the investor's hands.

Compatibility of Properties

But taking possession can mean the dissolution of the current form of the company and the redefinition of its limits in conjunction with other companies that are simultaneously held by the investor. When he or she—or more often they (in the case of an agreement between shareholders)—wants to reshape the company, a shareholder can choose to merge their newly acquired assets (both material and intangible) with other of their current assets. This strategy is only possible if the two companies demonstrate a sufficient degree of compatibility. From the compatibility of the capital brought together in the case of a merger, to the compatibility of product lines or even of customer portfolios, the points of compatibility or of redundancy of two firms are multiple. The *security compatibility* of two companies can ignore altogether their underlying capital if investors consider the titles they hold to be lists of irreducible properties. In such cases, investors limit their investigation of the bank at securities themselves. Their prices lend themselves to endless scrutiny and can be broken down into infinite statistics. This mode of compatibility always operates under a regulating principle: neutrality across price changes, maximization over time. Such a metric guides the investor through the many possible securities he or she could acquire, but they are seen as irreducible entities. Stopping the investigation at the level of the price of the security, investors do not conceive of the underlying company as an aggregate that can be reconfigured to improve the properties of the security itself. Instead, they simply adopt a portfolio manager strategy in which companies are the basic elements. When they are faced with risk areas in their portfolio, they diversify by canvassing new potential companies, presenting adequate risk assessments that are complementary and compatible with the securities already held.

Whereas financial *security compatibility* has a direct impact on the level of securities valuation through the effect of portfolio diversification sought by major investment funds, it does not have a direct impact on the body of the company. Two companies with compatible property titles need not have anything in common in terms of their productive organization. Financial compatibility is only a matter of portfolio strategy, not industrial enterprises. The pursuit of *industrial*[10] *compatibility*, in contrast, has a direct impact on this body. The shrewd strategy of the desk managers at the exotics desk— who traded the assets held in their portfolios with other desks—played on the specificity *and* compatibility of its capital. As a publicly traded company, the bank maintains an openly accessible capital, and investors can seek majority positions *sharewise*. But the internal and technological organization of the bank does not make it easy to *merge* a successful desk with other companies of the same type. The trick is performed by playing on the two levels mediated by the security. As a set of properties in a financial portfolio, the company is compatible with many other matching companies, and the burden of compatibility is borne by the composition of the portfolio itself (a couple of reasonably risky securities, a few risk-free bonds, even fewer very risky mortgages packaged by financial firms). As a set of industrial components, the bank cannot be divided up as easily as could be done with the securities.

This resistance has been learned from the economics of standards: the operators who chose to integrate their desk and activity within the bank— through the information system installed as a protection against the coming economic storm of the 1980s and 1990s—built mutual dependence between their products and the rest of the bank. They knew well that the bank is an economic entity made up of different activities whose unity faces tough challenges. Nearly a decade after its implementation, the disappearance of the emerging markets room reminded exotics desk traders how much the makeup of the bank can be questioned when results do not meet the expectations of the upper management. This is no longer Frederick Winslow Taylor's

"one best way," defined by the optimum combination in production management, but rather the "one unique way"—resisting a competition waged no
longer exclusively on the market for financial services but also, increasingly,
on the capital bodies of companies through their securities. The Taylorist's
concern for a rationalization of production (minimizing waiting times,
improving integration between processing centers) is not absent from this
choice of technology: it addresses the increasingly demanding requirements
of the clients, who are offered similar services from the ever-growing number of competitors. Of greater interest—and speaking more directly to the
current wave of corporate governance—is the resistance strategy nested in
the TRADE information system. The choice of using TRADE represents a
form of competition both by standards and by production systems compatibility.[11] By designing its information technology system in such a way as to
make it difficult to replace, and just as difficult to sell, advocates of TRADE
sent a message to the investors: *Do not* subvert the securities principle, and
do respect the division between ownership and management as much as the
unity of our business venture. This strategy of a reinforced *integration* of the
company does not necessarily put it at a disadvantage on the securities market; the securities maintain the same secondary properties (e.g., fungibility,
scalability, etc.). Once they are bought, they can be resold, but the engineered
glue of TRADE stops liquidity at the threshold of the bank's capital and re-
stricts its use to the bank's own securities.

Clashing Claims on Means of Production

The reaction documented here is noteworthy for at least a few reasons. First,
the resistance against the process of liquidating the bank's units allows us to
question a picture long held by economists of the motives animating economic actors. The managers who devise the conservative scheme of an integrated company do not think primarily in terms of their immediate monetary
payoff. Their strategy may indeed harm their future if it is to be construed
in these purely monetary terms. If they rise working against the growing
modularization of the bank and engineer it with TRADE, they show a concern for the future of their enterprise taken as a collective project. TRADE
was in many ways a failure. It was not adopted widely by all the desks and
it assumed—some thought "forced"—user preferences instead of reflecting
them. There was no consensus either on the global net gain achieved by this
solution. In no way can we read this episode as something that just dawned
on the employees of General Bank, an organic collective awareness. Yet, the
alternative reading supplied by the *principal–agent* economic theory does
not capture the meaning of this reaction. Principal–agent deals with delegation and the risk entailed by the distance between who owns passively and
who operates by delegation.[12] Owners have to trust managers and can only

rarely supervise their actions in order to adjust compensation according to performance. They cannot claim both property *and* command of the production tool under a system of shared ownership of capital. But the principal–agent theory mostly addresses appropriation under its monetary form. Typically, in the economic fictions favored by economists of this school, a manager can cheat the company's owner and take in more than what he or she is rightly owed. He or she can thus profit at the owner's expense. In such a situation, and when the terms of the opposition are set accordingly, it does not make any sense that a manager would feel concerned about his or her work environment, as our managers did. If one sticks to the agent's behavior as predicted by models, it makes little sense that an agent would want to shape his or her environment for reasons other than trying to exploit it personally. As for considering the possibility that he or she would want to make this environment more close-knit and intimate in order to protect it from the view of the owner for reasons other than pecuniary ones, this approach would not make sense either because of the overly narrow anthropological creed of the principal agent economic theory. Reading the principal–agent models in light of a case where the managers have actively contributed to the current form of their business points to the limitations of a theory that edits out any form of collective investment.

Once one relaxes the stringent rules that this economic theory has set for itself, these phenomena can actually be thought through. What needs to be kept in mind is the entrepreneurship of managers. The principal–agent theory reveals its limits in that it rules out creativity in these agents and consequently rules out the possibility of strong attachments to their collective enterprise, if these attachments cannot be framed in terms of profit maximization.[13] Once creative entrepreneurship is granted to these managers, it becomes possible that they may develop split allegiances: for the owner, by fructifying the means of production; and for themselves, by paying attention to dimensions of these means of production that standard measures of productivity and profit maximization adopted by owners do not easily factor in. Although these two modes of engagement look orthogonal, they do not necessarily pull the firm in opposite directions. This apparent divergence of motives only comes from a cursory assessment based on the unique and narrow metric of maximization that owners and economists strive to force on the company.

The "self" of the manager in this creative mode of engagement with the bank's means of production is not the narrow calculative agency of the economic actor fancied by principal–agent theorists. This view of the manager's self shows an actor in motion and easily encompasses collaborators who were part of a project. This self can be a collective self—a "themselves"—as when engineers who started the exotic derivatives activity right after finishing up at Ecole Polytechnique recollect their glorious boot-camp days spent inventing from scratch what became a success story of financial engineering. By identifying General Bank with this success, the small group of engineers who created the desk started to identify with the bank as a whole. General Bank became a second nature to these few engineers, and the future morphology of their extended self consequently became a matter close to their hearts.

French sociologists Luc Boltanski and Eve Chiappello, (2005) have elaborated on the notion of project and its explosion in the post-Fordist, post-1968 world. Further challenging the openness of metrics of maximization, projects are assessed on the basis of the inner quality of their unfolding. They require time, not only as a Kantian substrate making possible the regular measures of success, but as one of the qualities of their expression. The other central quality of projects is their involvement of different hierarchical levels, even their subversion of Taylorist notions of hierarchy. Friendship is central to projects' ontology inasmuch as the drive is the project itself and not the immediate and calculable pecuniary reward attached to it. People working on a project do sacrifice for it. They do not measure and count selfishly at its outset. In comparison to Boltanski and Chiapello's sweeping descriptions of postindustrial forms of management, General Bank offers us a case both similar and unique. Post-1968 glorifications of projects have been thrust on salaried workers more than they have been embraced. For the authors, these new forms of management have ridden the ambiguous appeal of a notion that had the flavor of resistance and protest against the old hierarchical modes of organization, but deep down they have exacerbated unequal access and alienation at work. By blurring the boundaries between work and leisure through all-absorbing projects, work has prevailed. By subverting old forms of domination, domination has thrived, only it is more insidious, more elusive, and more difficult to prosecute. In *The New Spirit of Capitalism,* projects are described as whirls dodging all forms of collective resistance by their very natures as mobile and morphing forms of coordination, and there is undoubtedly a version of that in the business of derivation championed by the exotics desk. In the realm of services, CGPs epitomize postindustrial projects: self-transforming, derivative, elusive, they sit well in the diagnosis of new capitalism offered by Boltanski and Chiapello. What does not feature so simply is the resistance displayed by the managers of the desk and their engineering of reverse finance. These engineers, who had dreamt of designing financial vehicles light and modularsenough to glide above the reality of industrial economies, have also become masters in the very opposite business: giving a body back to the company. Yet, instead of avoiding calculation by maintaining that body in a constant state of emergency and by keeping it on the move and on the morph so to speak, TRADE makes the exotic business unit so heavily and solidly tied to the larger body of General Bank that it can no longer be seen as a unit, let alone a calculable unit.

CONCLUSION

What Good Are Derivatives?

From Fieldwork to the Question of Value

In conclusion to what has primarily been an ethnographic journey into General Bank with few forays outside of its walls, it is necessary to go back to one of its main protagonists to extract general insights about finance.[1] The CGP has been the organizing principle of this narrative. Tracking it closely has offered a glimpse of the bank rarely enjoyed by the previous ethnographers of finance, who have too often circumscribed their objects of study to either populations of the world of finance (Abolafia, 1996; Godechot, 2000; Ho, 2009) or to organizations (Baker, 1984). In doing so, they have not always justified how these two entry points would either cast new light on finance itself or how new financial configurations would disrupt what is already known of such phenomena as power, gender, organizations, or networks. By contrast, investigating the circulation of a new class of products such as CGPs allows one to leave ajar the potential for consequences that are at stake there.

The main finding of this journey through General Bank is the character of quantitative finance's elusiveness: values and prices, topographies and roles, quantities and qualities, distance and intimacy all slip between our fingers as we try to seize them once and for all. One solution to tame that wild design is the invention of codes and models. The risk of the code is that of circulation and transparency. There may be secret codes, protected by other codes, possibly *ad infinitum*, but the problem remains the same whatever the number of additional layers of codes. They are still vulnerable because they are out there, up for grabs by anyone who can decode, that is, unleash the power of the formalism. A code does not make space for hesitation: either an operator knows the key (the codebook) or does not, but even a small variation will make it lose its power. Opposite to that form of exclusion achieved by a fully literal formula is the domain of tacit knowledge and embodied practices. There, too, exclusion rules but its mode of success is totally different. While the power of codes was a function of the once-and-for-all articulation between the object of enquiry and the code book, the power of embodied knowledge of a trader who has been dealing on a market for a long time is a function of layered memories and habits, all much more difficult to formalize and transport or transfer than literal codes. General Bank intentionally engineered products that could neither be decoded with a simple magical formula—that magical code book offering access to the ultimate characteristics and risks of the product—nor could they be embodied because their composition kept changing as engineers tempted clients with ever newer packages and these latter did not shy away from asking for further transformations to the perimeters of their products. This endless escape was the only way of dodging the competition aroused by the prospect of fat profits, but it also hampered the full control of its cost by a bank forgetful of its organization.

In their attempt to devise new sources of profit, financial engineers have created what appears to be a "monster product" that not only challenges the ability of the room to assign it a clear value, but also put to the test a firm that now finds itself invaded by its customers and investors, desperately in search of solid accounts. Living and exploiting temporary profits on the edge comes close to subverting the firm's form, that is, the orderly conduct of business organized along rules. Yet, this mode of value creation does not equate with a *market* mechanism as theorized by economists since Adam Smith (1776) as it eschews all forms of reciprocity.

Without leaving behind the detailed investigation conducted so far, I want to turn CGPs around and look carefully at their economic mechanisms: derivation. In question here is their constitution and destruction of value. What kind of goods are derivatives and what good are they?[2]

Decentering Derivatives and Recentering Derivations

Derivatives cover many different types of product but what they have in common is the process of derivation, where the value of a new good is derived from already existing and public values.[3] What is new and what finance has exploited successfully stems from the way derivation is defined. The definition of derivation is both captured and exhausted by this relationship of dependency on the underlying good: nothing else interferes with the derivative, which comes down to the monetary amount produced by the derivative formula itself. Financial derivatives are the purest engineering experiment of economic derivations. They come close to the purity allowed by the crafting of the mathematical notion of a derivative, itself central to the mathematical intuition used by traders who hedge derivatives.

A derivative product, such as the CGP, creates value from the existing values of underlying assets, such as securities or indices. It is tied to outstanding products but simultaneously derives its specificity and its value from the lack of any prior integration between these carefully picked underlyings. Its value stems from the existence of gaps and discontinuities, and its ability to bridge these gaps while also maintaining them. Derivatives stand at the fringes of existing values and only their peripheral position makes them viable candidates for becoming economic goods.

As chapters 1 and 2 made clear, CGPs are wagers based on the decorrelation of the underlying assets. Correlation translates into potential capital loss, so that the design of the formula is of the utmost importance for the room engineers. New enterprises launched around smart formulas whose components turn out to be incompatible are plentiful.[4] The strength and survival of the formula depends on the composition that it tries to bring to life. As formulas draw upon existing securities with their own momentum, their success hinges upon the possibility of a peaceful coexistence of these forces. These components, *bent* by the formula, are as much "worlds" in their own right as the formulas that enroll them. Although they are indeed starting points for the CGP formula, they are also the results of other *bending processes*. A formula is the tipping point of a series (or family) of existing formulas, but it can be enrolled by subsequent formulas that graft onto it and derive from it. This inheritance is both a curse and a blessing. It means that a past has informed the building blocks from which the bank assembles new products. The memory carried by these bricks is what makes them such useful ingredients of a new recipe. They are already in shape; they carry excess information that need not be generated again and can be captured by the derivative formula. But this past can also resist the particular *bending* that the new derivation tries to achieve; it can derail the blueprint. I would like to suggest in this conclusion that the systematic study of the mechanisms of derivation can shed new light on the old question of the creation of economic value. One advantage to the concept of derivation is the fact that it establishes an intelligible relationship between different critical components of mechanisms of value creation.

Derivation and Innovation

Markets activities can be viewed from two different but complementary angles: first, as organized exchanges around constituted goods and services whose values have been tested and recognized; second, as sites of innovations, that is, of new goods whose values are problematic and undecided. Western economies are such sites of intense innovation that simultaneously involve products, processes, and forms of organization, as is well known since Schumpeter (1942). The concept of innovation is central in the economic and sociological literature devoted to markets. It serves to name and to emphasize the creative dimension of economic activities and of the institutions that frame them. But it is also misleading in so far as it suggests that innovations are in stark and exclusive opposition with situations in which goods are stabilized—with their qualities established and their value simply needing to be calculated by the laws of supply and demand. This view presents innovation as challenging existing structures, whether social, economic, or cognitive: to prevail, an innovation has to find a way of getting rid of the old. This literal process of elimination is expressed aptly in the Schumpeterian notion of creative destruction. Many researchers have since endeavored to describe its various modalities or, as Abernathy and Clark (1985) put it in the title of a seminal article, to map the winds of creative destruction, which do not always blow in the same direction nor with the same force. Simpler classifications, such as those between incremental innovations and breakthrough innovations, adopt the same idea: an innovation is characterized as much by the intensity of the novelties that it produces as by the amplitude of the destructions that it induces (Dosi 1988). In any case, whether it is a violent storm or a gentle breeze, innovation has to destroy to succeed. The concept of derivation has the advantage of not confining the analyst to this dialectic of novelty and destruction. Deriving means creating new values, making them exist and making them acceptable, yet basing them on existing (economic) values that may be strengthened if the derivation is successful.

The value of goods is determined and measured during commercial transactions. Only when these goods are known can forecasts be made. In these rare cases, the so-called law of supply and demand, complemented by price elasticity calculations, applies satisfactorily and makes it possible to anticipate price variations. When, on the other hand, the good to be valued deviates from the pool of known goods, value calculation is more difficult. The existence of these difficulties does not mean that no calculation can be made; on the contrary, these calculations are the fuel of economic transactions and they generate new solutions to pricing issues. The agents apply a great deal of cunning to designing and implementing tools or procedures that enable them to define, anticipate, and even enforce the value of the new goods that they propose. Here again, the notion of derivation is useful for furthering the understanding of calculative behaviors in situations of innovation and uncertainty.

Agents who strive to take advantage of disjunctures tap into the repertoires of available solutions tried and tested by others—in other places and at other times—and transform, combine, and adjust them to suit new situations. The notion of formulas explicitly used by financial markets and by designers of derivative products is similar to that of *transactional forms* that Jane Guyer (1998) proposes to capture the ready-made qualculation modules, and which economic agents tinker with to solve problems and value conversions.[5] Linking these two worlds, it is possible to talk of *transactional formulas*, and say that the calculation of the value of a derivative good (in Paris, or in Jane Guyer's Nigeria) operates by establishing one or several transactional formulas. These usually draw on existing formulas serving as repertoires. For

CGP, the two master formulas that frame the design of the product are pure insurance (nothing but the guarantee) and pure investment (nothing but the return). The grammars of each of these transactional regimes are well in place: the prospectus of figure 1 weaves them in such a way that the notions of insurance and investment are within sight of one another but still sufficiently bent through the CGP formula that the product stands as unique.

The analysis of derivations illuminates the nature and scope of the calculation of economic values. Unlike prevailing conceptions rooted in the seminal analysis of Franck Knight (1921 [1997]), it is in situations of great uncertainty that calculations are the richest, the most complex, and the most sophisticated. The analysis of economic calculation must not start with situations of stability and certainty. On the contrary, to analyze these situations that seem the simplest, it is more fruitful to start with derivation and the notion of transactional formulas.

Derivation and Production

Production usually designates the set of human activities—most often highly equipped—that lead to the existence of goods or services meeting certain needs. In this case, production entails a precise and stable definition of goods.[6] They move about, are transferred and change hands in a space already equipped with metrological infrastructures (assessment of qualities and performances). This infrastructure reduces valuation to the numeric, and generally monetary, calculation of their value. This implies goods that are distinctly framed and well-positioned in relation to one another. We can call the process and the goods definitional.[7] Drugs exemplify the standard set by definitional goods, both up and downstream. On the upstream end, a minute variation in the quality of the components can turn out to be lethal. The supervision of these components—for instance, the role of the FDA in the United States and the scandals over the lack of control of these drugs in less regulated countries—has been one of the milestones in the regulation of this industry. They are, similarly, definitional goods downstream. The distribution of any drug is strongly regulated in many different ways. In the United States again, the FDA sets stringent limits on the populations entitled to take given drugs, and makes doctors gatekeepers of these provisions. The value of drugs is strictly framed by the matrix of inputs and uses that is allowed.[8]

Yet other configurations also proliferate, fueled by the rise of the service economy (Gallouj, 2002). In these other configurations, goods are constantly being revised, from the moment of their conception to that of their final consumption. The continuous transformations that they undergo represent the index of their quality calibrations and their value fluctuations. This trajectory is well captured by the notion dearest to financial operators: each new inflection of the good's path is a new qualification that can be understood as a derivation. This new good never ceases to be a function of the previous goods from which it comes. It is tied to them but it has been qualified into a different good altogether. In this new configuration, the notion of production as we understand it so far becomes irrelevant. Instead of being the generation of well-defined and stabilized goods, production is now the uninterrupted yet discontinuous series of derivations that accrue value on the economy. It picks up and enrolls an already existing set of goods and services. It adds qualities to these goods by securing them, but it does not create them from scratch. This dependence on preexisting goods limits the control that derivators can entertain. Yet, it is also one of their major assets as they lean on a world already in place, with its routines set.

This extension draws on economist Jean-Baptiste Say, who once defined production as *all* the actions turning things into goods.[9] Extending this notion of production so far, however, may be counterproductive and bring more confusion than analytic clarity. If the previous understanding of production is to be discarded, it is because it lumps together different modalities of value creation and does not provide us with the analytical tool that sorts differences between these modalities. It is clearer to keep the notion of production for definitional goods and to see this mode of economic activity as a subset of derivation. Derivation becomes the general mechanism through which goods become valuable.

The definitional process is characterized by the fact that it combines inputs and integrates them to the extent of making them disappear as individualized goods. They have to be consumed in order for new value to exist. This black-boxing is shrouded in industrial and commercial secrecy, making it difficult to access knowledge on what could be called the productive formula containing the combination of elements that went into making the good. Derivatives also combine existing values and goods, but the modalities of this combination are different. This is by no means black-boxing; on the contrary, the neologism, white-boxing, is more appropriate. The CGP formula is literal, although engineered. It explicitly and deliberately reveals the underlying assets of the derived product. Yet, more than revealing the formula in a gesture that marks its difference with other forms of financial service management, a product like CGP confirms the existence of its underlying assets. The notion of "underlyings" might be misleading as it assumes a precedent and hints at a foundation: a particular index or share, chosen as underlying, when acting as a derivative carries on its existence as an index or share. Derivation maintains it at a distance, rather than integrating and making it disappear as such, as in the productive combination of definitional goods.[10] Confirming the existence of the goods that it draws upon does not mean that it simply accompanies them. It can undermine and challenge them as well—it can interfere with them. But in either case, derivation does not dissolve them through a process that consumes them. The distance designed by engineers assumes the form of a "making visible"—derivation constitutes the initial values as underlying assets—whereas in the case of definition, opacity is the rule of the game: definition consumes and integrates them. The derivative formula keeps the derived good distant from the goods that it draws from; the productive formula eliminates this distance by organizing the consumption of the inputs that it combines.

From this perspective the notion of derivation is more fundamental to value creation than that of production, which is but one specific modality of derivation. However, it does not mean that there are two distinct economic spheres, each one ruled by different mechanisms. These two forms of value creation are highly intricate. Going back to the composition of the CGP will clarify this coexistence. It weaves together underlying assets. One of the underlying assets of the CGP may, for example, be a Sanofi Aventis share, which epitomizes definitional goods. As we pointed out, the CGP reinforces the definitional character of its underlying assets, and of the Sanofi Aventis share in particular. But the CGP may also be transformed into an underlying by a derivation that chooses to strengthen its definition. Hence, there are not simply two economic poles—that of the real economy and that of the financial economy—but subtle relations of constitution and interdependence of values. Derivations create and structure definitions; conversely, existing definitions are the building blocks of derivation. A good defined in a stable way, like the Sanofi Aventis drug, can hardly survive and last unless it is included in operations of derivation that confirm and enhance its value.[11] A derivative good may have a future only if it serves as a base for new derivations.[12] The tension between underlyings and derivatives leads to fascinating situations of overlapping dependencies as the case of commercial derivative licensed goods suggests. Take the value of footballer David Beckham. His value is constantly reactivated and enriched by the value attributed to the multiple derivative products—whether licensed or illegally produced—which in turn derive their value from him. For example, the Beckham hair wax product attempts to succeed over its competitors by deriving excess value from its association with the footballer, while the proliferation of products bearing his name adds to Beckham's value. In this case, relationships of valuation reach such a high degree of symmetry that the ageing Beckham can but become the derivative of his own line of derivative products. Derivation works both ways: Beckham's value is defined better, and in a sense is more stable, when a large number of products derive their values from him. Beckham can be sold and transferred from one club to another, without his value really being dependent on his scoring ability: his price is the product of all his derivations. Consequently, if the derivation is the general operation through which value is created, then the object to focus on is the constitution of chains of derivation.

The Violence of Derivation

Financial derivatives thrive nowhere better than in spatial discontinuities, those that they manage to create or that are offered to them. They play here on the assumed existence of groups of countries, which, like emergent countries, afford possibilities of conversion, elsewhere in the gaps between Exchanges situated in different time zones and countries with differing regulations. The notion of a circulation's space (like that of a sphere of exchange) has to be excluded, as it implies that the equivalences are not problematic. In reality, equivalencies and the possibility of circulation comes after the conversions achieved by derivations. To start to understand the world in which derivations operate and thrive, it would be necessary to find antonyms to "space" and "circulation." The lack of a preexisting space entails the generation of as many new spaces by the emerging goods.

A new good like CGP introduces disruptions into the state of possible interests, demands, expectations, and attachments. Regardless of its intensity, this disruption raises the problem of the existence of values and, consequently, of the terms of their qualculation. Derivations can fail for many reasons but two of these can be easily pinpointed and described in more detail.

Too much distance from the underlying assets is the first source of failure. This excessive distance can also be understood as *over bending* of the formulas. It is easy to imagine a formula adding other clauses to the ones exposed earlier. The 120 percent performance can be further tortured and bent so as to give the payoff another profile. Each additional bending forces a mental exercise the client and additional marketing prowess for salespeople. The multiplication of these clauses detaches the new service from existing services to a point where the novelty payoff is offset by the concerns raised by exoticism. It loses sight of the common world of financial actors—their expectations, their understanding of a financial service are suddenly derailed by a formula that stretches the world of finance too much and too far. If the possible outcomes of over-bending derivations are too distant from the underlying assets, then violence becomes the only alternative, as the derivative has lost its legitimacy. The victims of financial engineering in the 2007 credit crisis experienced nothing less than violence when their retirement plans lost 70 percent of their value in a matter of a few weeks.[13] When these losses are not understandable by those who are on the bitter end of the oscillating yo-yo of speculation, finance becomes subject to the criticism of hubris and is associated with two more basic and unsavory forms of circulation and transfer of goods: abduction and theft. When there is too much distance between the new derivation and the established values and formulas, discontinuity becomes inevitable as the derivation turns into predation.

But the derivation may also fail for the opposite reason, when it is too close to its underlying assets. In this case, the new good is reduced to nothing more than a predictable combination of existing goods: no new value is created and, rather than shifting and broadening competition, derivation simply increases its intensity by a repetition of existing goods. This is a case of *under bending* wherein the formula is not only transparent but its composition is also too linear. Imagine now a financial service offering nothing but an average of a set of only two stocks. Where is the service, one might legitimately wonder? What does the bank offer other than the trivial investment in two stocks (within the reach of even the least sophisticated investor) without a guarantee? By insisting on repeating that which already exists, *under bending* paves the way for violence, but of another kind: mimetic violence, that philosopher Rene Girard (1979, 1989) has described so well.

Derivation needs to be distinguished from the Marxian account of abstraction developed in *Capital* (1867). The Marxian description of the invention of ever new instruments of tokens of general exchange values takes place in the framework of an absolute topology; on the contrary, the act of derivation can take place anywhere in the long cascades of transformation of economies. Abstraction is an absolute index of distance between the original source of value and its final extraction. Derivation, on the contrary, operates by designing and sustaining a differential of properties between the underlying(s) and the derivative itself.

The romantic flavor of the sweeping account offered by *Capital*, through the description of the absolute extraction and exploitation carried out by the innovations of exchange value tokens, disappears from a landscape where labor is no longer assumed to be the unique source of value. The lack of an absolute index also blunts our critique of derivation, as we can no longer point to this absolute distance and need instead to show the collection of cascading derivations and their resulting devastation. If one focuses on only one such derivation, it may appear irrelevant to the dynamics of the economy and it may not look like a possible candidate to sweeping transformations: it is too close to its underlying, especially if it is a successful one that controls this distance and avoids direct competition/pusillanimity or the hubris of the excessive leap, to look like anything disruptive. Yet—and this is the challenge of a critique of finance that refuses to fetishize labor and a prefinancial world of legend—these little differentials add up to major transformations, regardless of their absolute distance from the elusive labor.[14] The challenge of looking at long moving chains rather than at solid Euclidean distances centered around an elusive foundational labor is compounded by the distribution of actors who can be found "responsible." This long-noticed feature of actor network studies is particularly problematic when transformations induced by derivations are indeed so devastating, as structured finance was during the first decade of 2000s. Once we leave the world of labor value, the description of financial products and financial intermediation is no longer—and exclusively—buttressed by the intent to decry its excessive abstraction, since we do not reckon any absolute origin point to value. Still, the question of financial hubris is more relevant than ever these days.

At the risk of oversimplifying, it is tempting to draw sharp conclusions to this investigation and see that civilization is a matter of skilled derivation. In derivation there is therefore an authentic civilizing dimension. It is indeed one of the mechanisms that forces us to clarify the inventory of the values that we feel bound to and that bind us (the underlying assets), and to simultaneously explore the new values that we are prepared to accept (derived goods). The political and moral dimension of derivation lies in the qualculation of the new value contained in the transactional formula. A good derivation escapes predation from the bottom (the prison of mimicry) and from the top (the hubris of excessive innovation). Well qualculated derivations re-enchant the world in which we live, whereas badly calculated ones tilt it over into chaos.

Derivation reminds us that, despite historian Edward Thompson's (1971) widely embraced thesis, ethics does not soften the harshness of economic relations, after the facts and from the outside.[15] Moral and economic values are entangled in the technical design of the formula. It is difficult to determine, a priori and in general, whether a formula will succeed. The search for the felicitous medium can be decided only on an ad hoc basis (even if certain tried and tested formulas allow for compromise to be reached more easily). This lesson of indeterminacy needs to be reasserted against the gut resentment expressed toward financial innovations in the wake of the 2007 financial crisis. The unregulated proliferation of new products, and above all derivative-based structured products, is fingered as the main cause. The descriptions and explanations proposed, often rich in images and metaphors—from wild beasts (Steinherr, 2000) to financial weapons of mass destruction (Buffet, 2002)—revolve around the idea that derivation is harmful and eventually produces uncontrollable and destructive excesses. Other voices are heard defending derivation, claiming that it increases the fluidity of economic activities, allows for a better allocation of resources, and favors change notwithstanding the associated risks. These voices demand only that the practices of derivation be framed better. This controversy in black and white is especially violent and circular because the very concept of derivation is not questioned.

I have taken the opposite track, starting with the observation that derivation is, or may be, a source of both destructive excesses and productive detours. Making sense of this ambivalence requires studying it as a process in its own right. I argue that derivation closely links the dynamics of production of economic values and their measurement. Financial markets have not invented derivation; they have gradually brought it into the foreground, focusing on it in an almost exclusive and obsessive way. They are not however exceptions or pathological forms; they act like magnifying glasses that make pervasive economic mechanisms more visible and easier to analyze. The fieldwork pursued here has shed comparative and complementary light on derivation, by proposing the reactivation of a concept whose general validity is thereby strengthened. Successful derivations serve as possible escapes from mimetic violence (or competition organized around fixed and determined values) and predatory violence (that resorts to theft, pillage, and war rather than commercial transactions). Central to their success is the right distance that formulas find—or not—between simply repeating underlying assets, and completely disregarding the effects of new values on existing ones. Moderate derivation, in the sense of moderate action between two extremes, hubris (predation) and pusillanimity (repetition), is a derivation that chooses the right transactional formulas.

A Capital Guarantee Product: The Full Prospectus

The World Wide Secured Exposure 8 Year EMTN
on Global Indices S&P 500, Nikkei 225, Eurostoxx 50

- 100% Capital Guarantee at Maturity
- 120% Participation in the Quarterly Average Rise of the Portfolio
- 120% Participation in the Best Performing Index in Case of Portfolio Underperformance
- In Euro with Exchange Rate Guarantee

The "Double Chance" Note—How Does It Work?

Thanks to the double chance mechanism, this note offers two chances to make a return on the global equity market. Indeed, contrary to a classic capital-protected investment, should the final value of the portfolio be below its initial value, the note will offer a second chance and pay the highest positive performance of the individual indices comprising the portfolio.

Redemption at Maturity

The first chance

- On the launch date, the value of the portfolio is set at 100.
- Every three months following the Start Date (each being a fixing date), the performance of the portfolio is calculated as a percentage of its initial value.
- The Final Value of the portfolio will be the arithmetic average of the 32 levels recorded on each Fixing Date.
- If the Final Value of the Portfolio is greater than or equal to its initial value, the investor receives 100% of his investment amount plus 120% of the Portfolio performance as calculated above.

The second chance

- If the Final Value of the Basket is less than its initial value, the investor receives 100% of the nominal amount plus 120% of the average performance of the best performing index in the portfolio.

Maturity date	February 25, 2008
Underlying	Equally weighted basket composed of the following indices: – DJ EUROSTOXX 50 (STX) – S&P 500 (SP) – NIKKEI 225 (NIX)
Issue Price	100% Nominal Amount
Reoffer Price	95% of Nominal Amount
Capital Guarantee	100% of Nominal Amount at Maturity
Redemption at Maturity	Maturity, the holder will receive the greater of the following: – Nominal x 100% – Nominal x (100% +120% [Max(BKT_m – 1;0)])

with

$$BKT_m = \frac{1}{32} \sum_{t=1}^{32} BKT_t$$

$$BKT_t = \left[\frac{1}{3} \times \frac{SPt}{SPi}\right] + \left[\frac{1}{3} \times \frac{STXt}{STXi}\right] + \left[\frac{1}{3} \times \frac{NIXt}{NIXi}\right]$$

where

t means the 32 quarterly fixing dates taken over the life of the note. SPt, $STXt$, $NIXt$ is the Closing Price of the Fixing Date t of the relevant index. SPi, $STXi$, $NIXi$ is the Closing Price on Start Date of the relevant index. BKT_i is the Closing Value of the equally weighted basket on Start Date.

Double Chance

If $BKT_m < BKT_i$, the Note pays

$$\text{Nominal} \times \left(100\% + 120\% \times MAx\left[\frac{SPm}{SPi} - 1; \frac{STXm}{STXi} - 1; \frac{NIXm}{NIXi} - 1;0\right]\right)$$

with

$$SPm = \frac{1}{32}\sum_{t=1}^{32} SPt \; ; STXm = \frac{1}{32}\sum_{t=1}^{32} STXt \; ; NIXm = \frac{1}{32}\sum_{t=1}^{32} NIXt$$

NOTES

Preface: Financial Innovation from within the Bank

1. The identity of the bank has been protected by the use of this nickname. In earlier articles (Lépinay, 2007a, 2007b), another nickname was used ($Bank instead of General Bank). The bank is the same.
2. Roberts Eccles and Dwight Crane (1988) are forbearers of this study.
3. See Bookstaber (2007:6) for a recent diagnosis of the paradox of financial innovations. "[I]t would seem there is a demon unleashed, haunting the market and casting our efforts awry: a demon of our own design."
4. Among many colorful characterizations, Warren Buffet (2002) calls financial innovations "financial weapons of mass destruction" in the *Berkshire Hataway Inc. 2002 Annual Report.*
5. Merton Miller (1986). Yuval Millo (2003) challenges this view in his detailed study of the Chicago Board of Trade and the complex dance between regulators and financial engineers who designed new products. Tufano (2003) disagrees with Miller on two counts: innovations have not slowed down, and their origin is much more difficult to pinpoint than Miller's cat-and-mouse account.
6. Karl Marx (1967) accessible at http://www.marxists.org/archive/marx/works/1867-c1/p1.htm.
7. *Pragmatic* refers here to the issue of accessibility (what can be studied and described empirically?) and to the American school of thought (James, 1907) that urges scholars to go back to the "pragma." Such a method has raised a question that needs an early response. The question asks whether tracking products forces us to accept a posthuman perspective wherein humans and nonhumans are treated equally and all ontological differences are loose. Because this book searches for greater understanding of the financial world and not for partisanship in a long, worn-out academic discussion, I set aside the ontological question and prefer to illuminate the sites of the most intense animation and change. These are the sites that are likely to shake the morphology of finance. Who would venture to explain the mortgage credit crisis without tracking the mechanism through which subprime mortgage contracts set an extended perimeter of action for new intermediaries and eventually created a situation in which borrowers and lenders were held at a

distance by ten degrees of separation? The claim here is a modest one. It does not amount to asserting that the contract alone carries the burden of *explanandum* in the complex unfolding of a financial crisis that obviously expresses many layers of past decisions. It simply points to the need to include in the narrative of this crisis a central character that holds many of the other parts together. So, no posthuman claims here; rather, the understanding that financial actors, in their diversity, coalesce with and through a rich variety of goods, services, equipment, and rules that cannot be edited out of the account of such an innovative business without losing the gist of it.

8. Offshore finance has been well studied by geographers (Agnes, 2000; Pryke and Allen, 2000; Roberts, 1995; Thrift and Leyshon, 1994). For an insightful study of offshore finance, see one of the rare anthropological attempts by Bill Maurer (1998).

9. I never saw or heard of a contract of less than €500,000 during my fieldwork in the bank. Early in the decade of the 2000s, a public version of these elite CGPs was already accessible to retail bank customers. A few banks—the most famous of which is the French bank, La Poste—were offering guarantees and investment to their clients, but they did not offer the whole suite of customized services. These secondary banks outsourced the management of these products to larger and more sophisticated banks like General Bank. La Poste would collect funds from daring clients who wanted the most up-to-date services but could not work with private banks due to lack of capital. They would transfer these funds to General Bank. From there the story of these products was the same, with the only exception being that a client was not given the right to modify the contract once it had been issued.

10. Private finance is now a specialty of some big banks offering specialized and customized services to wealthy clients, thus going back to the first days of finance. If retail banking aims at catching the savings of individuals who are not necessarily rich through a public outlet, private banking has no public face. There are no ATMs for millionaires, only personal relationships with specialists who handle a small portfolio of clients who want to be pampered and offered personal solutions.

11. On these questions, see Kopitoff (1986).

12. Unless otherwise stated, the documents presented in this book come from the trading room. They were public documents—as was this prospectus—or if they were not public during the time of my fieldwork, they have by now become common knowledge among the financial community. As sad as it may be for readers in search of inside tips, none of the documents in this book contain secret pieces of information. Obsolete, outdated, or made irrelevant by the fast pace of financial innovation, they are presented here as an archaeologist would present his or her findings. All diagrams are mine.

13. This initial fee came under the name "commercial margin."

14. Combining indices, stocks, and currencies from different national markets was not new when General Bank launched the product. Portfolio managers, hedge funds, and even some services for individuals were already crossing the boundaries of national economies and combining securities exchanged in remote financial places. Yet the real innovation came from the transformation of a service (just like the ones provided by portfolio managers and hedge funds) into a quasi continuously negotiable new security. This was not N services provided simultaneously, as when a wealthy investor asks his or her fund manager to buy Coca Cola and Telefonica stocks to balance the risk of his or her portfolio, but a single service covering the

places of each component. CGPs transform the dispersion of local financial exchanges and their respective activities (brokers, traders, trading rules, dividend payment rules) into a tradable service provided by one bank.

15. In addition to fees allowed in mutual funds and hedge funds, a reward mechanism makes the hedge fund managers interested in the performance of the client's capital. Each (positive) performance is shared between the fund and the client.

16. Latour defines black boxes in his book *Science in Action* (1987). There, he repeatedly uses economic metaphors that we will discuss in subsequent parts of this book. Annelise Riles (2010) works on similar objects as our white boxes when she studies the Japanese regulators designing collateral rules. Collateral rules—like CGP terms in relation to their underlying securities—are literal.

17. In the conclusion, white boxes are theorized at greater length. They offer a form of asymmetry that operates at a different level than that of black boxes.

18. Timothy Mitchell (2005, 2008) offers a related argument in his discussion of the history of "the economy" as a generic whole. He points to the role of economics in the engineering of the economy by the State.

19. One previous attempt (LiPuma and Lee, 2004) at theorizing derivatives as instantiating a culture of global circulation fails to recognize what authorizes this massive deployment. Although the authors are correct when they characterize the massive wealth inequalities that buttress the current financial landscape, they do not grasp the premise of finance in a gesture that is different from circulation, namely derivation.

20. Such a reading of the dynamics of the economy has already been offered by French philosoper Michel Serres in his book *The Parasite* (1980). This conclusion elaborates on the theory of the parasite contained therein.

21. The performativity thesis is first and foremost engaged in a discussion with mainstream economists and their relative lack of interest in questions of designs. Market microstructure has long shown interest, but design has remained slightly peripheral in the hierarchy of economists.

22. For two critical views of Callon's thesis, see Mirowski and Nik-Khah (2007) and Daniel Miller (2001).

23. In this text, the term *Exchange*, capitalized, represents the site of organized transactions. It is the institutionalized version of the process of exchanging. Many exchanges do not take place on Exchanges. General Bank's trading room has an interest in dealing both on Exchanges and through over-the-counter (OTC) relationships, outside the boundaries of the Exchange.

24. "Exotic" is the name given to financial products that are innovative and not traded on Exchanges. This qualifier carries the idea of an unknown, uncharted territory explored by bank operators.

Prologue: A Day in a Trader's Life

1. John Maynard Keynes (1936) distinguishes these two motives as investment and speculation. In chapter 2, we will analyze the extent to which the design of these products hindered speculation.

2. Some traders invest for other motives. They may want to support a business they perceive as beneficial to the community, even at the risk of losing money. Alan—as all traders who will be studied in this book—may also have these altruistic moods, but in his daily activities working for the bank he seeks profit, not soul-soothing.

3. See Makaye et al. (1998).

Introduction: Questioning Finance

1. Although I was accepted into the program, I only sat in on the classes and never took any of the exams that my peers had to endure.

2. "Education" deserves quotes because it carries a meaning not necessarily accepted in U.S.-based financial institutions. Education is more than training and sometimes it substitutes for training. Where I had been educated weighed more, to the traders and the human resources person who recruited me, than my experience. On the role of education in the French system, see Bourdieu's *State Nobility. Elite Schools in the Field of Power* (1996 [1989]). As opposed to Bourdieu's analysis, *Codes of Finance* pushes the investigation of the social beyond schools and early socialization.

3. There is now a rich literature on quasi-expertise gained by observers of a field. Collins and Evans (2007) bravely engage a question that most social scientists prefer not to raise explicitly for fear of losing credibility. Despite my training in mathematical finance, mine was still an interactional expertise, in the sense of Collins and Evans. I could make sense of the product formulas and could engage engineers and traders, but I was also trying to expose some of the deeply engrained assumptions that they worked from.

4. General Bank was awarded the Equities Derivatives House of the Year award several times in the 2000s.

5. Kevin Voldevieille was recognized as guilty at his trial in September 2010. He still challenges the account that his managers have given of his misdeeds.

6. For a book that makes stronger use of the cultural topos, see Mitch Abolafia's classic, *Making Markets: Opportunism and Restraint on Wall Street* (1996).

7. The topos of the end of geography ushered in by financial integration is the object of many fine studies, first among them, *Global Financial Integration: The End of Geography*, by Richard O'Brien (1992).

8. For a personal memoir of a quant who went through the quantitative revolution that brought mathematics and physics into the bank, see Derman (2004), Patterson (2010), and Lindsey and Schachter (2007).

9. Brownian motion is the movement of a tiny particle subject to random collisions with the molecules of the fluid or gas in which it is suspended. There are strong similarities between how financial economists model price movements and how physicists model Brownian motion.

10. This diagram presents one topography of the front, middle, and back offices. As the story unfolds, other topographies will emerge.

11. Olivier Godechot's (2000) early study of traders' skills in a Parisian trading room shows how chartists, mathematically inclined traders, and fundamentalists cannot communicate over the same products. The language that they develop to describe the dynamics of these products does not find an easy common ground. However, informed by a framework taken from the work of Pierre Bourdieu, Godechot tries to relate these disagreements to macro factors without acknowledging that the lack of a common language can come from the products' variety itself.

12. When clients face standard financial risks such as currency fluctuations, they do not have to approach the bank seeking ad hoc products tailored to their needs; they can simply resort to liquid securities, the kind of securities, such as Exchange-traded "futures," that do not raise as many definitional conflicts and can be described in a language that allows the two sides of a transaction to communicate easily.

13. When traders deal with standardized products, records of their transactions are automatically routed to the back-office managers. In some extreme cases, traders disappear from the picture when their actions can be automated (i.e., when buying or selling can be made to follow a simple rule), as in the case of treasury bond auctions.

14. Front, middle, and back office are functions, they are not sites, but these functions are often allocated to separate sites.

15. The puzzle of defining CGPs has received the most extreme solutions in science studies approaches of technoscientific controversies. Although my concern here recalls the challenge that Garfinkel (1967) addressed to the positivist social sciences à la Parsons, I side more easily with recent actor network approaches of the question (Latour, 2005; Law et al., 1999). This is made relevant and easier by the rather narrow network covered by the product. Unlike more controversial issues studied by scholars leaning toward actor network theory, I came across a relatively narrow variety of actors voicing radically different positions.

16. Douglas Holmes (2009) offers an original study of the conversational nature of finance policy.

17. David Stark (2009) has recognized the risk of closing the wild enquiries launched by explorators (as opposed to exploiters) "The first temptation for the leaders . . . is to immediately address ambiguous situations pregnant with interpretive search by using the clearly defined problem solving strategy of analytic search. A managerialist strategy of early top-down control entails the risk of forgoing the big opportunities represented in innovations such as cellular phones." (p. 5).

18. More than anyone else, historians know the sad promise of codes, luring them into mourning the whole of the document for its relevant features.

19. Influential to this interest in languages is Peter Galison's *Image and Logic* (1997). He shows how the two major approaches afforded by twentieth-century philosophy of science have unfortunately eluded the most crucial sites of scientific changes and continuities. Empiricists looking at experiments and paradigmatists looking at theories missed the interplay of these two modalities of scientific insight. Galison's *trading zone* finds these meeting points to be their pivot and he draws on the layered structures of these zones to account for the multiplicity of paradigms and the continuity of changes in physics post–World War II. The parallels between the worlds of postwar physics and 1990s finance are multiple and their shared terms are also numerous. In both cases, models are necessary as some properties of products' and atoms' reactions cannot be observed full scale until some of their lethal consequences are determined.

20. Miller and O'Leary (1998, 2002) and Veron (2006) illustrate the ductility of accounting techniques.

21. Michel Callon (2009) elaborates on this type of experimentation, as opposed to the *in vitro* experimentation performed in laboratories.

22. That is a difference of degree rather than nature. Both natural native languages and formal codifications create unmistakably social gradients by including their experts and excluding those who do not master them. The difference is one of the cost of access: a native idiom used to capture a unique reaction can be learned quickly and on the fly, whereas some codes are impossible to master without a formal training.

23. For an insightful application of this strategy see Miller and O'Leary (1994). For the debate it sparked in the community of critical accountants and critical political economists, see Froud et al. (1998), and Arnold (1998), and the response by Miller

and O'Leary (1998a). In parallel to this growing trend of scholarship in critical accounting—that looks closely at the (mis)application of the formal models of economists and accountants in firms—another source deserves mention as it nourished a sound conversation during this fieldwork. Financial economists have increasingly adopted methods akin to inductivism to probe the relevance of the otherwise strictly deductivist tools of the profession. One manifesto is to be found in Tufano (2001) and Chako, Tufano, and Verter (2001).

24. Economists no less than sociologists have had a preference for Exchanges. Among the former, the microstructurists (O'Hara, 2003) have come closer to what sociologists trained in the social network school have accomplished (Baker, 1984). Other approaches, outside of the dominating social network analysis, have peered into the history of Exchanges (Cronon, 1992; MacKenzie and Milo, 2003). At their best, these accounts offer a unique perspective into the joint design of securities and market structure. The historical sociological enterprises, launched by Donald MacKenzie and Yuval Millo at the Chicago Board of Trade and pursued more recently by Daniel Beunza and Millo (2011) at the New York Stock Exchange, follow these tracks.

25. Sociologists (Uzzi, 1999) have shown how firms develop all sorts of ties, up and downstream, to survive in competitive environments. Relationships of quasi-familiarity feature in the "portfolio of ties" of successful firms, particularly in fundraising efforts. The cost of loans can change significantly with the composition of the ties, but what we document here is yet another level of familiarity. The discretion granted to the client is not exclusively about the price but rather the overall components of the service.

26. "Firms will emerge to organize what would otherwise be market transactions when their costs were less than the costs of carrying out the transactions through the market" (Coase, 1988: 7).

27. The tension between "trust" and "distribution/distance" has been the focus of much of the new histories of the sciences in the 1980s. For a brilliant analysis of the conditions in which an early global enterprise managed to hold together and maintain trust relations in the context of distant transactions, see Miles Ogborn's *Indian Ink* (2007) on the use of documents by the East Indian Company.

28. Broader than the focus on the body—the human envelop with its two arms, two legs, ten fingers and ten toes, one head with its pair of eyes and ears—that scholars trained in the Wittgensteinian tradition have simultaneously made (arbitrarily) the center of action only to wonder at its ability to reach beyond its enclave. For that version of the body, see Lakoff and Johnson's *Philosophy in the Flesh* (1999).

29. On this theory of the extended body, see the illuminating insights that Gabriel Tarde (1902) offered, in vain, at the turn of the twentieth century in his College de France lectures, collected in the two-volume *Psychologie Economique*. For a quick presentation of Tarde's economic insights, see Latour and Lépinay (2009). The Tardian lesson was not lost on Gilles Deleuze, who articulated it in two major works, *Difference and Repetition* (1994), originally published in 1968 and *A Thousand Plateaus* (1987), originally published in 1980. Another source of insights comes from the Deleuzian (1970) reading of the Spinozian prophetic statements around the body and what it can do; see *Ethics* III, prop. 2, sc.2.11 [". . . no one has hitherto laid down the limits to the powers of the body, that is, no one has as yet been taught by experience what the body can accomplish"] (Spinoza, 1677).

Annemarie Mol's (2002) experimentation with the genre of ethnography and the related description of the body was also influential to the current study. In her case, capturing the multiple modalities of being a body is more naturally oriented toward the living bodies, which are twice at the center of her fieldwork with the patients' and doctors' bodies struggling to discover the most felicitous common world. But her experiment is compelling because she expands bodies beyond their personal envelope and tracks felicitous coexistences around the risky "enhanced bodies" of technological environments.

30. Bodies are here studied for their role in the communication of finance, or more appropriately, finance as communication. Michel Serres's learned contributions to the theory of communication in the *Hermes* series are the most relevant references. On the tension of angels' bodies and their claim to ubiquity, see his *Angels, a Modern Myth* (1995). Helene Mialet has used Michel Serres's insights to address the body-impaired physicist, Stephen Hawking, in her forthcoming book, *Hawking Incorporated* (forthcoming 2012; 1999).

Part I: From Models to Books

1. There are different options, some giving the right to exercise the right at any time up until the expiration date (American options); others giving the right to exercise on that date only. For definitions of the italicized terms, see www.investorwords.com.
2. The existence of arbitrageurs rule out the possibility of an option expiring with a positive value or, in traders' parlance, "in the money."
3. *Easily* and *market* would deserve to be put between quotation marks. Some factors are tricky to obtain, and their meaning can be ambiguous. The volatility that measures the variability of a price is one of these slippery magnitudes: it features prominently in the pricing equation (think of it as the magnitude of an extreme event when one tries to insure against it: the greater, the more expensive), but it is not clear whether one needs to use the historical volatility of the underlying security or the implied volatility reflected by the price changes of the derivative.
4. See www.riskglossary.com for articles related to the italicized terms.
5. The distinction between confined exploration and exploration in-the-wild comes from Michel Callon (2009). Our investigation shows that this opposition is challenged by quantitative finance research. The proximity between the sites of research and the markets where models are being tested—the speed with which information trickles back into the confined sites of research from the markets, and the amount of experimentation that markets offer the researchers—all contribute to inflecting the Callon thesis.
6. In order not to overuse the word *market*, which would tend to suggest that one can easily draw up a list of the actors and assets involved, let us instead say that each of the products sheds light on characteristics of those entities interacting in the trade. In the course of this book, markets will always carry this uncertainty. The population working in the bank is in search of the market, and unlike most popular accounts of markets, traders would be at a loss to give a definition of the market. See Karin Knorr Cetina and Urs Bruegger (2002) on the ambiguities of the market location and perimeter.
7. Daniel Beunza and David Stark (2004) have described the work of association in the case of modern arbitrage.

Chapter 1: Thinking Financially and Exploring the Code

1. This chapter expands Lépinay (2007a). I thank Donald MacKenzie for fruitful discussions of some of its topics.
2. It is also a major concern for scholars attempting to delineate the perimeter of their discipline.
3. John graduated from the École Normale Superieure in mathematics. He finished his dissertation while on a three-year stay in London during which he worked for a Japanese bank. After this experience, when he was "struck by the sensation that his quality of life was declining," he returned to France and began teaching at a Parisian university and at a business school. This trajectory is common of a trend that has only recently been challenged: up until physicists started to apply for quant jobs in banks, quantitative finance meant *applying* mathematics to finance. Most researchers in quantitative finance had a dominant training in mathematics, as had John. Yet, he also had a special interest for the challenges that financial contracts created for mathematical toolkits and was critical of a mathematical imperialism in banks. He worked as a quant on a derivatives trading floor (equities, bonds, commodities). He had arrived on this trading floor at a time when the R&D information technology apparatus was not yet in place. During the course of his first months there, he had to program using Turbo Pascal, and he built a group of pricer software systems for products that were not yet in the traders' software system.
4. "Nonstochastic" refers here to financial models where prices are solutions to partial differential equations (PDEs). Many scholars in mathematical finance use PDEs and stay away from stochastic processes.
5. Pierre had been at the desk for eighteen months when I arrived there. Following his studies at a Parisian business school, he had been accepted for an internship in the bank and had remained.
6. As the sketch of the room shows in figure 4, there are two distinct zones of passage. Within a desk, the aisles are narrow and occupied by chairs: operators can talk to one another without having to leave their chairs or by simply sliding the chair a few feet and spinning it gently 90 degrees. Beyond the desks, the aisles are more generous, marking the passage from one specialty to another. In general, operators leave their chairs around their desk when they move beyond their area.
7. In parallel to the search for information during coffee breaks, lunches were privileged moments of networking and searching as much for operators as for the financial engineers. Finding a lunch partner was an important task for operators during the morning.
8. Chapter 2 will delve into the hedging problems.
9. There are a variety of "digitals." For some, the underlying needs to break and stay above (or below) the threshold for the payoff to be made; for others, the threshold has to be hit only once.
10. Conversation recorded in early March 2000.
11. Ochs and et al. (1994) present a more sophisticated account of physicists struggling with the spaces they both occupy and refer to, the blackboard on which they write their phase diagrams, and the space they are constructing beyond their diagram. Unlike the physicists, our financial operators rarely have a blackboard, and their fleshing out takes place as if on a transparent blackboard separating the interlocutors.

12. This language is no longer as commonly used to write pieces of code. It has been taken over by object-oriented C++, but a few operators who have a cursory training in code still use C.

13. See Zaloom (2006) for a study of body codes in a pit and a room. Natasha Myers (2008) offers a fine description of crystallography's calls to the bodies of scientists who enter the structure of protein molecules. She differentiates the coding of protein structures and their embodiment, as if the body could relate *immediately* to the protein when it performs the folds of the structure. The body is a code operating between (at least) two milieu, even if it dreams of negating this gap.

14. Hands-on finance is a privileged site of what Gabriel Tarde (1902) saw as the key to capital growth. Hand gestures are the first vectors of understanding through a momentary figuration that does not immediately burden the flimsy thought process with too durable a model. Tarde, in his recently rediscovered 1902 *Psychologie Economique*, distinguishes between germ capital and cotyledon capital, praising the former for its ability to redirect its course and innovate constantly when cotyledon capital is stuck with a blueprint and cannot derail from it without risking entirely disappearing. See Lépinay (2007) and Latour and Lépinay (2009) for a discussion of some of the capital insights offered by Tarde.

15. For some earlier approaches to formalisms pedagogy and the embodiment of abstraction, see Lave (1988), Lave and Wenger (1991), Rosental (2008), and Verran (1998).

16. There is now a rich tradition of studies of the body resources at work in demonstration. Claude Rosental (2008) has recently approached demonstration practices of a theorem in fuzzy logic by looking at the full repertoires of body involvement, from the blackboard where visual resources are mobilized to flesh out more analytical insights to the commercial fairs where the theorem is already at work in devices as foreign to logic as elevator queuing priorities. The quality of this study is its consideration for all the resources that are necessary to demonstrate the validity of a theorem.

17. On arbitrage, see the two different accounts of Daniel Beunza (2008) and Hiro Miyazaki (2003).

18. The tacit knowledge at play here is of great interest: tt is indeed the tacit embedded in the formal; not the tacit against the formal. See Michael Polanyi (1958, 1966), and Harry Collins (1983) for two seminal but different theorizing efforts of describing tacit knowledge.

19. In a series of books, scholar Brian Rotman (1993a, 1993b) has offered a sharp critique of a view of formalisms—mainly mathematics but also other technologies of representations such as perspective and paper money—that makes no place for the body. Rotman offers what is missed most in the history of science by pointing to a theory of abstraction systems (algebra, perspective, fiat money) that makes space for the role of interacting bodies.

20. In chapter 5, the role of salespeople will be documented at greater length.

21. John breaks down mathematical intuition into at least two strands. One deals with partial differential equations (PDEs) as a way to solve a price unknown in a system; the other deals with Brownian motion.

22. This space is most often noncontinuous. It can have strange properties that appeal to mathematicians who love challenging theoretical entities.

23. "Bourbaki" was composed of a group of French mathematicians that set out to found mathematics in a most rigorous way. This legacy is still very much active in the French educational system, particularly in the elite engineering schools. For a recent analysis relating Bourbaki to French structuralism, see David Aubin (1997).
24. Calling that *accounting* represented one of the local fits of humor. For the quant, expansions were straightforward and could not be taken as the quant's display of expertise. Accounting was also a wink at a back-office exercise that the quant had no business with and not much interest for. In chapter 6, accountants become the primary actors of *Codes of Finance*.
25. The quant and his assistants are the only ones to use mathematics software. The other operators, including financial engineers, use Excel to simulate price dynamics.
26. This change in hedging strategies is the subject of chapter 2.
27. For a similar line of investigation into the transparency/articulation trade-off created by the use of models, see Chadarevian and Hopwood (2004) and the contributions to their third dimension modeling studies.
28. Benoît Mandelbrot is credited for having rung the bell in the 1960s when mathematicians were getting carried away by the amazing tractability of the Gaussian distribution of events. The Levy distribution (also dubbed fat-tailed distribution), a family distribution that encompasses as a subcase the Gaussian distribution, makes more space for events that depart from the mean and for infinite variance: in terms of financial modeling, it factors in more crises and crashes than that of the Gaussian models.
29. Recently, the normal distribution versus fat-tailed distribution contention has heated up with the real estate–based financial crisis. Levy distribution advocates finger-pointed normal distribution addicts for having favored tractability against fit.
30. Mary Morgan and Marcel Boumans (2004) present a nice example of these material constraints facing models that venture beyond the world of two dimensions. The Philips machine takes off from the letter of the Keynesian text and strives to incarnate the macroeconomic circuit, but it faces a whole new range of problems triggered by the tubes, tanks, valves, and engines powering the circuit.
31. By "academics," Franck means finance professors who publish finance textbooks and specialized review articles.
32. The R&D team of the bank would also send them a survey of the model.
33. Calibrating entails setting the parameters of a simulation model so that it really becomes the simulation of a phenomenon.
34. Franck used to attend *les Petits Déjeuners de la Finance*, organized by a young scholar from Ecole Polytechnique, Rama Cont. It was a monthly gathering of academic scholars and bank professionals where problems were presented and networks were created.
35. A "manageable product" will get its full meaning when the hedging activities of traders are introduced.
36. This isolated—although quite disorderly and noisy—price production has been singled out in the more recent mortgage crisis in the United States. The subprime products that many mortgage lenders have designed had been pooled together and purchased by commercial and investment banks as well as a few major hedge funds, but no one could assess the value of the mortgage absent a secondary market and at least a few transactions taking place on a regular basis. Because all the banks

and funds were sticking to them for fear of not finding a match on the market, the only valuation was based on a model that underestimated the lack of confidence among investors.

37. For a more constructivist approach to formalisms, see Berg (1997).

Chapter 2: Hedging and Speculating with Portfolios

1. "Manufacture" here does not denote any foundational stratum of reality. It is simply a less purified piece of the economy, seized by this invention of finance. It can itself be finance. In the conclusion, these cascades of derivations are discussed more fully.

2. See Mallard (1998) and O'Donnell (1993) for two case studies of generalizations.

3. Karin Knorr Cetina and Urs Bruegger (2002: 911) elaborate on the difficulty created by face-to-screen interactions, and elegantly phrases the dilemma: "the question that lies at the core of the notion of a response-presence-based social form that extends across global distance is, what are the possibilities of its inherent connectivity and integration as the key to overcoming the geographical separation of participants?"

4. It is important to note, though, that this slow and pedagogical reading is at this stage nothing but an artificial trick; possibly, a reading that no one ever accomplished along these specific terms and this decomposition of the formula. The preliminary and artificial reading given here is only meant to serve as a neutral baseline for highlighting the variety of interpretations and the practice of hedging by traders detailed at the end of this chapter.

5. The number of underlying financial securities (national debts, interest rates, stocks of major worldwide companies, national stock market indices) could vary significantly and substantially. Starting from 3, it could go up to as many as 10 in some cases. In addition to this variability in the number of its components, the formula was also very flexible in the range of securities that could contribute to making up the payoff.

6. At http://www.stoxx.com/indices/components.html?symbol=SX5E, "The Dow Jones Euro Stoxx 50 Index, Europe's leading Blue-chip index for the Eurozone, provides a Blue-chip representation of supersector leaders in the Eurozone. The index covers 50 stocks from 12 Eurozone countries: Austria, Belgium, Finland, France, Germany, Greece, Ireland, Italy, Luxembourg, the Netherlands, Portugal, and Spain" (as of December 3, 2009). For these three indices, big is understood in terms of market capitalization (i.e., the value of its publicly traded capital).

7. The comparison between an Exchange and the situation created by CGP is only meant to set the possibilities between the two opposite poles of a face-to-face price production and a trader-to-model value production. Prices come to being with actual transactions; values surround these rare moments. Exchanges also equip buyers and sellers in many ways and they filter and frame their contact, yet models allow—with more or less success—to do away with the counterpart until the term of the product.

8. I am grateful to Marc Lenglet for pointing out this second spelling.

9. Professional traders have long *pause*. They actually last several years, but they are constantly modified and played with. Day traders close their pause every night. They do not stay exposed overnight to price changes in other financial places. See Lépinay and Rousseau (2001).

10. The perimeter will become a central notion in chapter 4 when the topography of the portfolio and the products' archives will become an issue for the bank.

11. The local term for checking the market value of securities on the day stated in the contract is "fixing." The fixing is then extended as the market value of the security, under strict conditions of observation that guarantee that the value observed is the actual market value and not either an outdated market value or even inaccurate value.

12. Caitlin Zaloom (2006) covers some aspects of self-discipline, but her account conflates the rules set by exchanges (the tick) and the work on oneself (taking a loss) that traders elaborate on to stay in control of the fast-changing markets. The formula is yet another form of disciplining taking place from within the trading collective—engineers write it and teach it to traders—and forcing restraint on the very motive of trading.

13. The challenges of "miskeying" product information and the bank's attempt at solving the ensuing problems are discussed in chapter 4.

14. Fabian Muniesa (2003) describes the production of prices of listed securities in the French and Spanish Exchanges with greater detail than offered here.

15. The deal was an inflation swap with a Spanish counterpart. The client would get a rate indexed on Spain inflation, and would pay General Bank a market rate plus an agreed-upon spread.

16. I could not figure out whether the choice of the acronym OST was one of the rare manifestations of humor in the bank. OST stands for Organisation Scientifique du Travail—the bank OST was anything but a scientific organization.

17. On these new arbitrage techniques, Daniel Beunza and David Stark (2004) developed an innovative approach that cast light on new forms of securities valuation by arbitrage traders.

18. Transaction cost analysis looks at the effect of the sheer costs associated with entering a market on the decision to enter it in the first place. When the trader needs to hedge his or her portfolio against a Japanese company stock variation, he or she contacts its broker and passes the order accordingly. The broker charges a fee for this transaction, a transaction cost for the trader. The portfolios are so big and the volumes traded either way (buy and sell) so important that the bank had negotiated special deals with its brokers to lower the costs per stock. Ordering 1,000 futures on Sony or 2,000 futures on Sony may turn out to be in the same overall cost range. An additional effect of the size of the portfolio is that the trader can hedge on a finer basis without incurring extravagant transaction costs.

19. It is casual because it does not take into consideration the correlation of the prices of these items.

20. When the client uses his or her right to change the contract, a new contract is issued and the bank continues to have monopoly over its pricing.

21. First-order and second-order risks are not necessarily correlated. You can imagine important shifts in underlying prices that do not translate into large shifts in correlation if all the shifts go in one and the same direction. It is also easy to imagine small variations in underlyings that trigger high second-order risks if these variations go in different directions.

22. We were working in the same aisle, back to back and facing opposite directions. Before interviewing her, I had had the leisure of observing her for a few months, as I was her co-worker.

23. Nontraders can have experienced this sense of playfulness when searching for air fare. After searching on any online broker, data are loaded onto a cache disk, which

allows you to search for more information for determining the best flight. When you have filled in the electronic purchase form—and it now takes some time with the additional information that is required—and submitted it to the server, the data that you were working with may already be outdated. You may learn that the price of the flight is either greater or lower than what your research had shown.

24. She sometimes equated it to her "intuitions" or "hunches."

25. In the years 2000 to 2001, the stock most traded by the desk was France Telecom. The French telecommunication company had undergone major corporate changes, with a majority of its capital publicly traded but a high portion of its equity in the hands of the French State. France Telecom had invested money in many promising "dot com" companies through its fund.

26. This strategy is obviously not available when the product is already a composition of exchange-based indices, as is the case of our product in Figure 1.

27. Daniel Beunza and David Stark (2004) have formulated the old and new modes of arbitrage in a series of insightful papers. The new arbitrage operates by breaking down financial products in order to extract discrepancies at a finer grain.

28. In that respect, CGP traders are closer to analysts than to other monospecialist traders.

29. One of the first comments the floor quant made to me was in praise of traders. He emphasized the efforts they put forth, at the conclusion of long and exhausting days, in analyzing their portfolios. The quant even used this late-afternoon exercise to explain to me the breakdown of his own day: It was customary for traders to make a "visit" to the quant to review unexpected portfolio reactions they had discovered over the course of the day. The frequency of these visits reached a point where the quant could not dedicate himself to solving questions demanding sustained concentration after 5:00 P.M.

Part II: Topography of a Secret Experiment

1. *Leviathan*, as celebrated as it is, does not lack critics. Barbara Shapiro (2000) offers a contrasting view of the emergence of facts in courts. She points to the overwhelming role of lawyers in the Royal Society and claims that their primary concern was to document rather than experiment. Harold Cook (2007) also adds fuel to the critique against the Royal Society–centered account of the emergence of facts by pointing to the role of trades in the birth of procedures that would subsequently lead to fact standards.

2. Galison and Thompson's edited volume (1999) on the architecture of science adds other cases of this tension between seclusion and confrontation. Galison and Jones (1999) is particularly relevant to our comparison between laboratories and bank trading rooms.

3. See Shapin (1988) for an early elaboration around these two themes.

4. See Soroya De Chadarevian (1996) for a controversy around the best site of experiments, pitting Sachs and Darwin around plant biology. Gary Alan Fine (2007) offers a riveting account of the seclusion of meteorologists in *Authors of the Storm*.

Chapter 3: The Trading Room as a Market

1. These territories do not carry the same prospect of profit. New markets, recently created, are fruitful niches that traders want to exploit, as they are not prey to too much competition. Markets that were opened long before are most often very com-

petitive. Innovative banks such as General Bank complicate the picture somewhat by designing products that graft onto institutionalized markets. Traders of these products straddle many of these markets and are specialists of none in particular.

2. The recent cases of trader fraud will remind the reader that there is much to be lost in a trading room, yet only for an operator who has been exposed to the intricate rules of the products' database and who is known to his superior.

3. Legally, the trader is not the owner of the workstation. It belongs to the bank, but the trader, once granted a workstation, has the right to exclude most other operators from it. The exclusion extends to a couple of feet radiating from the screens and the telephone.

4. For a rich ethnography of secrecy in modern military-industrialized America, Hugh Gusterson (1998) is a useful reference. Joe Masco (2006) explores the environmental consequences of the paranoid organization around the most secret and also most publicized enterprise in Cold War America.

5. This episode will be analyzed in-depth in the last chapter of the book.

6. This fall must be understood in both its literal and metaphorical sense. During my first visit to a trading room (bond and foreign currencies trading room), while I was waiting to be taken to my station, I witnessed the fall of a young intern whom I met later. He was in charge of writing economic reports for the traders every morning and would spend early mornings scrutinizing even the slightest piece of information that could make his report stand out. On the day of his fall, he suffered a seizure that he attributed to a series of exhausting days and to the effect of staring continuously at his screens.

7. An early but still relevant study of these mediations is in Heath et al. (1995). Karin Knorr Cetina (2002) has performed sophisticated analyses of the change affecting marketplaces for financial transaction and its consequences on the location of the market. She pays less attention to the market in the room though.

8. *Online* is a convenient term that will receive further specifications as the analysis unfolds. As a proxy for more elaborate specifications, it is meant to remind us that traders are in conversations with other financial operators out of the room. This conversation takes place by office phone, on online platforms such as Bloomberg or Reuters terminals, or sometimes through the traders' bank e-mail accounts. Each channel of communication shapes the conversation in ways that are not trivial. But for now, *online* means beyond the walls of the bank trading room.

9. After the previous note, *physical* does not mean that the online conversation is not physical. It is in many ways as physical when traders need to coordinate actions on their desks to combine several tricky orders in a very short time span. Traders are also physical when they shout in their microphones to get their orders accepted or to show their anger when it has not been accepted on time. *Physical* is only a flag word in this chapter meant to point to the space defined by the limits of the room.

10. Sociologist Erving Goffman (1959, 1969) has drawn attention to the theater stage–like structure of most social interactions and the need to study the dynamic of local social adjustment to understand macro situations. As many commentators have already pointed out (Latour, 1996), the Goffmanian perspective deserves to be amended at least on two related grounds. The order of interaction never takes place in an ethereal void; rather, social interactions are always enmeshed in material situations with points of resistance and responsiveness of a different magnitude com-

pared with purely face-to-face situations. When material frames are brought into the picture —such as in *Gender Advertisements* (Goffman, 1979)—they are rock solid. Goffman sticks to a clear distinction between the world of humans and the material world of things that never surprise us. Hence, the technological networks that make space for these dynamics of interactions deserve serious scrutiny as they organize them in non-neutral ways. These networks challenge the Goffmanian topography and help us document the construction of intimate distances and other challenges to Goffman's formulations. For a series of studies that take seriously the transformations imparted to financial markets by the technological networks, see Knorr Cetina (2002), and Knorr Cetina and Preda (2005).

11. The "structuring" team works closely with the financial engineers and the legal department.

12. In this bank, two floors were fully occupied by the trading rooms.

13. Chapter 5 describes the encounter of sales and clients around the properties of the CGP.

14. Daniel Beunza and David Stark (2004) document spatial organization of a trading room in Lower Manhattan's financial district. The head of the trading room that they studied was as attentive to the morphology of the room and the consequent dynamics of its interactions as to the ability of a room's design to control and arbitrage the market.

15. There was still variety in terms of education but it did not cut along the various desks. The exotics desk was occupied by more highly educated staff than the others, but this initial gap was quickly being closed by the other desks, which were recruiting more and more prestigious engineering school graduates. Most traders were even critical of the scholarly education metric and claimed that the expertise gained on markets was far more important than formal education. Olivier Godechot (2000) has tried to excavate a pattern of correlation between education and trading style, but the categories used to qualify these styles do not follow the same line as my investigation of the room strategies. In Godechot's study, there is no place for the room as a stage where competition takes place. There is even less space for online markets as venues where notoriety is gained.

16. Airplane pilots in their cockpits and air controllers in their towers, are also put in these preposterous situations where they are withdrawn to better connect. See Hutchins (1995) for illustrations of such distribution of actions.

17. Adequacy, that is, in a nonreferential framework but in a pragmatic one. Adequate is the action that will survive and inserts itself in "its" environment without triggering a revolt.

18. Ernst Kantorowicz (1957) provides us with a distant but fruitful comparison to the traders' extended bodies. The two bodies of the king studied by Kantorowicz in his commanding analysis of medieval political theology provide us with an insightful topography articulated around the king's body. The question that besets monarchy is that of the continuity of the spiritual body in the face of mortal natural kings. How does one establish a spiritual mode of existence when kings do not last more than a few decades at best? Kantorowicz documents this institution and points to the very mundane artifacts that sustain the spiritual fiction. Traders are also trying to maintain that double body, in completely different ways of course and with resources that never compete with the casuistry of English lawyers. The imperatives

of presentation of self and that of expert market intervention are homologous to that of the spiritual figure and the mortal body. Here, the spiritual is in the room *and* in the network of online transactions that carry the name and identity of the trader. The mortal body struggling to manipulate the market shares these two spaces as it seizes the variegated fabric of the room *and* the many relays located outside of its immediate reach in the online network.

19. This ordering of the two bodies is pedagogical. In a universe driven by profit, it is expected that compensation prevails over manipulation, but manipulation helps accurate trading moves, so the oscillation between the two bodies' activation is quite complex.

20. See Olivier Godechot's work (2007) on high paychecks in French trading rooms for a detailed description of mechanisms at play.

21. There is a tension between salespeople, financial engineers, and legal consultants on the one side and traders, quants, and middle-office operators on the other. The first group aims at hyperprofessional identity, similar to the diplomatic personnel in embassies. They deal with surfaces. The latter ones deal primarily with products rather than people. When traders communicate with clients, it is always only via the salespeople.

22. Henri Bergson (1896) describes ably this felicity in *Matter and Memory*, when he conceptualizes the relationship between matter and representation through the notion of images.

23. Paul did not identify the trader by name, nor did he mention whether the trader was still working in the room.

24. One could argue that there are not two bodies but three in competition there. The performance put up for the peers in the room also takes place online: reputations are made and broken locally but they also emanate from the community of traders beyond the room proper. Traders need to protect their reputations if they want to be well served by their brokers. The distinction between the local performance and the manipulation of trades online is thus affected by the performance taking place online. The reason why this latter performance does not bear so much on the initial distinction comes from its resource: the body is not directly at stake in these distant performances.

25. As was shown in the previous chapter, the art of trading entails mastering the psychology of one's market. It is an expertise long in coming, and it cannot easily be achieved when traders—such as, CGP traders—need to trade on various exchanges. Having an intimate grasp of multiple markets is practically ruled out for CGP traders: they necessarily remain generalists.

26. Prestige and fame are important dimensions in markets. A famous trader is followed by less expert market participants. It is a symbolic asset, and it can be priced on the labor market, but it comes with many drawbacks in the daily activities that await the traders. The famous trader is monitored and questioned, and is at a pain to disappear enough so that orders will not be tracked nor strategies deciphered. Remaining quiet is as important as being loud, and it is sometimes more difficult.

27. For a discussion of the twists to the philosophy of action that the equipped environment creates, see Dodier (1993).

28. This complex architecture of moving bodies and stable instruments in a fragile state threatened by chaos could also be described in more technically Deleuzian (Deleuze, 1987) terms as "agencements," or sociotechnical arrangements.

29. On these questions, Laurent Thévenot (1994, 2002, 2006) and his students have been conducting a daring and arduous task of disentangling meanings between property, appropriation, and appropriateness.

30. On this figure of property, see Maurer (1998).

31. Exchanges that are not yet electronic (as of 2011: New York Stock Exchange, New York Board of Trade, Chicago Board of Trade) have tried many different versions of handheld calculators/terminals allowing brokers to communicate with their booths while on the pit. The remote trading station increases the market exposure of the broker, making possible swarming with other brokers while taking care of the back-end aspects of the deals. Confirmations are sent to the other brokers to rule out mismatch, and margins requirements are set. See Beunza and Millo (2011).

32. David Kaiser (2005b) offers a thorough analysis of agent-based model contamination in the case of the Feynman diagram.

33. These skills are attached to the operators, and they illustrate the notion of tacit knowledge coined by Michael Polanyi (1959, 1966). For a more recent use of this notion and its consequences for the study of scientific practices, see Collins (1983), and Collins and Kush (1999) and his focus on the social and embodied nature of scientific activities.

34. Graham Jones illustrates the necessary investment around secrecy among magicians. Only the community of magicians (coming, among other things, with a formal certificate) can disclose the recipe for a successful trick. It can go from explicit guidelines (get the coin in your sleeve) to more elusive ones (distract the audience's attention). See Jones (forthcoming 2011).

35. David Kaiser (2005a) discusses a *fetishization* that has much in common with this blind focus on the formula. During the Cold War, the "atomic formula" was created by media analysts who liked to think that there was *one* equation from which everything else originated.

36. As mentioned in the introduction, most of the traders dealing with exotic and complex derivatives came from the generalist model of the French Grandes Ecoles. Polytechnique, Centrale, Mines, and Ponts & Chaussées provide the largest draft of these traders, as well as of financial engineers. The quantitative engineers were more university based, but they had all gone through the *classes preparatoires* training. On the culture and mystique of classes preparatoires in France, see Jean Francois Sirinelli (1988).

37. Interview, December 2000.

38. This includes the quant and his or her assistants, the financial engineers, and the computing R&D engineers.

39. The presentations were printed on transparent plastic sheets projected to the audience.

40. It is not only the trading rooms that must be protected from disunity and excessive internal competition. As we will see later, this tension is pervasive in the bank's various units.

41. This absence of articulation and the consequent difficulty experienced by risk auditors in assessing the traders' positions does not lead to the kind of infinite regress à la Collins. The burden of proof is immediately accepted by the traders, and the risk auditors interrupt their investigation immediately when "due process" has been respected. The overriding proof still lies within the trader: generating profit is a good enough proof. The investigations launched after Kevin Voldevieille was caught

cooking the books concluded that various levels of management were complicit in letting it go on as long as the borderline strategies of their traders were paying off, only to distance themselves when it appeared publicly that the leash had not been tight enough.

42. The notion of exit strategy is Albert Hirschman's (1970). In the case of finance in the mid to late 1990s, the "outside" making the defection strategy so appealing may be forgotten in the current, dire times. This had been a decade of fast-growing financial market indices, reflecting one of the most bullish of markets.

43. When a trading operator is fired, the rule is that he or she must leave the position within 48 hours so as to not interfere with the operations. He or she is still paid but is no longer in charge of the bank portfolio.

44. Outstanding results are as problematic for traders as can be really bad results. Out-of-norms results attract attention and call for accounting. Heads of desks are asked to look into the methods of out-of-norm traders and to explain why they perform so much better than regular traders. This situation is an embarrassment for both the trader and his or her level of hierarchy within the group, as one loses the privacy of methods learned and has to spend time learning what they ought to know considering their hierarchical position. The recent Voldevieille scandal has shed light on the fact that outstanding results had to be concealed so that the rogue trader could keep on manipulating his trades. It has also brought to the attention of the public that managers in trading rooms usually turn their backs on illegal practices as long as they enrich their desk. However, another dimension creates incentives to disclose the outstanding results: by making these practices public, a trader initiates a conversation with other banks and not only with his managers. By becoming a crack trader, he makes himself available to banks in search of outstanding traders and hence detaches himself from his home institution.

45. Andrew Lo (2005, 2008) captures the specificity of hedge funds and the appeal that they represented to investors in search of alternative and less regulated forms of investments.

46. *Felicity* is an Austinian term in this context. It refers to the debate opened up by Austin (1962) with his performative utterances. In our context, even a loose version of performativity has important bearings on the disclosure policy adopted by banks and enforced by authorities. In a nutshell, if the financial sphere is stable thanks to the belief that most actors have in a few models, then everybody is better off if these models become public goods.

47. Non-outstanding players have all kinds of interest in undermining the valuation models defended by banks.

48. See Paul David (1985) for an early theorization of standards in economics. Delphine Gardey (1999, 2001) adds historical depth to David's account. She details these mediations and the competitive twists in the selection of the best keyboard. Contests definitely framed the expectations of the userswho were engaged. The keyboards were not to be appraised using aesthetic criteria.

49. Gabriel Tarde (1902) has a still innovative argument on trust and market conversation. In his little-read book, *Psychologie Economique*, he insists on making conversation on markets a crucial indicator of trust. This is only an insight that he does not develop further and it is indeed a tricky question. Tarde remarks that prices need nothing more than the beehive-like interactions of purchasers and that, ab-

sent this character, they may disappear altogether. The point of this call is well taken, but the relationship between conversation and liquidity is more complex. A silent market is not necessarily illiquid; it can also denote one where all uncertainties have disappeared and traders do not even need to ascertain the quality of what they buy and sell. In between these two extreme silent states, many possible nuances of conversations would indicate a growing distrust or a growing unanimity, the type of Durkheimian effervescence. See Latour and Lépinay (2009) for an introduction to these questions.

50. In chapter 6, the value at risk will feature centrally in the account of CGP. By designing risk models that fit precisely its risk structures, the bank is also forced to let external auditors step into the bank and snoop into its activities.

51. Long Term Capital Management (LTCM) was similar to the trading room studied here, composed of a collection of Wall Street wunderkinds who were convinced that they knew how to make money by studying the market closely with the latest, most sophisticated quantitative tools available. This arrogant stance and loner attitude drove them to bankruptcy, but the portfolios that they had built during their long and successful honeymoon were of such magnitude that their collapse nearly pulled down all the other major financial firms involved in LTCM-complicated financial deals. Unlike the Enron fallout, which proved to be based on fraud —with even looser standards of fraud—the LTCM fallout was mostly due to the lack of control that these hedge funds enjoyed. For a simple introduction to the rise and fall of the LTCM fund, see Lowenstein (2001).

52. Science & Finance (S&F) has three related activities: it is a quantitative research group, a software developer, and a hedge fund.

53. Marc Potters, director of S&F research, December 2000.

54. Jean Philippe Bouchaud, the cofounder of S&F, complained that his own demonstration of the Black–Scholes theorem, obtained using a different set of assumptions and expressing a physicist's take on random variables, had not been given the attention it deserved by a community of quantitative engineers, who were still under the spell of clean mathematical theorems as opposed to tractable and useful physics models. Bouchaud and Sornette's model (1994) claims greater generality than that of Black–Scholes, belittling it by making it a subcase.

Chapter 4: The Memory of Banking

1. The operators use several terms to describe the contents of their portfolios (either assets or liabilities), but they always refer to a state of rest, as opposed to the circulation they otherwise undergo. See chapter 2 for an anlysis of *pause* and *pose*.

2. On the metaphor of the body that is at play in this chapter, François Dagognet (1992, 1993) is the most relevant reference. Invagination is the action or process of something being turned inside out or folded back on itself to form a cavity or a pouch.

3. The term "little hands" comes from the people in the front office with whom I met. It was meant to be as disparaging and belittling as possible. Its use reveals an organic segmentation of financial work: the head (and face, of the face-to-face trader) for the front office, and the hands and arms for the back office.

4. Annelise Riles has been a relentless advocate for a *documentary turn* in anthropology. I do not do justice here to the sophisticated arguments and sweeping conse-

quences for the self-disciplining of social scientists of her enterprise. She has applied her approach to the study of financial regulators in Japan (Riles, 2004).

5. This episode looks innocuous to readers of the late 2000s, with traders and fund managers engaging in much bigger fraudulent activities. Only the biggest fraud cases are brought to the public attention. When they do not jeopardize the bank activities, traders are usually fired directly, and investigations are conducted discretely. Making these frauds public discredits the internal supervision system of the bank and weakens it on the debt market, should it need to raise capital to fix the failed wager of its fraudulent traders.

6. Kevin Voldevieille was exposed in January 2008, but the nature of his crime was still the subject of much debate in 2010. Like the traders who bump up their prowess by initially depressing their portfolio, he continuouslyclaimed that he never made any money on his illegal trades, if not indirectly by beating flat all his colleagues and making General Bank itself richer. He only expected the bonus system to pay him off for his adventurous and fictitious trades.

7. A payoff formula that was initially and contractually Max (Infn/Inf0; 0) × nominal was entered in the following form: Max [(Infn/Inf0) % + 5%; 0].

8. Several risks were entailed. The first one was obviously the cost of the manipulation itself on the bonus unduly granted to the trader. More important, in the longer term, was the trading room's— where traders set their rules—subsequest bad reputation, which affected the bank's potential for profit. There was a clear strategy at the bank—that I cannot say didn't fool me at first—of revealing bad cases, although rather innocuous ones, to emphasize the clean-up of the new organization entailed by a linkage of back-and front-office databases.

9. In the final chapter, we will explore other motivations that led to this choice.

10. That is, the value of a call option at its expiration is zero if the stock price, S, is below the exercise price, K, and is $S - K$ if $S \geq K$.

11. LIBOR is London Inter-Bank Offer Rate, measured each working day by a firm employed by the British Bankers Association and broadcast via systems such as Bloomberg. LIBOR as ascertained in this fashion is the average rate at which a panel of leading banks report other banks as being prepared to lend them money in a given currency for a fixed period (in this case three months).

12. That is, a form of reasoning in which it is posited that the only patterns of prices that can be stable are those that permit no opportunities to make riskless profits with no net capital outlay.

13. Each trading room (equities and derivatives, fixed income, commodities) had its own back-office database. The other hubris expressed by TRADE was to think that a smart application could bring all these traders and back-office managers to the same table and override decades of latent conflicts and cultural clashes.

14. Then Kevin Voldevieille appeared on the scene. His exposure to the back-office software mechanisms came from his stint there, before his promotion to the front office. His ability to trick the system came from his knowledge of the two sides of the wall and of the two applications.

15. The counterparts are asked to speak in *back-office terms*; they are asked to mention this code during each communication relative to the product. This code leaves the bank and is the common language of the two contracting parties. Here, we again have the bank's market topography overturned: although the early stages of con-

tractualization put the client in contact with the salesperson in a process consisting of payment formulas and flow volumes, the follow-up to this relationship is situated at a different level. The contract is stabilized, the formula and its parameters are fixed, but, above all, a code has been set on this initially fluctuating set under negotiation.

16. The issue of local transaction between desks belonging to the same legal entity is not minor. To be precise and anticipate what we will analyze more thoroughly in the last chapter, it is not only a budgeting trick, as it redistributes power relations in the room and can lead to major organizational revamping of the bank.

17. ODBC stands for Open Database Connectivity. Initially developed by Microsoft, it was meant to offer connectivity between various databases, regardless of the languages used. SQL, Structured Query Language, is a standard language used to manipulate databases.

18. "Procedures" is too extensive a term, and "routines" is too limiting, in describing the sequence of actions followed.

19. In a series of meticulous studies, JoAnne Yates (1989, 2005) has documented meticulously the role of the file folder in the transformation of management and control of the American insurance industry.

20. Identical, that is, to a certain extent. The two offices relied on one other to keep one other informed of any relevant changes. They expected the other side to communicate whenever it was necessary and to photocopy any relevant document.

21. For a history suggestive of the hope invested in the disappearance of these paper mediums, see Brown and Duguid (2000). Chapter 7 considers some experiences in the switch to all-digital records, by clearly showing how the paper file has remained the point around which the operators coordinated.

22. Susan Leigh Star and Karen Ruhleder (2001) offer a similar account of a collaborative project, the Worm Community System (WCS), which placed resources for biologists sequencing the gene structure of *Caenorhabditis elegans*, a nematode, online. In line with Star's interactionist creed, their account focuses primarily on the multiple interpretations of the collaboration project.

23. The alleged distance is yet very problematic. As we saw earlier, the topography of these actors moves during the stages of the product's life.

24. On the governmentality of the spaces in which accounts and calculations are done, a Foucauldian analysis of this type of system has already been proposed in many fine studies by a new school of critical English accounting. Seminal articles in this respect are Miller and O'Leary (1993, 1994, 1998a, 1998b, 2002).

25. When these documents were digitalized within the bank, they were easily attached. When only a paper version was available, it was scanned by the back-office managers' staff, who were even further removed from operations by the new software.

26. William Cronon (1992) provides a fascinating description of the work needed in the commercialization of grain, standardization, the creation of silos, and all the devices that transform the grain taken from the plant into a commodity. It is both the customized nature of the contracts that I study here and the markets in which they develop that are pitfalls to all the "silos" that have been attempted in the banking industry.

27. On the rise of multidivisional firms, see the classic by Alfred Chandler (1977).

Part III: Porous Banking: Clients and Investors

1. Never did wage negotiations question the organization as a whole. Financial operators were mostly using the counteroffers of competitors to negotiate their salaries or positions within the organization upward. When these negotiations involved management-level positions, equity compensation would be considered: stock options would be offered in addition to a salary and a bonus. Yet, these would consist of promises of money, never transformations of the organization as such. Similarly, the securities used for hedging were listed on these Exchanges and were beyond negotiations.

2. In the rest of the book, the terms *investors* and *shareholders* are used indiscriminately. They are opposed to clients who could in many ways also be characterized as investors but who negotiate their products with the bank. Investor shareholders negotiate the governance of the bank as a whole. Nothing rules out the possibility that an investor holding General Bank equities is also a client of the General Bank exotics desk.

3. General Bank was indeed a unique case to study, having located itself at this conflicted intersection. Other big financial firms were never as creative as General Bank on the products side; as a consequence, they were not as active on the underlyings markets, nor were they paying large remunerations to their trading rooms, which would have made them hot sites of job-market traffic. Hedge funds are not publicly traded and can protect their accounts from the gaze of investors.

4. The economics of asset specificity informs the general approach of this study. As the emphasis on the formula of the financial product has made clear, the specificity is central to the economy of its circulation. These products have no precedent in the bank, they require a special organization, and there is no way the bank can be understood without paying due attention to the profile of these products. If anything, this book takes too seriously this call for attention and extends the specificity category beyond what Williamson would see fit.

5. The conclusion will discuss this aspect at greater length.

6. This authorization has a gray existence. Some of its modalities are laid down in the contract, but most of them follow the etiquette. When clients bring hundreds of millions to the table, they expect to be treated accordingly, and the bank has to live up to its reputation as a financial engineering powerhouse.

7. Companies are authorized to move some of their deals outside of their public balance sheets. When they are off the sheet, their values do not appear in the same way as on-balance sheet activities. An example of that difference is given in chapter 6.

Chapter 5: Selling Finance and the Promise of Contingency

1. Only short term inasmuch as even products that have been quite successful with clients can turn out to be disastrous for the trading room if it is unable to hedge them and meet the payoff. The measure of success only comes after the last dime of this payoff has been made.

2. The private banking arm of General Bank was launched in 1997, a few years before I started the fieldwork at General Bank.

3. Denominations change. They sometimes refer to the population that they serve as "ultrahigh net worth individuals" (UHNWI).

4. The western districts of Paris—a rectangle stuck between Place Clichy, Place de l'Etoile, Porte d'Auteuil, and Place de la Concorde—contains most of the city's top-rated three-star restaurants. The business meetings would oscillate between the

historical headquarters of General Bank in the 8th district, the high-end services (hotels and restaurants) located in the immediate area, and the more up-to-date venues of its headquarters in La Defense.

5. The Monaco private banking office offers advice on yachts and other assets in which locals may want to indulge.

6. One can argue that no good or service ever delivers completely at the very moment of the transaction and always produces surprises as it is used, consumed, or put into yet another cycle of transaction. Even the most straightforward and standardized good as a can of Coke or a MacDonald's hamburger can deliver more than what its initial description could hint at. But a financial contract such as the CGP exacerbates the uncertain side of the service.

7. A quick comparison with a recipe or a menu highlights the nature of that discrepancy: nothing more distant than the list of ingredients (plus instructions) and the actual taste of the food in your mouth. But if you follow the instructions closely, you may hit the target more easily than the client hoping for a huge return.

8. This conversation took place in December 1999. I met this financial engineer through the courses in mathematical finance that I attended at Universite Paris 6 Jussieu. He gave a presentation of several new methods that young apprentice quants and traders needed to know before setting foot in a bank.

9. Michel was the head of sales in this trading room. He had a long experience of new financial services and knew how to proceed by respecting the various intermediaries.

10. *Les Échos* is the daily financial paper, similar in many respects to the *Wall Street Journal*.

11. On indices, see Muniesa (2007) and Paul Kockelman' (2006) learned analyses of Peirce.

12. The work of Paul Samuelson (1953) lurks behind the debates that have been raging in the community of scholars around the existence of preferences and the best way to measure them. The notion of revealed preferences that—among other things— made him famous, looks toward the products to derive a preference function.

13. Richard Bookstaber (2007) tells the story of portfolio insurance from the perspective of a trader in New York City in the early 1980s. Portfolio insurance was in the air.

14. Leland (1980). The structure of this article is most interesting: the conclusion and introduction read like sales prospectuses that surround the body of the article, which is nothing short of a finance theory piece.

15. By 1980, portfolio insurance had only been advertised for a year or so, and not even aggressively. Leland and Rubinstein are academics, and they do not have the salesman's guile. For a lively first-person account of the invention of portfolio insurance, see Leland and Rubinstein (1988).

16. Portfolio insurance does not initiate the return/risk couple. Harry Markowitz (1959) formalizes the intuition of many portfolio managers at the time. It is beyond the scope of this book to write the genealogy of such a strong couple of notions in the modern history of finance.

17. The convexity of the portfolio describes the reaction of its value to a variation of the underlying's value. When the underlying's value falls, the portfolio insurance guarantees that the overall portfolio's value falls proportionally less. If the portfolio of underlyings was not hedged, the two losses would be proportional.

18. Investigating various modalities of preference building is the great quality of Franck Cochoy's (2002) recent work. Through an analysis of both economists' theorizing of preference and marketers' close monitoring of clients' behavior in stores, Cochoy shows how preferences are always notions in-context: as marketers take into consideration the scene of the client's choice, they enrich preferences with more and more contextual dimensions, moving them from the client to its surrounding (the display, the good package) in a move that owes much to the distributed cognition approach.

19. We already faced this product earlier. Its name comes from the fact that it is an all or nothing product: under a threshold, the payoff is 0, above it is maximum. There is no continuity in the payoff, making it a difficult product to price and hedge.

20. It does not mean that the portfolio insurance providers do not differentiate the service depending on the expectations of their prospective clients. But this differentiation has no serious consequences on the process. One service is packaged— in marketing terms, not in engineering terms—whereas for CGPs, each service is designed.

21. We had already documented this reconfiguration during the archival puzzle episode, when two solutions were neck and neck. The salespeople were already bypassing the implicit hierarchy of the room and reaching out to the clients with pieces of information that were not supposed to circulate so freely.

22. I was working across from sales, and served the United Arab Emirates, Greece, Cyprus, Malta, Israel, and Lebanon.

23. In the room, "vol" stands for volatility.

24. The remuneration body was already at work in the trading room (chapter 3) when traders were on the mode of self-presentation—as opposed to intervention on the market. A telling example of the tension between appropriation and generality is given by Claude Rosental (2008) in his study of fuzzy logic demonstration practices. The dilemma pits the virtuosity of manipulations that delight prospective customers while making them aware of their own inability to reproduce these skillful hand plays *and* a demonstration that asserts the generality of its use and runs the risk of killing the spell of novelty.

25. New Yorkers who have walked through the Union Square farmers' market on Saturdays have certainly witnessed the expert in carrot and potato peeling. Joe Ades died in 2009, having for many years mesmerized passersby with his simple potato peeling choreography.

26. Hiro Miazaki (2006) has a sophisticated argument about promise, hope, and finance from his Japanese fieldwork. The sophistication comes as much from his subtle analysis of financial endeavors that recall the future and the past equally as from his engagement with anthropology as a project of hope.

27. The client is interested in the conditions of production insofar as they guarantee that the bank will not go bankrupt. Whether they are optimal or not is a minor issue for him or her, so long as the bank can live up to its commitment to turn in the payoff when the product comes to term.

28. Resorting to the clues as taught by Carlo Ginzburg (1980, 1992) is a good counterpoint to the protography stance.

29. When Bruno Latour (1979) reactivates the notion of inscription and popularizes it for the description of scientific activities, he is engaged in a discussion about reference—its tools, and its extensions. Inscriptions of protographies also work at stabi-

lizing and capturing properties, but they do so with *things* that are not yet present, only anticipated. Their existence-to-come is obviously a mode among other possible ones, but the important difference between the inscription of a particle and that of a financial payoff is that the latter will come to a different mode of existence in the near future. Inscriptions build objectivity and detach it from its context; protographies project time.

30. As mentioned earlier, the irrelevance of the underlyings' return to the cost of hedging was a surprise for the first economists (Black, Scholes, and Merton) who came up with the derivative valuation equation.

31. It is good to state once again that these comments on liquidity are valid for monetary transactions in the context of investment banks. There are many transactions that do not operate on the assumption of a liquid outcome or even imagine the unwinding of the transaction into a liquid asset. Liquidity assumes currency.

32. In the conclusion, the notion of white-boxing is attempted as a way to contrast the strategy of contingent products based on derivations and what should be called definitional products. Articulation entails keeping together most of the elements and putting them in place. It is about ordering, whereas derivation is about drawing on one element and simplification.

33. Let us remember the Tardian lesson and the role of conversation on market prices. See Latour and Lépinay (2009).

34. The consequences of ordinality are the high competition and the equally high turn-over. See the discussions that Jane Guyer's *Marginal Gains* (2004) has helped launch for a recent focus of anthropology on ordinality. The conclusion joins this discussion.

35. That is, with mutual funds or hedge funds. One recent and painful case in point is the Madoff hedge fund Ponzi scheme, which survived so long because it was operated in a financial environment that was still bullish enough that clients would not reclaim their interests at the end of each year but would prefer instead to roll them over into the next investment phase, thereby transforming them into nominal. There are nontrivial similarities between the Madoff guarantee and the guarantee provided by CGP, only that Madoff's should have been called a return guarantee product.

Chapter 6: The Costs of Price

1. These documents are public information. They are available on General Bank's website.

2. In addition to Veron's (2006) fine presentation of the conundrum of creative accounting techniques, the reader can go back to Mary Poovey's (1998) more ambitious take on the artificial. James Aho (2006) offers a learned counterpoint to the all-terrain and somewhat misguided use of Weber on the rise of capitalism through double-entry bookeeping.

3. The Fair Value and Full Fair Value accounting standards try to gradually outdate and outlaw the use of the off-balance-sheet by assessing all assets and liabilities at their market value. For all its allure, such a transformation comes with serious complications, some of which are instantiated by CGPs. If some products are off the balance sheet, it may not be only because they are intentionally hidden from investors' gaze to trick them into holding onto the company's securities. Some

structured products resist instant and continuous calculations as both engineers and traders know well.

4. On the plurality of performance measurements and the social critique that it fuels, see Michael Power (2004).

5. There is also a stage of very intense innovation in science. It is indeed its trademark, but unlike commercial ventures, scientists do not gain credit until this chaotic stage is tamed down, polished, and phrased in acceptable scientific terms. Bankers can make money, for long stretches of time sometimes, even if they cannot account for their "martingale." This is market credit, as opposed to another form of credit, and is entirely based on bankers' ability to account for their deeds and the organization that supports them. This other credit is not only symbolic: the accreditation given by regulatory agencies marks the green light for investors to buy more equity or lend money through corporate bonds. The need to police themselves is caused by this twofold structure of credit in publicly traded companies.

6. By examining three alternative cases of modeling, it will become clear that new operations led to the blossoming of a customized internal accounting system.

7. See chapter 4 for the back-office role and the reversal of the issuance topography.

8. *Simple* is the term used by the woman who told me what the cost problems were.

9. The heads of trading rooms had a nonaggression pact: they were not supposed to accept the application of a General Bank employee who was currently working in another room of the bank.

10. During an interview that I conducted with one of them, the term "bohemian" was used to describe their mode of appearance in the bank. It seemed like a paraphrase of some of the description of the new spirit of capitalism that Luc Boltanski and Eve Chiappello (2005) had recently offered.

11. Following the Cooke ratio, the Donough ratio broadened the scope of this risk metric and factored into the measure of overall risk the sources that had been overlooked in the first installment of the VaR.

12. This is particularly the case of the volatilities. Central to the hedging plans of traders, they are not used by the back-office employees. But assessing the value of these volatility-sensitive products midway through the course of their life span demands this information.

13. The equity-linked swaps are swap contracts with one of the pay-off flows based on the performance of a stock.

14. Unlike the back and front offices, the accounting department does not support its own database. It only derives information from existing ones.

15. The simplest explanation for this discrepancy in the terms of the trade can be found in a bad front entry or in the anticipation of a deposit of the flow to the back office.

16. Critical analyses of these approaches of accounting can be found in Carruthers and Espeland (1991) and Aho (2006).

Chapter 7: Reverse Finance

1. See Berle and Means's (1932) study of the growing crisis between management and ownership.

2. It is beyond the scope of *Codes of Finance* to study the diffusion of corporate management, organizational theories, and real option theories from academia to companies. Business schools have been sites of cross-fertilization for these initially separate fields of study. Rakesh Khurana (2007) elaborates on that confluence.

3. If its outstanding equities value was worth €150 million in 2001, detaining €15 million in General Bank property titles would amount to owning 10 percent of the firm. The invention of securitization kept separate the division of the firm in units (and even finer industrial functional divisions) and the nominal ownership in terms of equities. The very term "equities" hints at this distinction between the two possible divisions of the firm, industrial and financial. When one owns 10 percent of a publicly traded company, this percentage does not translate into any other functional divisions. Rather, it is 10 percent of the performance of the felicitous collaboration of the production factors. Even 10 percent of each and every factor (if we were to go with the usual division of production factors between land, labor, and capital) would not come to the same result as 10 percent of its product.

4. These revisions were in tune with the European Interbank Offered Rate.

5. Other studies making national claims involve similar projects aiming at scientific and industrial autonomy. Paul Rabinow's (1999) study of French biotechnology firms claiming to revolutionize the way of doing science and Gabriel Hecht's (1998) analysis of the French complex of energetic autonomy both point to a strong engineering tradition. When it comes to solving a problem, engineers are never very far away in France.

6. Peter Hall (1986), Jack Hayward (1986), and Michael Loriaux (1991) provide useful analyses of the complex combination of patriotism, intervention, and claim to liberalization of the succeeding French governments since the mid-1970s.

7. "Solid cores" (in French *noyaux durs*) were the shares of a company (groups of securities) belonging to another French holding. These solid cores were deemed safer than the usual dilution of property among a large number of shareholders because merger plans could be handled through a more simple conversation among CEOs of these companies and holdings. A high premium offer can easily appeal to shareholders who are looking for short-term profits. Countering the premium can sometimes be an expensive solution for the minority shareholders. The conversation that the French State had in mind when it came up with the model of the solid core was influenced by the conversation long entertained by engineers coming out of the most prestigious application schools after Ecole Polytechnique (Ecole des Mines, Ecole des Ponts et Chaussees, Ecole Centrale). These engineers have a sense of recognition; they know who is to be trusted and who is to be questioned. The ministry of economy's higher administration enjoys this conversation with the CEOs of the most prestigious French companies.

8. *Saint-simonisme* is a doctrine that took hold of the French elite in the 1830s and that propagated into the higher French bureaucracy to the present. A simplified version of the doctrine of its founder, Claude Henry de Rouvroy, the Comte de Saint-Simon, saint-simonism looks to establish the foundation of the economy on a strong industrial network. Various brands of saint-simonism diverged after the death of Rouvroy, but until fairly recently French technocrats have always navigated the tension presented by a political theory articulating organization and freedom. Michel Albert theorized the Rhénan capitalism, pitting it against U.S. capitalism around 1991, but these ideas of a specifically European path to market economy were already shared by many economists close to the policy-making circles. Jacques Delors, who was Economics, Finance and Budget minister from 1981 to 1984 and steered the reform of the French banking industry of 1984, was a strong advocate of the solid cores. The treasury head working during the Delors waves of

reforms, Jean-Yves Haberer, also pushed for solid cores and ended up putting some of his ideas into practice when he took the lead of Credit Lyonnais in 1988. For a solid study of Saint-Simonisme and its relationship with the French tradition of engineering, urban and social planning, see Picon (1992, 2002a, 2002b).

9. Interview, May 2001.

10. Industrial compatibility does not exclude the consideration of financial assets of the companies being merged. But it is no longer the market finance at play earlier in the title compatibility; rather, it is corporate finance. With corporate finance, the weight of the various assets is now possibly in question.

11. The economy of standards blossomed when compatibility became a relevant question for investigation by economists. Although compatibility between goods had already been on the agenda of economists in the past, the rise of networks triggered this renewed interest. Compatibility was added to the list of goods' characteristics in such a way that goods were made to communicate with each other, behind the backs of economic agents: compatibility became a characteristic relative to the space of goods, not to the intimate colloquium being played between goods and economic agents. The standard's economic structure can be summarized as follows: a *relationship made necessary* between two goods or services. Whereas two goods, X and Y, are developed in, and belong to, two apparently independent economic series, they actually need each other absolutely, and neither would be able to survive without the other. They form a *mutual necessity* relationship. One might believe that the assets are independent and individual, but this relation actually binds them tightly. As soon as commodity X is sold, it guarantees the commercialization of commodity Y through the technological compatibility that lends these two commodities a single configuration and a guaranteed outlay.

12. In addition to casting light on the economic tension created by the uncertainty of investment between ownership and management, principal–agent has also described and prescribed solutions out of this uncertainty. Principal–agent theory enjoys the status of being among the most performative economic theories. It is difficult to think of a large organization whose mechanisms would not be, more or less directly, informed by principal–agent models.

13. Creativity has been the motto of middle managers since the mid-1970s, in what some observers have called a new spirit of capitalism, reversing the old tenet of hierarchical structure by letting in the bohemian spirit of the 1968 revolts. Luc Boltanski and Eve Chiapello (2005) draw on the notions of inspired and artistic modes of behaviors transplanted in the corporation to account for the quite radical shift in values that now run the corporate world. There is undoubtedly an aesthetic dimension to their clinging to the business enterprise they had launched.

Conclusion: What Good Are Derivatives?

1. This chapter owes much to discussions with Michel Callon.

2. Readers who are not afraid of continental philosophy may want to read the highly insightful recent work of Elie Ayache (2010).

3. The dependence of a good's price on other goods is obviously not new. Economists have long played with the notion of price elasticity between goods.

4. The success of this new product depends on the stability of the hosts on top of which it is built. Crucial in this respect is the continuity of price measurements. If a stock price came to be disrupted on the date and at the time of measurement, the

whole architecture of derivation would be shattered and would demand at times complex procedures of substitution to guarantee the survival of the derivative beyond the hiccup of the underlying.

5. We owe the notion of qualculation to Franck Cochoy's (2002) studies of consumers' strategies. It reconciles the two approaches of goods as bundles of *qual*-ities subject to judgment and goods as items that feature in chains of cal-*culation*. Qualculation is a way of making space for the historicity of calculative practices. It also stresses the tight coupling between our ability to count and our ability to judge.

6. Guyers calls these goods "conveyed goods."

7. A first attempt to lay the properties of definitional goods—as opposed to derivational goods—is in Lépinay (2007).

8. Definition shares the spirit of the accounting revolution: each piece coming in and going out is a discrete and describable entity. See Mary Poovey (1998) for an elaborate analysis of the role of double entry bookkeeping on the stabilization of the category of fact.

9. Michel Callon (2002) drew attention to the fruitfulness of Say's views and by its compatibility with the dynamics of qualification of goods.

10. The distinction between the two combinations can be captured by the following comparison. Averaging a set of numbers, once accomplished, makes you lose sight of the originals. This is in all accounts a combination that creates a number irreducible to the initial set. The series {2, 4, 3, 7, 4} averages at 4 if I use the arithmetic operator. From 4, I have no way of figuring out the initial set as there is an infinite number of possible 5-number sets {a, b, c, d, e} averaging at 4. Critics of the all-pervasive use of statistics are eager to point to the loss of information due to the reduction performed by the average operator. Yet this widespread use also points to the political significance of taking the combination for the individuals. The figure produced by the operator empowers public agencies that try to categorize the population into subgroups; it creates "outliers" and "average men and women." Consider a set of colors that you combine to produce a new color. It may be difficult for a nonexpert to go from the result to the initial pool of colors that have been stirred together, but each combination will result in a unique new color. Starting from the primary color, and repeating the operation enough times, it will probably even be impossible to decipher the components. Yet the point of this comparison is to highlight the two different trajectories of numbers and colors undergone by this putting together, this bringing close, and the result of it. With colors, the combination does not erase the specificity of the ingredient. The result maintains this specificity in the production of a unique new one. Derivation works only through that particular filtering.

11. Cori Hayden (2007) analyzes the strategic organization of downstream derivation in the case of drugs circulating beyond their domains of regulations.

12. That is why many derivations do not project themselves in the future and refuse to invest, preferring instead to rip the low hanging, easily accessible fruit. Production (as defined above) qua cautious derivation injects the future into this ephemeral and risky present. Derivation as degenerate production rules itself out of any future.

13. The violence—material/monetary and intellectual—is interestingly experienced in both ways. Upward, when luck strikes, the lack of understanding comes with a much warmer feeling of sudden wealth, but as documented by Viviana Zelizer (1989),

these unaccounted sources of income are channeled toward special consumptions and are clearly set apart from the more routine circuits of income/expense.

14. On legends of prespeculative worlds untouched by the plague of finance, Marieke De Goede (2006) offers a refreshing analysis of a few key moments in financial history.

15. Opposing market economy and moral economies, as Thompson does, is misleading as it supposes that there would be one and only one formula of economy under the market regime whereas there would be plenty of them under the moral regime. As this case study exemplifies, it is not a good starting point, as there are actually as many economies as one finds configurations of goods/services. What needs to be put under close scrutiny is not the amorality of market economies (as they all have highly specific morals) but the way they affect populations—politicizing them again, in short.

BIBLIOGRAPHY

Abernathy, William, and Kim Clark. 1985. "Innovation: Mapping the Winds of Creative Destruction." *Research Policy* 14: 3–22.

Abolafia, Mitchel. 1996. *Making Markets. Opportunism and Restraint on Wall Street.* Cambridge: Harvard University Press.

Agnes, Pierre. 2000. "The 'End of Geography' in Financial Services? Local Embeddedness and Territorialization in the Interest Rate Swaps Industry." *Economic Geography* 76: 347–66.

Aho, James. 2006. *Bookkeeping and Confession: The Religious, Moral, and Rhetorical Origins of Modern Accounting.* Albany: State University of New York Press.

Akerlof, George A. 1970. "The Market for 'Lemons': Quality Uncertainty and the Market Mechanism." *Quarterly Journal of Economics* 84(3): 488–500.

Appadurai, Arjun, ed. 1986. *The Social Life of Things. Commodities in Cultural Perspective.* Cambridge: Cambridge University Press.

Arnold, Patricia. 1998. "The Limits of Postmodernism in Accounting History. The Decatur Experience." *Accounting, Organizations and Society* 23(7): 665–84.

Aubin, David. 1997. "The Withering Immortality of Bourbaki. A Cultural Connector at the Confluence of Mathematics, Structuralism, and Oulipo in France." *Science in Context* 10(2): 297–342.

Austin, John. 1962. *How to Do Things with Words.* Oxford: Clarendon Press.

Ayache, Elie. 2010. *The Blank Swan: The End of Probability.* New York: John Wiley & Sons.

Baker, Wayne. 1984. "The Social Structure of a National Securities Market." *American Journal of Sociology* 89: 775–811.

Balzac, Honore de. 1998 (1835). *Père Goriot.* New York: W.W. Norton and Company.

Barnes, Barry. 1983. "Social Life as Bootstrapped Induction." *Sociology* 17(4): 524–45.

Beck, Ulrich. 1992 (1986). *Risk Society. Towards a New Modernity.* London: Sage Publications.

———. 1996. *World Risk Society.* Cambridge: Polity Press.

Bensaid, Bernard, Jean-Philippe Lesne, Henri Pages, and Jose Scheinkman. 1992. "Derivative Asset Pricing with Transaction Costs." *Mathematical Finance* 2(2): 63–83.

Berg, Marc. 1997. "Of Forms, Containers, and the Electronic Medical Record: Some Tools for a Sociology of the Formal." *Science, Technology & Human Values* 22: 403–33

Bergson, Henry. 1990 (1896). *Matter and Memory*. New York: Zone Books.

Berle, Adolf, and Gardiner Means. 1932. *The Modern Corporation and Private Property*. New York: Harcourt, Brace & World.

Bestor, Theodore. 2001. "Supply-Side Sushi: Commodity, Market, and the Global City." *American Anthropologist* 103(1): 76–95.

———. 2004. *Tsukiji: The Fish Market at the Center of the World*. Berkeley: University of California Press.

Beunza, Daniel, and Yuval Milo. 2011. *Politics of Liquidity*, Working Paper, LSE Accounting and Management Departments.

Beunza, Daniel, and David Stark. 2004. "Tools of the Trade: The Socio-Technology of Arbitrage in a Wall Street Trading Room." *Industrial and Corporate Change*. 13(2): 369–400.

———. 2008. "Reflexive Modeling: The Social Calculus of the Arbitrageur." Working paper, accessed in December 2008 at http://papers.ssrn.com/sol3/papers.cfm?abstract_id=1285054.

Boltanski, Luc, and Eve Chiappello. 2005 (1999). *The New Spirit of Capitalism*. London: Verso.

Bookstaber, Richard. 2007. *A Demon of Our Own Design: Markets, Hedge Funds, and the Perils of Financial Innovation*. New York: John Wiley & Sons.

Bouchaud, Jean-Philippe and Didier Sornette. 1994. "The Black-Scholes Option Pricing Problem in Mathematical Finance: Generalization and Extensions for a Large Class of Stochastic Processes." *Journal de Physique I*, 4: 863–81.

Bourdieu, Pierre. 1991. *Language and Symbolic Power*. Cambridge: Harvard University Press.

———. 1996 (1989). *State Nobility: Elite Schools in the Field of Power*. Palo Alto, CA: Stanford University Press.

Brown, John Seely, and Paul Duguid. 2000. *The Social Life of Information*. Boston: Harvard Business School.

Buffet, Warren. 2002. Berkshire Hathaway Inc. Annual Report.

Burawoy, Michael et al. 2000. *Global Ethnography: Forces, Connections, and Imaginations in a Postmodern World*. Berkeley: University of California Press.

Caliskan, Koray. 2010. *Market Threads: How Cotton Farmers and Traders Create a Global Commodity*. Princeton: Princeton University Press.

Callon, Michel. 1998. "Introduction: The embeddedness of economic markets in economics," in Michel Callon, ed., *The laws of the markets*. Oxford: Blackwell, 1–57.

———. 2007a. *Market Devices*. Oxford: Blackwell.

———. 2007b. "What Does it Mean to Say that Economics is Performative?," in Donald MacKenzie, Fabian Muniesa, and Lucia Siu, eds., *Do Economists Make Markets? On the Performativity of Economics*. Princeton, Princeton University Press, 311–57.

———. 2009 (2001). *Acting in an Uncertain World. An Essay on Technological Democracy*. Cambridge: MIT Press.

Callon, Michel, and Koray Caliskan. 2009. "Economization. Part I: On Search of Economization." *Economy and Society* 38(3): 369–98.

———. 2010. "Economization. Part II: Some Elements for a Research Program on the Study of Marketization." *Economy and Society* 39(1): 1–32.

Callon, Michel, Cécile Méadel, and Vololona Rabeharisoa. 2002. "The Economy of Qualities." *Economy and Society* 31: 194–217.

Carruthers, Bruce G., and Wendy Nelson Espeland. 1991. "Accounting for Rationality: Double Entry Bookkeeping and the Rhetoric of Economic Rationality." *American Journal of Sociology* 39(1): 31–69.

Chacko, George, Peter Tufano, and Geoffrey Verter. 2001. "Cephalon, Inc.: Taking Risk Management Theory Seriously." *Journal of Financial Economics* 60(2–3): 449–85.

Chadarevian, Soroya. 1996. "Laboratory Science versus Country-House Experiments. The Controversy between Julius Sachs and Charles Darwin," *British Journal of History of Science* 29: 17–41.

Chadarevian, Soroya, and Nick Hopwood. 2004. *Models: The Third Dimension of Science*. Palo Alto, CA: Stanford University Press.

Chandler, Alfred D. 1977. *The Invisible Hand. The Managerial Revolution in American Business*. Cambridge: Belknap Press.

Clark, Colin and Trevor Pinch. 1995. *The Hard Sell: The Language and Lessons of Street-Wise Marketing*. London: Harper Collins

Coase, Ronald. H. 1937. "The Nature of the Firm." *Economica* 4(4): 386–405.

———. 1988. *The Firm, the Market and the Law*. Chicago: University of Chicago Press.

Cochoy, Franck. 2002. *Une Sociologie du Packaging ou l'Ane de Buridan Face au Marché*. Paris: PUF.

Collins, Harry. 1983. *Changing Order: Replication and Induction in Scientific Practice*. Chicago: Chicago University Press.

Collins, Harry, and Robert Evans. 2007. *Rethinking Expertise*. Chicago: University of Chicago Press.

Collins, Harry, and Martin Kusch. 1999. *The Shape of Actions: What Humans and Machines Can Do*. Cambridge: MIT Press.

Cook, Harold. 2007. *Matters of Exchange: Commerce, Medicine and Science in the Dutch Golden Age*. New Haven: Yale University Press.

Crackhardt, David. 1992. "The Strength of Strong Ties: The Importance of Philos," in Nitin Nohria and Robert Eccles, eds., *Organizations in Networks and Organizations. Structure, Form, and Action*. Cambridge: Harvard Business School Press.

Cronon, William, 1992. *Nature's Metropolis: Chicago and the Great West*. New York: W.W. Norton.

Dagognet, François. 1992. *Le Corps Multiple et Un*. Le Plessis-Robinson: Laboratoires Delagrange.

———. 1993. *La Peau Découverte*. Le Plessis-Robinson: Synthélabo.

David, Paul A. 1985. "Clio and the Economics of QWERTY." *American Economic Review* 75: 332–37.

Deleuze, Gilles. 1994 (1968). *Difference and Repetition*. New York: Columbia University Press.

———. 1970. *Spinoza. Philosophie Pratique*. Paris: Editions de Minuit.

———. 1987 (1980). *A Thousand Plateaus. Capitalism and Schizophrenia*. Minneapolis: University of Minnesota Press.

Deleuze, Gilles, and Claire Parnet. 2002. *Dialogues*. New York: Columbia University Press.

Derman, Elliot. 2004. *My Life as a Quant: Reflections on Physics and Finance*. New York: John Wiley & Sons.

Dodier, Nicolas. 1993. "Les appuis conventionnels de l'action." *Réseaux* 62: 63–85.

Dosi, Giovanni, C. Freeman, R. Nelson, G. Siverberg, and L. Soete, eds. 1988. *Technical Change and Economic Theory*. London: Frances Pinter Publishers.

Eccles, Robert G., and Dwight B. Crane. 1988. *Doing Deals. Investment Banks at Work*. Cambridge: Harvard Business Press.

Fabozzi, Franck J., Henry A. Davis, and Moorad Choudhry. 2006. *Introduction to Structured Finance*. New York: John Wiley & Sons Inc.

Fine, Gary Alan. 2007. *Authors of the Storm: Meteorologists and the Culture of the Prediction*. Chicago: University of Chicago Press.

Fox Keller, Evelyn. 1983. *A Feeling for the Organism: The Life and Work of Barbara McClintock*. New York: W. H. Freeman.

Froud, Julie, Karel William, Colin Haslam, Sukhdev Johal, and John Williams. 1998. "Caterpillar: two stories and an argument." *Accounting, Organizations and Society* 23(7): 685–708.

Galison, Peter. 1997. *Image and Logic*. Chicago: Chicago University Press.

Galison, Peter and Caroline A. Jones. 1999. "Factory, Laboratory, Studio. Dispersing Sites of Production," in Peter Galison and Emily Thompson, eds. *The Architecture of Science*. Cambridge: MIT Press, 497–540.

Galison, Peter and Emily Thompson. 1999. *The Architecture of Science*. Cambridge: MIT Press.

Gallouj, Francois. 2002. *Innovation in the Service Economy*. London: Edward Elgar.

Gardey, Delphine. 1999. "The Standardization of a Technical Practice: Typing (1883–1930)." *History and Technology*, 15 (2): 313–43.

———. 2001. *La dactylographe et l'expéditionnaire*. Paris: Belin.

Garfinkel, Harold. 1967. *Studies in Ethnomethodology*. Englewood Cliffs, NJ: Prentice-Hall.

Geertz, Clifford. 1978. "The Bazaar Economy: Information and Search in Peasant Marketing." *American Economic Review* 68: 28–32.

Gibson, David. 2005. "Taking Turns and Talking Ties: Networks and Conversational Interaction." *American Journal of Sociology* 110(6): 1561–97.

Ginzburg, Carlo. 1980. "Signes, traces, pistes. Racines d'un paradigme de l'indice." *Le Débat* 6: 3–44.

———. 1992. *Clues, Myths, and the Historical Method*. Baltimore: The Johns Hopkins University Press.

Girard, René. 1979. *Violence and the Sacred*. Baltimore: The Johns Hopkins University Press.

———. 1989. *The Scapegoat*. Baltimore: The Johns Hopkins University Press.

Godechot, Olivier. 2000. *Les Traders*. Paris: La decouverte.

———. 2007. *Working Rich*. Paris: La decouverte.

Goede, Marrieke de. 2006. *Virtue, Fortune and Faith: A Genealogy of Finance*. Minneapolis: University of Minnesota Press.

Goffman, Erving. 1959. *The Presentation of Self in Everyday Life*. New York: Anchor Books.

———. 1969. *Strategic Interaction*. Philadelphia: University of Philadelphia Press.

———. 1979. *Gender Advertisements*. London: MacMillan.

Goody, Jack. 1977. *The Domestication of the Savage Mind*. Cambridge: Cambridge University Press.

Greenspan, Alan. 2008. Prepared Statement before the Committee of Government Oversight and Reform, October 23, 2008; accessed at http://oversight.house.gov/documents/20081023100438.pdf.

Gusterson, Hugh. 1998. *Nuclear Rites: A Weapons Laboratory at the End of the Cold War*. Berkeley: University of California Press.

Guyer, Jane. 2004. *Marginal Gains: Monetary Transactions in Atlantic Africa*. Chicago: University of Chicago Press.

Hall, Peter. 1986. *Governing the Economy: The Politics of State Intervention in Britain and France*. Oxford: Oxford University Press.

Harper, Richard. 1998. *Inside the IMF: An Ethnography of Documents, Technology and Organizational Action*. San Diego: Academy Press.

Hayden, Cori. 2007. "A Generic Solution? Pharmaceuticals and the Politics of the Similar in Mexico." *Current Anthropology*, 48(4): 475–95.

Hayek, Freidrich. 1945. "The Use of Knowledge in Society." *American Economic Review* 35: 519–30.

Hayward, Jack. 1986. *The State and the Market Economy: Industrial Patriotism and Economic Intervention in France*. Brighton, UK: Wheatsheaf Books.

Heath, Christian, Marina Jirotka, Paul Luff, and Jon Hindmarsh. 1995. "Unpacking Collaboration: The Interactional Organization of Trading in a City Dealing Room." *Computer Supported Cooperative Work* 3: 147–65.

Hecht, Gabriel. 1998. *The Radiance of France: Nuclear Power and National Identity after World War II*. Cambridge: MIT Press.

Heimer, Carol. 2006. "Conceiving Children: How Documents Support Case versus Biographical Analyses," in Annelise Riles, *Documents: Artifacts of Modern Knowledge*. Ann Arbor: University of Michigan Press, pp. 95–126.

Hertz, Ellen. 1998. *The Trading Crowd. An Ethnography of the Shanghai Stock Market*. Cambridge: Cambridge University Press.

Heston, Steven L. 1993. "A Closed Form Solution for Options with Stochastic Volatility with Application to Bonds and Currency Options." *Review of Financial Studies* 6(2): 327–43.

Hirschman, Albert O. 1970. *Exit, Voice, and Loyalty: Responses to Decline in Firms, Organizations, and States*. Cambridge: Harvard University Press.

Ho, Karen. 2009. *Liquidated. An Ethnography of Wall Street*. Durham, NC: Duke University Press.

Holmes, Douglas. 2009. "Economy of Words." *Cultural Anthropology*, 24(3): 381–419.

Hughes, Thomas P. 1987. *Networks of Power. Electrification in Western Societies, 1880–1930*. Baltimore: The Johns Hopkins University Press.

Hutchins, Edwin. 1996. *Cognition in the Wild*. Cambridge: MIT Press.

James, William. 1907. *Pragmatism. A New Name for some Old Ways of Thinking*. Accessible at http://www.gutenberg.org/cache/epub/5116/pg5116.html (accessed Feb. 2011).

Jones, Graham. 2011. *Trade of the Tricks. Inside the Magician's Craft*. Berkeley: University of California Press.

Kaiser, David. 2005a. "American Suspicions of Theoretical Physicists during the Early Cold War." *Representations* 90: 28–60.

———. 2005b. *Drawing Theories Apart. The Dispersion of Feynman Diagrams in Postwar Physics*. Chicago: Chicago University Press.

Kantorowicz, Ernst H. 1957. *The King's Two Bodies: A Study in Medieval Political Theology*. Princeton: Princeton University Press.

Keynes, John Maynard. 1936. *The General Theory of Employment, Interest and Money*. London: MacMillan & Co.

Khurana, Rakeh. 2007. *From Higher Aims to Hired Hands: The Social Transformation of American Business Schools and the Unfulfilled Promise of Management as a Profession*. Princeton: Princeton University Press.

Knight, Frank H. 1971 (1921). *Risk, Uncertainty and Profit*. Chicago: University of Chicago Press.

Knorr Cetina, Karin. 2002. "Inhabiting Technology: Features of a Global Lifeform." *Current Sociology*, 50(3): 389–405.

Knorr Cetina, Karin, and Urs Bruegger. 2002. "Global Microstructures: The Virtual Societies of Financial Markets." *American Journal of Sociology*, 107(4): 905–50.

Knorr Cetina, Karin, and Alex Preda, eds. 2005. *The Sociology of Financial Markets*. Oxford: Oxford University Press.

Kockelman, Paul. 2006. "A Semiotic Ontology of the Commodity." *Journal of Linguistic Anthropology* 16(1): 76–102.

Kohler, Robert, 1994 *Lords of the Fly. Drosophila Genetics and the Experimental Life*. Chicago: Chicago University Press.

Kopitoff, Igor. 1986. "The Cultural Biography of Things. Commoditization as a Process," in Arjun Appadurai, ed. *The Social Life of Things. Commodities in Cultural Perspective*. Cambridge: Cambridge University Press.

Kuhn, Thomas S. 1962. *The Structure of Scientific Revolutions*. Chicago: Chicago University Press.

Lakoff, Georges, and Mark Johnson. 1999. *Philosophy in the Flesh: The Embodied Mind and its Challenge to Western Thought*. New York: Basic Books.

Latour, Bruno. 1987. *Science in Action: How to Follow Scientists and Engineers through Society*. Cambridge: Harvard University Press.

———. 1995 (1993). *Aramis, or the Love of Technology*. Cambridge: Harvard University Press.

———. 1996. "On Interobjectivity." *Mind, Culture, and Activity* 3(4): 228–45.

———. 2005. *Reassembling the Social. An Introduction to Actor-Network-Theory*. Oxford: Oxford University Press.

Latour, Bruno, and Vincent-Antonin Lépinay. 2009. *The Science of Passionate Interests. An Introduction to the Economic Anthropology of Gabriel Tarde*. Chicago: Prickly Paradigm Press.

Latour, Bruno and Steve Woolgar. 1979. *Laboratory Life. The Social Construction of Scientific Facts*. Beverly Hills: Sage Publications.

Lave, Jean. 1988. *Cognition in Practice: Mind, Mathematics and Culture in Everyday Life*. Cambridge: Cambridge University Press.

Lave, Jean, and Etienne Wenger. 1991. *Situated Learning: Legitimate Peripheral Participation*. Cambridge: Cambridge University Press.

Law, John and John Hassard. 1999. *Actor Network Theory and After*. London: Blackwell Publisher.

Leland, Hayne E. 1980. "Who Should Buy Portfolio Insurance." *The Journal of Finance* 35: 581–94.

———. 1985. "Option Pricing and Replication with Transactions Costs." *The Journal of Finance*, 11(5): 1283–301.

Leland, Hayne E., and Mark Rubinstein. 1988. "The Evolution of Portfolio Insurance," in Don Luskin, ed., *Dynamic Hedging: A Guide to Portfolio Insurance*. New York: John Wiley and Sons.

Lépinay, Vincent-Antonin. 2007a. "Articulation and Liquidity in a Trading Room," in Donald MacKenzie, Fabian Muniesa and Lucia Su, eds., *Do Economist Make Markets*. Princeton: Princeton University Press.

———. 2007b. "Parasitic Formulae. The Case of Capital Guarantee Products," in Michel Callon et al. eds., *Market Devices*. Oxford: Routledge Sociology Monograph.

———. 2007c. "Economy of the Germ: Capital, Accumulation and Vibration." *Economy and Society* 36(4): 526–48.

Lépinay, Vincent-Antonin, and Fabrice Rousseau. 2001. "Les Trolls sont-ils incompétents? Essai de sociologie des financiers amateurs." *Politix* 52: 73–97.

Lewis, David. 1969. *Convention. A Philosophical Study*. Oxford: Blackburn.

Lindsey, Richard, and Barry Schachter. 2007. *How I Became a Quant. Insights from 25 of Wall Street's Elite*. Hoboken, NJ: John Wiley & Sons.

LiPuma, Edward, and Benjamin Lee. 2004. *Financial Derivatives and the Globalization of Risk*. Durham, NC: Duke University Press.

Lo, Andrew W. 2005. *The Dynamics of the Hedge Fund Industry*. Research Foundation of CFA Institute.

———. 2008. *Hedge Funds: An Analytic Perspective*. Princeton: Princeton University Press.

Loriaux, Michael. 1991. *France After Hegemony. International Change and Financial Reform*. Ithaca: Cornell University Press.

Lowenstein, Roger. 2001. *When Genius Failed: The Rise and Fall of Long-Term Capital Management*. Random House Trade Paperbacks.

Lynch, Michael. 1991. "Laboratory Space and the Technological Complex: An Investigation of Topical Contextures." *Science in Context* 4: 51–78.

Mackay, Wendy, Anne Laure Fayard, et al. 1998. "Reinventing the Familiar: Exploring an Augmented Reality Design Space for Air Traffic Control." *Proceedings of the SIGCHI conference on Human factors in computing systems*. 31: 558–65.

MacKenzie, Adrian. 2006. *Cutting Code. Software and Sociality*. New York: Peter Lang.

MacKenzie, Donald. 2006. *An Engine, Not a Camera: How Financial Models Shape Markets,* Cambridge: MIT Press.

———. "The Credit Crisis as a Problem in the Sociology of Knowledge" (under review at *American Journal of Sociology*).

MacKenzie, Donald, and Yuval Millo. 2003. "Constructing a Market, Performing Theory. The Historical Sociology of a Financial Derivatives Exchange." *American Journal of Sociology* 109(1): 107–45.

MacKenzie, Donald, Fabian Muniesa, and Lucia Siu, eds. 2007. *Do Economists Make Markets? On the Performativity of Economics*, Princeton: Princeton University Press.

Mallard, Alexandre. 1998. "Compare, Standardize, and Settle Agreement. On Some Usual Metrological Problems." *Social Studies of Science* 28(4): 571–601.

Markowitz, Harry H. 1959. *Portfolio Selection. Efficient Diversification of Investments*. Hoboken, NJ: John Wiley & Sons.

Marx, Karl. 1867. *Capital*. Accessible at http://www.marxists.org/archive/marx/works/1867-c1/ (accessed Feb. 2011).

Masco, Joseph. 2006. *The Nuclear Borderlands: The Manhattan Project in Post–Cold War New Mexico*. Princeton: Princeton University Press.

Maurer, Bill. 1998. "Cyberspatial Sovereignties: Offshore Finance, Digital Cash, and the Limits of Liberalism." *Indiana Journal of Global Legal Studies* 5(2): 493–519.

Mauss, Marcel. 2002 (1924). *The Gift: The Form and Reason for Exchange in Archaic Societies.* London: Routledge Classics.

Meehan, Albert. 1997. "Record Keeping Practices in the Policing of Juveniles," in Max Travers and John F. Manzo, eds., *Law in Action: Ethnomethodological and Conversation Analytic Approaches to Law.* Brookfield VT: Ashgate, 183–208.

Mialet, Helene. 1999. "Do Angels Have Bodies? Two Stories about Subjectivity in Science: The Cases of William X and Mister H," *Social Studies of Science,* 29(4): 551–81.

———. (forthcoming 2012). *Hawking Incorporated.* Chicago: University of Chicago Press.

Miller, Daniel. 1998. *A Theory of Shopping.* Cornell: Cornell University Press.

———. 2001. "Turning Callon the Right Way Up." *Economy and Society* 31(2): 218–33.

Miller, Merton. 1986. "Financial Innovation: The Last Twenty Years and the Next." *Journal of Financial and Quantitative Analysis* 21: 459–71.

Miller, Peter, and Ted O'Leary. 1993. "Accounting Expertise and the Politics of the Product: Economic Citizenship and Modes of Corporate Governance." *Accounting, Organizations and Society* 18(2–3): 187–206.

———. 1994. "Accounting, 'Economic Citizenship' and the Spatial Reordering of Manufacture," *Accounting, Organizations and Society* 19(1): 15–43.

———. 1998a. "Finding Things Out." *Accounting, Organizations and Society* 23(7): 709–14.

———. 1998b. *The Factory as Laboratory in Accounting and Science,* edited by Michael Power. Cambridge: Cambridge University Press, 120–50.

———. 2002. "Rethinking the Factory: Caterpillar Inc." *Cultural Values* 6: 91–117.

Millo, Yuval. 2003. *Where Do Financial Markets Come From? Historical Sociology of Financial Derivatives Markets.* PhD thesis. Edinburgh, University of Edinburgh.

Minsky, Hyman P. 1982. *Can It Happen Again? Essays on Instability and Finance.* Armonk, NY: M. E. Sharpe.

———. 2008. *Stabilizing an Unstable Economy.* New Haven: Yale University Press.

Mirowski, Philip, and Edward Nik-Khah. 2007. "Markets Made Flesh: Performativity, and a Problem in Science Studies, augmented with Consideration of the FCC Auctions," in Donald MacKenzie, Fabian Muniesa, and Lucia Siu, eds., *Do Economists Make Markets? On the Performativity of Economics.* Princeton, NJ: Princeton University Press, 190–225.

Mitchell, Timothy, 2005. "The Work of Economics: How a Discipline Makes Its World." *European Journal of Sociology* 46(2): 297–320.

———. 2008. "Rethinking economy." *Geoforum* 39(3): 1116–21.

Miyazaki, Hirokazu. 2003. "The Temporalities of the Market." *American Anthropologist* 105(2): 255–65.

———. 2006. *The Method of Hope: Anthropology, Philosophy, and Fijian Knowledge.* Palo Alto, CA: Stanford University Press.

Mol, Annemarie. 2002. *The Body Multiple. Ontology in Medical Practice.* Durham, NC: Duke University Press.

Morgan, Mary, and Marcel Boumans. 2004. "Secrets Hidden by Two-Dimensionality. The Economy as a Hydraulic Machine," in Soraya De Chadaverian and Nick Hopwood, eds., *Models: The Third Dimension of Science.* Palo Alto, CA: Stanford University Press.

Muniesa, Fabian. 2003. "Des marchés comme algorithmes: sociologie de la cotation électronique à la Bourse de Paris." PhD dissertation, *Centre de Sociologie de l'Innovation*. Paris: École Nationale Supérieure des Mines de Paris.

———. 2007. "Market Technologies and the Pragmatics of Prices." *Economy and Society* 36(3): 377–95.

Myers, Natasha. 2008. "Molecular Embodiments and the Body-Work of Modelling in Protein Crystallography." *Social Studies of Science* 38(1): 163–99.

Nohria, Nitin, and Robert Eccles. 1992. *Networks and Organizations. Structure, Form, and Action*. Cambridge: Harvard Business School Press.

O'Brien, Richard. 1992. *Global Financial Integration. The End of Geography*. New York: Council on Foreign Relations Press.

Ochs, Elinor, Sally Jacoby, and Patrick Gonzales. 1994. "Interpretive Journeys: How Physicists Talk and Travel through Graphic Space." *Configurations* 2: 151–71.

Ochs, Elinor, Emmanuel A. Schegloff, and Sandra A. Thompson, eds. 1996. *Interaction and Grammar*. Cambridge: Cambridge University Press.

O'Connell, Joseph. 1993. "Metrology: The Creation of Universality by the Circulation of Particulars." *Social Studies of Science* 23(1): 129–73.

Ogborn, Miles. 2007. *Indian Ink. Script and Print in the Making of the English East India Company*. Chicago: University of Chicago Press.

O'Hara, Maureen. 2003. "Presidential Address: Liquidity and Price Discovery." *Journal of Finance* 58(4): 1335–54.

Patterson, Scott. 2010. *The Quants. How a New Breed of Math Whizzes Conquered Wall Street and Nearly Destroyed It*. New York: Random House.

Pickering, Andrew. 1995. *The Mangle of Practice: Time, Agency and Science*. Chicago: University of Chicago Press.

Pickering, Andrew, ed. 1992. *Science as Practice and Culture*. Chicago: University of Chicago Press.

Picon, Antoine. 1992a. *French Architects and Engineers in the Age of Enlightenment*. Cambridge: Cambridge University Press.

———. 1992b. *L'Invention de l'ingénieur moderne. L'Ecole des Ponts et Chaussées, 1747–1851*. Paris: Presse de l'Ecole des Ponts et Chaussées.

———. 2002. *Les Saint-Simoniens: raison, imaginaire, et utopie*. Paris: Belin.

Polanyi, Michael. 1958. *Personal Knowledge: Towards a Post-Critical Philosophy*. Chicago: University Of Chicago Press.

———. 1966. *The Tacit Dimension*. London: Routledge.

Poovey, Mary. 1998. *A History of the Modern Fact: Problems of Knowledge in the Sciences of Wealth and Society*. Chicago: University of Chicago Press.

Porter, Theodore. 1995. *Trust in Numbers: The Pursuit of Objectivity in Science and Public Life*. Princeton: Princeton University Press.

Powell, Walter W. 1990. "Neither Market Nor Hierarchy: Network Forms of Organization." *Research in Organizational Behavior* 12: 295–36.

Power, Michael. 2004. "Counting, Control and Calculation: Reflections on Measuring and Management." *Human Relations* 57: 765–83.

Pradelle, Michèle de la. 2006 (1996). *Market Day in Provence*. Chicago: University of Chicago Press.

Pryke, Michael, and John Allen. 2000. "Monetized Time-Space: Derivatives—Money's New Imaginary?" *Economy and Society* 29(2): 264–84.

Rabinow, Paul. 1999. *French DN: Trouble in Purgatory*. Chicago: University of Chicago Press.

Riles, Annelise. 2004. "Real Time: Governing the Market After the Failure of Knowledge." *American Ethnologist*, 31(3): 1–14.

———. 2006. *Documents. Artifacts of Modern Knowledge*. Ann Arbor: The University of Michigan Press.

———. 2010. "Collateral Expertise: Legal Knowledge in the Global Financial Markets." *Current Anthropology*, 51(6): 795–818.

Roberts, Susan M. 1995. "Small Place, Big Money: The Cayman Islands and the International Financial System." *Economic Geography* 71: 237–56.

Ross, Stephen. 1976. "Options and Efficiency." *Quarterly Journal of Economics* 90(1): 75–89.

Rosental, Claude. 2008. *Weaving Self-Evidence: A Sociology of Logic*. Princeton: Princeton University Press.

Rotman, Brian. 1993a. *Ad Infinitum . . . the Ghost in Turing's Machine: Taking God out of Mathematics and Putting the Body Back in*. Palo Alto, CA: Stanford University Press.

———. 1993b. *Signifying Nothing. The Semiotics of Zero*. Palo Alto, CA: Stanford University Press.

Samuelson, Paul. 1953. "Consumption Theorems in Terms of Overcompensation rather than Indifference Comparisons." *Economica* 20: 1–9.

Schumpeter, Joseph A. 1942. *Capitalism, Socialism and Democracy*. New York: Harper and Brothers.

Serres, Michel. 2007 (1980). *The Parasite*. Minneapolis: University of Minnesota Press.

———. 1995. *Angels, a Modern Myth*. Paris: Flammarion.

Shapin, Steven. 1988. "The House of Experiment in Seventeenth Century England." *Isis*, 79: 373–404.

Shapin, Steven, and Simon Schaffer. 1985. *Leviathan and the Air-Pump: Hobbes, Boyle and the Experimental Life*. Princeton: Princeton University Press.

Shapiro, Barbara. 2000. *A Culture of Fact: England, 1550–1720*. Cornell: Cornell University Press.

Shiller, Robert J. 2008. *The Subprime Solution: How Today's Global Financial Crisis Happened, and What to Do about It*. Princeton: Princeton University Press.

Simmel, Georg. 1906. "The Sociology of Secrecy and of Secret Societies." *American Journal of Sociology* 11: 441–98.

Sirinelli, Jean-Francois. 1988. *Génération intellectuelle. Khâgneux et normaliens dans l'entre-deux-guerres*. Paris: PUF.

Smith, Adam. 1776. *An Inquiry into the Nature and Causes of the Wealth of Nations*. Oxford: Oxford University Press.

Sombart, Werner. 1953. *The Quintessence of Capitalism*. New York: Howard Fertig.

Spinoza, Benedict. 1677. *The Ethics*. Oxford: Oxford University Press.

Star, Susan Leigh, and Karen Ruhleder. 2001. "Steps Toward an Ecology of Infrastructure. Design and Access for Large Information Spaces," in JoAnne Yates and John Van Maanen, eds., *Information Technology and Organizational Transformation. History, Rhetoric, and Practice*. London: Sage Publications.

Stark, David. 2009. *The Sense of Dissonance: Accounts of Worth in Economic Life*. Princeton: Princeton University Press.

Steinherr, Alfred. 2000. *Derivatives. The Wild Beast of Finance: A Path to Effective Globalisation?* Chichester, NY: John Wiley & Sons.

Steward, James B. 1991. *Den of Thieves*. New York: Simon and Schuster.

Stiglitz, Georges, and Arnold Weiss. 1981. "Credit Rationing in Markets with Imperfect Information." *American Economic Review* 71(2): 393–410.

Tarde, Gabriel. 1902. *Psychologie économique*. Paris: Felix Alcan.

Tett, Gillian. 2010. *Fool's Gold. The Inside Story of J.P. Morgan and How Wall St. Greed Corrupted Its Bold Dream and Created a Financial Catastrophe*. London: Free Press.

Thévenot, Laurent. 1994. "Le régime de familiarité. Des choses en personne." *Genèses* 17: 72–101.

———. 2002. "Which Road to Follow ? The Moral Complexity of an 'Equipped' Humanity," in John Law and Anne Marie Mol, eds., *Complexities in Science, Technology and Medicine*. Durham, NC: Duke University Press.

———. 2006. *L'action au pluriel. Sociologie des régimes d'engagement*. Paris La Découverte.

Thomas, Nicholas. 1991. *Entangled Objects. Exchange, Material Culture and Colonialism in the Pacific*. Cambridge: Harvard University Press.

Thompson, Edward Palmer. 1971. "The Moral Economy of the English Crowd in the 18th Century." *Past & Present* 50: 76–136.

Thrift, Nigel, and Andrew Leyshon. 1994. "A Phantom State? The De-Traditionalization of Money, the International Financial System and International Financial Centres." *Political Geography* 13(4): 299–327.

Tsing, Anna Lowenhaupt. 2004. *Friction: An Ethnography of Global Connection*. Princeton: Princeton University Press.

Tufano, Peter. 2001. "HBS-JFE Conference Volume: Complementary Research Methods." *Journal of Financial Economics* 60(2–3): 179–85.

———. 2003. "Financial Innovation," in Georges Constantinides, Milton Harris, and Rene Stulz, eds., *The Handbook of the Economics of Finance, Volume 1A– Corporate Finance*. North Holland: Elsevier, 307–36.

Uzzi, Brian. 1999. "Embeddedness in the Making of Financial Capital: How Social Relations and Networks Benefit Firms Seeking Financing." *American Sociological Review*, 64 (4): 481–505.

Veron, Nicolas. 2006. *Smoke & Mirrors, Inc.: Accounting for Capitalism*. Ithaca, NY: Cornell University Press.

Verran, Helen. 1998. *African Logic*. Chicago: Chicago University Press.

Weber, Max. (1904–5) 1976. *The Protestant Ethic and the Spirit of Capitalism*. New York: Scribner.

Weiner, Annette. 1992. *Inalienable Possessions. The Paradox of Keeping-while-Giving*. Berkeley: University of California Press.

Williamson, Oliver E. 1985. *The Economic Institutions of Capitalism*. New York: Free Press.

Wise, Norton. 1995. *The Values of Precision*. Princeton: Princeton University Press.

Yates, JoAnne. 1989. *Control through Communication: The Rise of System in American Management*. Baltimore, MD: The Johns Hopkins University Press.

———. 2005. *Structuring the Information Age: Life Insurance and Information Technology in the 20th Century*. Baltimore, MD: The Johns Hopkins University Press.

Zaloom, Caitlin. 2006. *Out of the Pits: Traders and Technology from Chicago to London*. Chicago: University of Chicago Press.

Zelizer, Viviana. 1989. "The Social Meaning of Money: 'Special Monies.'" *American Journal of Sociology* 95(2): 342–77.

INDEX

accounting, xvii, xxi, 12, 13, 15, 27, 45,
94, 154–55, 156, 158, 182, 184–86, 188,
196–203
aggregation, 72, 74, 76, 81, 83–84, 120, 124,
131–2, 147
articulation, 21, 23, 47, 54, 85, 161, 163–64,
175, 223, 251n41, 259n32
artifice, 35, 37, 129, 185, 203, 245n2, 259n2
assemblage, 21–22, 73
assets, ix, xii, xv, xviii, 15, 41, 59, 60, 62–64,
69, 73, 91, 106, 111, 123, 131, 158,
163–64, 173, 183, 195, 208, 213, 216–18,
223–24, 227–29, 231–32; specificity, 106,
213, 218, 256n4
asymmetry, xx, 25, 56, 57, 59, 114, 148,
203; information, 56, 57
Austin, 252n46

back office, xi, xiii, xiv, 4, 5, 7, 9–13, 16,
49, 72, 94, 95, 119, 121–22, 124–25,
127, 129–50, 157, 170–71, 181, 188–92,
197–202, 205, 214, 253n3
balance sheet, 156, 183–85, 202, 259n3
banking: private, 158–59, 236n10, 256n2;
investment, xv, xviii, 115–16, 158,
193–94, 212
bending, 76, 164, 224, 229, 230
body, 20–21, 37–39, 96–105, 118, 151,
173, 221, 240nn28–29, 243n13, 243n16,
243n19, 249n18, 253n2

bottom line, xix, 60, 64, 115, 186, 203

calculation, xix, xxi, 3, 9, 14, 21, 25, 39, 45–
46, 104–5, 153, 170–71, 184–88, 190–92,
196–97, 199–202, 215–16, 225–26
Callon, xvii-iii, 237n22, 239n21, 241n5,
263n9
capital, xiii, xv, xvi, 23, 61–62, 78, 93, 97,
115, 180–81; industrial, 213–21, 261n3;
requirements, 194–96, 209–10
capitalism, x, xi, xv, 55, 158, 182, 186,
211–12, 221, 230, 259n2, 261n8, 262n13
cash flow, 130, 161, 175, 200–201
center of calculation, 186–87, 191
conversation, 9, 11, 13, 15, 27, 29, 31, 35–
37, 81, 98, 100, 103–4, 113–4, 171, 173,
180, 239n16, 248n8, 252n49, 259n33
correlation, 3, 41, 45, 55, 61–62, 65–66, 69,
72, 75, 77–78, 80, 82, 172
Coase, Ronald, 18, 20, 205, 240n26
Cochoy, Franck, 173, 258n18, 263n5
code, 14–16, 34–35, 37–39, 45, 47–54,
222–23; professional, 100, 107; software,
130, 134, 136–37, 139, 186, 191
cost, xvi, 18, 20, 70,74, 75, 77, 155–56,
182–83, 185, 187–96, 202–3, 254n8
confirmation, 68, 70, 126–27, 133, 136,
138, 140, 142–45, 148, 171, 199, 251n31
creativity, 129, 140, 167, 182, 202, 220,
262n13